BIOGRAPHICAL SERIES · VOLUME III

THE NORWEGIAN-AMERICAN HISTORICAL
   ASSOCIATION

   LAWRENCE O. HAUGE, *President*

Nelson in the early 1890s, around the time he served as governor of Minnesota.

Norwegian Yankee

Knute Nelson and the Failure of American Politics, 1860–1923

by Millard L Gieske
and Steven J. Keillor

1995
The Norwegian-American Historical Association
NORTHFIELD · MINNESOTA

Gieske, Millard L. and Steven J. Keillor
    Norwegian Yankee: Knute Nelson and the Failure of American Politics,
1860–1923

In Memory of Two Scandinavian-American Immigrant Farmers
Olaf Hjelde (1893–1988) and Jens K. Krabbe (1904–1994),
and Those Who Preceded Them in Settling the Upper Midwest

Foreword

The Association is pleased to present as volume three in its Biographical Series *Norwegian Yankee: Knute Nelson and the Failure of American Politics, 1860-1923*. It is a work of great merit, well researched and skillfully written. Norwegian-born Knute Nelson (1842-1923) was the first Scandinavian-American politician to attain national prominence, as congressman, as governor of the state of Minnesota, and as United States senator. He became the object of much ethnic pride as he made his way in the American political system within the Republican party. But the study transcends the bounds of political biography to paint a very human portrait of a man who came to personify for many of his compatriots the American dream, moving as Nelson did from inauspicious beginnings as a poor immigrant boy to the heights of political power. His career symbolized treasured images in the iconography of American political culture.

The genesis of the work extends over a number of years and has required sustained effort by several persons. It is therefore appropriate to trace the circumstances that resulted in this work of scholarship in some detail. In 1987 I invited Millard L. Gieske (1931-1991), professor of political science at the University of Minnesota at the Morris campus, to prepare a definitive biography of Knute Nelson. Gieske was well qualified to take on this assignment. His doctoral dissertation in political science at the University of Minnesota in 1965 is titled, "The Politics of Knute Nelson, 1912-1920, " and in 1979 he published the incisive and widely praised monograph *Minnesota Farmer-Laborism: The Third-Party Alternative*. As a political activist in the Democratic Farmer Labor party, he had personal experience and knowledge of Minnesota politics. Work on the biography of Knute Nelson commenced the summer of 1988 with a concentrated effort during the period of Gieske's sabbatical leave of absence that academic year, 1988-1989. Good progress continued even after his return to the classroom at the end of his leave and in spite of failing health. At the time of his death of leukemia in January, 1991, Gieske left an impressive first draft of nearly 600 pages.

Emily Gieske, Millard Gieske's widow, graciously gave me a free hand to bring her husband's manuscript to completion and to have it published. To do so would demand the services of a trained scholar familiar with Minnesota and national political history. The required revisions entailed rewriting and radically shortening portions of the manuscript, additional research, and the writing of some final chapters. In the summer of 1992, Steven J. Keillor at my urging agreed to assume responsibility for bringing the study to a successful conclusion. We are grateful for the dedication, expertise, and talent he brought to the task. Keillor resides in Askov, Minnesota, where he works as a writer and part-time college instructor. He has written the biography of another Scandinavian-American politician, *Hjalmar Petersen of Minnesota: The Politics of Provincial Independence* (1987). Keillor has earned a doctorate in American history at the University of Minnesota, and he is currently completing a book on Minnesota's rural cooperatives.

In his investigations of Knute Nelson, Gieske had as his research assistant Jostein Molde, who earlier had ably assisted in research on the Norwegians in Chicago and at present is assistant editor of *Heimen*, the Norwegian journal of the local history societies.

Molde served as Gieske's competent and experienced researcher in the United States in January-April, and in Norway in June-August, 1989. His assistance was made possible by grants-in-aid from the Minnesota Historical Society and from the Andrew E. and G. Norman Wigeland Fund of the American-Scandinavian Foundation. A grant from the Norwegian Emigration Fund of 1975, established by the Norwegian government, enabled Millard Gieske to pursue research in Norway in the fall of 1988, with visits to Voss and Evanger, Nelson's birthplace, in western Norway.

Major financial support, with grants to both authors, came from the Association's own Thedore C. Blegen Fellowship Fund. This fund has proven to be of inestimable value in ensuring the completion of the present as well as of earlier manuscripts. It provides the resources and the flexibility that make it possible for qualified scholars to assume responsibility for a meritorious project and to carry it forward to publication.

My capable assistant in the editorial work, Mary R. Hove, continues to serve the Association with dedication, sensitivity, and good humor. I am grateful for her expert assistance in preparing the manuscript for publication. As in past publications, she is responsible for the index.

Odd S. Lovoll
St. Olaf College and
The University of Oslo

Preface

Completing the unfinished manuscript of a deceased author is an unusual assignment which requires some explanation. I never had the privilege of meeting Millard L. Gieske, yet we have co-authored a book!

Professor Gieske had largely finished a first draft of his planned biography of Knute Nelson, except for the final chapter on Nelson's last years. Building on his Ph.D dissertation on Nelson and his article on Nelson's Civil War letters, he had developed initial interpretations of Nelson's career. He had not had the benefit (as I have) of reviewers' comments or the chance to do further research and revision.

After consulting with Odd Lovoll, I have undertaken that research and revision where appropriate. Where I did little additional research (Chapter 1), I served as editor. Where I uncovered new information (other chapters), I served as co-author, adding new passages, revising old ones, using Gieske's interpretations or revising them as the new facts warranted. He thoroughly examined the 79 boxes of Nelson's papers at the Minnesota Historical Society. I have not duplicated that work, but have added other personal papers, newspapers, published works, and government documents to the data base. Gieske was a political scientist who might view historians' insistence on leaving no book unopened, no letter unread, no microfilm unused as obsessive-compulsive behavior, but we will let the two disciplines debate research strategies. I admit to what David Hackett Fischer called "a-wandering in the dark forest of the past, gathering facts like nuts and berries."

Throughout, I expanded on Gieske's interpretations—e.g., on the frontier's importance to Nelson's career—while cutting the number of events and issues presented to focus more closely on those we do present. I have also interpreted Nelson's personal life and feelings, admittedly a difficult task. He was not one to talk about himself or his inner feelings. Responsibility for the stress on Norway as his mother country, America as his fatherland, and American politics as his masculine mentor rests with me.

The title is also my responsibility, my attempt to do what I think Millard Gieske the political scientist would have wanted: to show how Nelson's career sheds light on current debates over American politics and government. Each generation seeks to understand history more accurately and fully than its predecessors, but as incentive for that effort it must be allowed to seek in the past explanations for its own dilemmas. We have written a more complete, factual account of Nelson's life than previous biographers, but we have examined it while knowing American political history since 1923. We know what came next and can't pretend we don't.

The "failure of American politics" does not mean Nelson failed. His career was remarkably successful. Without losing an election, he blazed a trail for succeeding Scandinavian-American politicians, aided his party, and accomplished many personal goals. His politics of settlement and development aided settlers and developers on the frontier. A broker, he taught Scandinavian Americans about American politics and government, and the government, about these immigrants.

A political system can hold elections, inaugurate winners, produce policies, fill government posts, and yet fail to accomplish important goals. Nostalgia about the Golden Age of political parties from 1865 to 1920 cannot hide the failure of many of their projects: tariff reform, slavery compromises, Reconstruction, Indian policy, enforcement of land laws, civil service reform, reform of political corruption, regulation of railroads, effective anti-trust law, a benevolent imperialism, conservation, and American leadership in a League of Nations.

Nelson knew of these failures, though he would not have called American politics a "failure." Still, two rival parties practicing a politics of patronage, perfecting an adversarial style using adversarial checks and balances, and often relying on lawyers' constitutional minutiae to mask underlying motives failed to solve the pressing problems of that age. It is not anachronistic to point that out. Nelson's contemporaries knew it. And, Nelson was part of that politics, which contrasted markedly with the consensus-building politics of his homeland.

That is what the subtitle means, and I must absolve the many people who helped me from responsibility for it or for what follows it. Special thanks go to Odd Lovoll for entrusting me with this project, and to Odd and Mary Hove for their editorial work. Jon Gjerde and Carl H. Chrislock read the manuscript and offered helpful comments. Thanks too to Ruth Crane at NAHA, Barbara Grover at the Douglas County Historical Society, Terry Shoptaugh and Korella Selzler at the Northwest Minnesota Historical Center, Lois Hendrickson at the University of Minnesota Archives, and the helpful staff at the State Historical Society of Wisconsin and the MHS Research Center. Ann Regan and Deborah Miller of MHS shared ideas and encouraged me in several conversations. Deborah suggested "Norwegian Yankee" as a title. J. Philip and Ann-Britt Keillor of Madison, Wisconsin, helped with lodging and photograph requests. Stan Keillor of the Minnesota Court of Appeals gave legal advice. My parents, John and Grace Keillor, provided free room and board on my research trips, which was greatly appreciated. Finally, I thank my wife Margaret for her faithful support of my historical research and writing, and Jeremy, William, and Amanda for bearing with my fascination with the life and times of Knute Nelson.

Steven J. Keillor
Askov, Minnesota

Table of Contents

Norwegian Yankee

Knute Nelson and the Failure of American Politics, 1860–1923

One

"Norway Was a Kind, but a Poor Mother"

Knute Nelson was born in Evanger, in the Voss district of western Norway, on February 2, 1842. That much is certain. Therein lies a tale, and a complicated one at that.

Throughout Nelson's life, the identity and fate of his biological father was an unresolved mystery. He was born out of wedlock. His mother's family responded by distorting the record, perhaps to the point of altering some of the evidence. Once in America, his mother, Ingebjørg, passed as a widow emigrating with her child. That was the official story throughout his political career, appearing in the numerous biographical sketches of this well-known Minnesota governor and United States senator. How much of the truth did Nelson know? When in his seventies, he still occasionally inquired about the "pedigree" of his ancestors, as he wryly put it. He was referring to his father, for he knew a great deal about his mother and her family.

Ingebjørg Haldorsdatter Kvilekval (1814-1908) was born in Norway's year of brief independence and constitution-writing. However, her birth on November 18 and her baptism on December 27 came after Norway had been compelled to submit to a union with Sweden. Such epochal events were far distant from Voss and the small *gård* (farm) of Kvilekval belonging to

3

Ingebjørg's parents, Haldor Jonson (1769-1853) and Brita Torbjørnsdatter Nedre Rasdalen (1787-1864).[1]

Kvilekval was an ancient farm—mentioned in medieval records as early as 1343. The name appears in documents by 1603 and regularly after 1647. Located near a fast-flowing river and a mountain pass, the farm was appropriately named. Kvilekval means a "high place by the road where one can rest in peace." A traveler might rest in peace but not Kvilekval's farmer. It was a precariously small *gård*, ranging from eight to twelve acres over the years. According to the agricultural census of 1840, it had seven cows, fifteen to eighteen sheep, and one horse. Its primary crop was barley (2,000 kilos that year), which was made into brown bread. It could barely support a family of nine.[2] Kvilekval left the farmer little margin for error.

In keeping with Norwegian custom, Haldor and Brita deeded the farm to their oldest son, Jon Haldorson Kvilekval (1810-1864). He purchased it from his father for 200 *speciedaler* in 1836. Life on such a farm was mere subsistence, with barter not cash payments characterizing the local economy. Jon Haldorson Kvilekval was an independent, landowning farmer, but landownership did not guarantee a living. Feudalism bypassed Voss and most of Norway, mainly because its economy was too poor to sustain the feudal system. A growing population on a small, fixed land base threatened to subdivide and parcel out landownership until it was small protection against poverty.[3]

As a young girl, Jon's sister Ingebjørg was considered to be talented. Some said that she was a genius, who wrote songs and poetry, committed them to memory, and performed them at weddings. Local traditions describes her as an unusually gifted musician and songwriter who was invited to entertain guests by singing and reciting her own compositions.[4]

Sometime in the spring of 1841, the twenty-six-year-old Ingebjørg became pregnant—by whom and under what circumstances are both uncertain. Perhaps a bachelor paid a customary Saturday night visit to the unmarried women's quarter. Custom

Senator Nelson at his birthplace, Kvilekval gård (farm) near Evanger, Norway, in early August 1899. Others unidentified.

dictated strict rules of conduct, but rules were sometimes broken. Perhaps the performer Ingebjørg had an encounter during a wedding celebration, which customarily lasted several days. Despite her talents, her future now appeared limited, for she had a pregnancy but no husband or suitor. She was unmarried when she gave birth to Knud (later changed to Knute) on February 2, 1842.

Knud Evanger was baptized on March 28, 1842, by his uncle Jon at Kvilekval—at home, not in the church—before his mother and at least five witnesses. Two witnesses carried the information to the parish minister who as a matter of duty recorded it in the "Kyrkjebok for presten," the parish book of births, marriages, and deaths.[5]

Baptized children must have fathers—at least in the record book—so Helge Knudsen Styve was recorded as the father's name. Seven years older than Ingebjørg, Helge owned part of the sub-divided *gård* Styve, some five kilometers west of Kvilekval—

5

very close to Evanger but higher up the hillside. Perhaps he was the biological father, for some Evanger sources reported that Ingebjørg claimed that Helge had promised her marriage.[6] As a bachelor landowner, Helge was certainly eligible, and capable of supporting a wife and son.

Why they never married (if Helge was indeed the father) is as uncertain as Knud's paternity. Local historians claim there was long-standing tension between the Kvilekval and Styve families, but they only speculate about the reasons. Perhaps there is a simpler explanation. Ingebjørg may have lacked the dowry or the financial resources desired in a bride.[7] Helge may have been too unsettled, too given to bad habits of carousing and drinking. Then again, Helge may not have been the true father, but only a stand-in recruited to be the official father of record—and unwilling to be a stand-in at a wedding.

Any possibility of marriage with Helge was ended when he pulled up stakes, sold his farm to his younger brother, and left Voss in May, 1844. Three months later, Helge sailed on the *Ørnen* for America and the Vossing settlement of Skoponong in Jefferson county, Wisconsin. There is little record of him thereafter. Knute Nelson never knew him. A brief note in Nelson's handwriting states that "father" died on Christmas, 1844, and was buried at Drogsvold farm near Bøvere church in LaGrange, Jefferson county, Wisconsin.[8]

Though she may have given Knute this information on Helge's death, Ingebjørg apparently never discussed with Knute her relationship (if any) with Helge. She left no record of it for biographers to consult. She lived the fiction that she had emigrated as a widow.

However, the tale of Ingebjørg's love child could not be so easily hidden in the small rural district of Voss—nor among the few tightly knit communities of Vossings in the Upper Midwest. One Vossing tradition was that his mother appeared sad immediately after his birth, but the local sexton predicted great things for young Knute.[9] The Vossing folklore about Knute Nelson's birth and parentage illustrates how Knute was raised in a highly local-ized community of oral, not written, traditions. Immigrants from Norway in the 1840s perceived themselves more as Vossings or Sognings or Telemarkings than as Norwegians. The numerous small isolated valleys and fjords claimed immigrants' loyalties and memories far more than did the sprawling kingdom under the authority of the union king.

The most romantic Vossing account suggested that Gjest Baardsen was Knute's father. Baardsen was a folk hero, a Norwegian Robin Hood of sorts—thief, con artist, swindler, se-ducer, and shadowy character who reputedly visited Voss occa-sionally. He was imprisoned at Bergen, where he wrote his autobiography in 1841, and was not released until 1845. That would seem to eliminate him from any role as Ingebjørg's lover in 1841.[10]

According to another Vossing oral tradition, her lover was Ivar Nelson Evanger, a local merchant, whose mother refused to allow him to marry Ingebjørg but instead recruited Helge to serve as paternal stand-in.[11] Still another account had a prominent Norwegian visiting Voss in the spring of 1841 and consummating a brief affair with Ingebjørg. He had no thought of marrying her and afterward arranged for poor Helge to be the father of record.

No Vossing males assumed the burden of helping Ingebjørg support her son. For the first year after his birth, they remained at Kvilekval. In the summer of 1843, Ingebjørg's brother Jon caught "America fever," sold the *gård* Kvilekval, and moved his family to Chicago.[12] Ingebjørg then rented a room or small house in Evanger, where she worked as a domestic servant and as a milk-maid on nearby farms, especially the *gård* Mugaas, where Knud was a regular visitor. In May, 1848, she moved to the coastal port of Bergen, some fifty miles west of Evanger, where she worked as a domestic servant.[13] At best, life was a continual struggle to sur-vive. It was at Bergen that Ingebjørg probably made the decision to travel to America with her young son. Often, emigration was a two-step process: first, internal migration from the rural interior

7

to a coastal city, and, second, the emigration to America. Ingebjørg appears to have followed this pattern.

The start of Norwegian emigration to America is commonly dated July 4, 1825, when the sloop *Restauration* left Stavanger for New York City. Most of the first wave of emigrants came from southwestern Norway, from ports such as Stavanger and Bergen. Among the first to leave were the poor—but not the poorest— and religious dissenters, including Haugean pietists and Quakers. By 1836, the summer migration became an annual occurrence, and in the following decade nine of the nineteen Norwegian counties (*fylker*) sent emigrants to America.[14]

In Norway, "America fever" spread from west to east, along fjords and other waterways and valleys. It was not long before it reached Evanger. Voss was an isolated rural area with a barter economy—unlike the cash economy common in the coastal areas. Despite those limitations, Vossings displayed a remarkable persistence in penetrating that cash economy—as peddlers, craftsmen, seasonal fishermen, and horse traders. Through these dealings with the coast, they apparently heard news of America and the Norwegians migrating there.[15]

As in other parts of Norway, overpopulation helped push Vossings to emigrate. Between 1825 and 1835, Voss's population jumped from 8,231 to 9,339, a 13 percent increase that placed additional stress on its limited supply of tillable land. The "crofter" class of renters and the day laborers, or "cotters," were crowded ever closer on their small holdings. Just for Voss's population to survive, local historian Johannes Gjerdåker estimates that Vossings would have had to clear and plant thirty-five to fifty acres of new land each year—"a sheer impossibility given the scant technology of that period." The typical Voss farm contained only nine to twelve acres, with between two and three acres of tilled land. Oldest sons purchased their fathers' farms, only to default on their loans. Farms changed hands frequently. Gjerdåker estimates that the pauper class numbered from 250 to 300 in the

1830s; they were totally dependent on the local parish and on charity.[16]

The first Vossing sailed for America in 1836. The following year 75 more departed. By the year 1843, 142 emigrants had left, and Voss was losing 4.5 percent of its population annually. Emigration became a business, with ship captains especially earning profits thereby. In the spring of 1843, a ship captain "declared that he had visited Voss in response to a request to come there to arrange for the passage of some fifty or sixty persons."[17]

When he left for America in the spring of 1843, Ingebjørg's brother Jon may have accompanied this large party. After he had been in the United States for several months, Jon wrote back to Evanger an "America letter" in which he discouraged emigration: "I do not advise anyone to come here who has a good *gård* and has a tolerable income for himself and his family, for it is a hard journey and there are difficulties." He noted the unhealthy condition of many immigrants: "everybody looks pale and worn."[18] At the time, Jon was working as a carpenter in Chicago.

This letter may have convinced Ingebjørg not to risk her already uncertain future in America. Or perhaps she lacked the financial resources to emigrate. It is estimated that each 1840s emigrant left with about fifty to sixty *speciedaler* ($38-$45), or nearly one year's wages.[19] That amount was more than Ingebjørg could accumulate.

Jon's discouraging letter was not the last word on conditions in America. Perhaps he sent more encouraging news later. In 1848 Vossings in Chicago "organized a Correspondence Society . . . to send regular 'America letters' to Norway"—to praise America and to counter her critics back home.[20] Specifically, they were responding to the criticisms voiced in an 1847 report written by the Swedish-Norwegian consul general in New York, Adam Løvenskjold. Their letters began arriving in Voss in the fall and winter of 1848-1849. They were copied and distributed in the community. Interestingly, given young Knud's condition, one letter described America in these terms: "Here you are not asked

9

what or who your father was; the question is: What are you? Do you have a good moral character? Are you imbued with a true patriotic spirit and do you have the required qualifications to pursue your lawful vocation—whether it be as a farmer or as a man in public office? Thus all are placed on an equal basis."[21]

These letters may have helped to change Ingebjørg's mind. In April, 1849, she borrowed the $45 for passage to America. On April 16 Ingebørg Haldorsdatter registered her intent to emigrate with her son Knud Helgeson Kvilekval to "Nordamerika."[22]

Ingebjørg and Knud left for Bergen and the seven-week crossing. Before they left Bergen, she purchased for young Knud a pocket-sized children's Bible (*Den norske børnebibel*). Knud was leaving his first life, the cottage on the cold mountain lake where he and a girl companion had nearly drowned. He later remembered leaving Evanger for Bergen and the old freight boat. Like the other passengers they carried their bedding and food supplies. They stored barrels of water on board. They suffered from seasickness.[23]

They arrived at Castle Garden on July 4, 1849. New Yorkers were celebrating independence—primarily their freedom to set off firecrackers. In addition to "the public fireworks," private citizens "all seemed alive to the privileges of the day, and girls as well as boys were burning powder in various forms."[24] The broad new land excited Knute, and he recalled the fireworks as though they were a greeting of personal welcome to him. His mother, however, faced a financial crisis: she had no funds with which to pay the disembarkation fee. She had to borrow the money from another passenger in order to get them off the ship. Over many years, the story was often told of how he comforted the fearful, weeping Ingebjørg: "Don't cry, Mother, we are poor now, but when I get big I shall be next to the King."[25]

Young Knute was mistaken about the title for the chief executive of the United States, where independence was so noisily hailed. He was not mistaken about his own future in this new country. Ironically, the lack of a father, which had hindered his past in Norway, would turn out to be an advantage to his future in America. Without a father's strong opinions about the new land, strong expectations for his son, or strong loyalties to the Norwegian-American community, young Knute would be free to adapt quickly, follow his own occupational path, and venture outside that community to find his future. The Americanization of young Knute was furthered by the absence of a father. As Chicago's Vossing Americans had reported, he would not be judged by his father's character or qualifications in America.

Two

Vossing American

When Ingebjørg and Knute arrived at Castle Garden, no one could mistake them for wealthy Americans returning from a European tour. They looked every inch like new arrivals, "green-horns," from Norway. Though she was still handsome, Ingebjørg was thirty-four years old, unmarried, with no knowledge of English. The myth was about to be created—and maintained until 1923—that she was a widow with a child. Seven-year-old Knute wore a homespun suit, long trousers, black jacket with wide collars, and a wide-visored cap. He seemed full of youthful confidence though he too knew no English and spoke only the Vossing dialect of Norwegian.

As Vossings, they did not melt into the general American population, or take Horace Greeley's generalized advice, "Go West, young man," or head for just any Norwegian-American settlement. Their destination was Chicago, where Jon Haldorson Kvilekval and a Vossing colony awaited them. [1]

Knute Nelson retold the story of their trip from New York to Chicago countless times. He reveled in this giant new land, stretching farther even than the imagination of a boy from Voss. First, they traveled up the Hudson River to Albany, probably by steamboat. Next, they traveled economy class on a passenger and freight boat drawn laboriously by two steady mules along the Erie Canal to Buffalo.[2] Occasionally, some unplanned excitement occurred. A passenger and his trunk fell overboard. The Erie Canal, opened in 1825, was a major route for immigrants trying their luck in the new prairie lands of the Old Northwest. Knute's luck turned when the boat captain's wife took a special liking to him and treated him to his first American apple pie. "You don't have to know English to eat American pie," she reassured him. Knute wasted little time picking up his first English words and phrases. He sensed that survival in the new land required quick mastery of the new language.

Traveling the nearly three hundred miles to Buffalo was slow, but they finally reached Lake Erie. There they boarded a sidewinder steamer, crossed the length of Lake Erie, went up the Detroit River into Lake Huron, passed through the Mackinaw Straits and down Lake Michigan to Chicago. It was late July by the time they reached Jon's home.

Though he and his wife Sigvor had three children, they offered Ingebjørg and Knute temporary shelter. Jon's home became a base from which to make a start in America.[3] A cholera epidemic swept through Chicago, killing people by the score. Two weeks after their arrival, Sigvor and two of her children came down with the dread disease. Sigvor and one daughter died. Young Knute was infected, but he recovered. To Ingebjørg fell the task of nursing the household's sick. For weeks, Knute watched as burial coaches passed by the house in what seemed a never-ending daily ritual.[4]

Shocking as this American greeting was, they had no time to engage in self-pity. Ingebjørg hired out as a household servant, the only work she knew. Part of her wages she set aside to repay her $45 loan for passage, which took one year. After six months, Knute moved to another household on the West Side, where he too worked as a servant. He carried water and wood, washed dishes, and drove the two family cows out to pasture on the nearby prairie in the morning and retrieved them at night for milking. "They were very kind to me and though they were poor working people, they gave me a good home," he recalled years later. Still, the lack of a father troubled him. In his own words, he had arrived in Chicago "worse than fatherless."[5]

When his host family's son became ill, Knute took over his job of selling the *Chicago Free Press* on the streets. His earnings helped pay his board. The job gave him the chance to build an English vocabulary and to gain an early mastery of common American street profanity.[6] The street became his school and the newspaper stories he hawked his first lessons in American civics.

He attended his first American public school, the "North School house." Yet his lessons came more from his mother and from the Chicago streets. The streets taught him self-sufficiency and a dutiful shouldering of burdens. His mother taught him the obligation to repay debts and to earn his own way in life. Later, these lessons would buttress his conservative ideology. Debts were to be honored, not repudiated by defaulting or through inflationary schemes. Sorrow or setback was to be met by plunging headlong into life's labors. Self-pity was equated with self-defeat. Late in life, he described himself: "as for me, I have been a hard plodder and worker all my days and have had little time to give to the social side of life. I have been a sort of drayhorse all my life."[7]

There must have been a social and religious side to Knute and Ingebjorg's life in Chicago's Vossing colony. They may have worshiped at Paul Andersen's First Norwegian Evangelical Lutheran church, which had been established in 1848.[8] In their poverty, they may have been aided by the Vossing Emigration Society, which collected money to help "needy and worthy families in America." One historian of Norwegian-American life, Theodore C. Blegen, writes, "Churches, fraternal societies, and other kinds of social and cultural groups tended to knit the Norwegians of Chicago into a unit."[9] But many of these ethnic institutions had not yet been created in 1849-1850.

After fifteen months in Chicago, Ingebjørg was ready to move on. Most Norwegians had come for the cheap prairie land and not to live in cities. The wide, often treeless prairies of Iowa, Illinois, and Wisconsin beckoned. At mid-century, America's population was 85 percent rural. Norwegian Americans were to become and remain the most rural of all European immigrant groups.[10] A Vossing wanted land, a wife, and children to help with the chores. He wanted experience as well. When he left Voss, he farmed with primitive plow, cradle, sickle, and scythe. Now, he faced sod thicker than he thought existed anywhere, and unfamiliar farm implements. By the mid-1830s, the reaper, harvester, binder, steel cultivator, and steel moldboard plow were arriving on American farms.[11] What the Vossing most wanted, however, was capital or credit. New implements cost money. Many failed at farming, not through sloth or inexperience, but through lack of credit and an inability to comprehend rudimentary principles of finance.

Nils Olson Grotland (or Grjotland) was one such Vossing. The third son of the owner of the *gård* Grjotland, Nils could not expect to inherit land.[12] Grjotland was located next to the *gård* Nesheim, whose owner, Lars Nelson Nesheim, was "given to . . . the dissemination of America-letters" as "correspondent from Voss for the Chicago Vossing group." Lars strongly favored emigration (though he never left himself) and undoubtedly told his fellow bachelor and neighbor Nils about the Vossings in Chicago.[13] Nils emigrated to America in 1845 and worked for two years as a pressman for the *Chicago Democrat*. The lure of cheap prairie land proved irresistible. In 1847 he moved to Skoponong, a Norwegian-American colony in southern Wisconsin.[14]

Vossings were numerous, perhaps a majority, in Skoponong. a rural offshoot of Chicago's Vossing colony. As Blegen notes, for Norwegian immigrants "it was not enough . . . to seek out fellow Norwegians," but "they went further and associated themselves with people who had come out of the very valley, the very *bygd*, from which they themselves hailed in the old country." Each rural district in Norway had centuries of its own tradition, its own culture, its own dialect. All these separated Vossings from Telemarkings, Sognings, and others—but especially the dialect, for "the dialect of another valley of the homeland marked a person off as not, in an intimate sense, belonging to one's own people." [15]

In these early years before the formation of common Norwegian-American institutions, Nils, Jon, Ingebjørg, and Knud were Vossing Americans more than Norwegian Americans.

Nils wanted a wife who hailed from the same valley and spoke the same dialect. Nothing is known of their courtship, but in the fall of 1850 Nils married Ingebjørg in Chicago. The groom was forty-nine, the bride thirty-six years old. No longer was Ingebjørg the single "widow" with son. Yet Nils Olson Grotland was hardly the optimum choice for a husband who could achieve the American dream. Though almost fifty, he was poor and just starting toward self-sufficiency and security. He was neither a skilled husbandman nor an astute financial manager. But for Knute, the marriage meant escape from the embarrassment of his beginnings. A Vossing male was now willing to claim him. In celebration, he dropped the surname Helgeson. Thenceforth, he was Knute Nelson. He left Chicago better than fatherless.

With his wife and stepson, Nils moved back to Skoponong, where he had worked as a hired hand. He still lacked land. For a month or two they lived with another family. That fall, Nils built a pioneer log hut on a 40-acre plot that was only partly tillable. It was across the road from the farm of Nils's nephew, Ivar Vikingson Grotland, who undoubtedly helped him to acquire it or let him have it "for the payment of taxes." It was located in northern LaGrange township, Walworth county, among several Vossing farms. [16]

A school built of tamarack logs lay about three-quarters of a mile down the road. [17] Here the Americanization of young Knute began in earnest, under the tutelage of a teacher of Irish-English ancestry, Mary Blackwell Dillon. Well-educated and modestly wealthy in Ireland, the Dillon family had been hard hit by the potato famine and depression of 1847, which forced them to emigrate to America. They settled in Skoponong, near the Norwegian Lutheran church founded by pastors J.W.C. Dietrichson and

17

A.C. Preus in 1848-1849.[18] Intellectually gifted, Mary Dillon was a linguist who knew Latin, French, and German. To supplement the family income, she began teaching in the log schoolhouse.

Mary Dillon was ideally suited to the task of educating and Americanizing a young Vossing. She served as a bridge from things Norwegian to things American and English. She apparently lacked the prejudice toward and ignorance of Norwegians that led some Wisconsin settlers to call them "Norwegian Indians."[19] She came to know pastors Dietrichson and Preus and learned Norwegian. From Dietrichson and his lectures she learned much about Norway and its people. She later recalled that the local Norwegians had befriended the Dillons "at a time when it was needed." She was a kindly go-between, helping a young Vossing to understand American society.

Arriving late, after the 1850 school session had begun, Knute quickly caught Mary Dillon's attention—not always for the right reasons. He was anything but an obedient student. A difficult personality, he was, by his own admission, "a turbulent fellow and ready to fight at the drop of a hat." A schoolmate observed, "Knute was the worst boy in school to play tricks on schoolmates, even in school hours, and got more spankings than any other pupil."[20]

Years of uprooting, relocation, and constant adjustment had produced a pugnacious personality, outspoken, quick to adapt, always ready to jump into provocative debate or combat. His ever-changing homes—Voss, Chicago, Skoponong, Koshkonong —he turned into playing fields where he tested his mettle against competitors and friends alike. Once, a local boy recognized Nelson's immigrant status by his homespun "newcomer clothes." He thought he would intimidate Knute and demonstrate his superiority by saying a few English words. Knute answered with such a rapid-fire volley of American profanity that the challenger fled from the battlefield.[21] Fun-loving, clever, talkative, Nelson set himself apart from the competition. People were drawn to him.

Knute Nelson's favorite teacher, Mary Blackwell Dillon of La Grange, Wisconsin, who helped to Americanize him and had a life-long influence on him. Photo by John B. Hawkins, year unknown.

He became Mary Dillon's favorite pupil. She found this diamond-in-the-rough teachable. "He was always resolute, persevering, and energetic," with "the best characteristics of the Norse type," she recalled thirty years later.[22] He was nearly nine years old, and had had only eight weeks of English-language instruction at Chicago's North school. She accepted the challenge. She imposed discipline. Nelson later recalled that she sometimes whipped "me three times a day, but that did not alter my liking

19

for her." The fondness was mutual. He learned how to cut a quill pen, to appreciate good literature, to set high personal goals.

After the three-month school term ended, she gave him advanced lessons, and he went to her home on Saturdays for private recitations. Only two other boys were admitted for private tutoring.[23] On her walks with him, she related "scraps of history" (English, American, and Norwegian), and taught him grammar. For three successive years, she worked with young Knute. She introduced him to the classics: Macaulay, Carlyle (whom she detested), Alexander Pope, George Eliot, Thackeray. She also introduced him to some Victorian refinements: a taste for some of life's luxuries and a large personal library brought over from Ireland, which was unusual in a frontier community.

The public school was an Americanizing force in a frontier area like early 1850s Skoponong. Here, the immigrant child had to use English, learned about American political traditions, and mingled with children of other ethnic backgrounds. As an Americanizing, non-Lutheran institution, it was attacked by some Lutheran ministers, who called it "religionless" and recommended that parochial schools be established. This sparked a bitter debate in Norwegian America, as more secular leaders accused the clergy of a "stupid imagined fear of everything American." Knute's public school education was largely finished when this debate began in earnest in 1858, but his instruction by the Catholic Dillon exemplified what the ministers opposed.[24]

Some Norwegian Americans sent their children to summer Norwegian-language parochial schools. Skoponong apparently lacked such a school in 1850-1853 when Knute lived there. Though he grew up in strongly Norwegian communities, they had not yet created strongly Norwegian-American institutions. Nils and Ingebjørg undoubtedly taught him Vossing values at home, but Mary Dillon faced no institutional competition for Knute's mind. His progress in Americanization was rewarded with an admired teacher's special treatment and praise. It was eased by his teacher's knowledge of Norwegian. It may have been eased by the absence of a strong-willed father who could object to the teacher's formative influence on his son.

Mid-nineteenth-century America faced little competition for Knute's mind when it came to political excitement and dramatic events. Voss had little political importance in Norway. There, history was being fashioned by gradual, undramatic, Malthusian factors; in America, by handsome orating senators, daring explorers, and dashing military heroes. It was no contest. From Dillon, Knute must have learned about the annexation of Texas (1845-1846), the California Gold Rush (1849), the Compromise of 1850, and California's admission to the Union (1850). After he left Skoponong, the debate over slavery in the territories intensified. Senator Stephen A. Douglas' Kansas-Nebraska Act (1854) repealed the Missouri Compromise line and substituted the principle of "popular sovereignty." The people of each territory would decide whether that territory would be "free" or "slave." Bleeding Kansas and Bleeding Sumner (1856), the Dred Scott decision, and the Lecompton Constitution (1857)—all undercut Douglas' substitute solution.

Teen-aged Knute became a Democrat and a strong admirer of Douglas. Uncanny coincidences and similarities were to link the two. Douglas was known as the "Little Giant," Knute Nelson acquired the nickname of "the little Norwegian." When Nelson moved to Minnesota in 1871, he moved to Douglas county. Nelson later served as a prominent member of the Senate's Committee on Territories, which Douglas had chaired. Nelson became a latter-day "frontier"senator, as Douglas had been. Even their personalities shared a few similarities: both were combative and full of self-confidence. Just as the frontier moved on, so too did Nelson's political loyalties move beyond Douglas. But that was far in the future. In the 1850s, the egalitarian nature of the frontier served to Americanize Knute—and Douglas was its embodiment.

In the summer of 1852, Knute and some Skoponong companions walked four or five miles to Whitewater to watch the July 4th

21

Knute, age 10 or 11, and his mother Ingebjørg, age 37 or 38, at the Goodman studio in Whitewater, Wisconsin, before their move to Deerfield in the spring of 1853.

celebration. Knute's schoolmate, Bjorn Holland, tells the story, a sort of parable of Knute Nelson's early experiences in America: "Upon our arrival we found to our surprise a vast concourse of people gathered around a speaker's stand [- the speaker was] delivering a 4th of July oration. . . . Well, our curiosity . . . was now solved . . . . At the close of the programme the people repaired to a nearby grove where tables were spread with a sumptuous dinner free for all. We Norwegian boys were too bashful and timid to venture up to the tables. In the meantime an elderly lady noticed us huddled around a large tree, approached and asked us if we had had our dinner, to which we of course answered in the negative. 'Why come along with me over to the tables, dinner is free for all; you are not excepted by any means, boys get hungry as well as the rest of us, if not more so.' We did not need a second invitation. . . . Dinner over, Knute remarked in his usual jocular manner, 'Oh but that was a good dinner, the best I have ever eaten. Cakes, pies, chicken, doughnuts, and not to forget the splendid lemonade. Yes, this meal I shall never forget as long as I live.'"[25] In this parable, the boy from a poor family in a Norwegian-American community without a rich cultural life surprisingly encounters an American frontier community full of the sumptuous drama of settlement, local politics, and the national slavery debate. He is unsure if he is included, but some Americans with an egalitarian spirit welcome his participation. Mary Dillon was like the elderly lady inviting him to partake. He would never forget that America gave him the opportunity—as well as the lemonade.

It also gave Knute the frontier male habit of chewing tobacco—a habit disgusting to Mary Dillon's Irish-English sensibilities. When he later sent her pictures of himself, she cherished them but asked that he send one with a beard unstained by tobacco juice! She admired his skills, but added, "I wonder that I have never lectured you on the heinousness of using tobacco."[26] In many other personal habits, Knute remained a simple Vossing farm boy. That was where Americanization never took hold—in the intimate matters of home and hearth, where a mother's early influence was strong. Even after he became a prosperous lawyer and successful politician, his eating habits remained spartan: oatmeal, cornmeal mush, and coffee for breakfast, coarse bread and coffee for lunch, and for supper, oatmeal, cornmeal mush, bacon, and tea. He never vacationed. He always walked to work. His private secretary "described his life as drab by the standards of most men for he only did three things: he read, he worked, and chewed tobacco."[27]

In the spring of 1853, Nils moved the family thirty miles north to the Norwegian-American settlement at Koshkonong. "Perhaps the most important of all the Wisconsin settlements," writes Blegen, "—certainly the most properous—was the 'Koshkonong settlement,'" which covered about seven townships near Lake

Koshkonong. Norwegians altered the name to Kaskeland.[28] Here was rich, rolling prairie land, with savanna outcroppings of maple, oak, and ash. Vossings had first settled here in 1839.[29] They were drawn by its lakes, fertile soil, and abundant hardwoods. It came to be the best-known Norwegian-American settlement in Wisconsin. Even the skeptical Løvenskjold praised it in 1847: "This settlement is the largest in Wisconsin and consists of between four and five hundred families from Telemark, Voss and Numedal. . . . The soil is very good."[30] The soil produced excellent crops of barley, wheat, oats, and tobacco.

Nils Grotland settled in a northern section heavily populated by Vossings. His poor luck in land-seeking followed him here. He initially moved to a farm in section 13 of Deerfield township, intending to purchase it. However, he sent the purchase money with another person, only to have the bearer turn thief and disappear with the funds. He then moved his family three miles south to section 27, where he bought 120 acres—"largely on credit."[31] Called "Tangen" after a turn in Mud Creek, which ran through the property, the farm lay a little more than a mile from the village of Deerfield.

In the Norwegian tradition of using gård names as last names, Nils sometimes referred to himself as Nils Tangen. However, when anyone mistakenly addressed young Knute as "Knute Tangen," he corrected them immediately. He wanted to be known as Knute Nelson.[32] That may have been to reassure his stepfather of his pride in bearing Nils' name.

Relations between the two were not untroubled. Nils (or, Nels, as he anglicized it) was a self-pitying hypochondriac. Knute carried much of the burden of farm work from an early age and also worked for area farmers to earn cash for the family. He recalled that his stepfather "was sickly and not able to do much, so that the burden of caring for the farm devolved upon mother and me."[33] He rebelled against any suggestion that farmwork should take precedence over schoolwork. Two sons, William and Henry, had been born to Nils and Ingebjørg in 1852 and 1854 respectively. Having sons of his own made the step-relationship more awkward. Nils apparentiy accused Knute of favoring his mother over his stepfather. Apologetically, Knute had to reassure him that it wasn't so: "Let him guage [sic] my conduct toward him by that toward mother and he will see that if I have treated him bad I have [treated] mother eaqualy [sic] bad." Unconvinced, Nils withheld love and attention, and worried that his stepson would not care for his natural sons after his death, which he always ex-pected to be soon.[34]

As a poor family with a "sickly" father, the Nelsons came under the strong influence of a neighboring farmer, Gullick Thompson Saue. A fellow Vossing, the successful Gullick presented a stark contrast to Nils, whose reputation was not that of a prosperous, progressive farmer. Inheriting $1,000 and acquiring $1,500 in the California gold fields, Gullick became the largest landowner in Koshkonong, though he was twenty years younger than Nils.[35] When Knute attended school in Koshkonong, he went to the Thompson school, located on Gullick's land. Favorably disposed toward the common school, Knute praised Thompson for getting this school built: "There is no one in the neighborhood except him who can see anything necessary beyond Lutheranism." The oth-ers regarded "the church and its poor pastor as the only correct means of instruction."[36] Knute, however, resented Gullick's local dominance. He felt that Gullick used his parents while seeming to befriend them.[37]

The Thompson school was a letdown after three years of Dillon's intensive tutelage and extensive library. Still, Knute con-tinued to take his education seriously — to the point of annoying his stepfather. Though public schools charged no tuition, the books were not free. Knute's efforts to acquire a book showed his dedication to education: "When the time arrived for me to begin studying Fifth Reader, I had neither the book nor the money. I was then working for a farmer, rooming on the fourth floor of his home, and he very kindly offered to let me have the oxen to haul wood to the town to buy the book. Arriving at the town with a jag

Built in 1852 about eight miles southwest of the Tangen farm, the West Koshkonong church was one of two citadels of Norwegian-American Lutheranism in Koshkonong.

of wood, I drove up to the store, went in and told the storekeeper I wanted a Fifth Reader. He told me the price of this book was $1.00. I told him I had no money, but had a jag of wood outside which I wanted to trade for the book. He came out, looked at the jag of wood and said he would let me have the book that day, so he looked me over, and said that he thought he could trust me until Saturday. When I walked out of the store with that book, I think I was the proudest boy that ever lived. You may be sure the second jag was delivered that Saturday."[38] He attended the Thompson school until 1858, when, he concluded,"I had got about as far as I could get at the district or common school, and was hungering for a better education."

No Norwegian-American colleges or academies existed in 1858.[39] As part of the early wave of Norwegian-American emigration, Knute Nelson grew up before the major Norwegian-American institutions were established. Instead, he chose "a good English Academy," about fifteen miles south of the family farm in a small village with the very English name of Albion.[40] Settled by New Yorkers and New Englanders, Albion had a grassy common, like a New England village. Seventh Day Baptists built a church on one side of the town common and an academy on the opposite side. Like good New Englanders, they kept intoxicating liquors out of their town. Opened in 1854, Albion Academy was a monument to New Englanders' strong desire to educate and Christianize the frontier West.[41] When he traveled on "an exploring expedition to the school" in the fall of 1858, Knute little realized what a stronghold of Yankeedom he was entering or what a cultural divide he was about to cross.[42]

He called at the home of Dr. Charles R. Head, a physician and president of the academy's board of trustees. "'Is the president at home?' he asked." Head looked at the "Norwegian immigrant boy" who "wore the home-made, homespun clothes characteristic of such boys" and who "had an open, eager face, with clear, penetrating blue eyes." He explained that he was not the principal but only a trustee. Knute replied that "he wanted to know if it

27

would be possible for him to enter the academy without any money." After asking some questions, Head determined that "he was a very deserving boy" and "told him to come right along when school opened and he would be taken care of."[43] Head was not making an exception for Knute. Albion "was an educational mecca for poor students." It had a policy that "No student is turned away on account of poverty."[44]

Four to six weeks later, Knute again walked the fifteen miles to Albion, accompanied by a pair of oxen pulling his Norwegian *kubberulle*, a crude wagon which "made an ungodly noise, creaking and groaning like a monster in agony."[45] It carried his supplies, an immigrant's chest and some books. This time he saw the principal, A.R. Cornwall, who was struck by "his small stature and boyish look." The principal told him he could start school at the winter term. Cornwall recalled Nelson's early days at Albion: "He told me at the outset that he had no money. He cut wood, built fires and took care of my horse, and in the spring worked in my garden to meet his bills—which he was very particular to have 'all up.' When the larder was empty, he walked with his basket the same fourteen miles [to his home] for a new supply. This he did every two weeks for the year, and I think much longer. I soon heard his name called over by the young men as they passed to and fro in the society rooms, and found that he was soon among the foremost in forensic struggles. He moved steadily on in his classes and his teachers almost uniformly gave him 'max' bills of standing."[46]

Although operated by the North-Western Association of Seventh-Day Baptists, Albion Academy was non-sectarian in admission and curriculum. It was coeducational, with an enrollment ranging from 200 to 300 students. Scandinavian-American students formed a small minority of less than ten percent. The campus consisted of three brick buildings on twelve acres. Most students boarded in private residences "off-campus." Albion's faculty was solid for the times, with the D.D., Ph.D., LL.D., and M.A. common among the teachers, some of whom were accorded

28

the rank of professor. For many years, Albion's preparatory education department supplied young teachers to the common schools in the surrounding area. Albion offered the four-year degrees of Bachelor of Philosophy (Ph.B.) for men and Laureate of Philosophy (Ph.L.) for women. The rules regarding "social relations of the sexes were of the most proscriptive type," as befitted a New England institution in the Victorian age. While a revised charter of 1863 forbade the teaching of sectarian tenets, Albion still had a "Christian atmosphere" and a morning chapel exercise. Rules for personal conduct were strict: no smoking, alcohol, gambling, profanity, or room visitation.[47]

Knute had little spare time for breaking any of the rules. He worked his way through school and studied hard. In later years he recalled studying English, grammar, higher mathematics, algebra, geometry, trigonometry, some physics, mental and moral philosophy, Latin, "most of Caesar's commentaries of [the] Gothic war, many of Cicero's Orations, and some 6 books of Virgil's Aeneid."[48] He prospered in the disciplined environment. He matured rapidly and was popular with both students and faculty. He continued a second year at Albion "till the Fall of 1860, when I went out in the country to teach a public district school among the farmers for the purpose of earning a little money so I could pursue my education further."[49]

The eighteen-year-old student turned teacher at the ungraded Melaas school in Pleasant Springs township, near the heavily Norwegian village of Stoughton in Dane county.[50] He instructed some thirty-five to forty students in that log schoolhouse for the fall and winter of 1860-1861. He struggled to maintain order among students who were not much younger than he: "Among my pupils were Agnes Frazer, Susie Laramore and Maggie McComb. Agnes Frazer was a little flirt, and I had to keep a cast iron face from being influenced by her glances. One day Susie Laramore snow-balled me, and as I had to keep the upper hand in my school, I picked her up and laid her down in the snow and washed her face good. She took it good naturedly, so it was all right."[51] He stayed with a Norwegian-American farmer, Johannes Melaas, who charged him "one dollar a week" for room and board.

This partly Americanized Vossing was now charged with Americanizing younger Norwegian Americans in the common school. In a recently-settled area, opportunities were as abundant as wildlife. Teaching opportunities could not be restricted to properly pedigreed New Englanders or to female graduates of Catherine Beecher's academy. The need for teachers was too great —and the method of choosing them too democratic. In a strongly Norwegian-American area like Pleasant Springs township, local Norwegian-American school boards could choose one of their own like Knute Nelson. He was perfectly suited for the role of educational broker: Norwegian enough to communicate with immigrant parents and students with little command of English, yet Americanized enough to teach in English and to satisfy old-stock parents' educational expectations for their children.

The meaning of "Americanization" changes as the context changes throughout an ethnic group's history in America. By the 1920s, Americanization meant loss of the Norwegian language and complete absorption into American society. In the 1850s and 1860s, both outcomes seemed highly unlikely. Command of Norwegian was too essential for daily communication, and the wider American society too resistant to complete acceptance of Norwegian Americans into its many circles and roles. In Norwegian America of the 1850s and 1860s, Americanization meant that the individual was sufficiently acculturated to perform the role of a broker, linking ethnic and Yankee societies. Both societies needed such go-betweens, and were willing to compensate them accordingly. Wisconsin's old-stock leaders needed brokers to communicate with the growing immigrant population. And, given the persistent language and cultural barriers, Norwegian Americans in Wisconsin needed brokers to communicate with the largely Yankee political, educational, commercial, and governmental institutions.

The Americanizing individual gradually moving beyond his ethnic origins was unlikely to obtain the complete acceptance needed for a leadership role in this Yankee society, and unlikely to turn down the compensation which both societies offered for assuming the broker's role.

In the late 1850s and early 1860s, Knute Nelson was attempting to transcend his narrow Vossing-American society. Many factors predisposed him to Americanizing influences. He lacked a strong father figure who might use paternal authority against Americanization. He had emigrated at a young age, before he had been educated in Norway or had adopted a Norwegian outlook on politics or culture. He had emigrated during the early history of Norwegian America, before its settlements had matured sufficiently to form a complete range of ethnic institutions—before its people thought of themselves as Norwegians more than as Vossings, Telemarkings, or Sognings. His family lacked status in Koshkonong, so he came to resent the superior status of the Lutheran clergy and the prosperous farmers like Gullick Thompson. Such resentments eased the way to acceptance of American ways. He came to a developing region where many opportunities both required some Americanization and resulted in further Americanization. The frontier's needs became the immigrant's opportunities.

Finally, he came to an America in sectional crisis. The country's needs became the immigrant's opportunity to serve and to be rewarded for service. While teaching in Pleasant Springs, Knute made friends with Johannes Melaas' son Christian, a student in Knute's school. They went skiing and snowshoeing on the winter Saturdays and Sundays. Knute turned nearly anything to some constructive purpose, and skiing was no exception. From a high hill, he would stop, look down upon an imaginary audience, and deliver an open-air address on the tariff, slavery, or Buchanan Democrats.[52]

Knute remained a loyal disciple of Douglas Democracy—opposed to slavery and Republicanism. He detested President

Buchanan. Douglas exhibited a kind of northern frontier bravado which fit quite nicely with Knute's pugnacious, Americanizing personality. In the 1850s, many Norwegian Americans supported the Democrats rather than the Whigs, whom they saw as a nativist aristocracy. Several Norwegian-language newspapers in 1850s Wisconsin were Democratic: *Democraten* (Racine), *Emigranten* (Inmansville), *Nordstjernen* (Madison), and *Den norske amerikaner* (Madison). Historian Odd Lovoll notes, "the Democratic party had without a doubt a strong appeal for the common people; it was the party of Jefferson and Jackson," and Jackson was "the living proof of the democratic principle of equality."[53] That appealed to Knute, with his growing resentment toward Gullick Thompson.

One morning at Albion's chapel, a professor read a comment from an English-language newspaper to criticize the Democratic party. Knute leaped to his feet and spoke out, "I should like to debate that point with the worthy gentleman and professor!"[54] He would soon get the chance to carry his frontier pugnacity beyond debating. Though exciting, with grand orations in the Senate Chamber, America's politics of white male democracy and constitutionalism failed to solve the problems of slavery and Southern separatism short of war. Democracy did not make men tolerant. It invited them to carry a pugnacious sense of honor into national debates. Insistence on their constitutional rights made them more contentious.

Three

Serving the Fatherland

In the mild southern Wisconsin climate, winter changed to spring, and Knute Nelson changed from teacher back to student. He returned to Albion Academy as a sophomore at the start of the spring term. He had earned money for his college education, and was determined to finish it. Much had changed in his adopted country as well. The fall 1860 campaign had ushered in a new era. He was still a low-tariff, anti-slavery, pro-Union Democrat, but he was in the minority. The Republicans' new candidate from neighboring Illinois won, after an exciting campaign with black-coated Wideawakes carrying torches through the streets for Lincoln, and a harried Stephen Douglas carrying a last-ditch appeal for Union through the secession-minded South. He stuck with Douglas, but the new states of the Northwest—Wisconsin (1848), Minnesota (1858), and Oregon (1859)—went with Lincoln.

Though the Republican platform and Lincoln's personal views did not envision action against slavery in the South, they were sufficiently anti-slavery to provoke the Deep South states to secede. By the time Knute returned to Albion in late February or early March, 1861, seven states had left to form the Confederacy. After Abraham Lincoln was sworn in as president on March 4, events moved precipitously. War-minded Southern hotheads overcame the opposition of Southern skeptics and fired upon Fort Sumter in Charleston harbor early in the morning of April 12. Two days later the fort surrendered. On April 15, President Lincoln requested the loyal states to furnish 75,000 volunteers to put down the "insurrection," which was "too powerful to be suppressed by the ordinary course of judicial proceedings."[1]

Individually and in groups, Albion's students considered whether they would volunteer for the extra-judicial proceedings. Any of them could construct a syllogism proving that secession resulting in firing on a United States fort had to be treason. The Union was in danger of disintegration. Young Knute Nelson discovered that Americanization had consequences when the adopted fatherland was threatened. As Norway was his mother, so henceforth America was his father. His ardent belief in American political institutions, his appreciation of the opportunities America had given him, and his own aggressive spirit—all made him a likely candidate for the Union's citizen army. He was not alone. He and eighteen other Albion students quickly made their decision. First, they began practice drills on the campus and the adjacent town common. In May, they enlisted in a state militia company, Racine's Black Hawk Rifles, commanded by a Captain Lohmiller.

The Albion boys soon realized their mistake. The Black Hawk Rifles was no New England-style, teetotaling militia company, but a freewheeling, hard-drinking group who hardly lived by Albion rules. Nelson described the commander as "an easy-going beer-drinking German, who kept little track of his men . . . the first and second lieutenants were bummers and toughs of the first water . . . when they were not drunk, they were continually swearing and God-damning the men."[2] The Albion volunteers rebelled at such goings-on. After six weeks of training with Lohmiller's "bummers," they showed their frontier democractic spirit by refusing to be sworn into federal service in the Black Hawk Rifles, despite threats of imprisonment. This time the Army capitulated, and agreed to transfer them to Company B of the Fourth Wisconsin Volunteers, an infantry regiment. The

34

Fourth Wisconsin was overwhelmingly "American," not Scandinavian American.[3]

Here, Knute's decision to enroll at Albion had the important consequence of throwing him into an "American" regiment. It kept him out of the all-Scandinavian Fifteenth Wisconsin, which he might have joined together with his neighbors if he had enlisted straight from his parents' Koshkonong farm. Thus, the Civil War served to further Americanize him in a manner unlikely if he had served in the famous Fifteenth. Separated from Colonel Hans Christian Heg's regiment with its 128 "Oles," he consistently underestimated Norwegian-American support for the war—and became embittered against slackers and lukewarm Lutheran pastors in Koshkonong.[4] Blegen noted, "The Civil War marked a new step in the identification of the Norwegian immigrants with the fortunes and ideals of their adopted country."[5] For Knute, that identification came as an individual—not as a collective experience shared with other immigrant soldiers. In fact, he came to doubt others' identification.

Nils (and probably Ingebjørg) opposed his decision to volunteer. In a later (1862) letter, he tried to explain to his stepfather: "I know that I caused you much grief in leaving you as I did; but my heart dictated it and I could not do otherwise."[6] In his many Civil War letters to his parents, he often expressed some guilt and concern over leaving them with all the farm work. Yet he never expressed regret over his decision to enlist.[7]

The Fourth Wisconsin took the train to Camp Utley in Racine, where they trained for one month. Very likely this was Knute's first train trip. He seemed exhilarated by the new experiences, by the drills, the good army food (better than at home!), and the wartime July 4 celebration. Perhaps to rebel against his Lutheran upbringing, he attended the local Norwegian Methodist church twice, and received newspapers and food from its pastor.[8]

On July 15, they left Racine by train for the Potomac front. Excited by the railroad, Knute used a farm metaphor to describe it to his parents: "The steam coach was our horse and a speedy

Private Knute Nelson serving the fatherland in his Civil War uniform.

one it was."[9] For them, he described each stop on the nine-day trip. Three months after Fort Sumter, civilians along the way still showed tremendous enthusiasm for the war and the troops. At Racine, "an enormous crowd of people had gathered to bid us farewell . . . . in a tremendous burst of hurrahs" we "immediately were traveling full speed toward Chicago." At Kenosha and

Waukegan, "men waved their hats high in the air, shouting 'Hurrah!' to us as we passed" and "ladies did the same with their handkerchiefs." The troops were suitably encouraged. At Chicago, the *Tribune* reported, "The arrival of the Fourth Wisconsin Regiment . . . was looked for by thousands of our citizens yesterday afternoon. They reached this city . . . at 4 P.M., and forming in column marched across the city . . . their entire route through Clark Street north and south being lined by spectators."[10] Still, Knute was disappointed that Chicago had not given them "so much as a cup of water," but perhaps that was because they did not arrive at suppertime. The next morning, Toledo made up for that with "a wonderful breakfast" of "good coffee, cake, pie, eggs, sandwiches, and ham" and Toledo's "ladies also filled our haversacks for the journey." Cleveland contributed "a wonderful dinner," Buffalo an ample breakfast, and Elmira, New York, "a wonderful evening meal." In Pennsylvania, the train traveled "through mountains, crossed trestles over valleys, and passed through thick woods." To Knute, "the country looked as if it were Norway."

Early on July 23, they arrived at their destination, Camp Dix, near Baltimore. Here they replaced some three-month volunteers who were guarding the rail lines in the area. Their term expired, these three-month men went home without having seen combat.[11] Two days earlier, the crushing Union defeat at Bull Run made it highly unlikely that the three-year 4th Wisconsin volunteers would avoid it. Elated to be so near the fighting, they were eager to put down local rebels.[12]

Knute felt some homesickness, but the enthusiastic reception on the way east had confirmed his patriotism. Despite his foreign origin, he was hailed as an advancing hero along with his comrades. That enthusiasm for the cause did not leave him. In the war's first few months, he formed the basic outlook which he would maintain throughout the war.

He expressed compassion for his family, and concern over their lack of farm workers. (The older of his brothers, William, was only nine when he left for the war.) Over half of his soldier's pay he sent home to pay for harvest help and to pay off the farm debt, which was accomplished by war's end through his help.[13] He provided advice on planting and on securing help for the harvest ("Where need wins one person to help, money wins ten.")[14] He promised to reward helpful neighbors "if I live." He appealed to their patriotism: "Let us hope that some of . . . your neighbors who have neither contributed man nor mite toward this mighty work now progressing will" consider "the cause of my absence and lend you a helping hand."[15]

From the start, he sarcastically criticized the stay-at-homes in Koshkonong. That was not due to war-weariness, but to his strongly Americanized patriotism. He recalled the Wideawake parades for Lincoln during the 1860 campaign: "But it surprises me very much that so few of the ones who paraded every night last fall in black coats, carrying torches high in the air on long sticks and yelling like crazy, were willing [to enlist]. One sees only a very few of them in the military ranks. They boasted that they could lick those Southern fire-eaters, all right. Easy. No trouble at all. But now the poor folk do not even dare come out and look the enemy in the eyes. From this we learn much that will be interesting in the future."[16] Throughout the war he complained about "Gunnar Torsen and Gudmand Lars . . . those big lummoxes" still at home, and about "all the friends of my youth who think more of their miserable limbs than the country's good." To such "friends" he sent this message: "I will not acknowledge or see them any more for they are not the country's friends and therefore are not mine." When Gunnar and Bjørn Torsen finally enlisted for a $500 bonus, he thought they did it "for money rather than because they loved the country." "Why could not such big strapping fellows have gone to fight for their country before now?"[17]

Through his parents, Knute tried to learn much about Norwegian Americans' attitudes toward the war. When inquiring about Gullick Thompson, he asked, "What is his opinion about the war?"[18] He wanted more news of "the neighbors": "Who is for the war and who is against it?"[19] Sending them stamps, he urged them to mail him copies of *Emigranten*, Madison's Norwegian-language (now strongly Republican) newspaper, so he could read up on the Koshkonong community's patriotism or lack thereof.[20]

Thoroughly aired in *Emigranten*, the Norwegian Synod's bitter debate over slavery caused Knute to blame the Lutheran Church for what he saw as a lack of Norwegian-American patriotism. The Synod had close ties to the German-American Missouri Synod, based in a slaveholding state, and sent its ministerial candidates to the Missourians' Concordia Seminary in St. Louis. When *Emigranten*'s editor, C.F. Solberg, inquired in May, 1861, about the war views of Concordia's faculty, a storm erupted. The Norwegian Synod's leaders engaged in "an abstract theological discussion" and concluded that slavery did not constitute "a sin in and of itself." Though their statement called slavery "an evil and a punishment from God," "condemn[ed] all abuses and sins connected therewith," and promised to "work for its abolition," the fateful words "not . . . a sin" encouraged misunderstanding and opposition.[21]

Probably in *Emigranten*, Knute "heard that the Norwegian Lutheran pastors sympathize with the South" and that "they regard slavery to be legal and moral according to the Bible." He asked his parents, "Is it true that they are indifferent to the war — to the Union's good cause?"[22] In another letter, he inquired "about what the Norwegian Lutheran pastors say and counsel about the war."[23] When a new bridge was built over Mud Creek, he joked about the pastor and the sexton being the first to use it — though they evidently had not helped to build it.[24] He criticized the Norwegian farmers' reliance on "the church with its poor pastor as the one and only means of instruction" in the community.[25]

Clearly, his perception that Norwegian Americans hesitated to enlist and Lutheran pastors sympathized with slavery and the South made his soldiering even more of an Americanizing experience. It distanced him from his Norwegian-American roots in

Koshkonong. It caused him to cleave more strongly to his American fatherland and its cause.

His growing cynicism about the Lutheran Church alarmed the devout Ingebjørg. When his parents asked if he went to church, he replied, "occasionally," and added a jest: "I was quartered in one for 4 days. I call this attending Church on a grand scale."[26] Responding to his mother's concerns, he wrote, "There is one thing I want to tell you about the soldier: He thinks less about eternity than about home, parents, and friends."[27] She was not reassured — especially when she realized that Knute was not looking to church and Bible for strength, but to Esaias Tegnér's *Frithjofs Saga*, an epic poem set in the ancient Norway of the old Norse gods and goddesses.[28]

Actually, Knute's strength in soldiering came equally from his zealous, civil-religious patriotism. He reassured his parents, "Remember now that, next to God, you have a good government to be thankful for — a country without equal in the whole world."[29] And, "I will be satisfied with whatever happens to me in this war, if only the country comes out of this peril safe . . . the finest and best government on earth."[30] The finest government could not fail in its future projects if only it could be rescued from Southern secessionism. To rescue it, he was willing to be sacrificed "on the country's altar . . . . If the country needs my blood and life I give them freely."[31]

Knute supplemented this patriotic devotion with romanticized tales of the Viking past. His less Americanized, more intimate side needed encouragement as much as the more public, Americanized side. He did not read stories of Revolutionary War heroes or take the Minuteman as his model. Perhaps he did not feel Americanized enough to personally identify with such heroes. The fatherland's civil religion had to be supplemented with the tales of the mother country.

In October, 1861, he asked his parents to send him a copy of *Frithjofs Saga*, which he was "very much gratified" to receive by November: "It is my constant companion and many a lonely hour do I spend with it by the side of my solitary fire when on picket guard in the woods with no other companion but my rifle."[32] "New Years day 1862," he noted, "was spent chiefly in perusing Tegners great Poem 'Frithjofs Saga,'" which "kept my spirits up during the day."[33] He lost the book later that year, and when his brother William sent another copy, Knute was relieved: "I felt its loss more than any book left at home; to me it was a happy companion."[34]

Frithjofs Saga is set in the eighth century, in Norway's Sognefjord, just north of Voss. Though merely the son of a wealthy farmer, Frithjof is much superior to Helge, the son of his father's friend the king. Like Knute, the young hero Frithjof loses his father. He also loses his love, Ingeborg, when her brother Helge forbids their marriage. Like Knute, the hot-tempered Frithjof leaves home for distant battlefields and dangerous missions, His pugnacity causes him to set fire inadvertently to the god Balder's temple, which forces him into an exile's life of Viking raiding. He eventually returns, reclaims Ingeborg, and is reconciled to Helge in a moving scene in Balder's reconstructed temple.[35]

A genius in his use of poetic meter, Tegnér wrote his epic poem in the 1830s, during the Romantic era. He softened the harsher edges of the Norse gods somewhat for his Christian-era readers.[36] Even so, Knute's mother was not at all reconciled to her son's strong interest in *Frithjofs Saga*, especially to the final scene in Balder's temple. In a letter to William, Knute praised that final scene, called "Forsoningen" (The Reconciliation), and added, "Tell mother to read it." He was "sure if she reads it carefully and understands it she will not blame me for being so fond of it, nor can she help liking it herself."[37]

Partly, Knute used *Frithjofs Saga* to distance himself from his mother's piety and sentimentality. When Ingebjørg asked Knute to send "a lock of my hair to remember me by," he called that "a verry [sic] silly notion." As an alternative suggestion, he quoted from Thorstein's dying words to his son Frithjof the Bold:

41

Du selv skal dø, og dø skal hvad dig tilhør';
men én Ting, ved jeg, Frithjof, som aldrig dør;
det er den Dom, vi over de døde høre.
Hvad ædelt er du ville, hvad ret du gjøre.[38]

[You yourself and what is yours must die,
Frithjof, but one thing I know which never dies—
That is the renown we hear about the dead:
Your noble desires, your good deeds.]

Displaying a growing ambition, Knute disdained to be remembered only by a lock of hair, but wished to be "remembered by 'what he has done.'"[39]

Thus, Knute tired of the 4th Wisconsin's do-nothing guard duty on the vital railroad link between Baltimore and Washington. For nearly four months they were stationed at Relay House, a rail junction south of Baltimore where a rail line also led west to Harper's Ferry. Complaining that "we are not only soldiers but cooks and washerwomen," Knute the bold grew impatient and looked hopefully for "the glory of quite a severe battle, which we very much desire."[40]

His hopes were aroused when the regiment was made part of the Army of the Peninsula and moved to the lower counties of eastern Maryland. But no renown or noble deeds resulted. Instead, the Fourth Wisconsin returned to Paterson's Park in Baltimore, where inaction allowed them to enjoy a three-hour-long Christmas (1861) meal "of the finest quality" at the home of a "rich Unionist."[41]

On February 18, 1862, they left Baltimore by steamer for Virginia, where they expected to join General Ambrose Burnside's troops near Norfolk. However, in early March they were reloaded onto the steamer *Constitution* for a six-day trip to Ship Island, Mississippi, on the way to New Orleans. It was a trip Knute would never forget or wish repeated, with an up-and-down motion reminiscent of Tegnér's singsong meter in "Frithjof on the Ocean." Packed in with other men from stem to stern, Knute betrayed his Viking ancestors, for he was embarrassingly seasick. From Ship Island, he confessed, "I have never valued ground as much as when I set my foot on this island. I'll take the solid land for mine, and let whoever will keep the sea."[42]

His regiment headed for New Orleans and the Mississippi River campaign of General Benjamin F. Butler and Admiral David G. Farragut. By late April, Farragut had breached the Mississippi delta fortifications and ascended the river to New Orleans. Butler then took command of New Orleans and lower Louisiana. On May 1, 1862, the 4th Wisconsin and the 31st Massachusetts were the first to enter New Orleans to take possession of the Customs House and Post Office.

In Louisiana, Knute witnessed an increasingly harsh military policy toward civilians. On May 15, Butler issued his infamous General Order 28 in retaliation for civilian, especially female, insults aimed at his troops. Any woman caught insulting Union troops would "be regarded" and "treated" as a prostitute. After the 4th Wisconsin left, Butler ordered the execution of a civilian who had torn down the Union flag. [43] He closed down the *Delta* newspaper office, imprisoned the mayor and "many other smaller lights," disbanded the city's police, forced merchants to open their stores, and threatened confiscation of the property of disloyal citizens.[44]

The hardening effects of soldiering became evident in Knute's hearty approval of these measures. When the 4th Wisconsin first marched into New Orleans, he reported, "a few drunken Rowdies" called them "'dam Yankees' or 'Abe Lincoln Monkies,'" but then Butler put "his iron grip around them" and now no one dared to "insult or speak disrespectively of a U.S. soldier or his flag."[45] After several months of Union occupation, he reported, "New Orleans is now as quiet a place comparatively as Cambridge [Wisconsin]." He approved of the confiscations: "This is summarily[sic] but yet it is needful and good—Severe yet wholesome—Hard yet effectual."[46]

After an abortive May expedition toward Vicksburg, the 4th Wisconsin left Baton Rouge on June 13, 1862, for Vicksburg as part of a 4,000-man brigade. On the way up the river, Confederates fired on them near Grand Gulf, Mississippi. After routing the rebels, the Union troops "set the town on fire and burned down every house as a warning to other small towns along the river." This small town "was about the size of Cambridge."[47] Knute clearly approved of this retaliatory act and warned of a similar fate for Vicksburg: "But Vicksburg is to be punished more severely than shot and shell can do it. It will remain a memento of this rebellion to the Rebells, mutely telling them to beware of how in the future they treat Uncle Sam."[48]

The 4th Wisconsin worked on Farragut's daring plan to dig a canal twelve feet wide and fifteen feet deep in order to bypass the Confederate cannon commanding the river at Vicksburg. Tough work it was digging a five-mile-long ditch to change the course of the Father of Waters. When the ditch filled with two feet of water, they turned the hard work over to 2,000 "contrabands" (former slaves), who dug for twelve hours a day while standing in water under the hot sun. Knute claimed that "they like it very well." He crowed, "We have taught the slaveholders that we can use their slaves as well as their own government can."[49]

His first real taste of combat came on August 15, 1862, when Confederate General J.C. Breckenridge "attacked us with about 6,000 men," giving the Confederates a 3-to-1 advantage. After a sharp fight, Breckenridge retreated, and the 4th Wisconsin helped bury the 320 Confederate dead. Though they were present at the battle, they had not fired their guns or killed any rebels.[50]

Military life is brief excitement and long monotony. After the battle, the regiment remained in Baton Rouge through December, and then into February. Knute longed for a decisive battle to advance the cause "of the finest and best government on earth." Such was his confidence in that government, that he rarely complained about its strategy or tactics. The March, 1863, "expedition" to Port Hudson, a Confederate fort on the Mississippi, was one exception: "The expedition amounted to this—The troops marched to within 3 miles of Port Hudson, camped over night, and returned by slow marches and far fetched maneuveres to Baton Rouge . . . . The plan and Gene[r]alship of marching to Port Hudson with 30,000 men and returning without even striking the least blow or having the slightest skirmish I can neither see the philosophy of nor account for. Doubtless there was deep strategy in it." Knute's comrades called these "Potomac tactics" in honor of General Nathaniel Banks, who had come from the Eastern theater to replace Butler.[51]

After an April 12th skirmish near Bayou Teche, the 4th Wisconsin marched toward Texas, and was converted into a cavalry regiment to correct a shortage of cavalry. Knute found cavalry duty hard: "I have been in the saddle every day on some duty or other hardly having time to eat and sleep."[52]

By the end of May, they were back on foot, and back east to attack Port Hudson. Knute saw his hardest combat yet in a May 27th assault on Port Hudson. The 4th Wisconsin formed the third line in the attack. The first two lines sustained heavy casualties. Nelson reported, "We advanced, the two lines ahead gradually melting into killed, wounded and an astonishing number of skulkers and cowards found laying on their faces hugging the ground shivering with fear. These we passed over kicking punching and damning them though a *very, very* small number of even our own Regt showed the white feather much to our regret. . . . When within 80 Rods of the Earthworks we found ourselves . . . encountering a storm of bullit, grape shell and canister." Here, the Fourth was ordered to halt. They looked back over the field at the dead and wounded. "The scene was not a happy one yet we looked upon it in the cold stoical spirit of a soldier—a slight chilling pang and then a return body and soul to the enemy before us." But no further attack was made.[53]

On June 2, they were temporarily relieved and reunited with their horses, but then were called back for another assault on Port Hudson scheduled for June 14. This was to be Knute's closest

45

brush with death in battle. The night before, he had a premonition of imminent death. The Wisconsin troops were to lead the next day's assault and "we knew very well what the morning had in store for us." They handed mementos to friends "who were sick and could not take part in the attack"—and who could mail the items to relatives and "could write to them of our death." For once, Knute worried and could not sleep. He thought about the contrast between the family's poverty when they first came to Koshkonong and their present nearly debt-free status. Like a land-hungry Vossing, he thought about his parents who now had "a good little farm," so "it seemed to me that my death could not injure" them. With those comforting thoughts, he fell asleep.[54]

Knute's premonition was not far off the mark. The next morning, he and three comrades advanced to within twenty yards of the Port Hudson breastworks before they were hit by Confederate fire. One was killed outright, a second was mortally wounded in seven places, and a third was unhurt. Knute was wounded deep in the thigh by a musket ball or shrapnel, which was never removed.[55]

They were found by three Confederates, who came out of the breastworks to look for canteens, haversacks, and other plunder. The Confederates, Knute recalled, "accosted us very civily— 'How are you all getting along, boys?'—'We were rather to[o] much for you I reckon'?" They tried to persuade Knute to allow himself to be taken into the fort: "'you had better come; we have good Surgens . . . . If you stay here you will die.'" But he "demurred saying I could by degrees crawl back til I could reach help from our men. And that I would certainly fare better [there] than within a beleaguered starving Fort." The rebels were undeterred. Two of them helped Knute as he "hobbled in" to the fort.

For over three weeks, Knute was held prisoner inside Port Hudson, where he met D.B. Arnold, the son of a rich planter from northern Mississippi. They became close friends—not unusual for persons who came to know Knute Nelson. Arnold's family

46

had lost everything when an Illinois regiment destroyed much of their property. The major had smashed his sister's piano for "refusing to play the 'Star-Spangled Banner' on it when requested." Three of his brothers had been killed. If anyone had been punished severely for the South's ill-treatment of Uncle Sam, it was Arnold. During their frequent conversations, Arnold told Knute that if he could just return home, "he would never fight Uncle Sam any more." Usually quite hostile toward the "Rebells," Knute seemed to forgive this "contrite and penitent" Confederate.[56]

After Port Hudson surrendered on July 8, Knute rejoined his regiment to take up the duties of a regimental adjutant's orderly. On September 1, 1863, he was promoted to corporal. He liked the orderly's position, "chiefly because it gave me opportunity for study and mental improvement."[57] As a garrison regiment guarding the lower Mississippi after the fall of Vicksburg and Port Hudson, the 4th Wisconsin faced fewer pitched battles. In the months before his scheduled mustering-out (July, 1864), Knute gave serious thought to re-enlisting as a lieutenant in a black regiment, but he dropped the idea: "It would take my enlistment time beyond the end of the war, and I do not like the black man well enough for that."[58]

He shared his fellow soldiers' prejudiced yet curious attitude toward blacks. As historian Reid Mitchell observes, "it was simply not the case that meeting the blacks of the South firsthand necessarily diminished the racism of the Union soldier."[59] Knute was impressed by black children who "learn faster than many White children I have seen." In fact, "both young and old are very anxious to learn."[60] Yet he still regarded them as inferior to whites. He thought it only right that "contrabands" were made to stand in water and dig ditches under the hot sun while white soldiers supervised. To honor Arnold's slave "Pud," he gave his new horse the same name: ". . .there is something odd and lugubrous in the comparison of Arnold's Pud and my Pud. His a Human being, mine a Brute. Yet both eaqualy dear to and beloved by and holding nearly the same relations to their masters."[61] His quick friendship with Arnold and his easy acceptance of a "personalized" master-slave relationship seen firsthand demonstrated that it was good for his pro-war zeal that his prewar acquaintance with slavery had been limited to talk of a distant "Slave Power." Up-close familiarity might have led him to agree with the Norwegian-American pastors that slavery was not a sin "in and of itself." But whatever his prejudices regarding blacks, Knute still supported Reconstruction.

The war changed his politics. It slowly eroded his Democratic loyalties, though he retained the egalitarian ethos of frontier democracy. After recovering from his wound, he wrote a lengthy essay which revealed his changing attitudes. He called for a future "War Democratic party," in the tradition of Andrew Jackson and Stephen A. Douglas. Yet his anger at the Copperheads presently in the party and at the past "political fossills of corruption and scurvy and nastiness of the Administration of Pierce, Buchanan & Breckenridge" did not bode well for his own future Democratic loyalties. He tried to argue that rank-and-file Democrats supported the war effort, though that "can not be said of the majority of its party leaders."[62] But a party's leaders could not be thus divorced from their followers. With each month, he drifted farther toward the Republicans.

The engine driving his continued Americanization and his Republicanization was his army service. In another essay, he contrasted the nationalistic army and the localistic politicians (Democrats were usually more localistic): "Our country is ful of little sectional politicians and statesmen. No place is more unfavorably and unhealthily to this species, than our army in the midst of a great war for the safety and integrity of the nation. The country as an agregated and indivisible whole is continualy before his [the soldier's] mind." Using Republicans' prewar talk of the "Slave Power," he compared the Civil War to the Protestant

Reformation. "Slavery like the Pope became avaricious of power," and the resulting conflict became far more revolutionary than first anticipated.[63] Certainly, the war eventually made Knute just as Republican as the Reformation made his ancestors Lutheran.

For Knute Nelson, the war was a life-changing experience, which he described for Nils, who evidently felt that Knute needed this "good school for his undutiful son." Knute assured him that the "careless reckless wild boy" of prewar years "will return if Providence wills it, with more experience and more thoughtful." The son "has learnt that the world is not the school house nor the narrow limits of the farm."[64]

In this "good school," he learned intense patriotism, self-discipline, patience, and other virtues. He became hardened to repression and suppression of civil liberties. Disloyalty he now associated with the Copperheads, whom he hated. He would later apply the same intolerance toward Spanish imperialism, German "Kultur," Bolshevik radicalism, and other alien ideologies. From Koshkonong's Norwegian-American young men's slowness to enlist, he wrote, "we learn much that will be interesting in the future." He would apply those lessons in World War I, but more immediately, he learned to move away from his Norwegian-American roots. Completing school brings rewards. His Civil War schooling would be an essential stepping-stone to political success in the postwar years. Serving the American fatherland would bring political rewards almost as great as being born in the mother country, Norway.

The nation's Civil War schooling would contribute to political failure. The war did not end with a reconciliation scene. For the next three decades, "little sectional politicians," North and South, would wave the bloody shirt of Civil War memories. An indivisible, centralized Union would depend on Republican victories. Its political and economic progress seriously retarded, the South would continue to oppose a strong central government.

49

Southern separatism would be "the fundamental issue facing the nation" for the rest of the century. It would delay and weaken workers' and farmers' attempts to make the "economic and social dislocations of northern industrial expansion" the major issue.[65] Knute would be enlisted to aid Republicans' delaying and weakening tactics.

Four

Frontier Broker between
Koshkonong and Madison

Mustered out at Morganzia, Louisiana, near Baton Rouge, Nelson was eager to return to Koshkonong, his family, and his studies at Albion Academy. When the Fall 1864 term began, he was one of the oldest students, a bearded "senior statesman," a toughened veteran with a clearer picture of what he wanted from life. He returned a new political convert. That fall, the former Douglas Democrat emerged as a Lincoln Republican, a metamorphosis facilitated by Lincoln's use of the "Union," not Republican, label that year. At the height of the presidential campaign, Nelson delivered his first campaign speech, which impressed the Albion faculty: "He gave a campaign speech in the hall of his Alma mater favoring the second election of Abraham Lincoln, which was called the most lucid candidate speech ever given by a politician [at Albion], notwithstanding nearly all the Governors of the state had spoken there."[1] No doubt, Nelson's soldierly disgust at Copperheads and "Potomac Generals" helped turn him against the Democrats and their candidate, the former commander of the Army of the Potomac, George B. McClellan. Also, he identified with Lincoln, though it is unclear if that empathy predated Lincoln's death.

Partly, Nelson identified with Lincoln because of the similarities in their poverty-stricken, migratory childhoods. In a later speech, he traced the Lincoln family's migration from Pennsylvania to Virginia to Kentucky, then to Indiana, and finally to Illinois. Nelson depicted them as peasants escaping a slave society which "had debased the white people of the South": "This peasantry though primitive, rude, and unlettered, was nevertheless in many ways far superior to its counterpart in the old world. It was courageous to a high degree, intensely democratic in spirit, and charged with a suppressed intellectuality. . . .From the very loins of this class, and as a crystallization of all the virile vigor that was in it came Abraham Lincoln— born the American peasant—died the American King."[2] Here, Nelson projected onto Lincoln his own intense ambition to rise from peasantry to "be next to the King," as he expressed it at Castle Garden. The courage, democratic spirit, "suppressed intellectuality," and "virile vigor" he praised were his own self-admiring qualities projected onto Lincoln's family.

Completing his studies at Albion was an essential step in fulfilling this ambition. College degrees were rare among Norwegian-American farmers' sons in the 1860s. Nelson was determined to earn his Bachelor of Philosophy (Ph.B.) degree. His last terms at Albion passed without significant incident. He was among the campus' most popular and academically talented students. When he graduated at the head of his class in 1865, he had a good general education to prepare him for a career in law and politics.[3]

In choosing the law, Nelson followed in the footsteps of Lincoln, Douglas, and numerous other American politicians. Yet he had more immediate practical reasons than political ambition with all its uncertainties. There were no Norwegian-American lawyers in Koshkonong.[4] He was certain to find clients among his fellow immigrants who lacked sufficient command of English or confidence in Yankee barristers. He had the English-language skills, college diploma, and patriotic war record which could serve as entrées into the Yankee-dominated legal world. Finally, the legal profession lay outside the authority of Koshkonong's

Lutheran clergy. It was safe territory for a dissident like Nelson. By contrast, his Koshkonong acquaintance and fellow critic of the clergy Rasmus B. Anderson faced severe trials in getting established in college teaching, which definitely fell within the ministerial sphere of influence.[5]

In the fall of 1865, Nelson moved from the Tangen farm to the bustling state capital, Madison, a city of some 7,000 people picturesquely located on the narrow isthmus between lakes Mendota and Monona. At one end of the isthmus loomed the new university buildings on College Hill. At the other end, on its own smaller hill, stood the yellow-brown three-story capitol building, still under construction, lacking its dome and looking hatless before the stiff lake breezes.[6]

Nelson began "reading law" in the law office of William F. Vilas.[7] There was no law school closer than Indiana, and he could not have afforded the tuition, so an apprenticeship was the only feasible approach. Though postwar Wisconsin was passing beyond the primitive frontier stage, it still partly subscribed to the "Western egalitarian views" of the frontier—"that every ambitious and honest young man had the 'immemorial right' to make a living and rise in his chosen profession" without formal academic credentials. Oratory rather than book learning swayed frontier juries, and a close acquaintance with that audience plus "rough and ready wit . . . counted infinitely more than subtle legal reasoning."[8]

Vilas was no mere glad-handing spellbinder, but a law-school graduate and a painstaking legal practitioner. The "only person in Madison with law-school training," he served as Wisconsin's reviser of statutes and as a distinguished mentor to many young legal apprentices.[9] For Nelson, "reading law" probably first meant copying Vilas's legal drafts, then drafting his own simple documents, reading law books, and listening to Vilas's counsel ("Never be afraid of your own conclusions"), which fit well with Nelson's self-confident personality.[10]

Lacking funds, Nelson suffered "privations" which were obvious to Vilas. He had saved little money, for over half his soldier's pay had been sent home for his stepfather's use. Fortunately, he received a soldier's bonus on July 28, 1866, just in time to see him through his legal apprenticeship.[11] While reading law, he took out his first American citizenship papers on October 23, 1866. His Vossing roots and veteran's status gave him no standing before American courts without citizenship.

In the spring of 1867, he was examined by a committee of the Dane County Circuit Court, and admitted by Judge Philip L. Spooner to the Wisconsin bar. In the fall he opened a law office "above Halle Steensland's store" on King Street in Madison. On the front page of *Emigranten*, he advertised himself as the "Norwegian attorney" (*Norsk prokurator*) connected "with the firm Spooner and Lamb, Attorneys."[12] Although he warned "our countrymen to avoid if possible all legal proceedings," *Emigranten's* editor obligingly stated that he could "highly recommend Mr. Nelson, Esquire, as an adviser and an attorney, should legal proceedings become unavoidable."[13] He repeated this endorsement several months later in an article titled "Norsk prokurator."[14] In 1867, those two words carried a connotation of improbability in Koshkonong—something like the term "Quaker general." Supported by an editor who was also a broker, Knute Nelson became a legal broker, linking the Norwegian-American farmers of Koshkonong to the American legal system's local branch offices in Madison.

He also aspired to the role of political broker, to represent Koshkonong's farmers in the legislature in Madison. Admission to the bar was an important first step in a political system stressing constitutionalism. Justice Joseph Story noted, "The discussion of constituitonal questions throws a lustre round the bar . . . which can rarely belong to the profession in any other country."[15] In his career, Nelson would often throw a lustre of legalism around his political opinions by phrasing them in constitutional terms impressive to Norwegian-American farmers.

In politics as in law, connections to both old-stock and

54

Norwegian Americans were vital. In Madison's small legal fraternity, he became acquainted with a Yankee lawyer and politician named Eli A. Spencer, then Wisconsin's Assistant Secretary of State.[16] Spencer encouraged him to run for the Assembly seat in Dane county's second district, and apparently persuaded some old-stock Americans to support him.[17] Meanwhile, Nelson pursued a separate, behind-the-scenes campaign among Norwegian Americans. He wrote to local Norwegian-American leader Lars J. Erdall of Deerfield to suggest that Erdall "urge me forward, after this fashion: That there are many Norwegians in that District. That the Norwegians have never yet had one of their countrymen as a candidate or member of Assembly from said District. That they are now anxious to have some one of their number up as a candidate. And that I am the man they propose." Nelson promised to support Ole C. Johnson, a Norwegian American, for the Republican nomination for Prison Commissioner at the upcoming state convention.[18]

Second district Republicans held their convention in the obscure hamlet of Token Creek on Saturday, October 5, 1867. The favorite for the Assembly nomination was Captain George Weeks, a farmer and Civil War hero of New England ancestry.[19] Despite Spencer's and Nelson's advance work, Weeks led on the informal ballot and the first formal ballot. Discouraged, Nelson tried to leave Token Creek in his borrowed buggy, but the horse, a neighbor's, would not obey his commands. Word came that the convention had given Nelson a narrow majority on the second formal ballot, and now wanted an acceptance speech. Nelson recalled, "I concluded I had better give the horse plenty of time to get started and went back to the hall."[20] Spencer's work among old-stock Americans—aided by Nelson's Civil War record—was probably more responsible for the victory than was Nelson's Norwegian strategy.[21] Without his military record, he could never have defeated the war hero, Weeks.

Local Democrats charged that Spencer had engineered the choice of "Knudt Nelson, an obscure Norwegian." Gleefully, the

Republican *Wisconsin State Journal* seized on that unfortunate phrase "obscure Norwegian," described his Civil War record, and praised Nelson highly: "Possessing the industry, perseverence and probity, which so prominently characterize the Norwegians, he has . . . acquired a good education, served his adopted country over three years as a private soldier, studied law, and been admitted to the bar."[22] Proud of this praise, *Emigranten* reprinted in full this response and called the Democrats' phrase—"obscure Norwegian"—a *skjældsord* (term of abuse).[23]

From October 23 to November 4, Knute Nelson joined other Republican candidates in giving campaign speeches in the rural schoolhouses of eastern Dane county.[24] Supported by the *State Journal*, *Emigranten*, and many proud Norwegian Americans, he won his first election with a large majority.[25] Norwegian Americans were especially proud that Nelson was "a fine speaker" who "speaks English like a native."[26] Such a fluent representative would do much to improve Yankee opinion of them.

Emigranten expressed the hope that a Nelson victory would "make him known, help him make a name for himself, and thereby increase his business."[27] It did not immediately do any of these things. He had to suspend his legal practice during the legislative session, which began January 8, 1868. The second youngest Wisconsin legislator, Nelson played only a minor role. By making him chair of the committee on enrolled bills, legislative leaders used his skill at drafting legal documents much as Vilas had—and perhaps asked his advice as little as Vilas had. He was a legal dray horse that first session. He secured the passage of only two pieces of minor local legislation.[28] He did, however, reward the Norwegian-American community by introducing resolutions to print a Norwegian-language translation of the Governor's address and to give *Fædrelandet's* correspondent the same free postage and stationery as the English-language correspondents received. Both resolutions passed.[29]

Nelson briefly interrupted his stay in Madison to return to Deerfield, where on January 22, 1868, he married Nicholina

Jacobson of Christiana township, just south of Deerfield. Born in Toten, Norway, on October 3, 1846, Nicholina had arrived with her parents in the United States in 1852. Because of Nelson's long-standing antipathy toward the local Lutheran clergy, Justice of the Peace Lars Erdall married them at his home.[30]

Nicholina was five months pregnant. Their first-born, Ida G. Nelson, was born May 23, 1868. As with the story of the "widow" Ingebjørg, so now Nelson (or biographers, family, and friends) scrambled the dates of marriage and birth to avoid social and political embarrassment. Either Knute and Nicholina were said to have married in 1867 or Ida was said to have been born in 1869. Still, the marriage proved to be a sound choice for both partners. Down to her death in 1922, Nelson commonly referred to his Nicholina "as a wonderful helpmate in life." A reserved Norwegian-American woman of simple tastes, Nicholina "had no desire for 'high society,' frills or furbelows."[31]

Marriage and fatherhood increased the economic pressure on him—and his interest in moving to the homesteading frontier, where lawyers were in demand in land-law cases. Earlier, while still reading law, he had weighed a possible move to Elk Point in the rich Missouri River bottomlands in southeastern Dakota Territory. Repeatedly, he wrote to a friend there about home-steading and opportunities for lawyers.[32] In July, 1867, he wrote to Erdall that he had "not fully decided" about "squatting down here" or "go[ing] west."[33]

He stayed in Madison, but he did not prosper there. Opening his Madison law office, he wrote to brother William for bed-clothes from home so that he could "save one dollar a week" by fixing up a bed in "a little room next to my office."[34] He was not overwhelmed with clients. He was largely sustained by his connection with the Yankee firm of Spooner & Lamb, which hired him to communicate with its Norwegian-American clients in Koshkonong. In the important Krogh case, involving one farmer's construction of a dam which flooded his neighbors' fields, Philip Spooner directed the legal technicalities, but

Nicholina Jacobson around the time of her marriage to Knute Nelson. Four years younger than Knute, she emigrated with her parents from Toten near Lake Mjøsa in southeastern Norway, in 1852.

depended on Nelson's knowledge of Norwegian and of the area farmers: "I should not be willing to try the case *without you*. With my ignorance of the witnesses, my difficulty in *conversing* with the parties and my want of acquaintance with the locus in quo [your absence] would place me under serious embarrassment."[35] Despite this connection, Nelson was in such financial straits that he had to use his brother William as a go-between to deliver messages to his clients in Deerfield.[36] He may have made some money, though, as the Dane county "emigration commissioner." People desiring to send their relatives in Norway a brochure about Wisconsin could write to him and he would send the brochures postpaid—at state expense.[37]

Postwar Madison was not a lucrative field for a young lawyer. From 1867 to 1871, the Wisconsin economy suffered a recession caused by "a shortage of money and credit." New federal legislation eliminated over $2,000,000 in state banknotes, while Wisconsin did not get its share "of the new national banks and national banknotes." Even the wheat market suffered a decline from 1869 to 1872.[38] The whole country was in a deflationary period. Wisconsin's young couples and Civil War veterans were looking west toward Minnesota and the Dakota Territory. Most good farmland had been already claimed in southern Wisconsin —and Nelson was still landless, a worrisome condition for a Vossing.

With both their families living in Koshkonong, Knute and Nicholina were not yet willing to move. His third soldier's bonus arrived in February, 1868, and helped greatly to finance their start as newlyweds. With Knute away in Madison at the legislature and his law office, Nicholina lived at Tangen.[39]

He decided to seek a second term in the Wisconsin Assembly. Legislative service had not noticeably increased his legal business, but then he was not so busy that he could not legislate three months out of the year. Assemblymen were paid $2.50 per day during the session, and a Madison resident like Nelson incurred no extra expenses.[40] At the Republican district convention in Sun

Nelson as the tousled, Lincolnesque lawyer of the Upper Country's frontier circuit courts. Photo by N.J. Trenham, Alexandria, ca. 1876.

Begun in 1857, the new state capitol did not receive its dome until 1869, and its interior was not finished until 1872, after Knute Nelson had moved to Minnesota.

Prairie on September 19, 1868, he again faced Captain Weeks and again won after the second formal ballot.[41] Once nominated, he went methodically about rounding up votes and won a relatively easy reelection.

When the legislative session opened on January 14, 1869, sophomore legislator Knute Nelson appeared more relaxed, more experienced, and a little more cynical. Among his new colleagues in the Assembly was Andrew Jackson Turner, father of the historian Frederick Jackson Turner, originator of the famous "frontier thesis" of American historical development.[42] In the first days of the session, Nelson reacted with Vossing humor to a legislative rule against smoking during sessions. Then a pipe-smoker, Nelson retaliated with a "sarcastic" resolution instructing the sergeant-at-arms "to enforce good morals by prohibiting the chewing of tobacco in the assembly chamber." To his surprise, it

61

passed. *Fædrelandet* questioned how the sergeant-at-arms could enforce it, however.[43]

His increased experience—or cynicism—was displayed early, when the resolution to print the governor's message in various foreign languages was introduced. In 1868, Nelson had himself introduced it. Now, he opposed it: "Mr. Knute Nelson said last year he enthusiastically advocated the printing of these messages in foreign languages, but he felt now that it was a humbug and a useless expenditure, at least as far as the Norwegians were concerned. It was simply a small subsidy to a party newspaper. He had seen none of these messages about the State last year." It was left to a non-Norwegian, a Mr. Hurlbut, to argue that many Norwegian-American constituents "were anxious for these documents."[44]

Assemblyman A.J. Turner also defended the resolution, which narrowly passed. Editor of the *Wisconsin State Register* in Portage, Turner was a skilled frontier politician from a wilder, more polyglot area than Koshkonong. He knew the importance of satisfying all ethnic groups. His son later recalled how his father "harmonized the rival tongues and interests of the various towns of the county, and helped to shepherd a very composite flock."[45] The famous son used his father's experience and his own childhood in Portage to hypothesize that "the frontier is the line of most rapid and effective Americanization." The "wilderness" found the settler "a European in dress, industries, tools, modes of travel, and thought," and made him an American. The advancing frontier thus "meant a steady movement away from the influence of Europe, a steady growth of independence on American lines."[46] Koshkonong's strongly Norwegian character, however, and the popularity of a resolution to print American political documents in European languages both argued against any "steady movement away from the influence of Europe."

Assemblyman Nelson was confronted by the continued influence of Europe in opposition to one Americanizing institution, the public school. He became embroiled in the common-school controversy which raged among Norwegian-American Lutherans in the late 1860s. It pitted the more conservative Lutheran ministers against a few liberals such as *Skandinaven*'s editor, Knud Langeland, Professor Rasmus B. Anderson, Pastor C.L. Clausen, and farmer and businessman John A. Johnson. It had flared in 1858-1859, had been temporarily overshadowed by the slavery controversy, then broke out anew in 1867-1869.

Conservative ministers distrusted public schools. Under frontier conditions, they and their teachers often did not meet the educated ministers' European standards. Teachers might be ignorant and inexperienced; there was a high turnover of teachers; discipline was sometimes lacking. Teachers might be Catholic or otherwise hostile to Lutheranism, thus endangering their students' Lutheran faith. Often, they were simply "religionless." Pastors tried to nudge their parsimonious congregations toward the creation of parochial schools to partly or fully replace this defective frontier institution.[47]

Some liberal critics accused the pastors of attempting "pastoral Norwegianization." They attacked what they saw as clerical promotion of "ignorance and superstition," and stressed acceptance of the English language and democratic American ways. Some stressed the conflict between Norwegian culture and American culture. Others stressed religious tolerance, even secularization, as a counterweight to what they saw as religious dogmatism.[48] The conflict had a third dimension: the class difference between the university-educated, elitist clergy and the minimally-- educated, anti-elite laity. The latter perceived the clergy as looking down their noses at common schools.[49]

A practical compromise would be to allow the teaching of the Norwegian language in largely Norwegian-American school districts. For defenders of the public schools, this compromise had the advantage of minimizing the Norwegian vs. American dimension in the debate, and thereby highlighting the secular vs. sectarian dimension. As a public school defender, Nelson introduced a bill in 1868 authorizing one hour of instruction in Norwegian. When it failed, he re-introduced it in the 1869 session.[50] *Fædrelandet* praised it: "Our countrymen owe Knute Nelson thanks for this attempt to help them . . .the law will be beneficial—in any case for the Norwegians among the state's foreign-born population . . . But the feeling among the Americans is against everything which might appear to preserve the immigrants' foreign character . . . [they say] that 'the public schools shall not Norwegianize or Germanize the Americans, but Americanize the Norwegians and Germans.'"[51] The bill passed. Norwegian Americans were urged to attend their fall 1869 district school meetings to vote for the one hour of Norwegian instruction.[52]

One week before the legislature adjourned, the school controversy erupted again—this time in Madison at a March 4th meeting at the Dane County Court House. Turning to higher education, the liberals, led by Rasmus Anderson and John A. Johnson, called a meeting to form a Scandinavian Lutheran Education Society. Over 200 persons attended. This was another attempt to make American public education more acceptable to Norwegian-American Lutherans by seeking "the establishment of Scandinavian Lutheran professorships" in American colleges and academies. It did not establish Norwegian-American unity. It simply carried the controversy beyond the elementary level to the secondary and collegiate levels. Conservatives walked out rather than agree to sign a pledge to support public education, and held their own meeting the following day. That "set off an explosive public discussion, and the controversy entered upon its most turbulent phase."[53]

Though his Norwegian-instruction bill was not the subject of debate, and though he played no public role in the March 4th meeting, Nelson could hardly avoid taking sides in this controversy. His respect for his public school teacher, Mary Dillon, his own experience teaching in a public school, his dislike for Koshkonong's Lutheran clergy, his Americanization—all these factors placed him squarely in the liberals' camp.

In mid-April letters to *Fremad* (Milwaukee) and *Skandinaven* (Chicago), ostensibly explaining the Norwegian-instruction law,

Nelson chastised the clergy and supported the common school. Though the Norwegian language could be taught, he explained, "certainly no instruction in dogmatics or in sectarian religion will be permitted." Ironically, the chief barrier to Norwegian-language instruction was a lack of suitable textbooks. He hoped the learned clergy would more profitably spend their time and talents writing such texts "instead of everlastingly getting stuck in dogmatic points of controversy (for example, the church's justification of slavery) which the whole Christian world has settled long ago."[54] The Norwegian-American community must act to make use of this law "unless it actually has come to the point that all of our educational instruction shall totally consist of sectarian religious education." His law would "avoid the necessity of maintaining private schools in addition to the legally-required district schools." And, it would give young Norwegian Americans a competitive advantage over old-stock Americans in finding teaching jobs in district schools, because they could teach both languages.[55]

The letter's sarcasm was dangerous for an elected official. Here, Nelson abandoned his customary caution and took sides in a very divisive controversy. Sometime that spring or summer he decided not to seek reelection to the Assembly.

Nelson's biographer Martin W. Odland and other writers have explained his decision by citing a story told by Rasmus Anderson in his autobiography, written some forty-five years after the events described. The story was that Nelson had failed to support a Norwegian-American candidate, Ole C. Johnson, for the Republican nomination for Secretary of State—but instead had supported "an American friend of his," Eli A. Spencer, his early political mentor. After a scandal about Spencer's handling of state monies, Spencer was defeated in 1869 "and both Spencer and Nelson were politically dead."[56]

Contemporary newspaper accounts disprove many details of Anderson's story. Scandinavian-American Republicans met on August 31, 1869, one day before the state Republican convention, to rally support for placing a Scandinavian on the state ticket. Most of those present were from Dane county. Nelson chaired the meeting, which quickly disintegrated into a bitter argument over whether Danes or Swedes could be considered, or only Norwegians, as the editor of *Fædrelandet* preferred. Nelson had difficulty keeping order.[57]

Moreover, Ole C. Johnson sought the post of State Prison Commissioner, not Secretary of State. The consensus of the August 31st meeting was to recommend Johnson to the convention as the one Scandinavian to place on the ticket. The final decision was left up to the Scandinavian delegates. The following day, Johnson was nominated and supported by the Scandinavians, but lost out to a Yankee, George Wheeler.[58] There is no evidence that Nelson failed to support Johnson, whom he had supported for the same post in 1867.

Eli Spencer did win the nomination for Secretary of State, but not against a Scandinavian candidate.[59] During the campaign, a scandal did arise about Spencer's handling of state monies. The Republican state central committee removed him from the ticket. He ran as an independent, and lost. Nelson likely supported Spencer at the Republican convention, and conceivably supported him as an independent. He was known to be loyal to his friends, and Spencer had yet to be proven guilty. Contemporary newspaper accounts, however, show that neither the Democrats, who pressed the scandal issue hardest and would not have protected Nelson, nor the regular Republicans, angry at Spencer's independent candidacy, nor the Norwegian-American editors, who would have rebuked Nelson if guilty, ever mentioned Nelson's name in connection with Spencer's downfall.[60] In short, no evidence points to Spencer's disgrace as the reason Nelson abandoned his political career in Wisconsin.

More likely, he abandoned it because of the divisive common-school controversy, in which he took a public position opposed to the clergy's position. Coming from Koshkonong, where the Norwegian Synod clergy were strongest, he may have felt politically vulnerable. Also, he was disgusted at the internal bickering over obscure points of dogma.

Knute Nelson grew up in Koshkonong before that settlement had developed a complete set of Norwegian-American institutions. His Americanization was partly due to that fact. After the Civil War and the initial pioneering were over, Koshkonong was ready to institutionalize its Norwegian-American cultural identity.[61] The clergy were sure to have a decisive role in shaping that identity and those institutions. Nelson's anti-clericalism endangered his roles as political and legal broker for Koshkonong. He could not be a go-between linking old-stock leaders in Madison and Koshkonong's Norwegians if the latter's church leaders opposed him. Now safe in academia at the secular University of Wisconsin, Rasmus Anderson could defy them, but a politician depending on Norwegian-American votes could not with impunity defy the voters' trusted pastors.

His political future was best served by moving to a frontier community at an earlier stage of development and less susceptible to ministerial influence. His law practice might also benefit from the many land-law cases arising on the frontier. In May, 1869, he had moved some, if not all, of his legal practice to the small village of Cambridge to be close to his wife and child and to combine farming with the law. This rural area proved even less lucrative for a lawyer than Madison. Nor did it offer much available land. For a Vossing who sought the security of land ownership, the frontier area of Minnesota would offer more possibilities.

For Knute Nelson, the frontier was a place of opportunity and Americanization, as Frederick Jackson Turner theorized, but not in the way or for the reasons he outlined. Turner wrote, "In the crucible of the frontier the immigrants were Americanized, liberated, and fused into a mixed race, English in neither nationality nor characteristics." The frontier turned the European into an American.[62] Reacting against theories of Anglo-Saxon predominance and coming from an old-stock pioneering family, Turner correctly observed that centuries of pioneering had made frontier old-stock Americans into something other than Englishmen.[63] He was wrong to claim that by the time he wrote the frontier had already turned the recently arrived Norwegian European into an American. The concentration of Norwegian settlers in Koshkonong enabled them to recreate Norway in Wisconsin. Turner's theory of rapid frontier Americanization was true only for some individuals, like Nelson, who grew up before Norway could be recreated—or for those who lived in communities like polyglot Portage—or for the ambitious, like Nelson, who saw Americanization as a pathway to success.[64] For the ambitious willing to be Americanized, Yankee leaders offered opportunities, not because they lacked anti-immigrant prejudices but because frontier conditions and the presence of so many immigrants required brokers who could communicate between two cultures.

Knute Nelson was not a passive object in the crucible of the frontier. For him, the frontier was a tactic, a choice to be used when needed throughout his career. By moving to the Minnesota frontier, he could avoid the divisiveness of settled Koshkonong. Later, by specializing in land law, Indian relations, and frontier Alaska, he could avoid the controversial issues of Populism, Progressivism, and socialism. He actively chose the frontier. It did not mold or "fuse" him.

Five

Nelson and Railroads
Come to the Upper Country

At least since 1867 Knute Nelson had been considering a west-ward move, but opportunities in Dakota Territory and Minnesota had seemed too nebulous for him to stake his young family's future on them. He was no rainbow chaser. He wanted a good location for practicing law—especially land-law cases for new settlers. He probably realized that a railroad attracted new settlers and made a location good. No railroad existed in Dakota Territory in 1867 when Nelson briefly considered moving there.

In March, 1870, a more concrete opportunity arose. Lars K. Aaker, a Norwegian-American friend, wrote to urge him to come to Minnesota.[1] Seventeen years Nelson's senior, Aaker had moved from Dane county to Minnesota in 1857. Two years later he was elected to the first of five terms in the Minnesota legislature. Like Nelson a Civil War veteran, his political connections to the new Grant administration landed him a patronage job in 1869 as register of the United States Land Office in Alexandria in Douglas county.[2]

Located in Minnesota's frontier "Upper Country"—everything northwest of St. Cloud—Alexandria lay on the stagecoach line eighty miles northwest of St. Cloud. The Norwegian-American journalist Paul Hjelm-Hansen, traveling there in 1869, reported,

69

"Alexandria has a very desirable location in the midst of a beautiful woods and surrounded by many especially pretty lakes." By that time, the three-year-old town had a flour mill, a hotel, a newspaper, eleven stores, four doctors, and four lawyers. Given Nelson's desire to escape the clerical domination in Koshkonong, perhaps its best feature was the absence of any Norwegian Lutheran churches. In all the Upper Country, Hjelm-Hansen reported, "are found neither [Scandinavian] minister, church nor school," because people had "not yet had opportunity to organize congregations or to acquire church buildings or ministers."[3]

Aaker offered practical arguments for moving to Alexandria. Nearby was "good Prairie Land" costing only $1.25 an acre, an attractive price for a poor, land-hungry Vossing. The land's value was sure to increase, according to Aaker, for "the Northern Pacific RR will run about through the center of our city." That would attract settlers, Nelson's future clients: "You could get yourself Land near the line of the new RR and practice your profession at the Land Office and act as Land Agent. Think of it."[4]

Having a friend as land office register augured likely success in the legal business, land speculation, and politics. Land officers were important political figures on the frontier, and had inside information useful for land speculation.[5] Aaker could refer puzzled or indignant land claimants to lawyer Nelson. Already, Aaker had given Nelson inside information about the Northern Pacific (NP) line—inside, but incorrect: Alexandria offered inducements to the NP, but it did not build there.[6]

Still, he hesitated. The railroad was Alexandria's dream, and nowhere near to a reality. Without it, Aaker was unlikely to do a land-office business—or Nelson much law-office business. Nicholina was pregnant by March of 1870, and the time was not right for a move. Their second daughter died not long after her birth in the fall of 1870, causing the young family sorrow and distress.[7] Soon after, Nicholina was again pregnant. In 1871 she delivered Henry Knute Nelson, whose healthy survival created a more favorable mood for a move.

Alexandria's railroad prospects became more promising by the summer of 1871. Thanks to vigorous lobbying at the legislature and in Congress by Edmund Rice, Congress passed legislation on March 3, 1871, authorizing the St. Paul & Pacific (SP&P) to switch its route westward to pass through the Otter Tail area. The Minnesota legislature concurred.[8] The *Alexandria Post* reported the "possibility that the road may be run *via* Alexandria." Arguing that "the company must be encouraged by substantial subscriptions" to make this a reality, the *Post* led a community campaign which culminated in a railroad meeting at the schoolhouse on April 29. At the meeting, Aaker read a letter from SP&P president George Becker, who tried to wring the maximum concessions from the railroad-hungry townsfolk. Recalling their earlier offer to the NP and threatening to choose "the most direct and cheapest line" (not via Alexandria), Becker warned that the precise location "will depend upon the inducements offered by the people interested in the location."[9] In their best frontier-democratic manner, the assembled townsfolk passed resolutions, and their chair appointed a "committee of correspondence" to mobilize township committees throughout the county.[10]

Within a month the effort collapsed amidst frontier-like wrangling over eight old-stock Americans' near-lynching of a Norwegian American suspected of a local murder. United at the railroad meeting, the Yankee group (the banker, the editor, and others) and the largely Norwegian-American "Aaker clique" now squared off in a bitter legal battle.[11] Despite this disunity, SP&P officials spoke encouraging words as they came through town in mid-June.[12]

Knute Nelson was another June visitor — at Aaker's insistence. To be certain before deciding, he rented a livery team and two-seat rig, and took the forty-five-mile trail to Fergus Falls to check out opportunities there.[13] Fergus Falls was also located on the possible SP&P route. In late June, the railroad's geologist wrote in the *St. Paul Pioneer* that the "new railroad will probably run to this place [Alexandria] or very near it." Convinced by this ac-

71

The source of much of Nelson's legal work, the first United States Land Office in Alexandria. Register Lars K. Aaker (right) and Knute Nelson (?left) stand inside. Photo by N.J. Trenham, Alexandria, ca. 1876.

count or by Aaker's private assurances, Nelson decided by July 6 to move to Alexandria.[14] His timing indicated that the coming of the railroad was uppermost in his mind. His move there and his political career there were closely tied to that important frontier cause—acquiring a railroad.

In mid-August, he, Nicholina, and their nursing baby Henry boarded the train for St. Paul, along with $100 in cash and $300–$400 worth of law books. Daughter Ida remained in Wisconsin with Grandmother Ingebjørg. At St. Paul, they boarded the SP&P train for Benson, where they caught a stage for Glenwood and Alexandria. They arrived on August 12. That same day, Nelson and Reuben Reynolds signed a law partnership agreement assigning one-third of their profits to Nelson.[15] Reynolds belonged to Aaker's clique and was soliciting legal business among the local Norwegian Americans.[16] No doubt he reasoned that Nelson could help secure it. By October, Nelson was admitted to the Minnesota bar. Reynolds & Nelson had the front rooms on the

Nelson & Reynolds, Attorneys at Law, with an office between clothing store and gun shop in the Centennial year, 1876. Note the Conestoga wagon at left. Photo by N.J. Trenham, Alexandria.

second floor of the bank building; Aaker's land office was in the rear room on the same floor.[17]

Almost before the ink dried on the partnership agreement, lawyer Nelson found himself accused of "claim-jumping," a serious charge on the land-hungry, litigious frontier. The lawyer was soon a client. The newcomer soon aroused some local anger. After staying two weeks with the Aakers and then briefly renting a house, the Nelsons moved half a mile south of town to a 120-acre homestead. Aaker informed them that the Commissioner of the General Land Office had canceled Leonard W. Kilbourn's claim to this land because of lack of the required improvements to the property.[18]

Actually, back in April, 1869, Kilbourn had jumped the claim of a protesting Robert McNeil. Kilbourn evidently paid off McNeil and then filed a "cash entry" with the Alexandria Land Office. Probably because Register Aaker complained that Kilbourn had not cultivated the land, the Commissioner in Washington canceled the entry on July 31, 1871.[19]

On October 10, 1871, Nelson filed a homestead claim to the property and, three days later, moved into Kilbourn's 14 x 18-foot shanty for the winter "after papering the walls with old newspapers." Challenging Nelson's claim, Kilbourn appealed to the Commissioner: Aaker had not informed him that he was in danger of losing his land. Unaware of Aaker's friendship with Nelson, the Commissioner sent the appeal to Aaker for a decision. Of course, Aaker denied the appeal. His "personal observation" of the land revealed no "visible improvement" except the shanty and no cultivation.[20] After Kilbourn took his case to the Secretary of the Interior, Nelson hired a Washington law firm to defend his interests. The case dragged on for two years before Kilbourn gave up and signed a quit-claim deed in exchange for $100 cash from Nelson.[21]

Though Nelson appears to have been innocent, Aaker did use his considerable power as Register to secure for his friend a 120-acre plot close to town—ideal for someone running both a law office and a farm. The appearance of claim-jumping and inside influence—together with the public's generally low estimation of land officers' ethics—all produced some indignation among Nelson's neighbors.[22] Legal delays kept lawyer Nelson living in the shanty for three years. The frugal Vossing American found some advantages to shanty life: "I could not buy furniture, because there was no place to put it." Thus, "I got ahead a little." For Nicholina, though, the mosquitoes and the heat in the two-windowed shack must have been terrible. Looking back, Nelson claimed, "my wife took those hardships of the pioneer days as a matter of course."[23] Still, daughter Ida had to remain in Wisconsin until they could build a house.

Though Nicholina had to wait for domestic comforts, her husband broke the prairie sod and began cultivation in the spring of 1872. The Vossing American finally had his own land to farm. That offered a degree of economic security. Owning a farm and doing farm chores also allowed him to deny that practicing law or holding public office made him part of the "official class" that disdained manual work.[24] He sidestepped the class antagonism of Norwegian-American farmers toward officialdom. Farming gave him some protection from attack.

The law gave him his main source of income. His casebook, where he meticulously recorded cases and fees, shows that by October, 1871, he was already busy. Reynolds soon moved to Otter Tail county, so he had both Reynolds' Alexandria clients and a legal ally in Fergus Falls. Much of his business came through the Land Office. The *Post* charged that Aaker "sends people in to Nelson's office in order that Nelson may get his $5 or $10 fee for information that [Aaker] should give for nothing."[25] With this help, he earned $506.81 in legal fees in 1873. (His 1868-1869 legal income in Wisconsin had amounted to just $52.50.) Only about 30 percent of Nelson's legal business in Alexandria came from Scandinavian Americans. Most came from leading Yankee land speculators and merchants.[26]

As a trial lawyer, Nelson was in demand because of his clear, convincing style and his skill at cross-examination. Still, it was difficult to collect legal fees on the frontier. Many clients gave him notes or paid him in farm produce. He once represented a Yankee farmer before a rural justice of the peace in a dispute over the ownership of a horse. After putting the fear of a jail term into the biased justice of the peace, he won a $125 settlement for his client, only to have his partner Reynolds keep the fee and leave town. Regretting this, the Yankee gave him two fine white shoats as a walking legal fee; however, the young pigs walked away from the Nelson place into town. Several days later, a hotel proprietor came to Nelson's office to ask whether the law required him to advertise two stray pigs found roaming near his hotel. "Let me see the pigs," said Nelson, who then took them home, where "his 'honoraria' remained this time."[27]

He could tell scores of such stories, often with an ethnic stereotype to them — in this one, the honest Yankee farmer, in others, Norwegians, Swedes, or Germans appeared. Like Lincoln, lawyer Nelson found that riding the circuit from one county district court to the next developed a man's repertoire of stories and friendships.[28] During the annual court week, an attorney was a public figure, as one of his friends once described it for the absent Nelson: "The 'Bar' was well represented in town yesterday on an attachment suit, all the celebrities of the upper country, Peck & Fulmer on one side Sheldon and Hawley on the other, wisdom flew you bet, but you can imagine the scene."[29] Elected Douglas county attorney in 1872, he earned a $500 annual salary—plus $30 for trying cases for the newly-elected Pope county attorney, a farmer without legal experience.[30]

Like many frontier lawyers, he also earned fees (almost $45 in 1873) as the local collection agent for farm implement companies, merchants, and other businesses. His fee was usually 5 to 10 percent of the money collected. Such cases put him in contact with cash-poor and credit-starved farmers, not all of whom were honest or good business managers. This experience was one reason he resisted agrarian protests that blamed farmers' woes on bankers, retailers, implement dealers, and manufacturers.[31] In the rapidly developing Upper Country, he was one of the developers who believed that rewards came deservedly to those who worked hard. To blame monopolies or banks for failure was to espouse an alien philosophy imported from Europe and used by demagogues. In America, success awaited the diligent.

Nelson's law practice supported his growing family. After settling up with Kilbourn in January, 1874, Knute and Nicholina built a little white frame farmhouse with three rooms downstairs and two upstairs.[32] In August, 1874, they sent for Ida to join them. Her departure fell heavily upon Ingebjørg, who sorrowed for days afterward. In good frontier fashion, the family grew. Joining Ida and Henry were Bertha Henrietta (born February, 1873), Maria Theresa (January, 1875), and Katherine Louise (June, 1876). They brought the family a full house, five children in all.

The Upper Country's politics was as unsettled and land-office dominated as its litigation. In 1872, Nelson campaigned with what the *Post* called "the clique which hovers around Lars K.

Aaker's office" against a group led by banker F.B. Van Hoesen. Disputes over delegates' credentials, non-residents allegedly voting at caucuses, rival Republican conventions nominating rival tickets, a propertyless "political adventurer" running for office, talk of "carpet-baggers"—all kept the 1872 campaign in a swirl of charges and counter-charges. In such a new territory, who could tell whether a candidate was "really a bona-fide citizen"?[33] With politics so personalized and faction-ridden, little dishonor accrued to a faction that "bolted" and held its own convention. With so many land speculators, claim jumpers, and drifters around, it was no wonder the postmasters and land office employees (with a permanent interest in their patronage jobs) were the most active participants in local politics.

With his Wisconsin legislative experience, Nelson became the Aaker faction's candidate for state senator in 1874. A non-Scandinavian, Van Hoesen, was his opponent; a "People's Mass Convention" at Glenwood nominated him; one Scandinavian American wrote him that "most of us are dissatisfied at having a banker for Senator." Still, Nelson needed land-office and old-stock backing to make him a viable candidate whom the Scandinavian-American masses could then support.[34]

Such support was not universal. The *Alexandria Post* opposed Nelson. *Nordisk Folkeblad* perceived him as the land-office candidate, not the "People's" Norwegian-American candidate. "[They] have now found a new method of taking our countrymen by the nose to support their evil corruption. . . They have become 'Anti-Monopolist' and 'Anti-Corruption'! Yes, men like Knute Nelson, that corrupt Land Office's corrupt lawyer in Alexandria."[35] The editor did not specify what "corruption" he thought Nelson guilty of, nor did he favor a true Anti-Monopoly candidate. Arising out of the Grange movement then sweeping Minnesota, the Anti-Monopoly party ran candidates in the 1873 and 1874 elections. It mainly sought state regulation of railroads and other corporations.[36]

Because Nelson ran against the "regular" Republican nominee,

Van Hoesen, some thought he was an Opposition or Anti-Monopoly candidate.[37] That was not the case. The Grange and the Anti-Monopoly party were weak in the Upper Country and among Scandinavian Americans. *Nordisk Folkeblad* attacked it as an anti-foreign "Know-Nothing" party after it failed to nominate any Scandinavian-American candidates in 1873.[38] Grange strength was in settled, wheat-growing, railroad-dominated southeastern Minnesota. For Upper Country farmers awaiting a railroad, Grangers' anti-railroad rhetoric made little sense. For a politician like Nelson, whose main legislative goal was to encourage railroad construction, the Anti-Monopoly party was not an option.

The Aaker faction's faith in Nelson's vote-getting abilities was well founded. He won large majorities in Scandinavian-American precincts such as Urness, Solum, Moe, and Osakis townships. After a *"very quietly* developed" campaign, he swept to victory with 59 percent of the vote, enough to win four of the five counties (Douglas, Grant, Pope, and Stevens—Hoesen won Big Stone).[39] His Albion mentor, A.R. Cornwall, hoped for even higher office. "I want you to strike for Congress," he gloated, "make a good impression in the legislature, but remember you must go to Congress."[40]

State Senator Nelson's first task in St. Paul was to help determine which Minnesota politician would go to the United States Senate. Old war-horse Alexander Ramsey, first territorial and second state governor, was seeking a third Senate term. He represented the Old Guard of territorial days. Young Governor Cushman K. Davis was eager to dethrone him. Minneapolis capitalist William D. Washburn, Chief Justice S.J.R. McMillan, and former governor Horace Austin were dark-horse candidates.[41]

Electing United States senators in the legislature involved a Byzantine intrigue in which factional alliances formed and faded like twilight mists in prairie muskeg. Ramsey won in the Republican party caucus, but then the battle went to the full legislature for thirty-one ballots and thirty-eight days of wrangling.

Nelson was in a difficult position. Douglas county Republican leaders backed Davis, but Aaker owed his land-office post to Ramsey. Claiming that "the caucus was binding on his honor," Nelson voted for Ramsey (though he called himself "a Davis man") for six ballots, then switched to McMillan on the seventh. Then he covered another political base by switching to Washburn for three days—only to return to McMillan, where he was at the weary end. He ended up with the winner, but he made a lifelong political enemy of Davis.[42]

There were charges of bribery.[43] In St. Paul, Nelson faced a rough-and-tumble legislative environment in which bribery and payoff were all too common when political speculators sought favors. In 1866, his friend Hanford L. Gordon had taken a $500 bribe offered by a Minneapolis colonel in exchange for dropping his support for Ignatius Donnelly. Gordon later told historian William Watts Folwell that he stayed with Donnelly and gave the $500 to Donnelly's campaign committee.[44] Contrary to *Nordisk Folkeblad's* charge ("corrupt lawyer"), Nelson avoided these bribery brambles. Though some were hurled, no charges of corruption ever stuck to Knute Nelson.

"A subject nearer and dearer to your readers, dear *Post*, than the Senatorial game of chance, is the St. Vincent extension of the St. Paul and Pacific Railroad," wrote Nelson in his weekly legislative letter for mid-February, 1875.[45] In September, 1872, construction on the SP&P's branch line, the so-called St. Vincent extension west from St. Cloud to Alexandria and beyond, had stopped just short of Melrose.

Slackening Dutch demand for SP&P securities caused the halt. Construction was financed by bond sales in Holland. After securities sales ended in the summer of 1872, the main contractor, De Graff & Company, "kept at work with their own funds" for three months, but finally had to stop. Earlier, the SP&P had completed the main-line track from St. Paul to Breckenridge on the Red River.[46] But the track to Alexandria lay unfinished, with no word of when it might be completed. The SP&P's credit was exhausted.

79

It had used its land grant sections as mortgaged collateral for the bonds held by its Dutch investors.[47] By 1873, its land grant had expired, wages were unpaid, and the company was in receivership. Local businessmen along the uncompleted line fretted about their towns' moribund prospects. The *Alexandria Post* worried that trade would be diverted west toward the completed main line running through Morris and Benson.[48]

His Upper Country constituents expected Nelson to bring about completion of the line. This crisis created local unity, softened frontier factionalism, and promised political rewards if he could deliver. One observer wrote that Nelson "came to the capital fully charged with the great duty . . .'to see to it that there was no more fooling about this matter,' and declaring his intention to prepare a bill which would *compel* the Railroad Company or the bondholders to go to work at once and finish these roads or get out of the way."[49]

Early in the session, he "moved to refer" the St. Vincent extension matter to a special committee of Upper Country senators. When a senator objected that it should properly go to the Standing Committee on Railroads, Nelson argued that it was a matter of local interest that the Upper Country senators should consider first. He won that argument. The special committee held "frequent and repeated conferences," including some "with several of our prominent railroad men."[50]

He soon found that prodding the SP&P westward was like pushing on a rope. "The company is *bankrupt* and *can* do nothing. The bondholders are *disgusted* and *will* do nothing."[51] And, "our lawmakers can make most everything but money. *In* the State we have no capital. From *abroad* we can get *none*." He blamed the 1874 "'Granger railroad legislation' in the northwestern States," for "repelling and frightening foreign capital, and I fear it will take years to undo the work."[52]

The 1874 Minnesota legislation set up a railroad commission to regulate rates, partly as a result of the 1873 Granger and Anti-Monopoly campaign for such regulation.[53] Though one

Alexandria friend wrote him to complain that blaming the 1874 "Granger" law was "narrow statesmanship," his Upper Country constituents and the 1875 legislature both regarded the 1874 act as a mistake. Railroad building had slowed to a stop, though this was largely due to continuing effects from the Panic of 1873. If the choice was between high fares and no railroad, his constituents preferred high fares. The state's promotional and regulatory functions conflicted. His fellow legislators and constituents gave priority to promoting railroad construction.[54]

Upper Country unity was offset by acrimonious debate and litigation among Dutch bondholders, unpaid contractors such as De Graff & Company, SP&P stockholders, unpaid construction workers, farmers settled on SP&P lands, and the court-appointed receiver, Jesse P. Farley. The state and federal governments were involved, for their land grants to the SP&P had expired. To protect the Minnesota contractors, the 1874 legislature passed the De Graff Act. It extended the time for completing the railroad, but "provided that no land was to be conveyed to the receiver until *all* the railroad's debts to citizens of the state were paid."[55] This act was unacceptable to the bondholders, who demanded its repeal before they would finance further construction.[56]

A regional rivalry further complicated matters. At the 1875 session, St. Paul interests, allied with the Northern Pacific Railroad, sought to declare the SP&P's land grants forfeited. They wanted a separate company to complete a branch line from St. Cloud to Brainerd, where it would meet the NP line. That would give the NP connections to the Twin Cities. It "would give St. Paul what she wants—a connection with Manitoba, and leave Alexandria and Fergus Falls out in the cold."[57] Upper Country legislators strenuously opposed this Delano bill. They feared that once the major parties were satisfied, no one would work to build the St. Vincent extension through Alexandria.[58]

This was the most important legislative matter Nelson had yet handled. On February 24 he introduced the Upper Country bill to extend the time allowed the SP&P for completion if it was to avoid forfeiture of the land grants. It provided for a step-by-step transfer of granted lands to the SP&P to match step-by-step completion, and reserved 300,000 acres to meet the claims of De Graff and other contractors.[59] It gave the bondholders the opportunity to proceed with construction, while it provided a carrot (granted lands) and a stick (a December 1876 expiration date for the land grant) to "*compel*" them to do so.

Opponents charged that it did not adequately protect the interests of unpaid construction workers, unpaid contractors, and the actual settlers along the future railroad track.[60] "Senator Nelson's reflection that some of the opponents of the bill were the paid attorneys of its enemies" (the NP?) sparked "excited dispute" and "considerable acerbity" in the Senate.[61]

When the Senate amended the bill to increase the De Graff reserve to 400,000 acres, Nelson, after a "somewhat excited speech," angrily moved for indefinite postponement of his own bill, although opponents' more extreme amendments had all been defeated. His motion carried, and the bill seemed lost.[62] After a recess, another senator successfully moved to reconsider the motion to postpone. After consulting Upper Country colleagues and a five-man Douglas county committee "chosen to assist him," the sponsor grudgingly acquiesced: "Senator K. Nelson said this was in no sense his bill [because of the amendments], and was not what he wanted, yet as some of his people had told him they would rather have that than none at all, he would like the bill passed, unsatisfactory as it was." The "Nelson bill" then passed, though Senator Nelson abstained on the final vote.[63] Ultimately "the united delegations from the northwestern [Upper Country] districts . . . strongly backed by petitions and lobbys from Alexandria, Fergus Falls and other localities," pushed it through—despite its sponsor's anger.[64] It passed both houses and the governor signed it.

Nelson's quick temper and his obsession with this one issue demonstrated that he had much to learn, yet he received no public criticism for his attempt to kill his own bill. On the contrary, he was hailed as a hero. Returning from St. Paul, he and Douglas county's state representative "were met by a large number of citizens who had awaited their coming . . . to congratulate them upon the success of their diligent labors during the session." The *Fergus Falls Journal* called the Nelson bill "a great improvement" over previous legislation. One Fergus Falls man wrote to give Nelson "the credit for all that was done in the Senate for this upper country."[65] Two Upper Country newspapers urged the Republicans to nominate Nelson for Secretary of State, as a reward for his services and for Scandinavian loyalty to the party.[66]

The decisive jury weighing the Nelson bill, however, was made up of SP&P bondholders. About a month after its passage, Farley notified Nelson of their verdict: "they do not think it possible to raise any money under the present legislation [the Nelson bill]" —despite Alexandria's willingness to sweeten the pot with some local aid.[67] The Nelson bill's failure seemed to confirm one opponent's sarcastic retitling of it as "An act to grant further time for proceedings in bankruptcy for the support of lawyers, and to prolong the agony of settlers and persons who made investments founded on the construction of a railroad. . . in 1871 and 1872."[68] Nelson was one such investor. Shortly after his bill passed, but before he heard Farley's bad news, he purchased, on mortgage, eighty acres along the projected SP&P line for just under $200.[69]

Nelson was not held responsible for distant Dutch investment decisions. Rather, his conspicuous leadership on the issue was a source of pride, especially for his Norwegian-American constituents. One wrote to him, "I am . . . proud to have a countryman who can be the equal of even the most educated and experienced Americans."[70] The 1875 SP&P battle was his first encounter with the fight between political agrarianism and corporate interests. His constituents' special needs and his emerging political philosophy pushed him toward concessions for corporations and criticism of agrarian radicals. He opted for a politics of settlement and development that stressed state promotion of private enterprise and questioned the need for state regulation.

His return home after the 1875 session was welcomed by his family as well as by Alexandria's citizens. Though his brother William had come up during the session to look after the family, Nicholina was eager for him to return. ("I hope you can come home it is so lonesome.") [71] His legal practice remained adequate to support them, but not as lucrative as it would have been had the SP&P's St. Vincent extension been built. He handled a few cases regarding railroad lands, but not the many cases actual track-laying would have brought. [72]

His popularity was confirmed when he was asked to deliver "the oration of the day" at Alexandria's celebration of the Centennial, July 4, 1876. Extensive preparations were made. "Flags and bunting profusely decorated the court house, hotels, private residences" and stores. At the grove, "the speakers' stand was festooned with evergreen and flags, and graced with several fine paintings," the largest one of George Washington. In front were seats for one thousand people. [73]

The day began with sunshine and a thirteen-gun salute. "Boys were out in full force, fire-crackers and torpedoes were snapping everywhere, and noise and hurrahs resounded in all directions." At the grove, the crowd sang "America," and Dr. Vivian read the Declaration of Independence. By then, "clouds had suddenly risen in the west." When Nelson rose to speak shortly after noon, "rain began to fall, and before the oration was [ended] one half the people had found shelter under the village roofs." Worse yet, the sale of "temperance beverages" at booths in the grove "was prematurely cut off," and "the trade in beer and whisky was stimulated by the unfavorable weather."

An "unimpassioned" chronological recital of Revolutionary-era events, Nelson's speech restated patriotic themes he had first developed as a Civil War soldier. Thoroughly Americanized, it let slip no hint that the speaker came from Norway. Referring to the Revolutionary generation, he boasted of the "pride that *we* come from such a race of men." He did not mention Norway's brief fight for independence in 1814. As in his Civil War letters, so now he spoke the language of civil religion and put religious terms to political uses. He called the Founders "political Protestants" and compared their revolution to Luther's. While he mentioned the Declaration's "double baptism of blood," he reserved his strongest praise for the second baptism in which he had participated, that of the Civil War. In "repressing and subduing the great slaveholders' rebellion"—the "one anti-christ of our republic"— his generation had shown great "strength and vital force." He cautioned his audience to "not forget, how many drops of blood have been spilt. . . that this republic might live, and have life everlasting."

His speech came during his 1876 campaign to secure the Republican nomination for Congress in the Third District. Unlike the speech, the campaign had much to do with his Viking ancestry and his fellow Scandinavian Americans. He followed a strategy he would use for decades: encourage others to advance his cause, so he appeared to be "drafted" by leaders or by a "spontaneous" people's movement. He used his newspaper contacts— the *Fergus Falls Journal*, the *Alexandria Post* (after 1874, firmly in Nelson's camp), and the Norwegian-American newspaper *Budstikken* (Minneapolis). They became his advocates.

Nelson began as the non-Twin-Cities candidate. To rural Republicans, he was sold as the man to break the Twin Cities' increasing hold on state Republican politics. His chances appeared promising. Minneaplis and St. Paul were intense competitors for political, social, and economic dominance. In 1876 each city had its candidate: Levi Butler, a state senator from Minneapolis, and Dr. J.H. Stewart, a longtime St. Paul surgeon. Nelson's backers urged him to bring "a good strong Northwest delegation" to the convention.[74] Then, Nelson believed, Minneapolis and St. Paul would battle to a draw and the convention would seek him as a compromise candidate. Even *Budstikken* touted him as the candidate who could secure justice for the under-represented "western counties." It also stressed that a Nelson victory would give under-represented Scandinavian Americans a deserved seat in Congress.[75]

Budstikken was overconfident because of the large number of Scandinavians in the Third District, which included the Twin Cities and everything to their north. A third factor loomed. Incumbent Congressman William King was thought to favor Dr. Stewart, so his patronage appointees stuck to Stewart in order to preserve their government jobs.[76] For regional, patronage, and ethnic reasons, old-stock Twin Cities' politicians and federal officeholders were not about to allow an Upper Country Norwegian-American upstart to win the nomination.

Butler dangled before Nelson's eyes the posts of national convention delegate and presidential elector.[77] Then, the Land Office Receiver in Detroit [Lakes] organized a pro-Stewart, anti-Nelson faction in the Upper Country. Taking advantage of Nelson's quiet campaign and use of surrogates, they spread the story that he was not actually a candidate. When the Becker county convention supported Nelson anyway, they bolted in true frontier fashion and selected their own delegation to the St. Paul convention.[78] When Nelson arrived in St. Paul, the politicians tried to convince him to withdraw, apparently in favor of Levi Butler. Nelson seethed at their condescending approach: "The Minneapolis man kindly called me to his [hotel] room and told me—of course sweetly—that I was an *able young man very able and worthy*, but I was a little to[o] new and to[o] young to expect it *then*, but next time would be my chance and that if now I would turn my votes over to him *he* would *appreciate* it . . . . I told that man in substance—though not in words: to go to H—l, and so did all my delegates."[79] On July 19, the convention began with a bitter four-hour debate over the rival delegations from Becker and Clay counties. With their majority, the Stewart forces seated their Upper Country allies, whom the *Minneapolis Tribune* called "the bolting land office seceders." With the bolters' help, Stewart won the nomination on the second ballot.[80]

The *Tribune* complained of "Land-Office Tactics" and denounced "the whole system of land office engineering" at conventions, but party regulars and Republican newspapers acquiesced in the result.[81] *Budstikken* and many Scandinavian Americans did not. They declared their independence from Stewart's endorsed candidacy. Starting with its August 1st edition, and then weekly into October, *Budstikken* urged Scandinavian Americans to bolt the Republican party and vote for the Democrat, William McNair.

Interestingly, although it accused Stewart's group of "Know-Nothingism" in opposing the immigrant Nelson, it did not argue primarily from wounded ethnic pride. Instead, editor Gudmond Johnson played to Norwegian Americans' dislike of officialdom by accusing federal officeholders of sabotaging Nelson's candidacy. Here, *Budstikken* claimed to be in line with the national Republican platform calling for civil service reform. Patronage corrupted "the American official class" (*embedsklassen*). Officeholders ("especially we mean the officeholders in the district land offices") constituted "a standing army of mercenaries who stand under the command of their common patron." *Budstikken* approvingly cited *Harper's Weekly*'s and the *Nation*'s support of civil-service reform, which alone could end "the nation's official corruption."[82] It charged that in the past year two land-office officials and one postmaster in Alexandria had been fired for supporting Nelson.[83]

A Goodhue county reader responded by waving the bloody shirt over Civil War issues and warning that *Budstikken*'s subscription revenues were in danger if it continued to support McNair. However, most readers apparently accepted the editor's position: he did not print many critical letters. One charged that a St. Cloud Land Office employee had been given sixty days off "to work in Dr. Stewart's cause."[84] Others reported on anti-Nelson Scandinavians, attacked the officeholding "ring," and complained that Yankee politicians excluded Scandinavians from all responsible positions.[85] One reader charged that some Norwegian Americans "are so Yankeefied [*Yankeeficerede*] that they regard themselves as too good to vote for one of their countrymen."[86]

This storm caused grave concern among Republican leaders.

Senator McMillan, W.D. Washburn, and Stewart urged Nelson to end this defection, to "use your influence," to come to St. Paul for urgent meetings, and to write "to say *fifty or a hundred* of your particular friends," especially "in the upper and western country," on Stewart's behalf.[87]

Typically, Nelson acquiesced, but ever so slightly. He traveled to St. Paul to meet with "Washburn, [John S.] Pillsbury," and "Johnson of the Budstikken." He wrote a few letters, and left a statement with Aaker—"We must do what we can to help Dr. Stewart through." Aaker went on an Eastern "tour" and did not release the statement for seven weeks.[88] Claiming illness, Nelson went into hiding for seven weeks also, traveling without his family to Deerfield, Wisconsin, Chicago, and other points. "The Dr. tells me that I need rest and must avoid all excitement or mental labor," he wrote his law partner.[89] He did not attend the convention to nominate a state senate candidate. He wrote Aaker that he wished someone else nominated but would serve if elected. Most likely, that was Nelsonese for "Get the nomination for me"—which they did.

Despite unrealistic advice from one Scandinavian American to run for Congress as an independent, he recognized that the intensely partisan nature of late-nineteenth-century American politics made that foolhardy. When the *Budstikken* editor came to Alexandria claiming he had Nelson's support for his "bolt" to McNair, the *Post* remarked that, if so, Nelson was committing "untimely suicide."[90] No, by traveling east, Nelson allowed *Budstikken* to continue its revolt, which he likely encouraged at first, while he avoided either declaring his independence from Stewart's candidacy or noticeably supporting him. If this sounds Byzantine, it was meant to be. He played a tough double game with his Twin Cities tormentors—a game he ended only when the election was little more than two weeks away.

Upon his return in mid-October, Nelson wrote to the *Post* to express studied "surprise" that his absence had been construed as an attempt "to give credence and force" to *Budstikken*'s anti-

Stewart campaign.[91] Evidencing that it had been precisely that, *Budstikken*'s editor, dismayed by his about-face, asked the returned convalescent: "How does this hang together; let us hear from you *immediately*."[92] Having used *Budstikken* to show Yankee politicians that they needed him, he left it hanging and hurried to repair his Republican fences by campaigning for Stewart. Relieved, Stewart told Nelson about his "beautiful faith" in his Upper Country friend whose seven-week silence had "put me in a tight place."[93]

After Stewart won, one of Nelson's Norwegian-American organizers summed up his strategy succinctly: "Stewart's majority . . . will be close enough to show that had you bolted him he would [have] been [in trouble]. . . . the bolting among the Scandinavians will help to open the eyes of some of our leading American politicians. . . . the day is not far distant when we shall reach the honor of having a representative in Congress of our people. . . . [We are] about the only nationality in America, who have failed to have a member in [Congress]. *Yet I live in hope* . . . Am expecting to see you pay Paul."[94] Yet who did pay Paul? After Stewart's victory, word came from Washington that the Alexandria Land Office would be moved to Fergus Falls. Nelson lobbied to reverse the decision. Though Stewart claimed he was lobbying for reversal and protested the injustice of holding him responsible for the removal, the transfer occurred by mid-December, 1876. Old-stock leaders may have played a double game to punish Nelson in the end.[95]

Alexandria lost its land office and still lacked a railroad. Dispirited at news that the SP&P was selling its locally-stored crossties, the *Post* lamented, "The St. Paul and Pacific R.R. Company has 'sinned away its days of grace.'"[96] The Nelson bill's December, 1876, deadline came and went, and the land grant was technically forfeited back to the state.

Nelson headed back to the legislature in January, 1877, for another election of a United States Senator—he supported William Windom, the winner—and another try at pushing the SP&P to completion. Railroad legislation remained of keenest importance.

89

Legislative possibilities had improved. The NP dropped its opposition to Nelson's new bill, which again extended the completion deadline. A settlement satisfied the De Graffs. The new Nelson bill passed.[97] Financially, prospects improved with the growing interest of James J. Hill and his associates in acquiring the SP&P, but Nelson and the general public were still largely unaware of on-going negotiations between Hill's group and the Dutch bondholders.[98]

Returning from the 1877 session to his law practice and spring planting, he confronted the deepest crisis of his married life. A diphtheria epidemic raced through the community and struck his household with a vengeance. In May, Nicholina and all five children came down with the dread disorder. Treating it was beyond the skill of nineteenth-century frontier physicians. "For three weeks I was at home all the time up most of the time day and night," he recalled, aided by "a couple of old women, who had no children in their families."[99]

First to die, on May 13, was Bertha Henrietta, "especially my pet and her loss affected me most deeply." On May 21 two-year-old Maria Theresa succumbed, followed the next day by Katherine Louise. Ida, Henry, and Nicholina survived, but Knute was left exhausted and grief-stricken. He penned a fitting epitaph for Maria: "Oh, we have gathered brightest flowers; But to see them fade and die." The *Post*'s editor expressed sympathy for Knute, "almost worn down with watching and sorrow." He recalled walking past the Nelson home "on the border of a natural grove, just without the village limits," where he saw Nelson's "little children playing in the shade of the trees, innocent, free and happy." Now three were gone.[100]

Toward the end of this disastrous year, Ingebjørg wrote to him in tones she had used in her Civil War letters. Her tone implied that he was suffering from depression. She concluded, "I have nothing more to write except to repeat my oft told story and advise that you must . . . not only take care of your physical welfare, but shape your course spiritually so that when your time is no

James J. Hill in the 1870s, around the time he was dispensing depots, jobs, and land purchase monies through Knute Nelson in the Upper Country.

more you may be reunited to your little ones gone before."[101] She perceived a lack of Christian orthodoxy in him, as she had during the Civil War. Certainly, rumors later spread that Nelson did not practice the faith which most Norwegian Americans practiced. A possibly apocryphal story was later told "that Knute Nelson's boy was asked if his father was a Christian. 'Yes, sir,' he replied, 'but he is not working at it much.'"[102]

One issue at which Nelson was still working was that of the

SP&P's St. Vincent extension. The 1878 legislature passed still another Nelson bill calling for another extension (until 1881) of the deadline and again offering step-by-step release of granted lands for step-by-step construction. This time, Hill's associates stepped in with a guarantee to the SP&P's small Minnesota creditors to take care of a last-minute snag.[103] Again, the *Post* gave "great praise" to Nelson for his role. This time, however, the Hill group's financial takeover, not legislative wrangling, dominated news accounts.[104] In early April, Nelson received assurances that "the road will be built . . . they intend to go to Fergus if possible this season . . . . [Norman W.] Kittson says they mean business."[105] Seven years of frustrating delay were nearly over.[106] To the last, Nelson kept pressuring the SP&P to complete construction to Alexandria as soon as rails could be secured from the steel-rolling mills.[107]

Under the heading "The Railroad at Last," the *Douglas County News* for November 7, 1878, reported, "The long deferred hope of our citizens is at length realized. . . . The tracklayers reached the townsite of Alexandria on Monday afternoon . . . and regular trains will commence running to Alexandria on the 15th of this month. . . . The completion of the road to Alexandria will inaugurate a new era in the history of both our town and county." The *News* prophesied "better times" for farmers, merchants and mechanics, "a great impetus" for trade, and "a great growth of our town." Buoyed by news of the SP&P's construction plans, the *Post* envisioned "long lines of through trains from the Atlantic to the Pacific, rolling . . . through Alexandria," now "midway on the grand, trans-continental railroad of North America."[108]

The railroad's arrival provided an impetus for great growth in Knute Nelson's legal and political career. Most importantly, he established a close alliance with James J. Hill, for whom he began to work on railroad right-of-way cases. By the fall of 1878, he was so busy with them that he declined repeated requests from his family to visit his ailing stepfather, who was mistakenly said to be dying.[109] He declined to run for Congress or for a third term in the

State Senate, and only halfheartedly and unsuccessfully pursued the Republican nomination for lieutenant governor in 1879.[110] Time was on his side, as the Upper Country filled with German and Scandinavian settlers, and as his prominent role in the SP&P's construction brought him a lengthening list of political contacts and IOUs.

Railroad construction poured thousands of dollars into the Upper Country, created new towns almost overnight and hundreds of very desirable new jobs, and permanently altered the economic geography. Through three years of this revolutionary process, Knute Nelson worked very closely with the chief revolutionary, James J. Hill, the "Empire Builder." One of Hill's chief aides wrote Nelson, "I am convinced that you have more influence with Hill than any one else with whom I am acquainted."[111] Nelson served as Hill's lawyer and as a broker between Hill and Upper Country farmers and businessmen—sometimes interceding with Hill on their behalf, but always keeping Hill's interests paramount.

His work began with negotiating the purchase of land along the surveyed right-of-way. This involved much traveling out into the country to talk to farmers. It could be arduous work. Near Fergus Falls, Nelson and a railroad employee were caught out in a hailstorm. Each man "took a driving line and their united strength was barely sufficient to hold the frightened team. They returned with their hands benumbed and almost paralzyed by the heavy beating hail."[112] In better weather, it was like campaigning with expenses paid, an excellent way to meet and greet folks who were future voters.

On a fee basis, he negotiated the purchase of nearly all the right-of-way along the St. Paul, Minneapolis and Manitoba (SPM&M, the SP&P's new name) from Alexandria to Fergus Falls. Sometimes this was easy. In Alexandria, public euphoria over the railroad's coming meant that "land-owners . . . cheerfully donated the right-of-way"; thus secured free by the town's Right-of-way committee it was donated to the SPM&M. If owners had balked, a town tax would have been levied to buy land to donate to the railroad.[113]

Localities granted land to the railroad as the state and federal governments had before. Several Grant county farmers approached Nelson and offered to give $800 to buy all the right-of-way through Grant county if Hill would agree to put a station there. Hill drove a tough bargain, for the farmers had to agree to help grade the sidetrack for a depot, donate a 100-foot-wide strip of land, and pay $800 in order to obtain their depot.[114] They came through, and the town of Ashby was created. By October, 1879, Nelson informed Hill, "Several parties are ready to put in stores or a hotel at this point" once the depot and sidetrack were ready. The SPM&M still had not built the depot by August, 1880, so the owner of Ashby's general store urged him to intercede with Hill "and I will make it all right with you." He wrote to Hill about Ashby's glowing prospects if they had a depot. Hill wrote on the bottom of the letter, "depot will be built at once."[115] Clearly, Ashby owed a significant political debt to Knute Nelson.

In some settled towns, such as Fergus Falls, landowners were less generous. They figured Hill's railroad had to come to them. Here, Nelson initiated condemnation proceedings. In Fergus Falls, he wrote Hill, "Head & Cutler ask $10,000—for their property in village and there are other ugly & high priced men."[116] The real-estate boom set off by news of railroad construction caused some landowners to become "ugly & high priced." In the spring of 1879, the Fergus Falls Land Office was so busy it had to close in the afternoons to catch up on the paperwork from morning sales. In the nearby village of Elizabeth, property values jumped fifty percent and the "townsite proprietor" had visions of becoming a "future millionaire."[117]

"Empire Builder" Hill didn't intend that the SPM&M build millionaires at his expense. Nelson often went up to Fergus Falls in the spring and summer of 1879 to handle the negotiations and to arrange for a court-appointed panel of commissioners to appraise condemned properties.[118] In August, Hill notified Fergus

Falls' citizens "that he should suspend work on the route through Fergus Falls" until he received a guarantee that the right-of-way and depot site "should cost the company nothing." He began negotiating for an alternate route. A week later, matters had been "happily adjusted," and several landowners (particularly Head & Cutler) had reduced their demands.[119] Nelson's behind-the-scenes work was vital to Hill, who later praised him: "I . . . desire to congratulate you on your success both in the matter of cost and time."[120]

Hill was also concerned about rivals building track into his Upper Country territory. When the Little Falls & Dakota railroad was organized in 1879 to build a line through Sauk Centre, Glenwood, and Morris, across the SPM&M's territory, Nelson quietly attended the company's meeting at Morris to safeguard Hill's interests ("I had to keep very shady . . . . I left when I did to avoid all suspicion").[121] By December, 1879, he informed Hill that rumors pointed to a likely "abandonment of the Sauk Center–Glenwood line." He promised Hill, "I will keep my eye on the matter and advise. Alexandria or no Alexandria I am for you in these matters." He placed Hill's interests above his own town's— even above his family's, for he reported that "I have been so busy [on railroad matters] that I haven't even kept Christmas."[122]

Once the right-of-way was secured and track laid, he interceded with Hill on behalf of Upper Country residents—to secure railroad jobs, to see that a station was given the name they wanted, to obtain permission to build a warehouse on the sidetrack, and to inquire about compensation for railroad-related injuries to horses and damage to crops.[123] All these services earned him political IOUs among farmers and merchants, which he could later collect during campaigns.

From Hill and the SPM&M, he received not IOUs, but cash, and more of it than he had ever seen. For his 1879 work, he received $540.75 from the SPM&M—more than his entire legal income in 1873. For work in 1880 and 1881, Hill's railroad paid him $1,134.53 and $812.50, respectively.[124] That was more than he had

95

ever earned. In addition, he was still earning legal fees from non-railroad cases. In 1880 alone he earned $244 in collection fees and $528 in legal fees—to bring his total income that year to over $1,900.[125]

Hill's track-laying success saved Nelson's 1875 land investment five miles east of Alexandria. It took seventeen years, but he ended up earning about $1,200 profit on his eighty-acre purchase, which he platted as the townsite of Nelson.[126] By 1883, he had accumulated enough wealth to begin speculating in a townsite along the SPM&M's route in Dakota Territory. He asked that Hill "remember me with a station at Northwood," his townsite, so property values might increase there.[127]

Completion of the SPM&M was a major political and financial boon for Nelson. As a broker, he served two constituencies: farmers and landowners and Hill's railroad. Both groups became indebted to him. Hill needed a negotiator to deal with Scandinavian-American settlers along his line. They needed a broker who understood them, spoke their language, and could deal with the SPM&M headquarters in St. Paul. Railroads were an economic boon to the Upper Country. Nelson found himself in a politician's dream world—handing out jobs, depots, sidetracks, and land purchase monies, none paid for with unpopular taxes. Apart from a few "ugly & high priced men," no one lost at this game. There seemed enough for everyone. Nelson liked this politics of settlement and development. Little anti-railroad sentiment yet existed in the Upper Country. Railroad service was a novelty well worth the fares and rates charged. Questions did not trouble many Upper Country minds: could a legislature tempted by bribes regulate railroads? could legislators hoping for legal work from them control them? could "land office" politics produce justice? Nelson came to power amidst the politics of settlement and development, which he liked.

Six

The Upper Country
Elects a Congressman

Late nineteenth-century American politics, according to historian Richard L. McCormick, was dominated by two political parties who favored "distributive policies." "Forever giving things away," party-dominated governments handed out public lands, franchises, charters, privileges, tariff protection, and state subsidies. Natural abundance, expanding population, and the growing number of governments all made for an ever-increasing supply of distributable "things," and a decreasing chance that any group of voters would be left empty-handed and disgruntled. Such practices were a "policy equivalent of patronage." Indeed, handing out government jobs was part of the politics of distribution. Well suited to building coalitions, the politics of distribution enabled political parties to "build bridges between their voters, leaders, and representatives in office."[1]

Knute Nelson was caught up in this intensely partisan and distributive politics. In 1876, he had failed to win either a congressman's power to distribute patronage or the distribution of one congressional seat to Norwegian Americans. However, he had gained some influence over the distributive policies of the St. Paul, Minneapolis and Manitoba railroad, a significant source of jobs, railroad depots, and economic opportunities. When, as a result of the 1880 census, the Federal government allocated one new congressional seat to Minnesota's Upper Country, he was favorably situated to claim it.[2]

As in 1876, he approached the Scandinavian-American (especially Norwegian-American) community for support. There was much agitation to place a Scandinavian American in some prominent political office. The new Fifth Congressional District could be the long-awaited chance. Nelson fit its demographics. Over sixty percent of its residents were foreign-born, and approximately fifty percent of the total population were Scandinavian Americans. Nelson carried these census figures carefully tucked into his small pocket notebook.[3] The old-stock Twin Cities politicians who had opposed him in 1876 were outside the boundaries of the new district.

In late 1881, Nelson approached Luth. Jaeger, *Budstikken*'s new editor, with some cautious suggestions regarding the upcoming campaign. He used the patented Nelson approach: let others—especially newspapers—promote his candidacy while he appeared uninvolved. He informed Jaeger, "I have received many suggestions to make an effort to secure the nomination for Congress in this district next year. I have not yet decided what to do .... I feel that in this Dist[rict] we are entitled to a Norwegian, and in case we are all united we could no doubt get our man. Now my platform is this[:] if the Norwegians cannot unite on me, I am willing to go in and do my best for another Norwegian whom our people would agree on for I have no claims beyond many others. Now would it not be a good plan for the Budstikken to agitate this subject from the Norwegian standpoint—in its general aspects—without in the first instance supporting any particular candidate. I am satisfied that this is none too early as several American candidates are already 'setting down their plans.'"[4]

Jaeger was warmly receptive to the idea. Two weeks later, Nelson followed up with more advice: "educate our people up to the point of the desirability and importance of being represented by one of our own nationality—without indicating anyone in particular." Once "our people" were "ripe," then "bring them to the particular man or men."[5] No sooner said than done. Little more than two weeks after Nelson's latest letter, *Budstikken* advanced the idea of a Norwegian officeholding quota as an equitable means to stop "ring" politics in Minnesota.[6] In the politics of distribution, one congressional seat ought to be given to Norwegian Americans.

To open his campaign, Nelson in January, 1882, secured from Governor Lucius Hubbard a coveted appointment to the University of Minnesota Board of Regents, thus adding to his public stature. As promised, on March 14 *Budstikken* endorsed Nelson, as the Normanna *Banner* had done the week before. Both newspapers asked Scandinavians to unite behind Nelson. They invited other Scandinavian-language newspapers, especially *Skandinaven* in Chicago, to join the Nelson campaign.[7] With a steady stream of letters to Jaeger, Nelson kept *Budstikken* well informed on the campaign's progress.[8] The newspaper dutifully took nearly everything he forwarded as unquestioned fact. It became a mouthpiece for his campaign.

Though Nelson was the only Norwegian-American candidate, at least nine other candidates sought the seat. No single city or rural region dominated the vast district, which sprawled across twenty-eight counties in the northern two-thirds of the state. A congressional victory could help the winning city or county obtain that dominant role. Thus, each major city or region had its "favorite son": Duluth, Charles H. Graves; St. Cloud, Lieutenant Governor Charles A. Gilman; Sauk Centre, former Lieutenant Governor Alphonso Barto; Perham, former state senator Andrew McCrea; Moorhead, Solomon G. Comstock; Brainerd, Charles F. Kindred; and Alexandria-Fergus Falls, Nelson.[9] Many of these hopefuls wilted and withdrew before the district convention in mid-July. Graves and Gilman remained candidates in the unlikely event Nelson should withdraw or the convention should seek a compromise choice.

The contest centered, though, on Nelson and Kindred. Nelson's

99

Scandinavian-American support and connections to Hill's SPM&M, and Kindred's financial resources and close ties to the Northern Pacific territory made them the strongest candidates. The Kindred-Nelson campaign has been extensively described by journalists and scholars—perhaps more than any other Minnesota congressional campaign.[10] Its drama was mainly due to Kindred's large campaign expenditures and highly suspect tactics, often described as abnormal and somehow peculiar to Kindred. Yet Kindred reflected his time and place—the late nineteenth-century frontier—and his occupation—land-office clerk. The Kindred-Nelson campaign reflected Gilded Age politics, especially as practiced on the frontier.[11]

When a *St.Paul Pioneer Press* reporter visited Kindred, who was "leaning slouchily against one of the pillars of the verandah" at the NP Headquarters Hotel in Brainerd, he found a tall "prepossessing" man, "well built," with a "ruddy complexion . . . light brown mustache, and hair just touched with gray."[12] Charles F. Kindred had come to Minnesota from Pennsylvania in 1872 as chief clerk in the NP land office in Brainerd under NP land commissioner James B. Power.[13]

A year earlier, the NP had finished laying track from Duluth to Fargo-Moorhead, and had begun to sell lands granted to it. Through advertisements, aid to immigrants, agricultural demonstration projects, and other means, Power vigorously promoted settlement along the Northern Pacific right-of-way. To promote land sales, bondholders (later, stockholders) were given the right to exchange NP bonds (or stock) for NP land. After NP owner Jay Cooke's bankruptcy resulted in its financial collapse and the Panic of 1873, NP bonds fell to 40 cents on the dollar, and its stock to 10 cents. That encouraged stockholders to trade shares for land, since the NP accepted the shares at full face value, not at market value. This absentee ownership frustrated Power's promotional goals.[14]

At the NP's land offices in Brainerd and Valley City, Dakota Territory, Power and Kindred did sell NP land to actual settlers.

However, settlers' ignorance of the stock-for-land exchanges encouraged "both Mr. Power and Mr. Kindred . . . in the habit of selling the company's land to settlers for payment in cash, usually on time with interest, and accounting to the company for the sales reported in the securities of the company."[15] In other words, Power and Kindred received cash payments for land or made mortgage-secured, interest-bearing loans to settlers for the purchase price. Then, they purchased NP stock at ten to twenty percent of its par value, paid the NP for the land with the stock (accepted at par value), and pocketed the eighty to ninety percent profit. Both men also "surreptitiously" sold desirable sections to their friends and relatives, monopolized scarce timber lands in prairie regions, and mortgaged unsold lands. In a few years, Kindred became wealthy, worth perhaps a quarter million dollars, with thousands of acres of land—including a large livestock farm near Valley City.[16]

Kindred could well afford to bankroll a congressional campaign, and his actions apparently did not disqualify him as a candidate in many voters' eyes, even though the NP removed both Power and Kindred from their posts. Voters seemed not to blame a government land officer for occasionally profiting at the government's expense.[17] Why should a railroad land officer be held to a higher standard? Power and Kindred acted as frontier promoters encouraging the region's settlement and development, from which nearly everyone profited. One defender argued that Kindred's "fortune was made by his faith in the future of the great Northwest" at a time when others were criticizing it "as colder than Alaska and bleaker than the steppes of Asia."[18]

Though critics saw his congressional prospects as bleak, Kindred's confidence remained unbounded. It was rumored that Kindred had indicated a willingness to spend $100,000 to win.[19] He was a master political organizer. To win caucuses and county conventions that selected delegates to the district convention, he recruited heavily. He undoubtedly offered bribes and often put local Republican chairmen on his sizeable paid campaign staff.[20]

Where his supporters failed to control a county convention, they bolted and held their own, in hopes that a Kindred-controlled district convention would recognize the bolting delegates. Nelson's men retaliated in kind, though he could not match Kindred's free-spending ways.[21]

The result was a "disruptive, confused, intensely combative, and highly personal form of politics." Historian Kenneth Owens has termed it "chaotic factionalism" and has argued that it occurred in each western territory.[22] At Ada (Norman county), Kindred hired Republican county chairman and editor Frederick Puhler and instructed him to give only one day's notice of the convention. Puhler "hired all the [livery] teams" to force Nelson's supporters to do their organizing on foot. When they secured a clear majority anyway, he ordered police to admit only delegates with Puhler-issued credentials. When the Nelson delegates forced their way in and nominated a convention chairman, Puhler refused to recognize the motion. Instead, he recognized a Kindred delegate. Two motions were put, two chairmen elected, two separate conventions held, and two delegations sent to the district convention.[23]

At Morris, in Stevens county, according to one report, "revolvers were drawn and knockdowns plenty." The police "had to clear the hall by force." Here again, two separate conventions were called to order. At Crookston (Polk county), the "disturbance" was "livelier than usual, the separate convention[s] declining to vacate the hall, and each going on with its proceedings, as if the other were miles away." One of the stormiest meetings, the Carlton county convention saw many charges of bribery and corruption, and "the usual bolt occurred." The St. Louis county sheriff refused to intervene in "the scene of considerable excitement" at the St. Louis county convention.[24]

Though participants and later observers blamed the donnybrooks on the two candidates, the Fifth District was a raw new frontier territory whose characteristics invited brawling factionalism.[25] Its population was small and scattered among many isolated communities strung across twenty-eight counties. The only thing linking many of them was a railroad track, and the Fifth was split between two rival railroad systems—the Northern Pacific and the St. Paul, Minneapolis and Manitoba. NP towns formed one region, and SPM&M towns another, competing region—each with its own identity and interests.[26] For example, the *Duluth Tribune* carried excerpts from NP-line newspapers in a column headed "Northern Pacific Kernels." NP-line churches organized themselves into the "Northern Pacific Conference of Congregational and Union churches."[27]

Kindred pulled most of his support from this NP region. Little wonder that "at the noon hour when the east and west bound [NP] passenger trains" stopped in Brainerd for dinner, he could "be generally found on the verandah" of the NP's Headquarters Hotel greeting folks.[28] Here, his argument was "You people along the Northern Pacific must support me against the Manitoba [line]." When campaigning in SPM&M territory, he argued that NP dissatisfaction with his conduct as land office clerk meant the "Northern Pacific is down on me" and he was actually pro-SPM&M.[29] The first argument was more credible than the second. Nelson's strongest political connections were to settlers along the SPM&M and to Hill, who provided railroad passes and other campaign assistance.[30]

Kindred was handicapped by the fact that, in Minnesota, the NP track mainly passed through logging country. The NP had only a narrow, 40-mile-wide swath of good farm country from Detroit Lakes to Moorhead, and part of that was also served by the SPM&M. The "pineries" in NP territory were sparsely populated, while the SPM&M's choice farm lands were rapidly filling up with settlers. Thus, the very different interests of a logging frontier and a farming frontier clashed in the Fifth District.[31] The two had different standards of political ethics. The Kindred-dominated pineries were accustomed to bribery and bosses, while prairie farmers resisted what offended their sense of virtuous, yeomanly independence.

Ethnic conflict between Scandinavian Americans and old- stock Americans also divided the Fifth. At the Polk county convention, the "Kindred men were especially furious at Paul Sletten, of the land office, whom they accused of fostering the race issue." Objecting to Sletten's appeal to Nelson's nationality, Kindred supporters "declar[ed] that there should be no Scandinavians, but all Americans."[32] One Yankee sarcastically criticized a "Scandinavian convention" for nominating a Nelson supporter for state representative: "Now, Mr. Editor, we simply desire to ask is there anything in the name, T.K. Torgerson, that caused his nomination? I would advise all American citizens of Clay County, if this sort of thing continues much longer, to emigrate to Norway immediately."[33]

The numbers heavily favored Torgerson's and Nelson's Scandinavian-American, SPM&M base of support. It would have been no contest, but for two "frontier circumstances." First, "for the great number of early settlers, political organizations had only a peripheral importance," whereas physical survival was paramount—and not guaranteed. Second, politics affected "the real and vital concerns" of only a few who sought to gain per-sonal advantage from it: federal officials, land office registrars, railroad agents, newspaper editors, and lawyers.[34] By distributing money, promises, and favors in this small universe of the politi-cally active, Kindred could hope to win in spite of his region's mi-nority status. Through his personal connections in this small universe, Nelson could hope to offset his rival's largesse.

The creation of the new Fifth District had unsettled this uni-verse by removing the gravitational pull of the incumbent con-gressman, whose power of appointment had kept all these patronage-hungry individuals in approximate alignment. Gone also was the organizing force of the old- stock Republican elite of the Twin Cities-dominated Third District. The Fifth was in chaos, until the order of greater and lesser political bodies—and their orbiting satellites—could be determined.

State government could not control this chaos within the

Republican party, since, in the 1880s, "no laws governed the actions of political parties" in Minnesota. The state controlled—merely counted—only the fall general election between the two parties. Before then, within each party, each committee was virtually sovereign at its own level. The Republican state central committee placed the Fifth's Republicans under the temporary control of an appointed nine-member district committee until the July 12th convention at Detroit Lakes, and then left them to flounder.[35] The Republican *St.Paul Pioneer Press* nervously wrung its hands over the impending "disgraceful spectacle" at Detroit Lakes, where frontier Fifth Republicans were about to throw off "the yoke of the political dynasties in the old Third."[36]

The July 12th convention at Detroit Lakes, an NP town, was indeed a "disgraceful spectacle." The *Duluth Tribune* termed it "the biggest political row ever heard of" and "the most disgraceful convention ever held in the northwest.[37] Alert to historical coincidences, the *Fargo Republican* compared it to the annual Catholic-Protestant donnybrook cum commemoration of the Irish Battle of the Boyne, also on July 12.[38]

Detroit Lakes was crowded with would-be delegates, political operatives, and spectators eager to see the show. East- and west-bound trains ("loaded down") brought hundreds to the village, mostly at the invitation of the free-spending Kindred. Appropriately enough for a territorial fight, about 150 pro-Kindred border ruffians and their brass band came on the NP train from Dakota Territory—all "talking, shouting and swearing for Kindred." Kindred brought additional brass bands from Brainerd and Little Falls, as well as several score of armed "police" commanded by former Crow Wing county sheriff Peter Mertz. Only a lonely male quartet made music for Nelson. Many lawyers supported him, but no police. The hotels were booked full of Kindred supporters, and drinks were flowing freely at the town's five saloons—often paid for by Kindred.

Acting like the people's choice, the outgoing, personable Kindred circulated among the crowd, pausing so frequently for glad-handing that he could not "keep his cigar lighted between talks." Reserved and cautious, Nelson stuck "pretty closely to his hotel" where he consulted with supporters—thereby unintentionally creating the image of a "smoke-filled room" candidacy. To house his delegates, Nelson "imported a number of tents," including one large white circus tent—ostensibly as sleeping quarters but also as a back-up convention site.[39]

Pre-convention bolting and disunity all but assured a disgraceful spectacle. About 150 would-be delegates laid claim to the allotted eighty delegate posts. Only about seventeen came with an undisputed right to their seats. The candidates failed to agree on a compromise. As chairman of the nine-member temporary committee, the Republican state central committee had appointed George H. Johnston of Detroit Lakes. The town's "founder," Johnston claimed to support Nelson but the Nelson camp greatly distrusted him. An anti-Kindred coalition controlled the temporary committee by a 5-to-3 margin, with Johnston as the ninth member. On the morning of July 12, Johnston refused to consider the Nelson camp's proposed solution to the problem of disputed delegates. The committee voted to dump Johnston and elected Alphonso Barto as the new chairman. Kindred's men refused to recognize Barto. Shortly after 1 PM, two rival chairmen headed for the convention hall, the Holmes Opera House, to organize the proceedings.[40]

They were late. The convention was supposed to begin at 1 PM. Anticipating trouble, Kindred's forces had occupied the Opera House by 9:30 AM with Kindred "strikers" and "shoulder hitters" (burly non-delegates) and their unofficial "special police," thirty men under Mertz's control. "Before 1 o'clock the opposition [anti-Kindred] delegates headed in an imposing procession" from the circus tent to the opera house. A "struggling mass of swearing, sweating humanity" tried to force its way in, some by the rear window. Soon, some 350 "howling gorillas" were inside. They "leaped on chairs, pushed forward to the stage, swung arms aloft, shouted . . . yelled till the power" of speech was gone, then just "wagged their jaws and rolled their eyes in a paroxysm of fury." All this before the competing chairmen arrived to start the proceedings.[41]

When the 300-pound Barto and the "ponderous" Johnston took the stage to organize the convention, the noise reached a crescendo. Though the bitterly divided assembly stayed united during a brief discussion of distributing admission tickets, unity soon disintegrated as Kindred and Nelson men rushed to elect separate temporary chairmen and committees on credentials. Soon two conventions were operating from one platform, which was overrun by shouting delegates. Two rival claimants fought for the secretary's table. To see the action, the newspaper reporters climbed on a table in the rear of the platform, while two masses of Kindred and anti-Kindred delegates noisily "writhed and coiled toward and about the front of the platform." According to one reporter, "There were probably a hundred men present in the hall with pistols in their pockets, and it was a wonder some one did not fire the first shot." Fortunately, at that moment the reporters' table "broke and landed them on the floor," which brought laughter and some relief from rage.

At a window, Fergus Falls land officer Søren Listoe relayed messages to and received orders from Kindred, who stood outside the building. When Listoe reported that Nelson's supporter, Solomon G. Comstock of Moorhead, had been elected temporary chairman, Kindred commanded, "God damn them. Clean them out. If you need help I will have plenty of it for you." Inside, "the Kindred crowd set up a howl of 'put them out.'" At Kindred's command the "special policemen rushed upon the stage, seized Mr. Comstock, and were about to pitch him headlong from the stage." Nelson's men came to his rescue, a man or two went "off the stage with his feet where his head belonged," and "a grand melee and smashing of heads seemed imminent."

But Johnston had rented the hall, and Kindred's police seemed to have the authority of law, and, most important, the Nelson men were badly outnumbered. Giving up the battle for the opera

107

house, the anti-Kindred "convention" approved a motion to adjourn to the white tent near the depot. It left the battlefield to the Kindred "convention."

Once separated, the two conventions went more quietly about their business. Inside the opera house, Kindred was unanimously nominated as the Republican candidate for Congress. Praising the Fifth like a promoter ("in natural resource [it] surpasses any other district in the West"), Kindred gave a short acceptance speech, in which he "regretted that the question of nationality has been raised for are we not all Americans alike?" Outside, in the tent, the anti-Kindred delegates first excitedly discussed the raucous proceedings inside, then settled down to nominate Nelson on the first formal ballot (Nelson–45, Gilman–8, and Graves–7) while Knute Nelson "stood outside the tent chewing a straw."

The second party-endorsed candidate entered the tent to give *his* acceptance speech. He raised no substantive issues for the coming campaign, only a criticism of Kindred's tactics. He claimed, "I am not your candidate so much as the exponent of a principle," which was "that the congressional office is not to be put up at auction." He could not defend that principle alone: "Every one of you are candidates. Your character, reputation and manhood are at stake." He warned them, "All manner of methods will be used against you," and assured them, "I will be true." His cause was "to maintain the integrity of the Republican party in this district." Fittingly, he closed with a reference to the grand old Republican: "I will live up to the utterance of Abraham Lincoln—'doing the right as God gives me to know the right.'"[42]

After speeches of support from the defeated Gilman and Graves, future United States Senator Moses E. Clapp presented the report of the resolutions committee, which did address several issues. In adopting it, Nelson's delegates committed him to support civil-service reform, a selective tariff reduction, legislation to encourage harmonious labor relations, and a reciprocity treaty with Canada. However, most of the resolutions' thunder was directed at Kindred, who bought men "like sheep in the shambles" and let loose "the strumpet of corruption" that hither-to had been confined to "other political parties in the slums and sink holes of the great cities." In their resolutions, Kindred's delegates addressed no public policy issues whatsoever, but loudly defended the regularity of their convention and warned the state central committee not to interfere.[43]

The ensuing campaign resembled a frontier mud-wrestling contest between two antagonists using different holds more than a civic-minded debate over public policy. Chaotic factionalism soon spread to local races, as the Kindred party squared off against the Nelson party for legislative seats and county offices. The distrust and hatred visible at Detroit Lakes was too great to permit the two sides to support the same local candidates. One Wilkin county Republican threatened that "if Mr. Childs [a candidate for state representative] proposes, through his Candidacy, to force upon the people a man so objectionable as Kindred," then he would run against him. After Childs supported Kindred, another Wilkin county man reported that a local caucus "appeared as Childs & anti-Childs, but was really Nelson vs. Kindred." In at least one case, Nelson intervened to ask a Nelson man to oppose a pro-Kindred legislative candidate.[44]

Kindred practiced the politics of distribution, while Nelson practiced the politics of connections. As a virtual political unknown with a bankroll, Kindred had little choice. He had few political connections. Like a ward heeler or Tammany boss distributing government jobs and Christmas turkeys, he distributed campaign jobs, new weekly and daily newspapers, promises of a new railroad and of government jobs, free liquor, and other distributable goods.

Nelson probably did not adhere to the high ethical standards he had announced in his 1875 speech to the Alexandria Library Association on corruption.[45] However, he lacked the funds to match Kindred's distributions, and had to rely on his connections. He was well connected to the many Scandinavian-American settlers, and to *Budstikken* and other Scandinavian-

109

language newspapers. As a popular frontier lawyer, he had scores of friends among the legal fraternity. Common people knew him, for he had handled hundreds of land conveyances. From his work for Hill, he had excellent connections in the towns along the SPM&M. As a former state senator, he had many political contacts in the Upper Country.

Though he was connected to a railroad builder, he lacked the money to be one. To win votes in railroad-hungry towns such as Princeton and Red Lake Falls, Kindred and other investors announced the incorporation of the Brainerd, St. Paul and Grand Forks Railroad. Offering Twin Cities shippers' boxed freight the luxury of a long, scenic drive through Mille Lacs county and past Gull Lake, the BSP&GF—which was never built—would have given voters in Mille Lacs county and the pineries railroad service. Announced a week after the Detroit Lakes convention, it was an obvious campaign ploy, though few could be sure that Kindred lacked the funds to construct it.[46]

Kindred had the money to develop a credible if misleading image by adroit investment in local newspapers. Obviously seeking to undermine Scandinavian-American support for Nelson, he started or subsidized Scandinavian-language newspapers such as *Tiden* (Fergus Falls), *Red River Posten* (Fargo), *Verdens Gang* (Chicago), and *Nordstjernen* (Grand Forks). He tried the same tactic with the American press. He started daily newspapers in Duluth (the *Daily Bee*) and Moorhead (the *Enterprise*), and subsidized the *Fergus Falls Daily Telegram* and *St. Paul Daily Globe*.[47] He also owned or subsidized many weekly newspapers: the *Perham Journal*, the *St. Vincent Herald*, the *Big Stone County Herald* (Ortonville), and others.[48] The pro-Nelson *Moorhead News* sarcastically observed that he was "the proprietor, in part or whole, of more type metal than any other man in the Northwest." Whether to secure subsidies or to please pro-Kindred subscribers, most newspapers on the NP supported him.[49]

Newspapers were the major source of political information in the Gilded Age. The Republican and Democratic parties insured

110

party loyalty by controlling information, most of which "came in the direct party form: newspapers were party newspapers, and political conversations . . . were among committed party newspapers."[50] A Democrat could almost go from cradle to grave without the contamination of reading a Republican opinion. In the factionalism of the "Bloody Fifth," most newspapers were Kindred or Nelson newspapers. They controlled the flow of political information on the campaign and twisted it for factional purposes. Thus, the battle for control of the press was vital.

The blame for a biased, subsidized press did not lie entirely with Kindred or Nelson. Many precarious local newspapers "bled" politicians by offering favorable news stories or editorials if the politician purchased stock in the newspaper, lent it money, or made an outright gift. Both Nelson and Kindred were victimized by these for-sale journalists. Politicians and press had a symbiotic relationship in late nineteenth-century America — each needed and used the other.

Lacking Kindred's deep pockets, Nelson relied on his connections to win press support.[51] His ethnic connections secured him the support of *Budstikken* and other Scandinavian-language newspapers. Nelson asked Luth. Jaeger of *Budstikken* to make Norwegian Americans "feel that it is odious and an insignia of purchase to be found in the Kindred ranks."[52] Jaeger did that and more. *Budstikken* defended Nelson against the attacks of *Verdens Gang*, reprinted an A.R. Cornwall letter extolling Nelson's character, and even criticized the pro-Nelson *Skandinaven* for being too friendly to Kindred. Kindred newspapers accused *Budstikken* of being under financial obligation to Nelson, which its publishers heatedly denied.[53] Nelson's cooperation with Upper Country newspapers in Alexandria, Fergus Falls, Sauk Centre, Moorhead, and Crookston to secure completion of the SPM&M helped him win their backing in 1882.[54] Congressman William D. Washburn and other Twin Cities Republican leaders helped him win the support of the *Minneapolis Tribune* and the *St. Paul Pioneer Press*.

The *Pioneer Press* greatly helped Nelson by publicizing

111

Kindred's record as NP land clerk. In early August, it printed verbatim the 1881 report of an NP committee outlining the land-office manipulations of Kindred and Power. The *Pioneer Press* detailed an NP lawsuit against Kindred, his trip to New York to reach a compromise settlement, and the restitution he was required to make. Said to be valued at $50,000, the restitution involved his relinquishing title to thousands of acres of company land in exchange for the NP's promise to drop the lawsuit and not publicize the affair.[55] These were damaging revelations. The Nelson campaign published them in a 46-page pamphlet—and distributed a reported 25,000 copies throughout the district.[56] But they carried more weight coming from the respected *Pioneer Press*. Nelson later credited *Pioneer Press* editor Joseph Wheelock for much of his 1882 success. Pro-Nelson weeklies loaded up with this ammunition and used it frequently.[57]

If these revelations were "heavy political thunder right over the head of C.F. Kindred," then little rain fell or lightning hit in towns with a pro-Kindred newspaper.[58] Bitter factionalism and factional control of the press insured that most Kindred partisans never heard such stories, automatically discounted them, or believed instead the articles and speeches defending Kindred's NP record.[59] With such press manipulation, it was impossible to have a real debate over this issue. Kindred simply ignored the charges, had surrogates issue vague and incomplete rebuttals, and tried to paint Knute Nelson as the real miscreant. His skilled publicity staff concocted charges about Nelson and incorporated them into plausible news releases printed by numerous Kindred organs.

Nelson's entire life seemed to be on trial. He was charged with being "an apostate, infidel, atheist" whom "no true Scandinavian . . . who properly respects himself, his church, and his God" could support.[60] Some digging in Dane county produced an anonymous letter, supposedly from one of Dane's most respected citizens. It accused "pettifogger" Nelson of filing debt-collection claims against poor farmers for trifling sums in order to collect the legal fees.[61] Charges of claim-jumping Kilbourn's homestead were hurled by Kindred newspapers and refuted by pro-Nelson ones.[62] Nelson's work for completion of the SPM&M was cited as proof that he had "sold himself to the Manitoba railroad for 1,280 acres of railroad land" while ostensibly serving the people in the Minnesota Senate.[63] Support from Washburn and Twin Cities leaders earned him the damaging title of "paid attorney of the great Minneapolis Millers' Association," formed to cheat the poor wheat farmer. (Earlier that year, he had received a modest fee from the Millers' Association for legal work on one case.)[64] He was guilty by association with former land officers H.L. Gordon and C.A. Gilman, allegedly members of a "pine land ring" stealing good timber lands from settlers and the government.[65] He was derisively called "Knuty Nelson" and "the little Norwegian," though the latter became a term of endearment in some quarters.[66] A scurrilous nativist piece ("Knute the Bolter") in Kindred's *Duluth Bee* distorted his past and insulted Norwegian Americans.[67]

The Nelson campaign denied or ignored these charges. To win the very important support of Civil War veterans, they publicized Nelson's war record—even going to the extent of contacting 4th Wisconsin comrades and persuading Ingebjørg to let them see Nelson's Civil War letters.[68] Mainly, they focused on Kindred's NP record and campaign tactics.

Both sides were shouting past each other—each to its own select audience of supporters. The *Fergus Falls Journal* claimed that another newspaper had committed "a most outrageous fraud upon the public" by printing a concocted quotation from the *Journal* falsely reporting "Nelson steadily losing" in Otter Tail county.[69] To a Norman county supporter, Nelson outlined his media tactics: "Then it is of utmost importance that you from time to time, send short reports of how the campaign progresses by letter or telegram to the Pioneer Press and Minneapolis Tribune. . . . For instance, a short dispatch saying,—'The feeling here is all for Nelson. Kindred seems to have no followers. His actions at Detroit [Lakes] disgusted every-body, etc.' would some-

113

times do much good. These newspapers will publish these reports if they are brief, curt and to the point. . . . Kindred will have lots of such reports, and we must not allow our side to be behindhand."[70] Given this strategy, it is hard to know whether to believe many of the contemporary newspaper accounts on either side. Though the *Pioneer Press* began the campaign with seemingly neutral reporting, few newspapers maintained neutrality throughout.[71]

Each side was often angered by what it could only regard as deliberate lies told by the other ("the dastardly sneak . . . an unmitigated, malicious LIAR of the BLACKEST DYE").[72] With discussion and debate useless, men sometimes resorted to dirty tricks or the threat of violence. When a leading citizen of Brainerd defended the NP auditor who had investigated Kindred and declared himself a Nelson supporter, an angry crowd marched to his home "with unearthly yells, insulting epithets, jeers and threats, winding up with smearing the house from top to bottom with rotten eggs."[73] A Kindred supporter in Alexandria shot a pair of oxen that Nelson's men had turned loose in his garden.[74] When Nelson spoke in Thompson (Carlton county) at the schoolhouse, "a gang of Kindred's retainers armed with eggs" entered the room and "immediately opened fire upon the speaker." They missed Knute and hit the blackboard. When he reluctantly spoke in Brainerd, twenty revolver-toting friends sat on the platform to protect him.[75]

Considering that women would not have the vote until the passage of the Nineteenth Amendment in 1919, it is not surprising that nineteenth-century politics was a very masculine world. From the revolvers and fisticuffs in Detroit Lakes to the eggthrowing at Thompson, the Kindred-Nelson battle was a man's affair.[76]

Once the exciting spectacle aroused the male public's interest, it was not hard to enlist many men in campaign organizations. They were eager to "join in." Though they lacked the sophisticated technology of twentieth-century campaigns, Gilded Age

114

politicians could mobilize an impressive army of campaign workers as election day drew near. In fact, "there was usually enough labor to conduct a full survey" of the voters and not merely a sample.[77] Nelson understood Gilded Age army-style campaigning: "it is as necessary in politics and state craft as in warlike operations . . . that men move collectively in large bodies, and not as isolated units."[78] In two letters to a Norman county supporter, he outlined his strategy for moving collectively: "That you, and two good men to be by you selected, . . . act as a county campaign committee . . . . That you at once appoint a subcommittee of three reliable and trustworthy men for each town, city and village in your county, to take charge of and look after the campaign in each precinct. That these sub-committees proceed as soon as practicable to make a canvass and list all republican voters within their respective precincts, putting the names of all voters on the list, and classifying them as 'Nelson' or doubtful as the case may be. . . . These termed 'doubtful' . . . should especially be labored with in time, as well as all democrats."[79] By such means, Gilded Age politicians made amazingly accurate predictions of vote totals.[80] Kindred's army did the same: "There are men out every day in Big Stone county with the poll lists of every town and plenty of Kindred's money in their pockets, setting up the pins for election day."[81]

Nelson closed his campaign at Fergus Falls on November 6. The Fergus Silver Cornet Band headed a two-block-long torchlight parade watched by "hundreds" of sidewalk spectators. At Bell's Hotel, he stood on the portico and received the crowd's loud "three cheers," which "made the Kindred men feel . . . the day of judgement was at hand." They paraded to the Opera House, where the "remarkable warm reception" caused the weary Nelson to temporarily lose control of his emotions. He managed to give a short speech.[82]

The Nelson-Kindred donnybrook was over—at least the legal campaigning was ended. Nelson had spoken in every major town. He had defended his entire public (and private) career. He had survived what Folwell called "the finest example of dirty politics known in America outside of certain great cities."[83] To defeat him, Kindred had spent between $150,000 and $200,000.[84]

The Nelson camp's great fear was the prospect of ballot stuffing, double-voting, and the use of ineligible voters by the Kindred forces, especially in the "pinery" counties. Such vote fraud was more difficult to pull off in settled counties—though Nelson workers were warned to be on the watch even there.[85] In the pineries, Kindred prepared to manipulate vote totals. Working through his legal counsel, Cushman K. Davis, he asked Governor Hubbard to establish by executive order voting precincts in sparsely-populated Itasca and Cass counties. Demanding that Hubbard refuse, Nelson pointed to Cass county's tradition of vote fraud, the itinerant lumbermen in Crow Wing county, and the likelihood of votes by fictitious pinery "residents." Pressure was intense from both sides, but Hubbard established the precincts in early October.[86]

The chaotic factionalism in the frontier Fifth would not have been complete without some frontier-style vote fraud. Despite Nelson's strong lead in settled western Minnesota, Kindred's managers sent a constant flow of news releases to the pro-Kindred *Minneapolis Journal*, all declaring Kindred ahead in the balloting. For a week after the November 7th election, the *Journal* announced Kindred's ever-widening lead. Outstate Kindred papers carried the same message. "Good-bye Knuty," warned the *Detroit Record*, as it reported that "The Final Result" was a 2,207-vote Kindred victory.[87]

Knowing Kindred's plans, Nelson sent three trusted campaign workers (including Gilman and George W. Benedict of Sauk Rapids) to oversee the counting in the pineries. The pro-Nelson *Pioneer Press* and *Minneapolis Tribune* sent reporters to Brainerd to check on Kindred's activities. They wired back stories of alleged Kindred frauds, from double-voting to destroyed ballots. Benedict braved daunting difficulties. From Brainerd he traveled north to Pine River (Cass county), where Kindred's men reported

116

that over 700 persons voted. Only 224 names were on the official poll list. At Clough Brothers lumber camp nearby, Kindred workers claimed 400 men at work, but the company showed only 120 employed. From Pine River, Benedict "attempted to cross [Leech Lake] in a birch bark canoe, was caught in a storm, had to make for shore and with his companion spent the night in an Indian tepee, but succeeded in reaching Lake Winnebagoshish and thence made down the [Mississippi] river in a yawl to Grand Rapids, arriving just as the polls were closed." There, Benedict encountered Peter Mertz and a brothel keeper from Aitkin supervising Kindred's interests in Grand Rapids. He found that "stupendous frauds were perpetrated," mainly by allowing people to vote in both Itasca and Cass counties.[88]

There was vote fraud in the NP region. Appropriately, at Northern Pacific Junction (Carlton county), Kindred workers used an NP gravel train to fetch track workers, who voted there and were then taken to two more polling places. Reportedly, men holding Nelson "tickets" (ballots) were driven away from the polls. The *Tribune* reported that 2,227 had voted at Brainerd's lone polling place, or 4½ votes every minute. Ballots were passed through a hole in the wall to out-of-sight election judges who counted (or destroyed) the "tickets." The *Tribune* charged that Indians were paid three dollars for each Kindred vote, and that liquor was also used as an inducement.[89]

Kindred planned to withhold the vote totals from Crow Wing, Cass, Carlton, and Itasca counties until he could determine how many votes he needed to overcome Nelson's lead in the western counties. When the official count showed that lead at nearly 7,000 votes, even fraud was useless. The four holdouts could never overcome that margin. Kindred finally capitulated on November 15, a sadder and much poorer man. Official returns showed E.P. Barnum, the Democratic candidate, with 6,248 votes (17.6 percent), Kindred with 12,238 votes (34.5 percent), and Nelson with 16,956 votes (47.8 percent)—for a victory margin of 4,718. Nelson carried nineteen counties, including all those along the SPM&M

tracks. Kindred carried six of eight along the NP tracks plus Mille Lacs and Itasca counties. Barnum won German-American, Catholic Stearns county.[90]

Kindred's official vote total was inflated by about 3,000 votes, making it proportionately the most fraudulent count in Minnesota history. The worst frauds were committed in four counties—Carlton, Cass, and Itasca with approximately 500 fraudulent votes each, and Kindred's home county, Crow Wing, with approximately 1,000 fraudulent votes.[91]

Kindred's money, tactics, and vote fraud, the stormy Detroit Lakes convention, the launching of Nelson's national political career, and the winning of Norwegian Americans' first congressional seat—all made the Kindred-Nelson campaign famous and seemingly unique in Minnesota history. Yet it was not unique. "Chaotic factionalism" was typical of the frontier. The ethnic dimension of this contest can easily be exaggerated. Kindred won the support of some Norwegian Americans, such as land officers Søren Listoe and A.A. Brown. Nelson relied heavily on his contacts among Yankee politicians and party activists. Fewer than 30 percent of the anti-Kindred delegates at Detroit Lakes had Scandinavian-American surnames.[92] Without old-stock support, Nelson could not have won even the "white tent" nomination. Given the organized, highly partisan, patronage-based nature of Gilded Age politics, it was highly unlikely that any single ethnic group, no matter how numerous, could storm the gates and snatch a congressional seat from Yankee politicians.

Though made possible by creation of the new district, this was a success for Nelson and his ethnic group. Yet the Kindred-Nelson fight revealed state government's failure to monitor and regulate nominating, campaigning, and voting. The state lacked the capacity, and violence could easily have erupted in Detroit Lakes or on the campaign trail. Republican state officials relied on fees levied on the lumber industry to build up their campaign war chests. They could hardly take a strong stand against vote fraud in the lumber camps. A larger population in SPM&M farming country, not state vigilance, kept the unscrupulous Kindred out of Congress.

Knute Nelson's role as broker between old-stock and Scandinavian-American communities enabled him to win support from both — and both were essential. His early Americanization in Koshkonong, his Civil War service and ardent American patriotism, his legal practice, and his work for Hill's SPM&M—all were essential in preparing him for his congressional victory. Yet, in his private celebration, public roles were joined by strong memories of the poor immigrant's arrival at Castle Garden and how far he had come. A fellow immigrant wrote of his prior conviction "that a Vossing would be the first Norwegian to enter Congress. It is a matter of congratulation to me and all other Vossings, that such is the case, but above all that that Vossing is Knute Nelson."[93]

Seven

Frontier Norwegian-American Republican Congressman

After the campaign, Knute Nelson looked "tired and worn out." In the last five weeks, he gave a speech "nearly every single day, and only once for a few hours on a Sunday afternoon could [he] come home and see his family." He thanked his friends and his Scandinavian-American supporters: "Allow me through *Budstikken* to express my sincerest gratitude to Scandinavians and the Scandinavian press inside and outside the 5th congressional district, for the fervour and force, with which they have embraced my candidacy, and thereby brought about my election."[1] Not all of them had embraced it, which added to his natural suspicion of people and politicians. Too many, he thought, justified Kindred's belief that every man has his price.

The campaign left him with debts, but unlike Kindred's, his were mostly political, not financial.[2] He thanked and acknowledged those allies who had marched loyally behind his banner. Those who felt they deserved more than thanks he could pay off with deftly distributed rewards of federal jobs, though job seekers outnumbered available positions. Most federal jobs were minor, like postmaster or railway mail clerk, but the demand for them exceeded the supply.

He could distribute one plum that would make everyone

happy: new post offices. As railroads, depots, and stores clustered around depots created new towns, new post offices were needed. The Fifth gained "nearly a hundred" of them during Nelson's three terms in Congress. "These were warmly welcomed by the settlers and added greatly to the congressman's popularity."[2] This was the popular part of the politics of distribution.

Patronage was not so easy. He dispensed patronage through a handful of trusted advisers. Appointments in northwestern Minnesota were filtered through Norwegian-born Paul C. Sletten, the Receiver of the United States Land Office at Crookston. Seldom were Sletten's recommendations overruled, and then only after consultation. In later years, Nelson referred to Sletten as the "boss of the upper country." In west central Minnesota, Lars Aaker did most of the field work on patronage. Here Nelson took a more direct hand because he knew this area and its politicians so intimately. At St. Cloud, he worked through Lieutenant Governor Charles A. Gilman, to whom he gave the tough task of finding job replacements in the pro-Kindred "pineries." That included the ticklish matter of a new postmaster at Brainerd. When Kindred supporter W.W. Hartley sought reappointment, Nelson secured Hartley's cooperation in persuading the *Brainerd Tribune* to take a more favorable view of him. He also asked Gilman to raise money to purchase stock in publisher A.J. Underwood's *Fergus Falls Journal* and his Norwegian-language *Ugeblad*, in order to keep both newspapers solvent.[4]

In patronage distribution, he had to balance several competing factors: the special needs of his frontier district, national Republican policies, his special status as the only Scandinavian-American congressman, and Gilded Age political realities. These four factors also influenced his position on such issues as the tariff, pensions for Civil War (Union) veterans, railroad regulation, and the related issues of public land and Indian policies. First priority went to the Fifth District's special needs. Since the first session of the 48th Congress did not meet until December, 1883, he faced the patronage problem long before he voted or spoke in Congress.

The 1880 Republican national convention endorsed the policy of merit-based appointments to civil-service positions, which passed Congress in January, 1883, as the Pendleton (Civil Service) Act. The Nelson faction's "circus tent" convention at Detroit Lakes had also voted to "heartily endorse the principle of civil service reform."[5] But Gilded Age politicians and the public measured a politician's power by his control of patronage. Nelson had to appear powerful to forestall another Kindred challenge in 1884. Patronage was especially important to him, because the 1882 battle was fought over factional and regional loyalties, not issues. Ideology tied no one to Knute Nelson. He had to use patronage to tie his supporters to himself. When Stillwater lumberman Dwight M. Sabin defeated incumbent William Windom for the United States Senate seat in January, 1883, observers warned him that Sabin was aligned with legislators friendly to Kindred. They feared that Sabin's victory gave Kindred a strong voice in Fifth District patronage and encouraged him to run again in 1884.[6] Fifth District friends echoed this fear and used patronage concerns to question Nelson's political manhood. One warned that if Nelson did not reverse a rumored postmaster appointment in Argyle (Marshall county), "people will lose faith in your influence & control of Patronage in this District."[7]

These considerations came together in his decision to remove Søren Listoe as Register of the U.S. Land Office at Fergus Falls. Nelson's longtime foe, Listoe had had a prominent role in Kindred's campaign. By Gilded Age political rules, Nelson was expected to remove Listoe. Before he was sworn in, his supporters were lobbying him over who the replacement would be.[8] The Otter Tail county register of deeds, George W. Boyington, an old-stock American, became the leading candidate. By mid-March, Nelson had requested President Chester A. Arthur to fire Listoe and appoint Boyington.

When the news reached Fergus Falls, a reporter found Boyington at home at midnight. "The interview was short and sweet." He exulted, "I wanted the office and, well, I got it, and that's all there is of it." Contacted at "a social gathering," Listoe "expressed surprise" and questioned, "whether this is in accordance with the new civil service rules."[9]

That was exactly the question raised by Minnesota's most influential Republican newspaper, the *St. Paul Pioneer Press*. It called this "a political decapitation, pure and simple . . . precisely as was done before the civil service reform bill passed." This was "an act which recalls the grossest political proscriptions of the old machine days."[10] Listoe's term expired in September 1883. Why not wait until then to replace him?, asked the *Pioneer Press*.

Nelson visited the *Pioneer Press* office two days after that editorial appeared. He did not answer that he had to prove his patronage power by removing Listoe before September, although that was likely his main reason. He argued that Listoe's removal was "strictly in accordance with the principles of civil service reform," for Listoe had "abandon[ed] his duties" to campaign for Kindred. The *Pioneer Press* questioned whether the congressman should be judge and jury in such cases.[11]

Folkebladet criticized Nelson's act as more appropriate for an executive officer than a legislator. However, more Scandinavian-American newspapers praised than condemned him. In 1876, *Budstikken* had opposed such land-office patronage politics when practiced by old-stock politicians. Now, *Budstikken* proudly claimed that Listoe's removal was "proof that Knute Nelson both has political influence and knows how to use it."[12] As the first Scandinavian-American congressman, Nelson could count on some support.

Fifth District grumblers questioned if he knew how to use it. As a Scandinavian American, how could he appoint the Yankee Boyington? One supporter asked, "Is it fair to take the *only* Office away from the Skandinavians, that they have had, that amounts to anything"?[13] Hurt, Nelson objected that he "ought to have a fair chance" before his friends got angry with him.[14] Adding to his "embarrasment" was the surprising news in early April that Boyington was declining the post![15] That renewed the local tug-of-war. The *Fergus Falls Ugeblad* editor nominated himself for the post, but the pulling and hauling soon centered on Scandinavian Americans H.G. Stordock and B.N. Johnson. A supporter wrote to warn Nelson that two rival lobbying delegations were headed for Alexandria: "I drop this line so you may have your Shot Gun loaded."[16] Nelson decided on B.N. Johnson, but he had offended civil- service reformers, some Scandinavian Americans, and several office seekers. Dispensing patronage was a messy business.

Congressman Nelson was also a University of Minnesota regent. That involved him in an even messier appointment dispute, featuring Norwegian-American religious quarrels he had come to Minnesota to escape. Nelson had asked to be named a regent so that he could promote Scandinavian studies at the University.[17] Political activities and congressional service made him largely an absent regent. In his first four and one-half years on the Board of Regents, he attended only one-third of its meetings.[18] At his and others' urging, the 1883 Minnesota legislature passed a bill establishing a University professorship in "Scandinavian" language and literature. As a regent and the leading Scandinavian-American politician, he was widely expected to choose the new professor. Prospective candidates and their supporters sent him letters. Scandinavian-American editors aimed their lobbying editorials clearly in his direction.[19]

First, the editors sparred over whether a Swede or a Norwegian should be appointed. *Svenska Folkets Tidning* wondered, "What is meant by the 'Scandinavian' language? Is that Swedish, or Norwegian, or maybe Icelandic, which lies at the root of them both?" Also Swedish-language *Skaffaren och Minnesota Stats Tidning* warned, "Our friends, the Norwegians, as always will certainly push themselves forward and get one of their own appointed if possible." In reply, *Budstikken, Norden,* and *Nordvesten* pointed to substantive reasons for Norwegian Americans' political success and accused Swedish Americans of bringing to America Swedes' traditional condescension toward Norwegians. *Norden, Svenska Folkets Tidning,* and *Fergus Falls Ugeblad* urged

125

that the professorship not become a political plum, which it might if it was seen as *krigsbytte* (spoils of war) in a Swedish-Norwegian conflict.[20]

A separate battle raged over whether or not the professor had to be a Lutheran. Could Norwegian Americans Luth. Jaeger, the freethinking editor of *Budstikken*, or Kristofer Janson, Unitarian minister and lecturer, be considered? *Skaffaren* pointedly reminded Nelson that Scandinavian Americans were "God-fearing and moral, and cannot reconcile themselves to the squalling freethinking which has found good spokesmen in Misters Jaeger and Johnson [sic]. Knute Nelson himself knows this fact, and, in so far as it is up to him, he dare not offend the people's religious beliefs by appointing anyone who denies God and his Word to teach the young at the University. . . . We expect that Mr. Nelson will consider our words, before he lets his word turn the scale in favor of an atheist's promotion to Scandinavian professor." [21] Private letters reinforced this point.[22] For the post, this group preferred the Conference minister, editor, and professor Sven Oftedal. It certainly represented the clergy's views.

Others supported Jaeger and Janson, and appealed to Nelson's dislike of clerical domination. In several previous battles, he had sided with this liberal wing, and they subtly reminded him of that. Willmar lawyer John W. Arctander wrote, "the Norwegian people of the State will certainly expect from *you*, that Jaeger be our Scandinavian professor." In words that recalled the 1860s common school controversy, Arctander assured him that Jaeger was "a warm friend of the *American* education of our young countrymen in opposition to the schools of our different religious sects." Also, "our mutual friend Bjørnstjerne Bjørnson would thank you" for supporting Jaeger.[23]

For years, Nelson had shown some degree of freethinking skepticism. His budding friendship with Bjørnson was one indication. Working through Rasmus B. Anderson, he had arranged a lecture by the iconoclastic Norwegian writer in Alexandria in early March, 1881. Then, he noted, "the clerical influence seems against us."[24] After meeting him, Bjørnson praised his "excellent English," his "most splendid Voss dialect," and promised, "I'm going to get drunk" in celebration once this "most outstanding politician" was elected to Congress.[25] During his 1880-1881 tour through Norwegian America, clerical influence was indeed against him for renouncing the Lutheran orthodoxy of his childhood.[26]

After the tour, they corresponded. The author sent a bust of himself to Nelson, who thanked him: "It is as if you were here with me all the time. . . . It is a bond that ties the heart of the farm boy to Norway and the spirits of Norway." Writing during the 1882 campaign, Nelson promised to visit Norway "when my little fight is over," and apologized for his Americanization and bad Norwegian handwriting: "My heart is Norwegian, but my mind and my hand are somewhat strange."[27]

Thus, Arctander's appeal was well calculated to win his support for Jaeger. However, Congressman Nelson was more cautious about antagonizing his fellow Scandinavian Americans than Attorney Nelson had been in March, 1881. In early May, Jaeger probably doomed his chances with a bitter editorial assaulting the Norwegian Synod for influencing the search.[28] In July, regents referred the choice to a general search committee, which reported out a compromise candidate in April, 1884. With Nelson probably influential in absentia, they selected Olaus J. Breda, who had scholarly credentials and the politically necessary experience as a Norwegian-American Lutheran pastor.[29] Congressman Nelson simply could not afford to battle the Lutheran clergy, as he had briefly done in 1869.

Nelson also had to mediate between the Grand Old Party and his fellow Norwegian Americans. Broker Nelson was especially needed in the 1883 gubernatorial campaign, when the Democrats nominated Norwegian-born Adolph Biermann, a Civil War veteran from Olmstead county. Republicans feared an ethnic defection to the Democrats. The panicky Republican state central committee pleaded with Nelson to rally the Scandinavians with speeches in Fillmore county and the Fifth District.[30] Republican candidate Lucius Hubbard warned him that Biermann had "seduced some Scandinavian Republicans in Otter Tail and northern part of Douglas" counties.[31] Budstikken's endorsement of Biermann kindled more worries.[32]

Though some Norwegian Americans asked him not to oppose Biermann, Nelson understood the partisan necessities of the Gilded Age.[33] Though Hubbard had aided Kindred by establishing the "pineries" precincts, Nelson loyally supported him a year later. On October 23, he delivered a widely reported address at Pelican Rapids. He reminded his ethnic audience, "We Norwegian Republicans of Minnesota have selected our party— selected it with deliberation and from principle," and pledged that they would "devotedly" and "permanently" support it. Democrats were the party of grumblers and obstructionists, who viewed Norwegian Americans as "a sort of voting cattle." Before, they "ridiculed us for the shortness of our jackets." Now they nominate a Norwegian in hopes the rest will follow. Equating loyalty to the GOP with gratitude to America, he concluded, "Most of us have come to these shores poor and destitute. Our chief capital has been our stout hearts and willing hands. America has received us with open arms, and treated us as though we were to the manor born. . . . on the whole [we have] been fairly treated."[34] Receiving the speech with open arms, the Republican state central committee had it translated into Norwegian, printed 100,000 copies, and distributed them throughout the state.[35]

Scandinavian Americans in the Twin Cities did not treat him so fairly when he spoke at Peterson Hall in Minneapolis on November 5. Fortified by whiskey, a contingent of Biermann's supporters crowded into the hall to jeer him. They shouted that he should speak in Norwegian, not English. Budstikken admonished them for their behavior and reminded them that speaking English was appropriate in an American campaign.[36]

This outburst did not hurt Nelson's standing or prevent Hubbard's victory. Nelson's standing with old-stock Republican

Nicholina (Jacobson) Nelson by the well at their Alexandria farm, no date (1880s?). Pumping and hauling water was a daily chore for a hardworking farm wife.

leaders was enhanced by his ability to stem the flow of Norwegian ballots to Biermann. The publisher of the *Fergus Falls Journal* wrote him, "I fully believe that Hubbard owes his election directly to your noble stand."[37] That may have been an exaggeration, but Nelson's "noble stand" demonstrated that he gave a higher priority to his Republicanism than to his ethnicity during a political campaign.

Following the 1883 election, he started for Washington in mid-November, tired and hoarse from campaigning, but heartened after a stopover in Wisconsin to visit family and friends. Thereafter, he always stopped in Deerfield, Wisconsin, on his way to the opening of Congress. He normally went alone, while his wife and children remained in Alexandria.[38] Like his traveling habits, his political beliefs and voting record were consistent throughout his three terms in the House of Representatives (1883–1889). His six-year congressional career is a study in personal consistency, not change over time or partisan consistency. He sometimes opposed national Republican policies, especially

129

its high-tariff protectionism. The needs of his frontier district came before Republican loyalty.

As the Whigs' successors, Republicans inherited their advocacy of high tariffs to protect American industries from foreign competition. Passing the highly protective Morrill tariff of 1861, Republicans had an added reason—high tariffs could finance the Civil War effort—and an added advantage—low-tariff southern Democrats were absent from Congress.[39] After the war, tariff revenues produced a budget surplus used to retire the federal war debt, which was reduced from nearly $2.7 billion ($77 per capita) in 1865, to about $1.4 billion ($26 per capita) in 1884. As the debt declined, the surplus rose. By 1884, the annual budget surplus reached $104 million.[40] The federal government's tax revenues were embarrassingly higher than what it could prudently spend.

Republicans built a political coalition to sustain this protectionism. It consisted of "industrial and financial elites" in the Northeast-Midwest industrial "core" (whose industries received protection), "industrial labor" (which received higher wages than European workers), and Civil War veterans (who received millions of dollars in pensions). The tariff's embarrassingly high revenues were spent on veterans' pensions, "in a fashion that encouraged fraudulent claims, to hundreds of thousands of Civil War veterans and their survivors." All three groups were concentrated in the northern core, which benefited at the expense of the southern and western periphery. (The South and West had few industries to protect. Confederate veterans were not eligible for pensions.) Westerners and Southerners opposed the tariff-pension system.[41]

The Fifth District was on the periphery. Of the three groups, only Civil War veterans were present in significant numbers. Even there, the Fifth had proportionately fewer pension recipients than did core areas in Illinois, Indiana, Ohio, and New England.[42] Thus, Nelson served his constituents' interests when he opposed high protectionist tariffs. He was also reflecting his 1850s views as a low-tariff Democrat.

130

Low-tariff Democrats had an opportunity in the 48th Congress. While Republicans had a bare four-vote majority in the Senate, Democrats had an overwhelming 201-to-119 advantage in the House.[43] Ways and Means Committee chairman William R. Morrison (Democrat-Illinois) presented a bill for a general twenty percent tariff reduction. However, core Democrats led a protectionist coalition which defeated the Morrison bill on May 6, 1884. Four low-tariff Republicans —all Minnesotans, including Nelson — voted for the doomed Morrison bill.[44]

Though the national Republican party opposed the Morrison bill, the lonely stand of the Minnesota Four was not unpopular among Minnesota Republicans. The one Minnesota congressman who voted against the Morrison bill, William D. Washburn, was defeated in 1884. The Minnesota Four won reelection. The influential *St. Paul Pioneer Press* asserted that "the Morrison bill was a move in the right direction." It claimed that the Four had "truly represented the opinion of the State of Minnesota."[45] Far from being courageous, Nelson's low-tariff stand fit Minnesota's, and the Fifth's, peripheral, nearly colonial, role in the national economy in the 1880s. There were few Minnesota industries for a high tariff to protect.

In the Fiftieth Congress, Democrats controlled the presidency and the House. Forcefully departing from tradition, President Grover Cleveland devoted his entire annual message of December, 1887, to tariff reform. Low-tariff Democrats supported the Mills bill, which provided for general tariff reductions and an expanded "free list" of duty-free goods. That set off the "Great Tariff Debate" of 1888, in which Nelson participated. Ultimately, tariff reformers again failed in 1888. Though Nelson and the House approved the Mills bill, the Senate passed a very different bill, and no compromise was reached.[46]

Not a tariff expert or spokesman, Nelson spoke nearly three weeks before the main debate on the Mills bill. He spoke only because the "committee on Indian affairs [of which he was a member] had the floor, which gave him the right, under a question of

131

privilege, to have his say."[47] "IT IS NELSON'S DAY" and "Knute Nelson Fires Off His Tariff Gun," trumpeted the *St. Paul Pioneer Press* and the *Minneapolis Tribune*.

Denying he favored free trade, he argued that it was not a "question of protection or free trade," but of whether to "get rid of our surplus by extravagant expenditures or by reducing taxation." He echoed most reformers in contending that the protective tariff "taxation" should equal the amount by which Americans' costs of production exceeded Europeans' costs. Tariffs should level the playing field, not require Europeans to run uphill—for that would keep American consumers running the treadmill of high taxes.[48]

Though he asserted that the debate was over taxation, not protection, he proceeded to dispute protectionists' arguments. He denied that protective tariffs produced economic growth or guarded higher American wages. A frontier immigrant, he argued instead that abundant, nearly free land "together with the immense tide of immigration, with all its capital of money and muscle," produced America's economic growth. As for high wages, "our great safety-valve" of western lands kept the labor supply scarce, because dispersed, and wages correspondingly high. "When our great West is filled up . . . when we begin to approximate Europe in density of population," then American tariffs would be as powerless to raise American wages as European tariffs presently were to raise European wages.

He did not use the Democrats' argument that high tariffs created monopolies. Nothing in his speech recognized the growing concentration of economic power. Everything rested on the assumption that, in home markets, American farmers, workers, and manufacturers bargained freely as equal individuals.[49]

On the House floor, Nelson's speech "disconcerted the Republicans generally and warmed the cockles of the Democratic heart."[50] Reporting on Minnesotans' sentiments, the *New York Times* emphasized, "The demand for [tariff] reduction is especially strong among the Norwegians and Swedes and generally throughout the agricultural regions." The "so-called Scandin-avian press" and Minnesota's Republican editors and politicians mostly favored tariff reduction.[51] Protectionism was not a princi-ple on which either Knute Nelson or the Scandinavian-American voter had been recruited to Republicanism. Neither felt obligated to "devotedly" support it. Republican anti-slavery, free-labor, and free-land principles had attracted both to the Grand Old Party— and the Civil War cemented the bond.[52] But they were not "voting cattle" who blindly followed the Republican high-tariff bell.

Civil War passions clashed on the pension side of a tariff-pension system. Here, he remained loyally Republican. President Cleveland strove to stymie Republican efforts to spend the em-barrassing budget surplus on veterans' pensions. When his ap-pointees at the Pension Office denied some pension claims, "the Republican members of Congress introduced an increasing num-ber of private pension bills." Each bill "added a specific individ-ual to the pension roll." He vetoed 233 of these bills in his first term (1885-1889), which caused "a terrific confrontation with the northern-dominated Congress."[53] Pensions figured prominently in the 1888 presidential campaign. Republican candidate Benjamin Harrison objected that it "was no time to be weighing the claims of old soldiers with apothecary's scales."[54]

Apothecary's scales and Civil War passions were present on June 1, 1888, when Nelson rose in the House to defend a private pension bill for one Theodore F. Casamer.[55] A House committee had very carefully weighed the medical report on and the Pension Commissioner's denial of the claim of Mr. Casamer, a wounded Fifth District veteran requesting an increased pension. In their re-port the House committee characterized the Commissioner's let-ter of denial as an "impertinent communication," an "inexcusable violation" of the pension law. Southern Democrats regarded this as "an insult to the Commissioner of Pensions." Southerners' sense of honor was offended. They refused to allow the Casamer bill to pass unless "the unwarranted attack" was removed.

Nelson called this southern sensitivity "fuss and feathers," "a bit of sentiment in respect to the commissioner of Pensions." "Is he above criticism? Is he the sacred white elephant? [Laughter and applause.]" Casamer was the one being unfairly attacked by the principal southern opponent, Kentucky Democrat Asher G. Caruth. Angered, Nelson challenged the Kentuckian, if he "is so terribly anxious to make a fight upon a Union soldier, here is an old soldier who is ready for him. [Laughter.]" He reacted with a Norwegian American's hatred of high-handed officialdom:" . . . for a man occupying the high position of Commissioner to use such language . . . to this old soldier . . . is an insult." The Commissioner implied that Casamer was a slacker who refused to work with his one good arm. If he had been sent such a letter, "by heavens and the eternal God I should consider it an insult, and should answer it as it deserves. [Applause]" "Are you satisfied?" he asked Representative Caruth.

Carried away by Civil War antagonisms and Norwegian distrust of officials, Nelson missed the chance for a compromise which would have given Casamer his increased pension. He half apologized with a frontier comparison: "I feel like a man at camp-meeting. We read in the Holy Writ of how pious men were carried away by their emotions, and can it be expected, then, that we poor mortals in the Fiftieth Congress should not occasionally get excited?" He was criticized for getting excited and for "making a political point" while forgetting the soldier. And the pension bill was referred back to the committee.

Nelson faithfully voted with his party to overturn Cleveland's vetoes of private pension bills.[56] This was a Civil War issue important to the Union veterans' organization, the Grand Army of the Republic (GAR). A turning point in his life, Nelson's Civil War service had recruited him to Republicanism. He could not vote against his old comrades.[57] Nevertheless, the sight of the House minutely weighing the medical report and arguing the pension claim of a single veteran revealed how Congress was hamstrung by intense Gilded Age partisanship, weak presidents, and inconclusive elections.

The Grand Army of the Republic (GAR) parade marches east on Sauk Centre's Main Street in June 1887. The day before, Congressman Knute Nelson spoke to this GAR encampment.

Nelson did not support all Republican attempts to spend the embarrassing surplus. When Republican Henry Bingham favored a subsidy to American steamship lines, his frugality and free-trade principles got the better of him. He recalled his native Norway, "one of the most poorly endowed countries on God's green earth." Yet "that poor little country, with free trade and free ships," and no shipping subsidy, "comes next to the United States of America in shipping and tonnage." Good management, initiative, and thrift were the reasons. No, a subsidy would only encourage American companies to "lie back on their oars" and enjoy their protected status.[58]

Angered by this unexpected criticism, the pro-subsidy *New York Marine Journal* viciously attacked Nelson's "terrible tirade . . . showing how Norway, of which God forsaken country he is a fine specimen of native," prospered without subsidies. The *Journal* charged that low wages on board Norwegian ships were the real cause of Norway's success. It would brook no interference from the likes of "Cute Knute Nelson": "Mr. Nelson, the Norwegian immigrant, who has been pitchforked into the American congress by the votes of his fellow immigrants who infest and overrun Minnesota, should bear himself more modest[l]y in the country of his adoption, through whose good natured laxity in her immigration laws he is permitted to enjoy all of the privileges of a native born American citizen. . . . The foreign born element in congress should sing smaller."[59] Democratic Congressman Edmund Rice and the Democratic *St. Paul Globe* gleefully seized on this diatribe from a presumably Republican newspaper to gallantly defend the popular Nelson and ingratiate themselves with Scandinavian-American voters.[60]

Nelson did not defend himself against the *Journal* attack, but he showed sensitivity to the anti-foreigner bias displayed during the subsidy debate. A California Republican, Charles N. Felton, sneered, "I only hope the gentleman's own country [Norway] will arrive at the same kind of civilization in time as pervades ours." Nelson replied, "Oh, I know all about the feeling in California. You have been hating the Chinese so long over there that you hate everything else in the shape of a foreigner." Felton felt the charge of Chinese-baiting was a "compliment," but Nelson refused to allow it to seem so.[61]

He reacted angrily when, after the Haymarket affair, Felton tried to restrict immigrants' rights to claim homestead land. Immigrants had built up Wisconsin and Minnesota and "are amongst our best and most law-abiding citizens." He was "out of patience with that maudlin sentiment" provoked by Haymarket. Why, the policemen shot at Haymarket Square were foreign-born themselves. "The very sheriff who . . . hung the anarchists in Chicago was a foreigner, who came over to this country on the same ship as myself. [Applause.]" He became more personal than ever before on the House floor: "In the year 1849 there was a poor widow and her boy six years old who landed at Castle Garden,

136

and if these new rules of modern reformers had been then in force we would have been shipped back, mother and I, to the country from which we had come." Immediately after he finished, the House rejected Felton's amendment.[62] When hit with anti-immigrant sentiments, Nelson struck back. His role as the first Norwegian-American congressman then became more important than his Republicanism.

To a frontier Norwegian-American congressman, the related issues of Indian policy and sale of public lands were the most important ones. Land ownership and land law were like hat and coat to his politics, as shown in his strong reaction to Felton's amendment. He had once been a land-hungry Vossing. He understood ordinary Scandinavian Americans' wish for a maximum distribution of tillable lands at minimum expense to actual settlers, not speculators. As a former land-office lawyer, he had professional expertise in this subject.

His Fifth District contained by far the largest share of Native Americans and reservation lands remaining in Minnesota. More than a dozen reservations remained, including the large White Earth Reservation of about 800,000 acres. The Red Lake band of Ojibway retained more than 3.5 million acres never ceded to whites by treaty. The Fifth was truly a frontier district. Extinguishing Indian land titles, surveying land, and opening large areas for settlement were still major issues among its voters thirty years after being resolved in southern Minnesota. By his choice, he was appointed to the House Committee on Indian Affairs, where he stayed for three terms, though he came to Congress with no special knowledge of Indian policy.

His primary task was to open reservation lands to white settlement. Like the SP&P completion in 1875, this was now his main assignment. He and other whites in the Fifth believed these lands were too extensive for the 1,100 Ojibway at Red Lake and the 1,800 at White Earth. He explained to the House that "over 60,000 voters" had "sent me here, and among other things desire me to secure the opening of these reservations."[63] They desired to secure agricultural lands there. Also, settlers in the treeless Red River Valley "have to bring their lumber from Minneapolis and Duluth, a distance of from two to three hundred miles," which was expensive. They were "anxious to have this pine [land] contiguous to that country opened, so that they may have the benefit of it."[64] Lumbering companies were eager to start harvesting this pine land, and were already logging near the White Earth Reservation.[65]

Already receiving post offices, patronage, and pensions from him, his constituents expected to secure through him the sale of this land, which they considered unused. They expected Gilded Age governments to distribute, not regulate. They were not too concerned if unregulated distribution of these lands resulted in defrauding their Ojibway owners.

Nelson partly satisfied them with a political coup in the summer of 1883. He convinced President Arthur to rescind an 1879 presidential order closing off pioneer settlement in thirteen townships around White Earth. Just how he lobbied Arthur has never been revealed, but on July 13 the President issued an executive order cancelling the prior one.[66] Thirteen townships meant almost 300,000 acres of potential homestead land, or some 1,800 farmsteads. Opening up this land would benefit towns like Detroit Lakes, Ada, and Crookston, where Kindred had been strong. "For a new member only 5 mon[ths] in office I feel that I have done pretty well," he boasted to Paul Sletten. He told Sletten to get the news into the leading Norwegian-American newspapers so "that our people may see how baseless and unjust were the lies and charges of the Kindred papers last Fall."[67] The newspapers quickly spread the news. Concerned that they gave *him* "too much credit" for the decision, Sletten wrote to them to insist "most emphatically" that "to Mr. Nelson is chiefly due the honor."[68]

The thirteen townships only bordered White Earth. Obtaining access to reservation lands would not prove as easy. That goal carried Nelson into the field of governmental policies toward the Indians, which reformers were struggling to change. Unlike the tariff battle, the struggle was not a partisan one. It pitted the "Friends of the Indian" against westerners, land-hungry settlers, and lumbermen. Primarily evangelical Christians in reform groups like the Indian Rights Association (IRA), the "Friends of the Indian" lobbied Congress, gathered facts and worked closely with the Indian Office. Their goals were: a breakup of tribal communalism; increased individualization through individual land ownership, Americanization, Christianization, and citizenship status; an end to the reservation system; and assimilation into American society.[69] In Minnesota, Episcopal Bishop Henry B. Whipple of Faribault was the most prominent reformer. Accepting the national goals, Minnesota reformers focused on consolidation of the scattered Ojibway in agricultural settlements on the White Earth Reservation as the best means to achieve them in Minnesota.[70]

The reformers' goals of ending communalism, breaking up reservations, and allotting land to individuals dovetailed with westerners' goal of acquiring access to reservation lands. The two groups differed in motives and the specific terms demanded, but there seemed room for compromise.

On December 11, 1883, Nelson introduced a bill to acquire the Red Lake lands, distribute 160 acres to each Indian household, and then sell the "surplus" to settlers. Pine lands would be sold to settlers or loggers. On January 7, 1884, he introduced a companion bill covering the White Earth lands.[71] Seeing his bills as good politics, he wrote *Budstikken* publisher Gudmund F. Johnson that he wanted "more homestead land for the Scandinavians of the Upper Country."[72]

To get it, he included reformers' preferred provisions: individual land allotments, guarantees that whites would not swindle them out of their 160-acre allotments, creation of a permanent trust fund with the proceeds from land sales, and annual payment of interest on the fund. In his opinion, "this is altogether too big a provision for these Indians." However, in obedience to the reform "sentiment and spirit now abroad" he had included these points in his bill.[73] He later attended one reformers' conference. He secured a railroad pass for Charles C. Painter, the reformers' chief Washington lobbyist, "for the purpose of getting his cooperation" on the bill.[74] Nelson likely agreed with the reformers' goals. After all, individual farm ownership, hard work, thrift, assimilation, education, and citizenship were vital to Americanizing Norwegian immigrants—which goal Nelson supported.

Despite his compromises, he failed to get his two bills passed in 1884. The June 10th debate on the Red Lake bill wandered off the subject into a sectional, occasionally humorous, often racist quarrel on Indian policy in general. Sniping at Nelson, southern Democrats charged that the bill was unfair to the Ojibway, whose "thrifty and energetic white neighbors" were covetously exaggerating their need for land. Unable to contain himself, a Colorado Republican accused the Southerners of harboring "a sentimental New England notion of the Indian": "if some of you philanthropic gentleman had traveled in a stagecoach over the plains, with a rifle across your legs, you would not have such profound sympathy for the Indian." He accused easterners, who had already stolen their land from its native owners, of hypocritically refusing westerners the right to do the same. Southerners and Coloradans could agree on the "pious Puritans'" hypocrisy here.[75]

Defending his bill, Nelson made several factual mistakes that prevented him from regaining control of the discussion. Fishing for support, he linked his bill to the more popular Dawes bill, which was to provide land ownership and eventual citizenship to Indians, claimed it would end the present timber frauds on the reservation, and charged that "the lumber men are opposed to it." He was forced to rely on the illogical argument that a government powerless to prevent whites from invading a closed reservation would somehow be able to prevent them from fraudulently exploiting an opened one.[76] That was the problem. Americans expected their government to distribute, not regulate. Gilded Age government was "indispensible" in distributing jobs and subsidies, but "an incorrigible bungler that presided weakly

Agent Simon Michelet (center, seated) distributes land allotments to the Ojibway at White Earth Reservation, ca. 1905.

over territorial government, Indian affairs, and the distribution of lands."[77] In 1884, Nelson bungled his two bills, which both failed.

Learning from his errors, in 1888 he combined the Red Lake and White Earth bills into one bill. He added the Minnesota reformers' goal of consolidating most Ojibway on the White Earth Reservation. He sweetened the pot for the reformers by increasing the minimum payments whites would make for timber rights and for agricultural land. He diplomatically accepted most proposed amendments, including one which contradicted the consolidation goal. Criticizing his bill, a southern Democrat stated, "I do not desire to antagonize my friend from Minnesota. The truth is, he has such a persuasive, clever manner about him that I can hardly find it in my heart to say what I am saying now."[78]

Ojibway opinion on his bill is difficult to ascertain. The *White Earth Progress*, a reservation newspaper published by the

Beaulieu family, praised it at first, and did not view it as a "pine ring" bill, though they thought it should be amended to more adequately protect Ojibway interests. It had been partly shaped by Ojibway protests over an earlier Northwest Indian Commission agreement, so it demonstrated, said the *Progress*, that "we can reach the ear of the House."[79] The *Progress* vigorously disputed charges made by the *Detroit Record* and the *Crookston Chronicle* that the Ojibway were not ready for the American citizenship which accompanied land allotments.[80]

More critical, the Indian Commissioner released a letter written to him accusing Nelson of representing the "pine ring" of defrauding lumbermen. Appearing before the Senate Committee on Indian Affairs to deny the charge, Nelson became "rather more warlike than was necessary." The Senate committee reported out a very different bill, which Nelson was forced to defend in the House to achieve passage of any measure at all.[81] His temper had cost him in the past and now cost him again.

His defense came down to this: "How foolish is the suggestion that frauds can be perpetrated under this law as under laws of the past." He had a lawyer's faith in words, but the government lacked the ability to enforce the words. He had a Republican's faith that the new Harrison administration would surely appoint honest men to appraise Indian lands, when Republicans too could be dishonest or corrupt. As a Michigan Republican noted, "There is nothing to prevent [the appraisers] making a false return." That is exactly what happened. Frauds were perpetrated, including gross underestimation of the timber on Indian lands and collusion between lumbermen bidding for it. The Ojibway received far less than the timber was worth. The Nelson Act's provisions were equally powerless to prevent whites from manipulating and cheating Ojibway out of agricultural lands.[82]

Though Nelson was well intentioned, he mainly considered constituents' land-hunger rather than what was best for the Indians. He did not issue racist slurs such as Congressman Washburn's "miserable, wretched, vagabonds of Indians."[83]

142

When the *White Earth Progress* criticized him, he humorously pointed to this "half a column of good abuse" as proof that the White Earth Ojibway were "making rapid progress in civilization."[84] He tried to accommodate reformers' demands. Yet the weak enforcement powers of the federal government rendered his carefully crafted "provisions" useless.

The sorry results came long after he had left the House, and he learned little from them. In the case of homestead land, he learned much from his stay in Congress: "For myself I can truly say that while I came here from my distant and far-away home in Minnesota, imbued with the narrow and provincial idea that the sooner we could settle up the unsettled portions of our country the better, yet now, sir, with the education I have received in this Chamber, and with an enlarged sphere of vision here acquired . . . I have come to the conclusion that we are . . . too prodigal of our public lands."[85] That was a rare occasion when he acknowledged the education he had gained in the House. In May, 1889, shortly after voluntarily quitting Congress, he expressed dissatisfaction with his time there: "I feel that I have wasted several good years. I have served a good people and would have been willing to have served them longer, but could not afford it. I am a poor man and have a family and it is my duty to provide for them. . . . No man has ever had a seat in the house but would like to continue in that position. It flatters one's vanity. But I saw the lives of others before me and constantly pictured for myself old age and failure."[86] By "failure" and "wasted," he may have meant that individual congressmen lacked influence, but debated for hours over private pension bills and tariff minutiae, giving set speeches which changed no votes. When the House acted, it passed laws which the federal government lacked the power to enforce.

No congressman's personal success could hide the government's failure. By 1889 Nelson had become a skilled politician yet the federal government remained "an incorrigible bungler"— except in distributing tariff protection and pensions. It could not adequately enforce its own civil service, land distribution, Indian

143

protection, or civil rights laws. Once an enthusiastic believer in "the finest and best government on earth," Nelson had invested too much of his life in American politics and government to admit their failures. Instead, he reinterpreted the waste of "several good years" as a personal failure, a weakness for the limelight that reduced his ability to provide for his family.

Another reason he decided not to seek reelection in 1888 may have been his recognition of his own mortality. He nearly lost his life in a boating accident in October, 1886. On Monday evening, October 11, he borrowed a neighbor's boat and went fishing on Lake Victoria, near his Alexandria home. After catching a large pickerel, he lost his balance and fell out of the boat. A "powerful swimmer," he remained in the water for some forty-five minutes, before a neighbor boy heard his cries for help. By the time he was pulled from the lake, hypothermia had almost killed him; his excess weight may have saved him. He did not regain consciousness until Tuesday morning.[87] The incident may have helped to convince him there had to be more to life than debating Theodore Casamer's medical report.

Eight

The Republican Elites
and the People's Party

On February 22, 1892, Knute Nelson wrote an impassioned letter to Anfin Solem, editor of the *Fergus Falls Ugeblad*. Suspicious and sensitive as ever, Nelson thought Solem was "quite hostile to me" because he had printed two submitted pieces which seemed "a studied effort to besmirch me." In fact, the two pieces criticized James J. Hill, Governor William R. Merriam, and other urban politicians for planning to run Nelson for governor in order to bring Scandinavian Americans back to the Republican party. Neither "Dakota" nor "M.A." directly criticized Nelson. Likewise, he felt that an editorial displayed Solem's "real animus" toward him when Solem had complimented him and had merely concluded, regretfully, that Populist Scandinavians could not vote for a Republican Nelson.[1]

The February 22nd letter showed that Nelson had yet to adjust to the new ideological politics brought to Minnesota by the Farmers' Alliance in the late 1880s. He charged that "Dakota"'s and "M.A."'s implication that he was "a corporation or railroad tool" was "only a feeble echo of the Kindred arguments in 1882," made in "the old Kindred papers." He ignored one great difference. The two Populists sincerely believed in their cause, whereas Kindred's newspapers printed whatever would aid their faction and keep Kindred's subsidies coming. Missing Solem's sincere commitment to the Alliance, he excused these "newspaper assaults" on him, "for as an alliance organ" Solem's *Ugeblad* had to print what it otherwise wouldn't "if your hands were free." He knew that his allies in Fergus Falls had founded the *Ugeblad* in 1883 as a pro-Nelson, Norwegian-language organ. Made cynical by the 1882 battle against a bribing opponent and purchased newspapers, he attributed the same insincerity to the Alliance's true believers.[2]

Replying, Solem claimed friendship and hoped "you realize that you have imagined a great deal which has no foundation." The editor believed Nelson's assurances that he "had not been a railroad attorney" and offered to publish them. Using a clipping he sent, Solem published a *St.Cloud Journal Press* editorial booming Nelson for governor and deftly handling the ethnic issue ("He has an American education and is totally Americanized," but if Norwegian Americans should support him out of pride, "we will as a rule have no reason to object to it").[3]

That editorial presented Nelson's own view of his personal identity, his public record, and his 1892 political strategy. It failed to mention the Alliance, any ideologies, or any issues. Nelson was still relying on Civil War issues and postwar demands for economic expansion, when many voters wanted more than the Union's preservation and development. The Alliance could not be ignored, nor issues so totally avoided as they were in the Kindred-Nelson campaign.

Nelson claimed to have quit politics altogether after March 4, 1889, when he left Congress. Later, he liked to recall that "except as a voter, I was done" with active political life.[4] That was not clear at the time. He hoped for a legislative deadlock in the 1889 election of a United States senator, and then his election as a compromise choice. The main contenders were David M. Sabin and William D. Washburn. John Lind broke the news of Washburn's election to him and received an angry tongue-lashing that did not square with his professed eagerness for political retirement.[5]

146

Little more than a year later, he explored a gubernatorial candidacy. His "retirement" meant that he recognized the current realities of Republican politics, not that he wished to be left alone. It meant practicing law out of his law office on Broadway and farming at his nearby farm. He was in great demand as a lawyer, and soon was pleading cases in the circuit courts at Fergus Falls, Morris, and Elbow Lake, and before the United States Land Office in Duluth.[6] There is no evidence to support the widely circulated rumor that, in 1889-1892, he was a railroad attorney receiving $15,000 per year from Hill's Great Northern, as the *St. Paul Daily Globe* charged. In the fall of 1889, he opened a hardware store in Alexandria.[7] He gave occasional speeches, such as the one at the Dane County (Wisconsin) Fair on September 24, 1889.[8]

Great changes were occurring in Minnesota in the late 1880s and early 1890s. Iron ore mining began on the Vermilion and Mesabi ranges. Large numbers of new immigrants flooded into the urban areas: Irish, Germans, Scandinavians, Slavs, central and southern Europeans. The Twin Cities' population continued to expand faster than that of rural areas. The state's farm population was about to reach a plateau, as the tillable homestead lands were largely taken. Railroad transportation brought markets closer, but commercial agriculture brought a cash economy and dependence on distant, impersonal markets. Credit was always short. Many small businessmen, including Nelson, lent their personal funds in land mortgages and contracts for deed. Cropping patterns changed. The wheat belt moved from southern to western and then to northwestern Minnesota. Soil depletion, lower wheat prices, insects, and crop diseases virtually forced farmers in southern Minnesota to turn to dairying and corn and hog production.[9]

Farmers' natural reaction to changed conditions was to blame someone else: bankers (interest rates too high), railroads (freight rates too high), manufacturers (prices too high), millers and grain elevators (wheat prices too low), the government (money supply too low), the "cities" (too much concentrated wealth), and the

147

upper classes (wealth too unfairly acquired). There was some truth in all of these charges. In the postwar economic expansion, demand for new railroads and new industries caused government to stress its promotional role, not its regulatory role. As long as entrepreneurs expanded the supply of goods and services, government and most citizens ignored expanding profits and inequities. By the late 1880s, many citizens took the goods and services for granted, and now expected low prices as well. Also, farm protest was strongest where there was geographic isolation from towns and villages: areas which goods and services had not yet reached, townships lacking stores or nearby railroad connections, and farming districts far from and antagonistic to the county seats.[10]

Farm protest and anti-county-seat antagonism led thousands of Minnesota farmers to join the Farmers' Alliance in the 1880s. Alliance supporters began forming local, township units, called sub-alliances, in 1881. By 1886, Minnesota had 438 sub-alliances. By May 1890 that number was around 1,200, a formidable political mobilization.[11] Open to all local farmers, sub-alliances met regularly (usually on Saturdays at rural schoolhouses), bargained collectively with area merchants, passed resolutions, and elected delegates to county and state conventions.[12] Local grass-roots associations, these sub-alliances mobilized voters more effectively than did the Republican clubs formed by county-seat leaders in election years. Sub-alliances threatened Republican elites' control of rural politics. The old top-down hierarchical political armies faced hundreds of platoons electing their own leaders and refusing leadership claims of county-seat elites. After almost thirty years' experience in organizing and addressing voters, Nelson too felt threatened when voters began organizing and addressing *him*, not individually, but in platoons.

Up to 1888, the state Alliance pushed its program within the Republican or Democratic parties, most often the former. In 1890, it voted to run its own candidates despite opposition from its more conservative members. Briefly, the platoons appeared ready to choose Nelson as their statewide leader.

The first Alliance convention to nominate a state ticket met on July 16, 1890, in the Minnesota House of Representatives chamber in St. Paul. Hotels that usually hosted Republican operatives during legislative sessions and conventions now housed farmers, "great stalwart men . . . with broad shoulders, full, bushy beards and bronzed countenances." Sub-alliances sent 452 delegates. But, reported the *St. Paul Daily Globe*, "farmers are not alone at the hotels . . . many recognized Republican wire-pullers" like Nelson's ally Charles A. Gilman were "putting in a word for the smooth corporation counsel from Alexandria."[13] They hoped for a joint Alliance-Republican nomination of Nelson.

On the first, informal ballot, he led with 104 votes, while Ignatius Donnelly was second with 98 votes. However, many delegates questioned his loyalty to Alliance principles and his ties to James J. Hill and the Minneapolis millers. Editor Everett Fish of the *Great West* rose to remind delegates, "There was no one in the convention who knew where Knute Nelson stood regarding the principles of the alliance, but they all knew Mr. Donnelly's position." Nelson's usual silent treatment of supporters doomed his chances in a party of principles. Where words counted for more than connections, principled Alliancemen preferred the eloquent Donnelly. Though several Alliancemen telegraphed Nelson to ask whether he would accept an Alliance nomination, he did not reply. The convention was left to consider conflicting interpretations of his stance. Alliance president R.J. Hall claimed that he had said he would not accept a nomination from an independent party. Supporters claimed to have a letter from him saying just the opposite, but it was never read to the convention.[14]

On the first formal ballot, the silent Norwegian's total fell to 56 votes, many from more conservative sub-alliances in southeastern Minnesota.[15] After the convention deadlocked between Donnelly and Hall, delegates chose editor Sidney M. Owen as a compromise nominee. Most likely, Nelson did not lament his defeat, if such it was. He could ill afford to risk his political career on a bolt to a new, untried party. In the mid-1870s he had seen the

149

political Grangers quickly come and go. If he joined the Alliance, he would never escape cries of "Knute the Bolter." The ideological Alliancemen would not tolerate a joint Alliance-Republican nomination of him. He had to remain with the party which had nominated and elected him for over twenty years. He was reported as saying, "I am a Republican and not a mendicant for office."[16] Offices would have to come to him. He would not go begging for them.

The Alliance could not be so cocksure. Though its grass-roots organizing had formed 1,200 platoons, it lacked an outstanding candidate for governor. Owen was a good candidate, who ran a competent campaign, but Nelson would likely have given it the governor's office. It did poorly at developing credible, consensus-forming leaders. It developed factional leaders and welcomed itinerant orators like Donnelly, but could not recruit the "name" candidate it needed.

When the Republican state convention met in St. Paul a week later, GOP elites toyed with the idea of nominating Nelson, partly because he was neutral in the bitter "census war" between Minneapolis and St. Paul. A caucus of Scandinavian delegates called for Nelson: "The situation demanded a man of great strength who could win back the large number who have gone over to the Farmers' Alliance." Nelson, however, did not work for the nomination. Republican elites were not yet sufficiently alarmed at Alliance strength to depart from their custom of giving an incumbent governor a second term. Merriam easily won renomination.[17]

Nelson also underestimated Alliance strength. In the fall campaign he reassured Republican regulars of his loyalty on the tariff issue more than he appealed to Alliance-tempted Scandinavians. His endorsement of the high McKinley tariff angered his natural Scandinavian-American rural constituency. The Alliance caused a powerful storm over Republicans' heads in 1890. Owen finished third with 24 percent of the vote. He took Scandinavian-American votes away from Merriam (37 percent), and left the incumbent with only a 2,267-vote margin over the Democrat Thomas Wilson (36 percent). A Norwegian-American Democrat and Alliance nominee, Adolph Biermann, was elected state auditor. Republicans were routed in the legislature. They won only 26 of 54 seats in the Senate and only 41 of 114 in the House. The Alliance captured 32 House seats and 13 Senate seats. In the congressional races, Republicans, who had controlled all five districts in 1889, lost four seats, and retained John Lind's Second District by only 482 votes.[18]

Minnesota politics would never be the same. The years of unquestioned Republican supremacy dating back to 1860 were ended. Old-stock politicians and Republican county-seat rings were shown to be out of touch with the popular mood. Republicans had always depended on the local merchants, bankers, lawyers, and more prosperous farmers. They joined together at campaign time, formed local Republican clubs, distributed Republican ballots, and then returned to their occupations. Local newspapers publicized in great detail the doings and sayings of these civic leaders, who hoped for state jobs for friends or relatives. Patronage was the oil that lubricated this machine.

Sub-alliances sidestepped these elites and organized farmers around an ideology opposing concentrated wealth and power. Scandinavian-American, especially Norwegian-American, farmers distrusted capitalists and their local allies. Alliance lecturers, who appealed to the old Haugean tradition of local democracy and rejection of officials, turned against local officeholders and "monopolists."[19] Scandinavian Americans flocked to join sub-alliances.

The Republican leaders' post-1890 panic changed their attitude toward Knute Nelson. They had perceived him as a handy Upper Country ally, useful but necessarily subordinate to Twin Cities politicians. Now he was a potential deliverer from the Alliance hordes.[20] The irony of this change of heart was not lost upon Nelson. A twenty-year veteran of Republican factional wars, he was cautious, distrustful, and very secretive. A longtime Fergus

Falls supporter recalled that when he "sent for me to come down and see him, he would take me down into the cornfield and whisper in my ear, to make sure that nobody would hear him."[21] Nelson's true goal was the United States Senate, but he dared not even whisper that in cornfields, lest incumbents Washburn and Davis act to block his way. In the elite's desperate need for a candidate to beat the Alliance, he saw a chance to achieve his goal indirectly, through the governor's office. Seeking the Republican nomination, he made that elite his main constituency. In cornfields, at home, in hotel rooms, and in "private" and "confidential" letters he kept from his secretaries, he whispered to them. His secretive style contrasted markedly with Alliancemen's public speechifying in schoolhouses, conventions, and rented halls.

So secretive was he that it is difficult to reconstruct his role in his 1892 campaign for governor. The first indication that there would be a Nelson campaign came in early February, in a letter to Solem's *Ugeblad* from Norwegian-American farmer Knud Bondy, who had questioned Nelson about his availability. He told Bondy that he had decided "to accept the nomination" but "not to work for it."[22]

Not only would he not work for it, but he would play hard to get. He hinted that he would accept only a unanimous nomination. He threw his supporters into agonized suspense with a report that he was considering a six-to-eight month trip to Norway, which would have made a Nelson campaign impossible. He talked of poor health. He sequestered himself in Alexandria. One frustrated St. Paul backer wrote, "Why in the dickens don't you come down and see a fellow & tell us what you want and where you want it." Another plaintively asked, "But don't you think it soon is time to give your friends a little *positive* encouragement?"[23]

The old-stock Republican elite were asking Nelson to appeal to Minnesota's many Scandinavian-American, Alliance-friendly farmers. That was a role he was familiar with, from Koshkonong days and from the 1876 Stewart campaign. If the elites needed him, then acting coy would serve to increase what they would be willing to pay him for his services. Officeholders would come to him, not he to them. Republican state employees could keep their jobs only if Republicans kept the governorship.

Officeholders did come to him: the chief deputy grain inspector, the state weighmaster, the deputy state insurance commissioner, the grain inspector, the insurance commissioner, and a dairy and food department worker. They all wrote to report on their campaigning for Nelson.[24] These state jobs were temporary, appointed positions. Jobholders were not permanent St. Paul residents. They retained strong political connections in their home counties, and made short campaign swings home on weekends. There, they used the arts of persuasion on county seat politicians, who usually dominated Republican county conventions. The state weighmaster assured Nelson, "Whatever is done by us is done quietly."[25]

They also donated money. One surveyor general of logs and lumber reportedly donated $7,000 to the 1892 Republican campaign.[26] The weighmaster attended a Nelson strategy meeting, at which Minneapolis lumberman Henry F. Brown encouraged the Nelson men who were working to control the Hennepin county convention: "Do not fear the expense. I will see that you have money to pay expenses. It won't be necessary to pass around a subscription list either." Brown later wrote to Nelson, "I ask nothing but the control of the Surv[eyor] Gen[era]l's office—which I have had through Merriam's terms."[27]

Their quiet activity did not go undetected. *Anoka County Union* editor Granville S. Pease reported: "It has been promised that if Nelson is elected there will be no changes in the appointive offices, and that is enough to transform the grain inspection department, the labor bureau and the food and dairy commission into a howling mob of political whangdoodlers, whose one cry and chorus is, 'Give us Nelson or we will lose our jobs.'"[28] Fear of losing state jobs to the Alliancemen was the engine driving the campaign to nominate Nelson. Republicans had held the governorship since 1860, and many could not remember what it was like to be out of power. No matter how strong, Scandinavian Americans' sentimental wish for a Scandinavian governor could never secure the nomination for Nelson. A Scandinavian caucus had failed miserably in the 1890 attempt.

The primary barriers to this pre-convention campaign were old-stock Americans' desire to retain control of the Republican party, conflicting ambitions among Republican elites, and doubts about Nelson's loyalty to the GOP.

Old-stock Americans wishing to retain control coalesced around the candidacy of former governor Andrew R. McGill. Coming from a strongly Yankee town, editor Pease led the McGill chorus and complained about use of the ethnic appeal: "Every cowardly little candidate for constable who wants to fortify himself with the Scandinavian vote thinks all he has to do is to yell for Nelson and walk away with the persimmon."[29] Instead of attacking Scandinavian Americans directly, Pease criticized politicians seeking to use "the little Norwegian" to win their votes.Likewise, the *Blue Earth City Post* opposed Nelson's candidacy because "nationality in politics is as dangerous to our republican institutions as knownothingism ever was."[30] Such attacks were cautious ones before the convention, for McGill would need Scandinavian-American votes if he received the nomination.

Conflicting senatorial ambitions also hindered the Nelson boom. In a March interview, Nelson cautioned, "I am advised that both Senators Davis and Washburn regard me as a possible rival for the senatorship," and were, thus, "averse if not positively hostile to my nomination and election" as governor. How could he run if he was "handicapped with hostility or lukewarmness in high quarters within our own ranks."[31] How could Republican elites beat back the Alliance masses if they were divided? He implicitly encouraged state jobholders to pressure Davis and Washburn to drop this hostile stance towards their champion. Davis faced a reelection battle in 1893, and Washburn one in 1895. A Democrat-Alliance legislature (like the one elected in 1890) would reelect neither of them. Both needed a strong candidate heading the ticket to ensure a Republican legislature in 1892, but both might fear that Republican legislators elected on Nelson's coattails would reward him with a Senate seat.

Recently, historians have emphasized the inarticulate electorate rather than the articulate elites traditionally overrepresented in historical accounts. Both must be understood. In the late nineteenth century, elites framed the choices that the inarticulate voter faced on election day. Minnesota's Republican elites were particularly effective in framing choices for Tuesday, November 8, 1892. First, they had to overcome internal bickering. It is important to understand how they did so.

Washburn resented Nelson's charge of hostility. "What in the world should have led you to say what you did of me?" he asked Nelson. Either someone had misrepresented Washburn's views "or you are a victim of morbid suspicion and without the slightest cause." They had been allies since 1878. "Now, my good friend from Evanger, I hope you will take back, in your own mind at least, the injustice you have done me." He told the *Pioneer Press* he did not oppose Nelson's candidacy.[32]

Davis refused to support Nelson before the convention. He and Nelson had been intraparty antagonists for seventeen years: Nelson did not vote for him for senator in 1875, and he worked as Kindred's legal counsel in 1882. After Davis's election to the Senate in 1887, Nelson refused to speak to him in Washington. Nelson suspected that he had spread rumors that Nelson's near-drowning in 1886 had been a contrived hoax.[33] Nelson sent Minneapolis millowner Charles A. Pillsbury to secure some apology from him, but the senator insisted that Nelson's cold-shoulder treatment made *him* "the aggrieved party." Davis reportedly told Pillsbury "that Mr. Nelson has seemed to take pride in parading himself as my personal and political enemy." Davis called a Nelson nomination "the height of political folly."[34] Pro-McGill Republicans argued that Nelson's nomination would endanger Davis' reelection to the Senate.[35] But, as Pillsbury predicted, Davis could do little to block Nelson: "any course except one of strict neutrality" would "make him more enemies than friends." If Nelson was nominated, Davis "in very self-defence" would have to work for his election.[36]

Alliance success in 1890 made open factional warfare between Republicans in 1892 too costly to consider. The *St. Paul Pioneer Press* editorialized: future senatorships should not "be introduced into the discussion of [Nelson's] gubernatorial candidacy." The Alliance had created what the *Pioneer Press* euphemistically called "the existing political situation," which did not permit "dissensions and divisions" or "personal rivalries" in the party that year.[37] Yet Davis' ultimate acquiescence and (especially) Washburn's support only turned open warfare into subterranean intrigue. To Washburn, Nelson's nomination was not "a question of choice but necessity." If chosen "by common consent," without any apparent "factional connection," Nelson could win: "the entire Scandinavian vote will swing into line." However, Washburn wanted *his* friends driving the Nelson bandwagon as a vehicle for *his* reelection in 1895. Alarmed at his friends' hesitancy in backing Nelson, he warned them, "Do not think you are to get on without Knute."[38]

They probably hesitated over questions of Nelson's loyalty to Republican protectionism. Opponents harped on his support for the Democrats' tariff-reducing Mills bill, perhaps to mask their underlying Yankee opposition to his ethnicity. With his Mills bill vote, "the Alexandria free trader" had played "holy havoc with the Republican party" in Minnesota. Republicans might as well endorse the Democratic candidates and "avoid the trouble and expense of a campaign" rather than support this renegade.[39] These attacks proved unpersuasive. Nelson was not running for Congress. The McKinley tariff of 1890 wrote protectionism into law. Nelson was running for governor. Republican jobholders wanted present rescue not debate over past votes. In March, the *Pioneer Press* published county-by-county reports "made up at the county seats . . . after interviewing the leading men of the

Republican party." Not surprisingly, they showed a strong Nelson lead, which July's county-seat survey confirmed.[40]

The Republican convention met on Thursday, July 28, to nominate candidates who could rescue the state from the Alliance-dominated People's party. The 709 delegates met in the flag-adorned auditorium of St. Paul's People's church. Delegates from the rural districts wondered at the coincidence in names. Was it appropriate to meet in a house of worship, with "caucusing among the pews," instead of in "a convention hall where smoking was allowed"? The purer atmosphere allowed "a number of the fair sex" to attend. Their presence turned an assemblage of smokeless politicians into "a most dignified and decorous body."[41] Nominating candidates was as free from discord as electing church deacons. Andrew R. McGill withdrew. Nelson's name was presented, and then seconded by a speaker who praised the "sturdy race" of Norwegians, but praised Nelson even more for having "so far eliminated foreign thought, foreign custom and foreign prejudices from his nature [as to] become so thoroughly American that the great American party of a great state is demanding by acclamation his nomination in this convention." If not as thoroughly American, he was as unanimously nominated as the speaker promised.[42]

Knute Nelson strode to the platform to make his acceptance speech, a double-barreled shotgun loaded with charges of Democrats' Southern secessionism and Populists' "utopian" radicalism. He aimed most of his fire at Populists: their program was "visionary and utopian in character, and involves organic or revolutionary changes in our system of government." They taught "that the capital of the wealthier classes is nothing but plunder." He criticized the famous preamble to their Omaha platform, a preamble written by his opponent, Ignatius Donnelly. "Their next aim," he thundered, "is to impress upon their followers that this government of ours—state and national—is the most corrupt and unjust government on the face of the earth, and that the people are as badly governed as bad can be." How strange, he

157

mocked. The masses had voted for the two old parties for twenty-five years, and they now say voters have "been engaged in a grand hari kari of self-destruction." He ridiculed their three main reforms: "[1] Government ownership of all railroads—as though nothing could be regulated or controlled unless owned—[2] unlimited free coinage of silver—thereby under the existing disparity of value between the two metals, paying the owners of silver bullion 100 cents in coin for 70 cents in silver; and . . . [3—the sub-treasury plan—] the federal government must turn pawnbroker and set up a great national pawnshop under the so-called sub-treasury scheme." He closed by telling Minnesota voters that he hoped "to become as intimate with you as with the people of the 'old Fifth,'" and by endorsing Senator Davis for reelection.[43]

He oversimplified and distorted several of these issues. Populists did not claim that "nothing could be regulated or controlled unless owned," but that railroads were so vital to the economy as to be an exception to the rule of government regulation. The pejorative term "pawnshop" did not accurately describe the sub-treasury plan, for farmers would not give up ownership of their crops. They would store crops in federally-owned warehouses while awaiting better market conditions and borrow money using the stored crops as collateral. They would pay the federal government 2 percent interest plus various fees.[44]

Optimistic, seemingly unified, Republicans left the People's church to battle the People's party. But Washburn was "absolutely astonished" that anti-Washburn "adventurers and free-booters" like Henry Brown had controlled the convention. His friends had hesitated too long and it might mean his defeat in 1895. Establishing a leadership role among Populists with his Omaha preamble and his oratory, Donnelly persuaded most Alliancemen to abandon their 1890 Alliance party in favor of a new Donnelly-dominated People's party. In mid-July, the People's party nominated Donnelly as its candidate for governor.[45] The party of ideological words selected the fiery orator, without considering that Donnelly's party-switching and gift of

Populist crusader Ignatius Donnelly as Don Quixote with Everett Fish, editor of the Populist Great West, as his Sancho Panza. Cartoon by Bart in Minneapolis Journal, 24 February 1891.

gab offended many voters. In early August, Democrats nominated Daniel Lawler, a St. Paul attorney. Donnelly and Lawler encountered prejudice because of their Roman Catholic backgrounds, although Donnelly had left the church.[46]

Republican elites confronted Protestant, Scandinavian-American farmers with an unprecedented choice. They could vote for the Irishman Donnelly, a former Catholic, former Democrat and frequent party-switcher, widely believed to be erratic. They could vote for another Irish Catholic, a loyal Democrat. Or they could vote for a farmer, a nominal Protestant, and make him the nation's first Scandinavian-American governor. Elites framed the choice so that it was difficult not to do the latter.

Nelson spent the month after the convention trying to unify Republicans. Prominent Republicans sent congratulatory letters and offers of support, but he remained suspicious of the commitment of even old supporters like Charles A. Gilman.[47] Perhaps at Hill's invitation, he dined at St. Paul's Minnesota Club soon after the convention with Judge D.B. Searle of St. Cloud, Hill, and Duluth banker Luther Mendenhall.[48] This dinner probably was James J. Hill's way of congratulating his friend and one-time attorney.

In the ideologically charged 1890s, dining with elites was dangerous. Populists and Democrats used the dinner to "besmirch" Nelson and to redefine voters' choices. The Populist *Great West* caricatured him as the tool of trusts and railroads. Editor Fish spared no sarcasm: "What a magnificent spectacle—in this day of murder and warfare between aggressive Capital and defendant Labor . . . listen to the gurgle-goo-goo of the champaign[sic] as it flows down the scarlet throats of millionaire frauds. . . . And yet, they tell us that Nelson is to pose as the marble Apollo Belvedere of Reform. . . . After the devil-crabs, Little-neck clams and sportive lobsters—and the wine kegs—are exhausted—and the plans laid —farmer Nelson steps nimbly forth, goes to the Merchants Hotel, and slobbers over his country constituents waiting to welcome their reform candidate."[49] Republican elites were on the defensive.

At first, Republican newspapers denied the dinner had taken place. Then, they claimed that it concerned the Great Northern's "legal business pending in Judge Searle's court."[50] The Republican candidate for Congress in the Sixth District, Searle saw that that explanation "reflects upon my judicial integrity," so he made fun of the *Globe's* and *Great West's* accounts.[51]

Knute Nelson was very careful not to dine with railroad presidents for the rest of the campaign, but he could do little about his Norwegian birth.

Disappointed Republicans and some Democrats criticized the Republicans' strongly Scandinavian ticket. Only the nominees for lieutenant governor and attorney general were old-stock Americans. Denying that he was guilty of Know-Nothingism, F.W. Seeley, a disappointed McGill supporter, criticized Yankee politicians for putting this virtually all-immigrant ticket together. He warned that old-stock Republican voters were angry enough to reject it. In printing his remarks, the Democratic *Globe* distanced itself from him and called him a Know-Nothing.[52] Other Democrats were not so hesitant in appealing for disgruntled Yankee votes—though they too were careful to have anti-immigrant words coming out of Republican mouths. The Democratic *St. Cloud Daily Times* quoted a Republican arguing that a Nelson win meant a perpetual Norwegian claim to the governorship: "Whenever we have elected a Scandinavian to an office, they have ever after claimed a warranty deed to it, and you couldn't get them out with a stump-puller."[53] Since the Constitution required that the president be native-born, the Republican *Rush City Post* claimed there was "a widespread feeling" that the state's chief executive should also be native-born.[54]

Nelson's backers used his Civil War service as their primary means to soften old-stock antagonism to his ethnicity. Support from the traditonally Republican Grand Army of the Republic helped among Yankee voters. At campaign's end, they circulated an article titled "Private Knute Nelson: A Brief Word to the Veterans of the Late War and Their Sons."[55] And, they did not blatantly

161

use his Norwegianness to appeal for votes in ways that would offend old-stock voters.

That appeal was made quietly. They circulated 30,000 specially printed copies of *Skandinaven*, strongly Republican and pro-Nelson. One Thomas Lajord traveled from farm to farm in Otter Tail county distributing *Skandinaven*, talking to farmers, and writing anti-Irish-Catholic and pro-Nelson letters to the *Fergus Falls Ugeblad*. He reported to Nelson that "real Alliancemen are becoming ours," including a sub-alliance president and another local Alliance leader.[56] In the *Ugeblad*, the Populist "M.A." charged that Republicans were using Nelson to round up "the 'strayed Scandinavian sheep' up here in the district." He asked, "Shall we let ourselves be taken in by these means?" If they did, others would "call us voting-cattle, who, led by familiar voices, now go here, now go there." Appealing to ethnic pride, Lajord responded that when Nelson becomes "our highest officeholder, then will the praise and glory of Norway and Norway's people ring out greater, and we will thereby be praised more in the nation's eyes than we can now imagine."[57] The ethnic appeal could be used in heavily Scandinavian-American territory, in the Norwegian language! Just before the vote, *Skandinaven* printed "Minnesota-Folkesang," a campaign song ringing out Norway's glory and pride in her favorite "gut," Knute the Bold:

> "Hurra for Knut, Hurra!
> Foruden Rigdoms gyldne Rang,
> Foruden Storfolks Gunst og Tvang
> Han fandt dog Vei til Ærens Maal . . . .
> Han drog som fordums Viking ud,
> Hurra for Knut, Hurra! . . . .
> Selv er han fattig, saa er vi,
> Og derfor vil vi staa ham bi. . ."

> (Hurray for Knute, Hurray!
> Without wealth's privileged place,
> Without elite's favor or force,

He found his way to glory's goal. . . .
He set out like a Viking of old,
Hurray for Knute, Hurray! . . . .
Though he is poor, so are we,
And that is why we stand by him. . .)[58]

Unconvinced of Knute's poverty, "M.A." renewed the charge that he was a railroad attorney greatly aided by *storfolk* like James J. Hill. Republicans countered by cleverly using letters written by Sidney M. Owen and Editor Fish in 1890 in support of the rumored Nelson candidacy on the Alliance ticket.[59] If Nelson was such a corporate tool, then why were the Alliancemen ready to nominate him in 1890?

To disprove the charges, Nelson gave the *Minneapolis Journal* an interview at his hotel room. This accusation was "the old chestnut that was used by Mr. Kindred" in 1882. He explained his right-of-way work for the St. Paul, Minneapolis, and Manitoba back in 1878–1881 without mentioning his connection to Hill during those years. He strongly denied having done any work for any railroad company since 1881. In fact, since then he had handled many cases for settlers *against* the Great Northern and the Northern Pacific. He had papers to prove it. He told the *Journal* reporter to "come up to my room for a moment." "Once in his room" he "produced the 'missing papers' from a recess in his trunk as triumphantly as though he was 'doing' the heroics for an adapted melo-drama." The papers proved that he was handling sixteen legal cases against the railroads in May, 1892. But nothing he could pull out of a trunk could disprove his earlier close business relationship with Hill, the main Populist charge.[60]

The *Alexandria Post* was more forthright in pointing out that sentiments toward the railroads had changed greatly since the 1870s, and that "suppressing all allusions to the great and direful need of railroads" in the 1870s was anachronistic and misleading.[61]

The "little Norwegian" began his formal campaign with an August 26th speech at a Republican rally in Minneapolis. Senator

163

A Syttende Mai celebration at John Larson's farm near New Richland, with Rev. O.A. Melby in front, the New Richland band, and the Norwegian flag with the mark of union with Sweden, ca. 1890. At their 1893 festivities for 17 May, Melby gave a Norwegian-language speech, as he probably did on this occasion.

Washburn introduced Nelson by recalling a visit to Norway where "he saw in the charming little valley the neat little house where Mr. Nelson was born." This sentimental reference so moved Nelson that he was momentarily unable to speak.[62] In his Minneapolis speech (and in later ones in conservative southeastern Minnesota), he mainly answered charges of disloyalty to protectionism and linked the Democrats to the South.[63] He quoted his 1888 tariff speech. Tying Democrats' tariff views to John C. Calhoun's, his short history lesson on the 1832 nullification controversy linked Democrats to South Carolina's secessionism. By a demagogic confusion of the broad contemporary use of the word "race," he linked Democratic opposition to a Norwegian-American candidate (here, "race" meant ethnicity) to Democratic opposition to black candidates in the South (where "race" meant race).

He was working the old Minnesota "solid south"—solidly Republican. Occasionally he met old neighbors from Skoponong or Koshkonong who had moved to Minnesota. A few he had harvested for or served as plowboy, and they would drive from miles around to see and hear him in his prime. Nelson made several trips, east to west, across the southern and central tier of Minnesota counties. He was often invited to speak at county agricultural fairs, normally run by the conservative county agricultural societies, not by sub-alliances. The Freeborn County Agricultural Society's secretary advised him, "there is no opportunity like the County Fair," and reported, "A large per centage of our Norwegian voters went into the Alliance two years ago and we are anxious to get them back." [64]

To live up to his pre-convention billing as the man to get them back, he had to leave the safety of the Republican south and campaign in northwestern Minnesota, the home of many 1890 Scandinavian-American defectors. Here, he faced a more hostile reception. On October 25, at Elbow Lake, which lawyer Nelson eleven years earlier had helped to preserve its status as county seat of Grant county, the Republican elite met the Alliance masses head on. The evening meeting began in the usual manner. The local band led a torchlight procession to the courthouse, where Nelson was to speak. Hundreds crowded into the courtroom and spilled into the adjoining rooms and corridors to hear him. Contrasting him with the witty Donnelly, the county-seat newspaper reported that he "presented his arguments without any embellishments of so-called funny stories or appeals to prejudice of any kind." [65]

He had to issue frequent appeals for order, however. Perhaps aided by some county-seat Democrats, the Alliance masses had evidently formed "an organized conspiracy to break up the meeting." He became "disconcerted with the unearthly crying of babies" held in Populists' arms. "Several dogs were scattered around the hall and their tails were stepped upon, resulting in the dogs howling and barking." More disconcerted, he "emphatically" noted that "between dogs and babies it was hard work to proceed." When this noise quieted down, "deafening cries of 'Hurrah for Lawler'" arose. He demanded that someone quiet these whiskey-soaked Democrats, and the county sheriff complied.

Only loud whispering remained, when a question on the tariff caused him to lose his temper. He was contrasting high American and low Norwegian wages, when an Elbow Lake man interrupted to ask if that was entirely due to the protective tariff. Mistakenly thinking the question came from Tobias Sauby, a burly Populist leader from Pomme de Terre township, Nelson vented all his frustrations on Sauby, who may have been guilty of whispering and stepping on dogs' tails. "Shut up, you demagogues from Pomme de Terre," he yelled. He tossed a disparaging remark about "Pomme de Terre reformers." Sauby angrily stood up, demanded an apology, and insisted he had not been the tariff questioner. Verifying that, the questioner "stood up and explained that he was from Elbow Lake, which anyone could see, but that accomplished nothing." Unconvinced, Nelson clenched his fists, shouted, "I will fix him," and headed for Sauby. He grabbed the township reformer by the collar and "crowded the disturber into his seat." Lawyer J.W. Reynolds seized Nelson and warned, "Don't do that, Knute!" The two men were separated, Sauby becalmed, and Nelson's speech resumed—until after 11 PM. Nelson retained control of the field of battle, a point the *Pioneer Press* emphasized.

After breakfast the next morning, Nelson left by team for Ashby, a town he had helped found by persuading Hill to locate a depot there. When he arrived in Dalton (Otter Tail county) on October 27 to give a speech, he was arrested for assault and battery, based on a warrant issued by "a populist justice of the peace" of Pomme de Terre township. He filed bond, two Ashby men signed as sureties, and his court appearance in Pomme de Terre was delayed until November 15 so that he could continue his campaign. The charge was later dropped.

Editorial opinion on the incident varied according to the newspapers' political loyalties: the Republican *Pioneer Press* ("Nelson Is A Brick"), the Democratic *St. Paul Daily Globe* ("the idea of electing such a man governor"), the Populist *Great West* ("Knute Nelson Punches a Farmer"), the Populist *Fergus Falls Globe* ("everyone who votes for him votes for a criminal"), and the Republican *Battle Lake Review* ("Hurrah for Nelson").[66] The incident typified the 1890s battle between isolated Populist farmers in the townships and Republican county-seat elites. County-seat leaders (county attorney, county auditor, local banker, and state senator) strongly supported Nelson's actions at the courthouse.[67] Opposition to the Republicans came, in this case, from Pomme de Terre township, not that isolated (it was west of Ashby and north of Elbow Lake) but certainly containing outspoken Populists.

From Elbow Lake, Nelson headed north to "talk sense" to Populist-leaning Scandinavian Americans in the Upper Country. The pace was grueling. After his 11 PM finish at Elbow Lake, he arose Wednesday "morning at 5 o'clock and was driven to Ashby, where a fresh team was taken" to haul him fifteen miles to a 2 PM engagement at Battle Lake. After a two-hour speech, "he took a freight train for Henning, speaking there at 7:30" Wednesday night to a crowd of 500 despite "a slight effort to disturb" his speech. Thursday noon, nearly 100 farmers were present to hear him at Underwood, "but Mr. Nelson was completely tired out and so hoarse that he could hardly speak." Proceeding to Dalton, he posted bond and held a large meeting in a "packed full" hall. On Friday evening, he was at Pelican Rapids; Saturday, at Rothsay.[68] He headed down the Red River Valley, speaking at Moorhead (Monday, October 31), Halstad (Tuesday, November 1), Ada (Wednesday), Twin Valley (Thursday), Fertile (Friday), and Crookston (Saturday, November 5).

He tailored his speeches to address "the wheat question" in this wheat-growing area, especially in the smaller towns. At Henning, which had a farmers' elevator, "he advocated the building of farmers' warehouses and a law that would give them sidetrack facilities." This was a "practical and business like" solution to wheat farmers' marketing problems. By contrast, when Donnelly

167

spoke at Henning a week earlier, the editor reported his "slur at the farmers elevators."[69]

Polk county illustrated Republican tactics in the Valley. At Crookston, the county seat, he spoke on the tariff, while the local Republican elites sold his campaign as a patriotic spectacle. Thousands watched a "serpentine march" through the streets: "over three hundred voters were in line, each with a torch and plenty of sky-rockets and they did make Rome howl in great shape." Crookston's Glee Club sang "a campaign song . . . 'Protection's Come to Stay'. . .while Johnny Carter stood behind them waving 'Old Glory' back and forth in perfect time." The "Crookston string band" played "two or three patriotic pieces." Then, they called on Nelson. Though he "was so hoarse with much speaking during the campaign that he could hardly articulate," he still gave "one of the best talks on the tariff," according to the local Republican editor.[70]

The county-seat band, Republican club, and torchbearers accompanied him to the small town of Fertile and used the same marching tactics to draw a crowd, but the audience and the speech were quite different. The "farmers drove for twenty miles, and some of them walked in for 6 and 7 miles to see and hear Mr. Nelson." Here, he concentrated on "the questions which the people's party like to discuss"—grain elevators, the sub-treasury plan, and free silver. The Republican county-seat editor reported, "He showed the fallacies of the arguments of the people's party orators, and showed it [sic] so plainly that many of the farmers said after the meeting that they saw where they were mistaken."[71] The Populist editor in Fertile acknowledged that Republicans thought Nelson's speech "a good one . . . but as a vote getter it was a dismal failure."

Knute Nelson was a matter-of-fact, commonsense speaker. As a former country school teacher, he excelled at explaining complicated tariff and fiscal matters in simple terms which farmers could understand.[72] He lacked Donnelly's oratorical style. At Moorhead, reported the *Daily News*, "He spoke in an unimpassioned and argumentative style, his speech being punctured, here and there, with a witty sally, an apt illustration, or a bit of cutting sarcasm."[73] A Halstad correspondent liked it when Nelson "gave the audience some cold facts in regard to the actual situation . . . there was no windpuffs."[74] A "windpuff" would never carry Nelson through his typical two or three hour speech. One "bit of cutting sarcasm" recalled by a Populist at Halstad was his charge that the 1891 Alliance-influenced legislature had "done nothing but grant large sums to doorkeepers, spittoon-polishers and assistant letter-writers."[75] That sally effectively appealed to farmers' skepticism about unnecessary government expenditures.

After his Upper Country speaking tour, he hailed a train for Minneapolis, where he closed out the campaign with three speeches. At the Lyceum, he reported on his tour: "'I have been trying for the past ten days,' said he, with a grim smile on his face and a merry twinkle in his eye, 'to hold the Republican banner aloft and gain the right of free speech, and I have generally managed to make myself heard.'" This allusion to "the Elbow Lake incident pleased the crowd immensely and they cheered wildly."[76] The *Pioneer Press* claimed, "Mr. Nelson has done great work in the last two weeks" when "he has left the larger cities and gone into the small villages" and spoken "largely to his countrymen."[77]

If Nelson had the right to free speech, so did Populist leaders. Many sub-alliances held pre-election meetings, especially "in the Scandinavian townships." There, leaders polled Alliancemen and pressed last-minute arguments on the wavering. "These meetings have been held very generally" in the Upper Country, warned the *Pioneer Press*, "and are much more efficacious than a speech on the issues by speakers of either of the old parties." Rather than listen to "farmer" Nelson, many farmers preferred to discuss issues with their neighbors at Saturday sub-alliance meetings at the local schoolhouse. Here, their leaders tried to build a democratic consensus and to minimize the individualism inherent in voting. At Rothsay on Sunday, November 6, Alliancemen met "to decide what we will do on election [day]." Usually, they passed a motion "to stand by the Populist ticket, though," in the individualism of balloting, "whether they will do so remains to be seen."[78] Republicans lacked such grass-roots meetings. Once the Republican bands and speakers fell silent, they resorted to that Gilded Age resource, the partisan newspaper. The last week, Republican newspapers ran a four-page "Supplement," featuring short biographies of statewide candidates, an attack on the Alliance-Democratic 1891 legislature, and a sample Republican ballot.[79] The "Supplement" was costly to print in such large quantities, but it was likely paid for by the state central committee with state jobholders' contributions.

Nelson and the Republican elites had done the very best they could, and that proved to be very good indeed. Their victory did not match "old time" Republican standards, but it was impressive given the political task they faced. With 109,220 votes, Nelson captured 51 of 80 counties and 42.6 percent of the vote. Lawler's 37 percent rekindled Democratic hopes, but Donnelly's 15.6 percent fell far short of expectations — and of Sidney Owen's 24.3 percent in 1890. The Populist carried six counties, only three (Kittson, Marshall, and Polk) in the northwestern, wheat-growing Red River Valley. "Beaten! Whipped! Smashed!. . . Our followers scattered like dew before the rising sun," lamented Donnelly.[80] The Sage of Nininger finished ahead of only the Prohibition candidate, William J. Dean (4.8 percent). Nelson was now "the rising sun" of Minnesota politics.

He rounded up enough "strayed Scandinavian-American sheep" to win. When he spoke in Halstad and Twin Valley, for example, he addressed Norwegian Americans who had voted overwhelmingly for Owen in 1890. North and east of both towns lay seven townships with heavy (75-100 percent) concentrations of Norwegian Americans. Owen had received 78 percent of the votes here, but Donnelly, only 42 percent. The Republican Merriam won less than 9 percent in 1890, but Nelson had 41.5 percent in 1892. He did not carry the area, but he cut the Alliance vote almost in half.[81] In Otter Tail county, he gained 10 percent over Merriam's 1890 vote. Among Swedish Americans in seven townships in Meeker and Kandiyohi counties, he gained thirteen percentage points over Merriam's share.[82]

Officeholders kept their jobs; Scandinavian Americans got one of their own as governor. Yet Nelson did not broker a simple deal. By 1892, he had the clout to act independently, not merely as a broker. He made concessions to Scandinavian-American farmers' demands, but he refused negotiations with their leaders that limited his independence. He refused to bargain over the 1890 Alliance nomination. He refused to bargain with jobholders in any way that limited his senatorial ambitions. Rather than mediating between two parties, he played jobholders' fears off against farmers' protests—to further his career. 1890s politics was too elite-led to allow popular leaders to dictate to him, yet too democratic to allow jobholders to ignore him. He played off its contradictions.

Bone-tired, Governor-elect Knute Nelson celebrated his victory in Alexandria, not in the limelight of the Twin Cities. On Saturday night, November 12, county-seat Republicans held a campaign-style celebration, complete with a torchlight procession, marching bands, and speeches by the Grant county attorney, a Glenwood editor, and a Fergus Falls ex-legislator.[83] Perhaps it was his Norwegian tendency to be economical in discourse, but Nelson spoke very briefly. He borrowed from Lincoln, as he liked to do: "I go in without having made any promises to any combine, corporation, or person, and shall endeavor to do right, because it is right, and I endeavor to give an administration of the people, for the people, and by the people."[84]

Nine

The Lawyer-Governor and the Reformers

In mid-December, 1892, James J. Hill wrote to Governor-elect Knute Nelson with words of congratulations "that you have done for your party what no other man in the state could have done." Hill regretted, "I have not had the pleasure of seeing you since last summer"—since the much-criticized dinner. Social pleasantries aside, he got to the point: "I wish to speak early of an important appointment that you will be called on to fill, i.e. Railroad & Warehouse Comm[issione]r." He recommended the reappointment of John P. Williams, and asked that Nelson make no decision "until I see you." Recognizing that public disclosure of the letter would embarrass Nelson, he did not entrust it to the post office, but sent "a special messenger from my office to deliver it."[1]

The governor-elect gave the messenger a note, evidently a refusal to meet with Hill about the matter. Hill destroyed it, and angrily replied, "During your entire public career, I have never asked you for any favor and I do not propose to begin or end your term as governor by asking for any favor." Nelson did not reappoint Williams.[2] After the controversy over the dinner, he could not appear to be doing Hill's bidding. The lawyer had to tell his former client that their connection had ended.

His 1892 victory brought a continuing risk. A reputation as the Republican who could defeat Populism would be useless if he failed to pilot the Republican state government through the troubled waters of 1890s protest. Though a useful stepping-stone to the Senate, the governorship was a risky office for a cautious politician like Nelson. It was hard to hold one congressman out of 356 responsible. Blame *could* be assigned to one highly visible governor, who risked antagonizing the state legislators who elected United States senators. The risk was even greater as Minnesotans increasingly demanded reform of the many perceived abuses of the Gilded Age. Minnesota's economy was becoming increasingly complex with the rise of manufacturing, iron ore mining, and urbanization. Not just farmers, but consumers, workers, and the lumber industry all demanded reform. Nelson would have to accommodate those demands while still preserving Republicans' Gilded Age political machine and their thirty-year hold on state government.

In his *The American Commonwealth* (1888), Lord James Bryce described a governor's powers as "more specious than solid." "A State Governor, however, is not yet a nonentity . . . a sort of perfume from the old days" of colonial and Revolutionary governors' power "lingers round the office."[3] Nelson took office before the governorship was reformed and strengthened by Progressives, but even 1890s voters and legislators might not accept "specious" powers as an excuse for inaction.

The state's five most important executive officials were directly elected and independent of the governor — "he is not responsible for their conduct, since he cannot control it."[4] About 16 percent of the state's employees were chosen by these independent officials. The governor directly appointed about 38 officeholders (41 percent), while they in turn appointed another 39 employees (42 percent). He could not supervise all state employees, for he had an office staff of only four. Under the patronage system, the state employee often had powerful allies who had secured the position for him and would oppose any governor's attempt to remove him.

174

Looking like a county courthouse on the grassy square in the county seat, Minnesota's second State Capitol shows state government's small size and close connection to county seat elites. Photo taken by E.A. Bromley in 1898.

The governor also appointed 106 unpaid members of sixteen policy-making boards, which supervised the major activities of state government: corrections, higher education, charitable institutions, conservation, property taxation, and licensing.[5] The governor could not give personal attention to so many boards, though he was an *ex officio* member of many of them. Moreover, the legislature oversaw all agencies and boards whose budgets depended on legislative appropriations. Bryce concluded that state executive "officers are the mere hands of the legislative brain, which directs them by statutes drawn with extreme minuteness . . . and supervises them by inquisitorial committees."[6] Threatening to assassinate the governor-elect, one man seemed to regard him as a mere underling when he offered to

The Governor's office in Minnesota's second State Capitol, which Nelson occupied from January 1893 to January 1895.

"take the head off of Knute Nelson" if anyone gave him traveling money plus $5.[7]

Nelson, reported the *Douglas County News*, left for St. Paul at noon on Saturday, December 31, "and a large number of our citizens were at the depot to see him off."[8] His inauguration was set for Wednesday, January 4, 1893. Two railroad cars full of Norwegian-American leaders from Chicago came up for the occasion.[9] Appropriately for a mere hand of the legislative brain, he was sworn in before a joint legislative session. There were no other inaugural ceremonies. One rural newspaper praised the "unostentatious way in which Governor Nelson takes hold of the reins of government . . . no inaugural ball, no fuss, no frills, no feathers, but just a plain, simple businesslike way." The editor claimed, "All this is tough on the 'sassiety' folk of the Twin Cities, but highly appreciated by everybody else."[10] Yet lack of ostentation might indicate that a governor did not actually hold the reins.

In his inaugural address, Governor Nelson gave a straightforward review of state government. He sounded like a frugal Scandinavian-American farmer when he called for cost-cutting economy in government. Reflecting his long-held view that education was the key to personal success, he described the "common school system" as "the priceless jewel of our liberty." He asked for a modest increase in the number of teachers, increased appropriations for teacher training, and a return to the practice of supplying free textbooks. Otherwise, his speech was a lengthy statistical review of such state institutions as normal schools, prisons, and insane asylums. At the end, he turned to a campaign theme: the agrarian revolt demanded some immediate, practical remedy. To end the worst abuses, he proposed state licensing and inspection of country grain elevators. To eliminate railroads' interference in wheat marketing, he would require railroads to allow anyone to build an elevator on their right-of-way or sidetrack.[11]

Legislators and "densely crowded" galleries responded "with so much applause that the governor looked disconcerted for a moment and evidently thought an encore was demanded." That might prove impossible. He had reported on all his major responsibilities. "He was allowed to escape, however, after accepting a beautiful basket of flowers." That ended his inauguration.[12]

Nelson proposed to undermine Populist protest with modest reforms achieved by a Republican administration. He would suggest the reforms, but legislators would have to enact them. He could attempt to persuade them. He had been his party's leader in the 1892 campaign, and his party's legislators might respect his views. He could use his patronage and veto powers to reward and to threaten legislators. Yet debate over the "Governor's Grain Bill" revealed how difficult that could be. Democratic and Populist legislators named it that to indicate disapproval of a governor initiating legislation. How could the hand tell the brain what to do? Yet, if Nelson desired a promotion to the Senate, he had to initiate.

177

Railroad and Warehouse Commission office in the second State Capitol. Little larger than a county auditor's office, it housed few employees, who had to retain Republican, hometown ties to keep their jobs.

The Governor's Grain Bill grew out of his listening on the 1892 campaign trail. He recommended that the Railroad and Warehouse Commission be given authority to license, inspect, and regulate country grain elevators.[13] Probably at his urging, the Republican House caucus "agreed to put through" this bill, introduced by State Representative Allen J. Greer, a Lake City Republican lawyer. In the Senate, Samuel D. Peterson, a Norwegian-American farm implement dealer from New Ulm, introduced a similar bill. Republican dailies hailed it as a wise means to deprive demagogues "of their chief political stock-in-trade," farmers' grievances, "the staple of campaign oratory for many years past."[14] Greer "wanted it passed in order to knock the political demagogues out of business."[15] That was likely Nelson's feeling also: it would force Democratic-Populist legislators to put up or shut up about reform.

Viewing it as the Governor's reelection bill, opposition legislators balked at giving Nelson a reform victory to campaign on in 1894. It "was fought all the harder by its enemies because it is directly from Gov. Nelson and is in the form as amended at the last moment by a suggestion from him."[16] A Populist farmer-legislator charged that "it had been drafted by a political farmer [Nelson], introduced by a legal farmer [Greer] and supported by an agricultural farmer [Peterson?], but the real farmers of the state do not want it."[17] They took offense when Nelson and the caucus made it "a party measure" mandatory on all Republicans. Alliance State Senator John B. Hompe of Otter Tail county hit the hardest. What if "Gov. Nelson favored the bill"? Nelson's hold on "the gubernatorial chair gave him no right to come in and dictate to the legislature and people what they should do." The executive hand should not dictate to the legislative brain. His opinions "were entitled to no more weight" than anyone else's. Like a southern secessionist, fire-eater Hompe threatened that enforcement of the bill's provisions "would be resisted at the point of arms" in "another civil war."[18]

That was extreme language peculiar to Hompe, but he reflected other legislators' concerns when he stated that his constituents "thought very little of the railroad commission and did not want their powers increased." The commission was thought to be "too arbitrary" and to show "favoritism." How the commission administered the proposed law was the key, argued State Senator Ignatius Donnelly. Its new powers "might not always be exercised to the benefit and advantage of the people."[19] Here, Nelson was on weak ground. He and previous Republican governors had used the Commission's twenty jobs to reward faithful Republicans. Several Commission employees had worked diligently for Nelson in 1892.[20] Early in the session, its chief grain inspector endorsed the Governor's Grain Bill in a very partisan way.[21] Would Republican appointees use these extensive new powers fairly? Five years later, a legislative investigation revealed that grain inspectors relaxed standards just before the 1898 election, probably to appease angry farmers with higher prices.[22] Wouldn't increased powers simply bring more Republican grain inspectors sifting their districts for Nelson support, Democratic dust, or Populist impurities?

Governor Nelson worked behind the scenes to overcome this opposition. The vote was especially close in the Senate, whose members were carry-overs from the Alliance-Democratic year of 1890. Twenty-eight votes were needed for a majority and Nelson had only twenty-four Republicans. To convince one St. Paul Democrat, Charles H. Lienau, Nelson may have threatened to veto a bill for a new state capitol building in St. Paul.[23] The grain bill passed on a vote of 28 to 23, with two Democrats and two Alliancemen joining all Republicans in voting aye.[24]

He used more "judicious maneuvering and planning" in the House.[25] There, Republicans from the "solid south" (including Representative Greer, the author!) threatened to kill it if northern representatives passed a reapportionment bill injurious to southern interests. Nelson, "alarmed at this movement," then recycled the veto threat used on Lienau. Still, ten Republicans, including seven southerners, voted no, and the bill was defeated. Then the House voted to reconsider the bill. All six St. Paul Democrats voted aye to save their new capitol and enough southern Republicans switched to give the Governor's Grain Bill a narrow victory.[26]

As a result of his judicious maneuvering and Republicans' fear of Populism, the Republican-controlled legislature passed most of his program. He could favorably contrast the 1893 session with the 1891 Democrat-Alliance session he had ridiculed at Halstad. Also successful were a farmer-supported bill creating a state-owned grain elevator at Duluth, a bill requiring railroads to provide elevator sites, a bill for free textbooks, an occupational safety act, and a workers' anti-discrimination act. Nelson signed the bill for a new capitol in St. Paul, over the opposition of some rural people who wanted the capital removed to a location away from the Twin Cities.[27]

The most controversial events of Nelson's first administration were not the bills, but the investigations of the "timber ring" and the "coal combine." Both provided a brief alliance of convenience between Nelson and his frequent antagonist, Donnelly. In 1893 he cooperated with Donnelly and the legislature to investigate abuses.

Somewhat unintentionally, lumber companies' demands for reform led to the "timber ring" investigation. As the Kindred-Nelson contest revealed, in Minnesota Gilded Age political corruption was most rampant in lumbering areas. Once allegations surfaced, Nelson was almost forced to support a legislative inquiry. Accused of "pine ring" loyalties during that 1882 fight, "Governor Nelson intended that no one should have a pretext for insinuating that he was affiliated with or was under the influence of any pine-land ring."[28]

He *was* "affiliated with" and "under the influence of" one "pine-land ring" in matters of patronage and campaign finance. Minneapolis lumberman Henry F. Brown played a prominent role in organizing and financing his 1892 pre-convention campaign. Henry's brother, S.S. Brown, surveyor general in the Second District, reportedly contributed $7,000 to the 1892 Republican campaign.[29] In return, Henry Brown had asked for continued "control" of the Second District surveyor general's post. When several politicians lobbied Nelson to appoint a different candidate to the Second District post, he replied that he was already committed to S.S. Brown, whom he did reappoint.[30]

It is no mystery why the Browns eagerly wanted to retain the post. Surveyor General Brown earned an estimated $18,000 in scaling fees in 1892.[31] He pocketed most of that, for his expenses were small. With the income, he was supposed to hire and pay "scalers" to determine the amount of timber cut. "Scalers" were to be state employees paid "for honest and independent service." Instead, surveyors general allowed lumber companies to hire and pay their own employees to guess the amount harvested! Lumber companies obtained a less than "honest and independent" esti-

181

mate, which lowered their payment to the state for timber cut on state land. Surveyors general obtained scaling fees without paying scaling expenses.[32]

But most timber was cut on private land. Here, the companies wanted reform. They rightly complained of paying a scaling fee but receiving little scaling, for the surveyor general's few deputies visited a given logging site only a few times a month and made only "a rough guess."[33] Republicans in state government used this pretext of a scaling service to maintain a lucrative office which then gave "of its large income freely to the party campaign fund." Republicans could run this rake-off because the lumbermen were so guilty of fraudulently acquiring public lands that they could not complain publicly. The scaling fee resembled "hush money" extorted by politicians in return for remaining silent on lumbermen's land frauds. Lumber companies lobbied for a House bill to limit the surveyor general's salary to $5,000. It would end the practice of having Republican "campaign expenses paid from the tax directly levied on the lumber interest."[34]

The lumbermen's bill set off a chain reaction of public exposure. Lumbermen exposed the rake-off. The Browns fought back. They likely used promises of campaign contributions or monetary gifts to legislators to secure defeat of the lumbermen's bill. Nelson apparently took no public position on the bill. As a warning shot, they probably leaked to State Representative Robert C. Dunn, another early Nelson backer in 1892, allegations of illegal timber sales to a Minneapolis lumber company that opposed them.[35] Dunn investigated and found the Democratic state auditor primarily responsible, but the lumbermen were effectively warned. Angered by the Browns' opposition, the *Mississippi Valley Lumberman* threatened court action: "It looks now as though the goose that laid the golden egg for the politicians had been killed." Some lumbermen apparently cooperated with Democrat Henry Keller and Populist Donnelly's Senate probe into "the entire field of suspected abuse in the lumber industry's relations with the state."[36]

The Keller committee's report described the surveyors general's misdeeds, especially in Itasca county, the Browns' bailiwick. It concluded that "the State of Minnesota has been robbed of millions of dollars' worth of its property" by "the most gigantic frauds." Its hearings focused on scaling and estimating. The amount of timber harvested was often five to ten times greater than what the surveyor general reported. Frauds long practiced against United States Land Offices had been used against the state auditor, who was the state land commissioner. Like United States land officers, the state auditor and surveyors general had connived with lumber companies to underestimate timber sales and allow rigged bidding at public auctions. Lumber barons such as John Pillsbury, Thomas B. Walker, the Kindred brothers, Loren Fletcher, and Charles M. Loring had fraudulently purchased state and railroad lands, which often contained the added bonus of iron ore deposits.[37]

A week after the Keller report was released, Governor Nelson asked the Senate to authorize a joint Senate-House investigating committee which could conduct a more thorough probe.[38] The investigation threatened the reputations of several well-known entrepreneurial Republicans, including Pillsbury, Walker, and Senator Washburn. That might strengthen Nelson's hand against the old-stock politicians. However, he was also involved with the lumbermen and surveyors general. His lieutenant governor, David Clough, a lumberman, opposed the cap on the surveyor general's income—probably because it was a cap on campaign contributions Clough would need for a future run for governor. Politics is partly a matter of luck. Nelson was lucky the "pine lands" scandal broke at the start of his administration. Citizens would be unlikely to blame a new governor, especially for misdeeds of the state auditor, an elected official independent of the governor.

A former land-office lawyer, Nelson knew the customary ways lumbermen and speculators defrauded the United States government. As a longtime Republican politician, he knew that Gilded

Age campaigns depended on officeholders' contributions. He may not have known exactly how the Browns were able to contribute so heavily. He was playing by the rules of Gilded Age politics, but those rules were changing under pressure from Populists and Progressives. He was playing the role of an attorney who saw no inconsistency in representing two very different clients. First, in 1892, he quietly represented Republican jobholders and favor-seekers like the Browns. Once elected, he represented the people of Minnesota. His first client sought privileges injurious to his second, but revealing that fact would violate his confidential relationship to the first.

He also played the lawyer in the second investigation, of the "coal combine." Donnelly started it by going after John P. Rhodes, manager of the Minnesota Bureau of Coal Statistics, a coal dealers association with an innocuous name but a practice of fixing anthracite coal prices. It enforced its policy by cutting off supplies of coal to dealers who sold below the Bureau's fixed retail price. Donnelly's Senate committee seized Rhodes's records, which revealed a price-fixing conspiracy and Rhodes's perjury before the committee.[39] A mass meeting of 2,500 citizens at St. Paul's Market Hall cheered another sage address by the great orator, who responded, "I seem to be the most popular man in the state— between elections." In democratic fashion, they passed a series of resolutions, one of which instructed the legislature to call a convention of all the states to combat the coal combine.[40]

The legislative brain delegated this duty to the executive hand. It acted. Consumers were demanding reform. Nelson found it easy to side with Minnesota consumers against a few coal dealers and their Eastern suppliers. Realizing that legislation could not be aimed at only one industry, he "broaden[ed] the approach by calling an interstate Anti-Trust Conference to be held in Chicago" on June 5, 1893.[41]

Meeting during the World's Columbian Exposition and overshadowed by the spectacular arrival of Spain's Infanta Maria Eulalia, more than seventy delegates from twenty-six of the forty-four states gathered at the Apollo Music Hall for the conference. They were a very heterogeneous lot. Populist governors appointed Populists, while Republicans and Democrats appointed their own kind. Illinois Governor John Altgeld sent noted reform journalist Henry Demarest Lloyd, among others. The Populists' 1892 presidential candidate, James B. Weaver, attended. Nelson selected trusted Republican ex-congressmen, ex-lieutenant governors, and ex-state legislators—and Donnelly. No rule equalized states' voting strengths. Minnesota had eleven delegates (and votes), while many states had only one. The delegates were deeply divided between advocates of government regulation and government ownership.

As convener, Governor Nelson gave the opening speech. Like a lawyer summarizing before a jury, he spoke at great length about his legislature's investigation of Rhodes, the lumber trust, and the defects in the Sherman Anti-Trust Act of 1890. He presented Rhodes's letters as exhibits in evidence and discussed Rhodes's replevin suit to recover the records that the Senate committee had seized. To prove the Sherman Act's inability to go beyond common law restrictions on monopolies, he recited a legal brief, complete with citations ("United States vs. Greene, 52 Federal Reporter 104") and lengthy quotations from judicial opinions. In this appearance on the national stage, he tried to impress by his legal erudition and expert grasp of the issue. At the end he gave a brief rhetorical closing argument, managing to sound condemnatory and conservative at the same time: "Comprehensive and exhaustive federal and state laws are needed to protect and defend our people against this, the most offensive and dangerous of all modern anti-Christs. We must check and repress this great and growing enormity by law and not by revolution. . . .We must leave no field open for the communist or anarchist. The evil must by cured in the true American way—by methods of law and order."[42]

The ex-congressman who had wielded the thin reed of unenforceable law to protect the Ojibway now would eliminate

185

monopolies by outlawing the legal device, the trust. Outlawing a form would not change reality. He wanted "simpler and easier forms of pleading and rules of evidence" in anti-trust cases. Yet the American legal profession was hiring itself out to the corporations. These corporate counsels could devise new legal devices or complicate the simplest forms of pleading.[43]

This narrowly legal approach brought him into direct confrontation with Donnelly, who had long since abandoned his law practice for radical politics. After the committee on resolutions essentially adopted Minnesota Republicans' very mild ones, Donnelly "took the floor" with some very different ones. "He had a bundle of manuscript in his hand and fire in his eye." He would have the United States government confiscate trusts' properties, deny them legal protection, and seize coal fields.

When a wrangle over parliamentary procedure produced a point of order, Chairman Nelson stated, "Mr. Donnelly is getting his resolutions before the convention, and that is what he is after."[44]

Donnelly erupted. "The chair has no right to sneer at me in that manner. Were it not for me this convention never would have existed, and I propose to say here what I believe." He "glared at the governor of his state through his spectacles."

Taken aback, Nelson denied "any intent of sneering at the speaker."[45] To him, Donnelly was grandstanding—presenting resolutions with no chance of passage or implementation, for political effect. Even worse, Donnelly attacked the principle of judicial review and the Supreme Court, whose opinions Nelson had so laboriously cited and quoted. Donnelly believed that governmental power "should rest with the great mass of the people, and not with a few lawyers." Later, he ridiculed the Supreme Court's dictum that corporations had the rights of persons, by wittily predicting that the courts would soon say "corporations have the right to marry and rear children."[46]

When the conference voted down Henry Lloyd's resolution for government ownership of coal fields, the radicals had clearly lost,

186

and it went on to adopt the Minnesota resolutions. In its hetero-geneity, it fell apart—into debate over Henry George's Single Tax, unlimited coinage of silver, and other issues. Finally, "after a vote of thanks to Gov. Nelson and the other officers of the con-vention," it adjourned *sine die*. Populists and radicals met that evening at the Palmer House to adopt the resolutions which the full conference had rejected. The full conference had tried to form a permanent antitrust association, but there were no funds avail-able for that task. It weakly "requested" delegates to report back "when they got home."[47] Donnelly ridiculed the "perfunctory res-olutions, calling on some one else to do his duty."[48] At least, by doing his duty to call it, Knute Nelson had a moment on the na-tional stage, in Chicago during the World's Fair.

By the June Anti-Trust Conference, the nation had been hit by the Panic of 1893, leading to a severe depression in the mid-1890s. Banks closed, credit tightened, unemployment soared, and agri-cultural prices declined. Fortunately for Nelson, voters did not yet hold governors responsible for a state's economy, as they would a hundred years later.

An 1890s governor's more limited responsibilities meant that Nelson had some time for personal affairs. He returned to his Alexandria home for Sunday visits about once a month; his wife continued to live there.[49] More extended visits were possible dur-ing the summer: weeknight meetings with the Sons of Veterans in June, and a little fishing in August.[50] In late August, the *Douglas County News* announced that "Gov. Nelson has leased his farm to John Felton for five years. The Governor will still reside on the place."[51]

1893 was a year of personal loss. In mid-May, his Albion men-tor, A.R. Cornwall, died—before Nelson reached the Senate seat which Cornwall had encouraged him to seek.[52] As the small grain harvest approached, he received the second personal shock. Mary Blackwell Dillon, who had set him onto a path of intellectual de-velopment and ambition, died August 5th in Whitewater, Wisconsin.[53] Nelson had been her prize pupil. Her picture always

187

sat on his desk, like a watchful English-Irish surrogate mother overseeing his daily activities, and reminding him of his ultimate goal. In response to Nelson's letter of condolence, Miss Dillon's brother reminded him, "Mary said she would not be satisfied until you were in the U.S. Senate. I hope you will get there."[54] The coming 1894 campaign took on a greater imperative than before.

Nelson had time to visit the 1893 World's Fair at least three times, though only one visit was a personal one.[55] His first visit brought controversy. He failed to realize that, if he lacked solid powers, he had the specious power of being a state symbol. And, at the World's Fair, symbolism was everything.

He accepted an invitation to speak at the Syttende Mai (May 17) festivities, which was also Norway Day at the World's Fair. By coincidence, Minnesota's newspaper editors planned to dedicate the Minnesota Building at the fair that same day, and they expected him at that event. His silent treatment of supporters carried over to editors and World's Fair officials. The editors only learned on their way to Chicago that he would not attend their dedication. Minnesota's World's Fair commissioners did not know he was in Chicago that day, so "no escort met the governor at the morning train."[56]

At the Norway Day ceremony, some 7,000 Norwegian Americans sang Bjørnstjerne Bjørnson's hymn, "Ja, vi elsker dette Landet." Other speakers offered some remarks. Then, there "was a stir on the platform . . . and a stalwart man, bearded like a Viking of old, stepped forward." Apparently no one introduced Nelson, for at first "few recognized him as one of the most distinguished Norwegians in the United States."[57] The day's chief speaker, he read a forty-five-minute, English-language account of Norway's history and its brief independence in 1814. As a politician needing Danish-American and Swedish-American votes, he trod historical ground cautiously. Denmark's rule over Norway was "mild," but brought too much warfare against the Swedes! He wistfully regretted the failure of one united Scandinavian kingdom (the Kalmar Union), which would have made life easier for Scandinavian-American politicians. As he continued, more of the audience recognized him. He closed with a call for Norwegian-American loyalty to the United States: "Let us remember that to the same degree that we lack true love and a sense of duty towards our adopted country, we do an injustice to ourselves and discredit the land of our birth."[58] When he finished, one leader cried out, "Long live Governor Nelson, the first Norwegian Governor in America," and the crowd shouted their pride.[59] He then left for St. Paul before many Minnesotans realized he had been at the fair.

Feeling jilted over at the Minnesota Building, the editors wondered just which land Nelson loved. Some felt he had discredited himself by lacking a sense of duty to his adopted state. Future governor John A. Johnson of the *St. Peter Herald* led a dedication program witnessed by some 400 onlookers—Minnesota drew a much smaller crowd than Norway. "Gov. Nelson was conspicuous by his absence, though in the city and supposedly on the [fair] grounds." Norwegian Americans had hailed him, but equally warm greetings "were awaiting him at the Minnesota state building had he chosen to appear, which he didn't." "Why Not, Knute?" asked the *Minneapolis Journal*. St. Paul's *North-Western Chronicle* charged, "Governor Nelson seems to have persuaded himself that he has been elected governor of Norway and Sweden instead of Minnesota." Defending him, the Republican *Journal* called this "a tempest in a teapot."[60]

The plain, matter-of-fact Nelson could not understand why all the "fuss and feathers." At the World's Fair, symbols and ceremonies were everything. For the state's first foreign-born governor to prefer to symbolize Norwegian Americans' success rather than Minnesota's success was unforgivable to some. His absence led to a wrangle over whether the editors' dedication had been official. He scheduled, then cancelled, an official dedication for the first week of June.[61]

He redeemed himself by appearing at the World's Fair for Minnesota Day, Friday, October 13. In the same Festival Hall where he had spoken on May 17, he fulsomely praised Minnesota ("this earthly paradise") and described her people of mixed ethnicity as her most "instructive" exhibit at the Fair. Minnesota's "great destiny" would be realized "when these different elements" became "fully assimilated into one people . . . intensely and truly American." Three weeks earlier, at the Redwood county fair, he had described them as "a new race" — "neither like the Anglo-Saxon of Great Britain, nor like the Yankee of New England." Using a wheat-grading term, he called them "a No. 1 hard specimen of humanity."[62] Ringing the fair's Liberty Bell, reviewing a Minnesota regiment, and greeting people in the hours-long reception line, the Governor fully met his symbolic obligations.[63]

At Minnesota Day, he praised Minnesota's "extensive" transportation network and "great headway and progress in manufacturing."[64] Little wonder, then, that he should have to face workers' demands for reform during his first term. In Minnesota, workers had not looked to the legislature for reform to the degree that farmers had. The strike was their weapon. For Nelson, supporting consumers was easy. Backing railroad workers' right to strike proved impossible.

The Panic of 1893 led Hill to order three successive wage cuts on the Great Northern (GN) from August, 1893, to March, 1894. Seeking assistance, angry workers contacted Eugene V. Debs's new American Railway Union (ARU), an industrial union of all railway workers. On April 13, the ARU struck the Great Northern.[65] Despite opposition from more conservative railroad brotherhoods, the strike spread along the GN's transcontinental route. On April 18, the charismatic Debs came to St. Paul "to take command of the strike," which was "spreading to new cities every day."[66]

Historian Bryce had noted earlier that when strikes or riots threatened, a governor "may at any moment become the pivot on whose action public order turns."[67] Nelson soon began "receiving appeals from citizens who are suffering from the strike to do something to have traffic resumed." The manager of the Northwestern Elevator Company wrote to the governor to complain that his company had "loaded and standing on sidetracks more than 500 cars of wheat . . . . We may suffer heavy loss from the failure to make shipment of this wheat. . . . we are entitled to the movement of our property, and that every means at the command of the state should be used — in proper ways of course, — to aid in the movement of the business."[68] A threat to public order existed at Willmar and St. Cloud, two important GN switching points. At Willmar, "strikers swarmed all over" two trains, separated passenger coaches and sidetracked them, then reconnected engine and mail cars to comply with an injunction against interfering with the United States mail. They obstructed attempts to put together a train. A GN manager was badly beaten.[69] At St. Cloud, they took similar steps to prevent trains from passing through that city.[70]

Nelson faced a dilemma. After a decade of criticism that he was too close to Hill, he could not risk seeming to side with Hill's Great Northern in a campaign year. Seeking the Republican nomination again, he could not risk seeming to side with Debs and the ARU, whom the Twin Cities' dailies regarded as radicals. Yet he could not abdicate a governor's responsibility for law and order. He had to appear evenhanded, yet Republican, and concerned with public order.

With literal evenhandedness, on behalf of his clients, the people of Minnesota, the lawyer-governor sent two nearly identical letters to Debs and Hill. He cautiously denied having sufficent knowledge of "the grounds for the strike" to qualify him "to sit as an umpire in the matter." Yet, "as the chief peace officer of the state," he was concerned lest Minnesotans' "law-abiding" reputation be "darkened." He suggested arbitration, but while that was pursued, "law and order must be maintained and the property of the company must be preserved from injury or destruction at all hazards." He did not mention workers' right of assembly or right to strike.[71]

When the Stearns county sheriff and county attorney met with him, he directed them to preserve law and order, to tell the strikers not to "in any way hinder the company from doing business if it could get men to run the trains."[72] Like the Anti-Trust Conference, he was telling other men to do their duty, but was very cautious about doing anything himself. He sent Tams Bixby, his chief aide, to Willmar to reason with the strikers. Commissioner of Labor Statistics L.G. Powers spoke to the strikers' mass meeting in Minneapolis. Nelson never addressed the ARU men, though he did meet once with Debs.[73] Using a legal technicality, lawyer Nelson largely evaded responsibility. Hill had appealed to the federal courts for an injunction, which Federal Judge Walter Sanborn had granted; therefore, Hill had "placed the matter in the hands of the federal government." United States marshals would have to arrest strikers who disobeyed the injunction, and United States troops would have to be called up if marshals were inadequate to the task. The state and Knute Nelson would stay out of it.[74]

He apparently stayed out of the settlement too. Twin Cities business leaders arbitrated the dispute. The ARU strikers won most of their wage demands, and the press portrayed it as a victory for Debs and the ARU. For Nelson, it was further evidence that caution was best. His handling of the 1894 GN strike confirmed a governor's limited role in the early 1890s. The Progressive era brought greater expectations of governors. When a strike hit Minnesota's Iron Range in 1907, Governor John A. Johnson played a prominent role in attempting to end it.[75] Johnson helped create the expectation that a governor would intervene personally in major strikes. Thirteen years earlier, Nelson's very limited role did not draw unfavorable public comment.[76]

The spring and summer of 1894 saw massive national labor protests, the Pullman boycott led by Debs' ARU and "General" Jacob Coxey's march of the unemployed on Washington. Nelson briefly worried about Coxeyites creating disorder in western Minnesota, but this movement was centered elsewhere.[77] In the

Pullman strike, the ARU shut down railroad terminals and stock-yards in Chicago, and the Santa Fe and NP railroads. Miners began the Cripple Creek strike in Colorado. Three days before the Republican nominating convention, the *Pioneer Press*'s front page was entirely filled with strike news.[78]

When the convention met on July 11, the Pullman strike had just been broken and Debs arrested.[79] With the outdoor temperature over 100 degrees, firemen sprayed the St. Paul Auditorium to cool it and prevent fire. Inside, things were cooler, as Nelson was renominated by acclamation. In his acceptance speech, he called strikes "ruinous and demoralizing in the extreme" and recommended arbitration of future strikes through the Republican-dominated Railroad and Warehouse Commission. Yet he offered no sweeping proposals. "I have aimed to be conservative, to keep within the beaten paths of law and precedent," he confessed in lawyerly terms. The executive hand admitted, "I have felt that if any radical change, any new lines of public policy was to be inaugurated, it should come from the people, through the legislative department, and not through the executive."[80]

Of course, a governor was also elected by the people, but Nelson was not as interested in achieving reform through the governorship as he was in achieving election to the Senate. In that regard, there was a curious omission. The 1892 Republican convention had endorsed Cushman K. Davis for legislative re-election, but the 1894 body simply voted to "commend" Senators Davis and Washburn, the six Republican congressmen, and Nelson.[81] Where did that leave Washburn? He continued to worry.

The 1894 gubernatorial contest was largely a replay of the 1890 and 1892 campaigns. The Populists nominated Sidney M. Owen, the 1890 candidate. Their 1894 platform was similar to the 1892 one: unlimited coinage of silver, woman suffrage, progressive income and inheritance taxes, government ownership of railroads, the initiative, and the referendum. Owen praised unions and Debs, deplored Coxey's arrest, and pilloried Pullman and Hill.[82] The 1894 differences were dramatic strikes, marches, and depres-

193

sion. All contributed to a fear of radicalism and anarchy which presaged the Armageddon of 1896. To keep their spot on the ballot, Democrats nominated old George Becker, Civil-War-era SP&P president and currently a Railroad and Warehouse Commissioner. Since he was allowed a *de facto* leave of absence from the Commission to campaign ("when the commissioners were appointed by the governor"), many suspected he was a Nelson-Hill token candidate to prevent Democrats from voting for Owen.[83]

Nelson began his campaign earlier than ever. Relying on statistics from the Census Bureau, the Railroad and Warehouse Commission, and other sources, he carefully crafted his basic message. On Saturday afternoon, July 28, he delivered it in Argyle, a tiny hamlet on the old St. Vincent Extension in Marshall county. He was "greeted at the depot by a large crowd" and serenaded by "the Argyle Cornet Band." Because the crowd was larger than expected, he spoke from the steps of the schoolhouse, "the audience being furnished with seats and chairs placed on the grass in the school yard."[84] The setting was fitting, given his experience as a country school teacher and his schoolmasterish speaking style. It was a Republican answer to the sub-alliances' Saturday meetings at schoolhouses.

Argyle's Populist editor truthfully characterized the speech as "remarkable for its dryness," "an array of dry statistics, compiled" as "a refutation of Populist theories."[85] First, lectured Nelson, it was not true, as Populist "I told-you-so reformers" charged, that the farmer was "the neglected stepson of organized society." Farmers received a smaller proportion of the nation's total wealth than they had in 1860, but they now formed a smaller percentage of the population. Their *per capita* share had not declined noticeably. "Our legislation" was not designed "to oppress the farmers." "No other class can point to any more or as much friendly special legislation": homestead laws, farm schools, agricultural experiment stations, grain inspection laws, and a dairy school. Statistics gave "proof positive" that low wheat prices re-

sulted from global overproduction and not a reduced money supply, high freight rates, or middlemen's extortionate profits. More
money circulated *per capita* than ever before. Wheat transportation rates had dropped greatly. The answer to overproduction
"must come from more diversified farming." He contrasted diversified, dairying Freeborn county ("a large and valuable variety
of farm products") with wheat-growing Polk county ("little to exchange for money except wheat").[86] Freeborn prospered while
Polk stagnated. The moral was clear.

He showed sensitivity to the contrast between his dry, statistical
style and the flamboyant style of such Populist orators as Mary
Ellen Lease, "The Kansas Pythoness," or Jerry Simpson, "the
Sockless Socrates." He half apologized for his "plain and homely
suggestions" when farmers could hear "the new style of reformer" with "an easy, flippant and demagogic way" of speaking,
and "perhaps more scientific remedies to propose." Here, farmers
were likely to favor the speaker more like them, the hard-working
Norwegian-American fact finder with his plain talk and plain
facts. Denying that Nelson was like the farmers, Argyle's editor
ridiculed his "dry statistics" and "wise explanation" of "*per
capita*": "It was nice to have a walking dictionary come to town."[87]

Nelson was poor-mouthing his style when he suggested that
reformers were more scientific. In fact, his speech reflected the increasing predominance of "systematic" and "scientific" farmers,
who used careful record-keeping, observation, and experimentation to improve farming practices. They read the fact-laden bulletins published by the university farm schools and experiment
stations that Nelson praised.[88] At Argyle, he sounded like a walking farm-school bulletin promoting dairying and diversification.
That is what agricultural experts promoted in their bulletins, and
they were as unsympathetic to Populism as he.[89] Their term "diversified farming" was misleading, for they really recommended
specialization in dairying. And, by April, 1896, Freeborn's dairy
farmers were hit with the same price decline — in butter — as a re-

sult of the same specialization and overproduction that Polk's wheat farmers had faced earlier.[90]

Nelson's speech provoked much comment. In reply, Owen pointed out that "diversification" was a necessary but not an all-sufficient remedy.[91] Appointing himself a one-man truth squad in his *Representative*, Donnelly reprinted it—one Nelson paragraph followed by several paragraphs of his rebuttal. He agreed with Argyle's editor that Nelson's sample of statistics was "very misleading." Let Nelson examine statistics on increased farm indebtedness. "Let the governor apply his fine front teeth to those figures and see if he can chew them into any shape that will demonstrate the prosperity of the farmers."[92] Similarly, Fergus Falls's Populist newspaper, *Rodhuggeren*, charged that "Knute the Vossing" had "explained away" farmers' problems "in a shrewd, lawyer-like manner" by "serving up bundles of statistics." Nelson, "with real lawyers' tricks defends his fine plutocratic clients." Appealing to Norwegian-American farmers' distrust of exalted officialdom, it called him "His Excellency" six times and "lawyer" three times in the one article.[93]

Delighted with their lawyer-governor's speech, Republicans, on the other hand, regarded it as the definitive answer to Populism. The *Pioneer Press* printed the full text of the "masterpiece." In a two-column editorial, the *New York Evening Post* quoted and paraphrased it at length and predicted that it "will produce a great effect upon the public mind." The *Post* reviewed Nelson's birth in Norway, emigration, and political rise: "Such a speech as this, addressed to people of an American commonwealth by a man who came here a poor boy from a foreign land, revives one's faith in popular government."[94] The Americanized Nelson could no more escape the immigrant's Castle Garden than the successful Lincoln could the Kentucky log cabin.

In the midst of the campaign, Nelson faced one more state crisis. The summer of 1894 was unusually dry. In fact, Nelson's meadow caught fire in early August, and His Excellency spent a weekend fighting the flames with a crew.[95] Far more serious was

196

the Hinckley Fire which swept east-central Minnesota on Saturday, September 1, killing at least 413 people. Nelson's secretary Tams Bixby received the news by telegram at 11:15 AM, Sunday, September 2. Nelson and Bixby then dispatched a special Sunday afternoon train to the disaster area. Lacking a state disaster relief fund, the governor had to call on private citizens to do their duty and contribute money toward "relief of prevailing distress." He did appoint a five-man State Fire Relief Commission to handle donated funds and supervise aid to the fire survivors. The legislature later appropriated $20,000 for the effort.[96]

When the governor and the commission inspected the area and the survivors the following week, Commission Chairman Charles A. Pillsbury took the lead as representative of the private donors. As a symbol of the state, Nelson's presence was deeply, tearfully, appreciated by survivors. "Many of them were from Scandinavian countries, and to them Gov. Nelson spoke in Norwegian." At Hinckley, he vowed, "Minnesota will never see her children suffer."[97] Yet, he had only privately-donated monies to use to fulfill his vow. Governor and commission were determined to limit relief and encourage home-building and farming (on the fire-cleared lands) as quickly as possible. Given the limited powers of late-nineteenth-century government, they managed fairly well (over 200 relief houses built, over 2,600 people aided), though Hinckley people charged that commission employees "have been hanging on like a lot of leeches, sucking the sustenance donated" for survivors.[98]

Not noted, except by forestry reformers, was that blame for the fire partly rested on the state government's lax regulation of the lumber industry. The state did not require loggers to clean up waste branches ("slashings"), which then became the tinder for damaging forest fires. A state investigating committee charged that the Hinckley Fire had been deliberately set by some loggers to "cover up their stealing of timber on state lands."[99] Failure to reform could have tragic consequences.

No disaster could suspend politics in the 1890s. Less than a month after the fire, two worried Hinckley Republicans went to state party headquarters to report that in Hinckley, "there were three Republican voters burned to death to every one Democrat."[100]

As in 1892, Nelson ended the campaign with a late October swing through the Upper Country. On the final day, a beautiful Indian-summer day, he made a sentimental journey back to Detroit Lakes. A large barbecue was planned. A torchlight parade helped draw several thousand people for the rally, which ended with an emotional Nelson speech in Holmes Opera Hall, the site of the tumultous convention in 1882.[101] November 6th brought another Nelson victory, a 60,000-vote plurality over Sidney Owen. Few could deny that he was the rallying point for Minnesota Republicans since their 1890 debacle. Owen carried only twelve farming counties—the Populist Red River Valley and a few southwestern counties. Republicans captured all seven of Minnesota's congressional seats and overwhelming control of the state legislature.[102] Republican elites had clearly beaten back the assault of the sub-alliances. Knute Nelson had survived the risks of being governor. Voters did not hold him responsible for failure —economic depression, lumber frauds, lack of regulation of lumbering leading to the Hinckley Fire, or the lack of effective anti-trust action. He was now ready to claim his reward.

Ten

Norwegian-American Country Lawyer vs. Yankee Aristocrat

Replying to Nelson's criticism at Argyle of office-seeking reformers, Ignatius Donnelly accused him of "straddling two horses" while "he objects to a People's party man riding one": "He is not satisfied, like the modest reformers, to run for one office at a time, he wants to be elected governor and United States senator by the vote cast at the same election."[1] Donnelly was exactly right. Behind the scenes of Nelson's public campaign for governor was a quiet campaign, a "still hunt," to elect legislators supporting him for the Senate.

In March, 1894, in a private conversation with James J. Hill's son-in-law, he showed himself "much in earnest in his desire to be chosen U.S. Senator."[2] At the same time, "in a long conversation," he told Senator Washburn that he had no idea of running for the Senate.[3] The utter contrast between these two conversations would ultimately produce charges of treachery when Nelson and Washburn squared off in one of the bitterest political fights in Minnesota history.

An utter contrast separated the two combatants as well. Nelson "was born in Norway . . . of a family so poor that . . . a property qualification for immigrants . . . would have prevented their coming to America."[4] Then, he had no father who would acknowl-

199

edge him nor any brothers. Though his mother's later marriage to a poor fellow Vossing gave him both, neither achieved great distinction. Born in Maine to a family with eleven children, William Drew Washburn had distinguished brothers. One served as Maine's governor, another as Wisconsin's governor, still another as minister to France. All four brothers were elected to Congress. Donnelly joked about William that "every young male of the gentleman's family is born into the world with 'M.C.' [Member of Congress] franked across his broadest part."[5]

Nelson was still living in a nine-room modest farmhouse on the homestead he purchased in 1874. Washburn's ten-acre estate, Fair Oaks, probably costing "well over one hundred thousand dollars," was the grandest in Minneapolis. Sixty feet high, the house had mahogany doors, "a marble floor with Washburn's monogram," walnut panels, and "onyx fireplaces." "The grounds . . . may have been even more spectacular than the house." All this ostentation led the *St. Paul Globe* to note that "there is a strong suggestion of royalty here."[6] He earned an ostentatious amount of money in the lumbering and flour milling industries. (He had got his start in lumbering as the United States Land Office's surveyor-general for Minnesota during the Civil War.) With large personal investments, he figured prominently in the beginnings of the Minneapolis & St. Louis Railroad and the Minneapolis, St. Paul & Sault Ste. Marie ("Soo Line").[7] Nelson could help to bring the St. Paul, Minneapolis, and Manitoba to the Upper Country as a state senator, but not as an investor.

Nelson had the advantage of his Civil War service, which contrasted favorably with Washburn's wartime patronage post as surveyor-general.[8] From Koshkonong and from the Upper Country court circuit, "Uncle Knute" knew how to mingle and chat with farmers and ordinary people. One Washburn intimate admitted, "Washburn was no politician. He did not like to travel from town to town, sleep and eat in dirty hotels and hob-nob with local bosses."[9] Five years of hobnobbing with his fellow United States senators had reinforced his senator-sized ego. Annually,

Senator Knute Nelson's house in Alexandria, c. 1890.

Washburn opened Fair Oaks to the public, but these one-dollar-a-head New Year's Day visits may have confirmed popular perceptions of Washburn the aristocrat more than they displayed Washburn the politician. One country editor described him thus: "Senator Washburn is a gentleman of commanding figure, his hair and sideburn whiskers liberally sprinkled with white and his face stamped with intelligence and firmness."[10] Nelson's short stature did not make him a commanding figure. Occasional farming duties sometimes undercut any image as a gentleman. In every way, the Yankee blueblood and the Norwegian-American lawyer-farmer stood markedly apart.

Politically, they differed as well. Because he had opposed protectionism while in Congress, Nelson was seen as somewhat independent of the Republican hierarchy. Because he lived in the Upper Country, he was seen as the rural candidate. An unalloyed Gilded Age Republican, Washburn had his political base in Minneapolis business interests who wanted the state's largest city to have its own senator. He argued that "the people of Minneapolis" should "feel very indignant" that his opponents would "deprive them of their U.S. Senator." Senator Davis was a

201

St. Paul resident.[11] His limited rural support came from his earlier federal patronage appointments and from businessmen friendly to him. He lacked Nelson's intimate connection to rural people and places. His Maine birthplace brought him fewer votes than did Nelson's Evanger.

Washburn was the obstacle in Nelson's path to the Senate. Washburn was vulnerable to an Alliance-style, grass-roots attack on his aristocratic character. That was not Nelson's style, and that could not succeed within the Republican party. Washburn was vulnerable to a challenge from an equally wealthy Republican who could contribute lavishly to Republican state legislative candidates, and then bribe legislators. Nelson lacked the funds to do these things. In 1888, he wrote to Donnelly that "the Yankee blue blood of the Twin Cities would never tolerate that a damned Norwegian without boodle should ever aspire to the U.S. Senatorship."[12] His only chance lay in using his ethnic appeal and his control of state patronage. To maintain that control he had to run for reelection as governor. So, he could not openly campaign for the Senate. He had to set out on a "still hunt," a quiet search for legislative support while the opposition was unaware of his candidacy. Such a course risked charges of treachery, but it was his only chance.

The state legislature elected the senator, so senatorial hopefuls sought to arrange the nomination of legislative candidates committed to them, and to aid their campaigns.

As the only announced Republican candidate for the Senate, Washburn could more or less openly manipulate legislative nominations. Kept in Washington at the 1894 summer session, he wrote almost daily letters to his chief aide, Major William D. Hale, to inquire about this candidate's loyalty or to insist on that candidate's selection or another's rejection. "J.M. Underwood is all right," and "Dr. Zier and Jim Griffin are favorable to me," but he did not "want Wash Elliot nominated under any circumstances." He flatly stated, "you do not want to nominate Geo. Savage," and instructed Hale to see to it that Stacy was "turned down."[13]

202

Yankee gentleman William Drew Washburn, United States Senator, Minneapolis industrialist, and scion of a very distinguished American political family.

Holding the key patronage post of Minneapolis postmaster, Hale had the clout to "see to it." Washburn wanted conventions to instruct legislators-to-be to vote for him for senator: "Any man who objects to being instructed cannot be trusted." Hale was to get the newspapers to demand instruction of candidates.[14]

Like a cat, Senator Washburn could hear and smell the Nelson-for-Senate mouse, but could never put his paw on it.

As the candidate for governor, Nelson was not supposed to be overseeing these nominations. Yet, Washburn heard, "efforts will be made" throughout the state "to secure nominees to the Legislature favorable to Governor Nelson" for the Senate. He doubted that rumor, for "Governor Nelson has said to me, both in personal interview and by letter, that he was not a candidate."[15] Still, he thought it "very suspicious" when a last-minute Norwegian-American candidate won a legislative nomination in Goodhue county after a "hot" fight and five ballots. Asked to investigate. Hale discovered the Nelson forces had engineered this surprise candidacy. Indignant over this raid into his sphere, Washburn wrote back, "If Nelson has been guilty of what you indicate, it seems to me it is about time for someone to 'read the riot act' to him."[16]

Washburn fumed when he heard "of the movements of Little Foot," that is, Hiram W. Foote, the state oil inspector appointed by Nelson. "I am informed, on the best authority," explained Washburn, "that he has been writing to" the thirty-four deputy oil inspectors "urging, and almost instructing them to do whatever they could in their respective localities to secure members of the Legislature opposed to me."[17]

Like the surveyors general, the state oil inspector earned sizeable fees from the regulated industry, paid his expenses and his deputies' fees, contributed a large sum to the party, and pocketed the rest. Here was another Republican rake-off. In 1894, Foote netted "the comfortable sum of $16,870.73." Much of it went to pay Republican campaign expenses, probably the expenses of anti-Washburn legislative candidates whom Foote recruited.[18] Almost as valuable as this war chest was the small army of deputies, who performed political services as they traveled and inspected. Nelson also appointed the deputies, and could demand their loyalty.[19]

Writing to Washburn, Nelson innocently denied any knowledge of Foote's movements, and promised to find out the truth. When Foote admitted working against Washburn and offered his resignation, Nelson refused to accept it. If unaware of Foote's movements, which seems unlikely, he was not opposed to them. Washburn remained convinced that Foote was "secretly plotting" and committing "such outrages."[20]

He suspected Norwegian Americans of secretly plotting anti-Washburn legislative nominations. An Otter Tail county supporter warned him that "the only thing [he] had to fear was a movement on the part of the Norwegians friendly to Nelson."[21] He was pleased to hear that "only one Norwegian" had been nominated in Fillmore county. Still, he warned Hale, "You had better see Kittleson and Andrew Haugen, and some other of the more prominent Norwegians, and ask them to keep a sharp lookout as to the talk among that nationality."[22] A Freeborn county supporter advised Hale that if Washburn "had some good active discreet Norwegian friend, who could spend a few days in this co[unty] he could find out what was going on, and also do him much good in the rural towns."[23]

Washburn's suspicions were not unfounded. In Goodhue county, a large turnout of Scandinavian Americans from the rural towns and townships nominated the surprise candidate, who went on to support Nelson for the Senate.[24] In Polk county, "the Norwegians were out in force. It was the largest convention we ever had in this county and two thirds of the delegates were Norwegian." Here, the county-seat elite lost control when Norwegian-American farmers flooded in to the convention in unexpected numbers. Polk's losing old-stock legislative candidate bitterly complained of Nelson's "dictations" and "active part" in the result.[25]

To counter Scandinavian Americans' and state employees' work for Nelson, Washburn had money, well-placed friends, and *past* appointments to federal positions. However, he could not promise *future* federal jobs, then controlled by a Democratic president and a Democratic Congress. He could offer campaign con-

tributions to legislative candidates. He assured a Fergus Falls editor, "If you can absolutely commit the two members nominated
for the House in your County, I think some of my friends here
would feel like contributing a small amount to your County
Committee." But he wanted this "kept very quiet."[26] Several candidates wrote to him or to Hale to ask for money.[27] The *quid pro
quo* was a pledge to vote for Washburn.

Dr. A.C. Wedge, a Washburn supporter in Albert Lea, could
not secure such pledges without a definite statement of non-
candidacy from Nelson. In strongly Norwegian Freeborn county,
he reported, "there is a disposition among the leaders among the
Norwegians to be non committal, perhaps because they do not
know but Gov. Nelson may be a candidate." Wedge suspected a
"quiet scheme even in this county to get a delegation in his
[Nelson's] favor." Washburn must secure a definite Nelson statement.[28] For months Republican leaders had been seeking that
very thing. They badgered Nelson to make a statement and announce his support of Washburn. Accusing him of a secret Senate
candidacy, the *Minneapolis Journal* and the *Minneapolis Tribune*
wanted a Sherman-like statement denying that he was—or
would ever be interested in becoming—a candidate against
Minneapolis' senator.

Wedge's letter produced results. Just a week before Freeborn's
convention, Nelson and Washburn appeared in Albert Lea for the
Freeborn county fair on Friday, September 21. Arriving late on the
afternoon train, Nelson largely missed the chance to join
University dairy expert Professor T.L. Haecker in praising
Freeborn's dairying success—which he had praised at Argyle.
Instead, he probably had Washburn and the Senate on his mind.
During a heavy thunderstorm that reduced attendance, they both
spoke that evening in the courtroom in the county courthouse.
Here, Nelson finally testified on the often-avoided question of his
senatorial intentions.[29]

There was no court reporter present, nor any written text, so
Nelson's exact words were later disputed. Very likely tipped off

206

that he would make a statement, the *Minneapolis Journal* printed a front-page report, credited to "Special to the *Journal*." That meant written by a news stringer or correspondent (not a *Journal* reporter), perhaps a local politician friendly to Washburn. The strongly pro-Washburn *Journal* featured the story because it appeared to contain a Nelson statement of non-candidacy.[30] The *Journal* story was phrased with extreme care, like a question put by a prosecutor to eliminate ambiguities: "The governor declared frankly and unequivocally and in the most public way before a large audience that he was not, never had been, and should not be a candidate for the United States senate." It paraphrased him: "He had been accused, he said, of being a candidate for the senate and the governorship at the same time. That was not true. He was a candidate for governor. He wanted to be elected governor, and if elected expected to serve out his term. But he was not, had not been, and should not be, a candidate for the senate. He hoped that some such man as Senator Washburn would be elected to fill that seat."[31]

That was the pro-Washburn paraphrase. But Washburn's and Nelson's supporters later agreed that his exact words in closing were: "to elect your Republican legislative ticket, so as to send my friend Washburn back to the United States senate, or if you do not like him, send some other good Republican."[32] That was Nelson the skilled lawyer, whose comments were neither frank nor unequivocal, but full of double meaning, curious omissions, and curious additions like "some other good Republican" and "some such man." He likely uttered them to put Washburn off guard. Very literally, he *was* only a candidate for governor. Since he could not know whom legislators would elect senator, he "expected" to complete his second term.

Albert Lea's Populist newspaper gave a more realistic interpretation. To be sure, he "expressly denied" being a candidate, and "declared the Republicans should re-elect senator Washburn 'or some other good man.'" Still, "officeholders appointed by Gov. Nelson" and others "throughout the state are working like

207

beavers to elect him governor and to the senate." Yes, he said he was "not a candidate," but "[n]either was D.M. Sabin when he ousted Windom" in 1883. "No one doubts that keen Knute would accept the senatorship if his diligent friends should succeed in controlling it and tender it to him."[33]

The November 6th election resolved none of these ambiguities, since the Senate seat was not on the ballot. Focus shifted to legislators-elect, to their faithfulness to their pledges, and to who might be tempting them to renege.

Washburn was unconvinced by Nelson's testimony at Albert Lea—or by the *Journal*'s interpretation of it.[34] Nor was Nelson his only possible opponent. Surrounded by several, he tried desperately to determine from whom the blow might come.

November and December were full of intrigue and suspicion. Two men went up to Moorhead to spy out ex-congressman Solomon G. Comstock's intentions.[35] Washburn tried to determine the positions of Lieutenant Governor Clough, former senator Sabin, whom Washburn had ousted in 1889, and former governor Merriam, among others.[36] Through third parties, Nelson called on others to do their duty and run against Washburn. His strategy was to block Washburn from gaining a majority, then to slide in as the choice of the Republican caucus. He sent a Gustavus Adolphus college professor to New Ulm to tempt John Lind to run. Angered that Nelson cast him as a stalking horse, Lind resigned from the University's Board of Regents in protest.[37] Two of Nelson's state officials wrote to Comstock to flatter and encourage. Soon the senatorial bee was buzzing around Comstock's head. When the Moorhead man asked about Nelson's intentions, one official innocently replied, "I have been unable to get any information as to how the Governor feels."[38]

On December 1, the *Chicago Tribune* reported Washburn in deep trouble, with many senate candidates and Nelson the leading one. No, responded the *Minneapolis Tribune*, Nelson had pledged at Austin [Albert Lea] not to run, and "Nelson is known to be an honorable man and he could not violate [his pledge] without infamy."[39] The subterranean warfare continued in the press. Sabin showed up in Washington, gossiping that "at the proper time Governor Nelson would be definitely placed in the field" as a candidate and "would be a winner." Washburn declared there could be "no possible foundation for such a report," for Nelson was "an honorable man" who was "not capable of anything of the kind attributed to him in the story."[40] The term "honorable man" was a thinly-veiled warning of the charges of dishonor which awaited a Nelson candidacy.

Privately, Washburn characterized Nelson in quite different terms. When told that he had discussed his possible candidacy with a state senator, Washburn erupted, "The young man seems absolutely to have lost his head."[41] (Washburn was 63 years old and Nelson, 52.) Sarcastically using the name "Moses" for the man Norwegian Americans looked to as their political leader, he ridiculed "the great claims of 'Moses' Nelson" to have saved the Republican ticket in 1892 and 1894. "I think it about time that the conceit be taken out [of] the young man. He is 'roosting too high.'"[42]

Over the holidays, the subterranean scheming erupted above ground. Shortly before Christmas, Comstock announced his candidacy. Many saw Nelson's hand here, for he had been a strong Nelson supporter for nearly twenty years, and was Nelson's chosen successor in Congress in 1888. A few days later, Congressman James McCleary of Mankato entered the contest. For Christmas, the governor's appointees gave him "a handsome silver fruit bowl" in appreciation of his services. This semblance of a going-away present to the recently-reelected governor seemed odd, but then his appointees had been working like beavers to win him a greater reward requiring his departure.[43] On December 27, while he was home for the holidays, the *Alexandria Post-News* endorsed Comstock: rural Minnesotans supported him "more fully than any person mentioned except Gov. Nelson."[44] Possibly only a hometown paper's obligatory praise for the local hero, that remark was interpreted by the *Minneapolis Tribune* as a sign of

Nelson's "arrant treachery and bad faith" in abandoning his Albert Lea "pledge." That January 2nd editorial also belittled Nelson's reelection: he would have been defeated "had not Senator Washburn and his friends worked for him with a will."[45] With that, the thunderstorm broke.

That night, Nelson and his advisers met in his hotel room and decided that he must declare his candidacy. Comstock and McCleary could not by themselves prevent Washburn from gaining a majority of Republican legislators.[46] Rumors of Nelson's candidacy circulated in the Windsor Hotel lobby the next morning. A state senator, and then Washburn, headed to the capitol to confront the governor about the rumors. Washburn began by restating his expectation that Nelson would support him. "Scratching his head for a moment and looking down at the carpet," Nelson answered, "'Well, I don't know about that. Last night I made up my mind to be a candidate myself.'" The senator cited his Albert Lea speech and several of his letters disclaiming any intentions of running. Nelson insisted he had never promised to support Washburn, and explained his last-minute candidacy as an angry reaction to the *Minneapolis Tribune*'s and other Minneapolis newspapers' abuse of him. Though busy behind the scenes directing the Minneapolis newspapers' coverage of the senatorial issue, Washburn now denied responsibility for press coverage. After more debate, Washburn left. That afternoon, Nelson told a *Tribune* reporter, "The *Tribune* made me a candidate yesterday."[47] The *Tribune* editorial may have sparked a premature announcement, but it hardly prompted Nelson's candidacy.

The *St. Paul Pioneer Press* correctly predicted "one of the hottest [fights] that has ever been fought" in Minnesota "for a seat in the United States senate."[48] For three weeks—all day and most of the night—Nelson and Washburn fought for legislators' support by flattery, pressure, and intimidation. The Three-Week War was also the Hotel Campaign, for "the seat of war" was St. Paul's major hotels, primarily the Windsor and the Merchants, where all four candidates had their headquarters.[49] By Saturday, January 5, the battle was on: "All day long the crowds surged about the Windsor and Merchants hotel lobbies and up to a late hour in the evening, the Windsor was especially thronged. A couple of Salvation Army girls vainly endeavored to sell their 'War Cry' in the Windsor lobbies and the various headquarters. . . .the republicans did not care to secure salvation."[50]

Republicans divided into two hostile camps. Congressman Loren Fletcher, former congressman Lind, Charles A. Pillsbury, Major Hale, and Republican luminaries from Minneapolis led councils of war at Washburn headquarters.[51] Lieutenant Governor Clough, Tams Bixby, Inspector Foote, Henry F. Brown, and former senator Sabin led Nelson's forces. The Washburn camp sent a spy to loiter around Nelson headquarters. One night at 11:30 PM, he reported, "Sabin and H.F. Brown [came] out of Nelsons private room where they had been having a consultation." Minus Nelson, his aides then played shuffleboard and pool until past midnight, and "they were drinking freely as they played."[52] Nelson was extremely busy receiving many callers, one of whom asked, "I wonder when Gov. Nelson sleeps?". "For three weeks" he and his aides "went to bed about two o'clock in the morning and were up very early, averaging but four hours sleep a night."[53] Typically, he was very closemouthed to the press: "We are saying nothing but sawing wood. In a contest like this we must keep at work, and keep our plans to ourselves."[54]

Legislators were the wood, and the sawing took different forms with different legislators. Both Nelson and Washburn promised government jobs in exchange for votes, though Nelson had more jobs to offer. The governor reportedly promised the positions of state prison warden, commissioner of labor statistics, and superintendent of the state census to supporters or their friends.[55] The names of several workers (or relatives of workers) in the Hotel Campaign were on a list of Nelson's appointees leaked the week after the balloting.[56] Washburn's men used their influence in Hennepin county to lobby for the reappointment of a state senator's brother as the county "poor farm overseer," but the senator voted for Nelson.[57] Washburn newspapers strongly attacked Nelson's use of state patronage: "Gov. Nelson peddled out, disbursed, and misappropriated" his powers, which he used "as a commissary department" in "the most wanton logrolling with official patronage that ever disgraced a state."[58] That biased account exaggerated the logrolling. State jobs were limited in number.

"Stories are going around in the [hotel] lobbies," reported the *Minneapolis Journal*, "connecting Gov. Nelson with boodle, but they are unsubstantiated." Yet, when the Washburn spy tried to entice a Nelson worker into offering a bribe to Representative John Dahl, who "was very poor," the worker replied that "the Nelson backers wouldn't let him have a bit of money to buy votes with." Still, unsubstantiated charges circulated that both camps were buying votes.[59] In December, Washburn had speculated that some legislators encouraging anti-Washburn candidates were "simply waiting for boodle" from him: "The idea that this thing [boodle] can be talked of in [this] shameless way . . . is simply a disgrace to our State."[60] After the Three-Week War, Washburn reported that fellow lumberman Earnest Arnold "has expended quite a large amount of money in my interests, much larger than he had any authority to do from me."[61] Most likely, it was not all spent on hotel rooms, liquor, meals, and cigars. Some was probably spent in less legitimate ways.[62]

Also suspected but unsubstantiated is James J. Hill's role. For years, historian William Watts Folwell sought evidence that Hill's influence and money were used against Washburn, builder of the rival Soo Line. By the start of the Hotel Campaign, Hill had left for Europe, which only proves where he was and not what he did. His son-in-law, Samuel Hill, probably was in the anti-Washburn camp, but Samuel years later wrote, "As far as I know J.J. never put up a dollar." During the "present contest," reported the *St. Paul Morning Call*, "the absence of any people connected with the Great Northern has been particularly noticeable about the hotels."[63]

Constituents' opinions were the main weapons used to convince legislators. Calling the election of a United States senator by the legislature undemocratic, as one historian has, is an exaggeration, especially if other elections are termed democratic by comparison.[64] Few late-nineteenth-century elections were as democratic as idealists claimed. In the Republican party, which dominated politics in Minnesota, county-seat elites, editors, and political jobholders dominated elections for congressmen, governors, and state legislators almost as effectively as elections to the Senate. These "wirepullers who manage the people and act in their name" managed and acted in all elections.[65] St. Paul's *Midway News* correctly argued that there was no difference in elections: "The people think that if permitted to vote directly on United States senators they then could knock out the boodlers, but they have every opportunity of a direct vote on members of the legislature and they can't knock out the boodlers right at home!"[66] In fact, the people did have an indirect, limited role in the Three-Week War. Washburn and Nelson "wirepullers" strained every nerve to pull public opinion to their side.

They used several tactics. County-seat leaders circulated pro-Nelson or pro-Washburn petitions. Pelican Rapids sent both kinds to St. Paul. An elitist tactic, petitions were often circulated only among "business men and leading citizens" or "leading Republicans."[67] Sent to the Twin Cities' dailies, they gave the impression of overwhelming popular support. To obtain greater democratic legitimacy, Washburn and Nelson supporters held public meetings and passed resolutions favoring their candidate. Such meetings were hardly democratic indicators of local public opinion. The *New Ulm Review* charged, "A few people got together here at private invitation . . . which they ridiculously figured as a mass meeting" and endorsed Nelson. At Little Falls, a few county-seat Republicans held a "mass meeting" in an office and passed pro-Nelson resolutions.[68] To create a popular pretext for several Washburn-pledged legislators to switch to Nelson, the Nelson forces arranged a meeting in south Minneapolis at Tollefson's Hall. They brought railroad workers, "Clough's followers," and sawmill workers from outside the district to the hall. Amidst "many exciting tilts and knock down arguments" and considerable "pandemonium," several pro-Nelson resolutions were finally passed—or so the chairman ruled.[69] Two of the legislators ended up voting for Nelson despite their convention pledges.

More effective were personal visits, group or individual, to the hotel lobbies. The *St. Paul Morning Call* reported the arrival of "a small army of country supporters of Washburn." "Urgent appeals have been sent all over the state to the Washburn strikers to come in when the legislature reassembles" after a weekend recess to counteract pro-Nelson petitions flooding into St. Paul.[70] Several days later, "The trains . . . brought into St. Paul leading Nelson backers from towns and counties where some of the more influential of the unpledged members live. . . . The visiting delegates are brought face to face with their representatives, and then the fun begins. The visitor says that he is just from home, and that within 24 hours there has been a great change of sentiment, Nelson now being the general choice of the people. The visitor, being a personal friend to the member, and not wanting him to make a mistake, got on the first train for St. Paul in order to . . . advise him to declare for Nelson."[71] More than twenty Granite Falls residents "went cityward to see the senatorial battle." The contesting forces were rumored to be offering free railroad tickets from Granite Falls to St. Paul. Little Falls's "mass meeting" sent a six-man committee to "the field of action," including future congressman Charles A. Lindbergh. New Ulm's John C. Randolph was "in St. Paul keeping close tab of the political chessboard" and did not "expect to return home until a senator is elected."[72]

The Nelson-Washburn contest aroused great interest, despite its location in hotel lobbies and legislative halls. In Le Sueur, it was the "chief political topic of conversation and wherever men meet the subject is discussed."[73] Talk was cheap, but some could afford the time and expense to go to St. Paul. Once there, "strikers" often misrepresented themselves as spokesmen for the entire county.[74]

214

They acted on instructions from Washburn and Nelson operatives seeking to maximize favorable publicity. Meanwhile, the candidates gave directions, wrote letters to country supporters, and met with individual legislators to "saw" them night and day.

For those being "sawed" the Three Week War was especially difficult. Many faced enormous pressure from several sides. One Republican leader advised a new legislator, "You can no more please all of them than you can fly."[75] Early on, legislators side-stepped the pressure by pleading that they could not decide until they could go home and talk to the voters.[76] A long weekend recess in mid-January allowed them "to get at the sentiment of the constituents," but they came back "forced to the conclusion that it was so mixed that they were unsettled in their minds just what to do."[77] Some legislators' declarations that constituents' overwhelming support for one candidate had made up their minds cannot be taken at face value.[78] It sounded good to say you voted according to public opinion back home, but which public was consulted? When Senator Jones returned to Morris "to feel the pulse of the Republicans of Stevens county," which wrists did he grab?[79] Returning legislators may have consulted only key financial backers, county officeholders, or the county-seat "ring."

Despite the wirepulling, Minnesotans had some chance to express their views. The *Red Wing Daily Republican* approved of "this declaration of their will by the voters of the several legislative districts." It was the "nearest approach" to direct, popular election of a United States senator.[80] Newspapers also conducted "man on the street" interviews.[81]

The arguments used to sway public opinion were many. Pro-Washburn men accused Nelson of "bad faith" in reneging on his Albert Lea pledge and "hoggishness" in seeking two offices at once. One pro-Washburn editor-legislator cleverly compared "our Governor Knute" to the arrogant eleventh-century King Canute, who "bade the advancing waves . . . stand still": he "will either have to retreat before the advancing waves of the popular will or be drowned by the indignation of a wrathful people."[82]

Nelson's supporters countered that Washburn, unlike Davis in 1892, did not receive an explicit endorsement at the 1894 Republican convention—partly because he was too aristocratic. And Nelson deserved the Senate seat for his valiant rescue of Republicanism from Populism.[83] They circulated stories of his Civil War heroism, and contrasted it with Washburn's wartime patronage job. They argued that rural Minnesota deserved a United States senator, and capitalized on the perception that Minneapolis was arrogant in insisting that it must have one.[84]

The one argument rarely used openly was that Scandinavian Americans must have a United States senator. During the three weeks, the Norwegian-American press in particular was noticeably silent on Nelson's ethnicity—except to defend it against Yankee sneering about the "little Norwegian."[85]

Some crude attempts to ridicule Nelson and his Scandinavian-American supporters were made, in rough dialect. One featured a Swedish-American farmer nominating him for President: "Knud Nelson . . . hay ben hard vorker . . . Any man like Knud Nelson, who can geep chinz bugs and kokle bur outen 640 aker land on Mansota can run hol United Stades like top." If Knute was nominated, "ve carry efery stade north side Mansota."[86] The *Waterville Advance* had Nelson telling Washburn, "Ay baen an dase country for long times, baen civilized an baen pruty slick feller al-round. En ay skol get ma plenty vote for U.S. senator . . . de best yob any Norwegian fellow can have in des country."[87]

Despite ridicule and claims that they were "roosting too high," the *Fergus Falls Ugeblad* insisted that Scandinavian Americans could "take this thing quietly." "The Scandinavian population's fate in Minnesota" was not "bound to either Senator Washburn or Governor Nelson," who were only politicians.[88] That disinterested pose helped to defuse opponents' charge that Nelson was using the "nationality issue."[89] Ethnic pride could backfire if publicly trumpeted. Not taking things quietly, one Norwegian American privately confessed that when he heard of Nelson's candidacy, he "became nearly altogether nervous with suspense over the out-

216

come," and fretted "that it should perhaps end in disaster."[90] Quietly, many Norwegian Americans worked for Nelson. One fellow Vossing from Becker county offered to help, though "we are too few of us against the opposition."[91] Iver Davidson, a seven-foot, one-inch Norwegian American, could not avoid public notice when he came to the Windsor hotel to lobby for Nelson.[92] In Granite Falls, Norwegian-American campaigning for Nelson caused "much bitterness" and "ill feeling" among pro-Washburn "Americans." A few, like Pastor M. Falk Gjertsen, proclaiming himself "a loyal Minneapolitan," supported Washburn.[93]

Nelson quietly used the "nationality issue" with some Scandinavian-American legislators, but it backfired when the Washburn newspapers publicized his efforts. State Senator E.K. Roverud told Nelson that he was pledged to vote for Washburn. The Governor insisted that, as a fellow Norwegian, Roverud's vote should rightfully be his. When State Senator Larson gave Nelson the same message, he exploded in anger: "'I am a Norwegian,' he exclaimed wrathfully. 'If I were a Swede, you would vote for me in a minute. That is the way with you Swedes, but I will show you yet who is master here.'"[94] Larson stuck with Washburn in the caucus and the formal legislative vote. Roverud switched to Nelson on the latter.[95]

Republican legislators caucused in the House chamber on Friday evening, January 18, for the first test of strength. The evening before, three reputedly pro-Washburn legislators from Duluth declared for Nelson. Early Friday, Major Hale noted in his diary, "Matters assume a very serious aspect this morning — and grave doubts may be expressed. Caucus tonight."[96]

Witnessed by Twin Cities reporters and seventy-five country editors, the caucus confirmed Hale's doubts. With 72 votes (out of 141) needed to nominate, Washburn picked up only 61 on the first ballot, to Nelson's 45 — and 35 scattered among other candidates. "Outside, in the lobby," sending notes in to legislators, "the Nelson managers were in active control of their forces within." On the second ballot, having fulfilled their Washburn pledges, several Scandinavian-American legislators switched to Nelson: Boxrud, Ellingsen, Anderson. Nelson picked up ten votes while Washburn lost two. On the third ballot, editor Jens Grøndahl of Red Wing's *Nordstjernen* switched to Nelson. By midnight and the sixth ballot, Nelson led Washburn 60 to 55, and observers expected his nomination on the seventh or eighth ballot. However, a motion to adjourn came "so suddenly . . . the Nelson managers in the lobby were utterly unable to rally their men," and the caucus unexpectedly voted to adjourn *sine die*. The Minneapolis newspapers put up a brave front ("MADE NO NOMINATION!"), but Hale confessed, "Bed at 4 this a.m. W.D. [Washburn] collapsed as usual."[97]

The contest now went to the full legislature, but insiders knew that Washburn was finished. Whether Nelson or a compromise candidate would win was still uncertain. "A dismayed feeling very apparent," noted Hale.[98] On Tuesday, January 22, the House and Senate met separately to vote. Nelson's total increased to 62, while Washburn's fell to 54. Sensing defeat, Washburn's friends held an evening meeting, discussed running John Lind, and tried to form an anti-Nelson alliance, but Comstock rebuffed them.[99]

The next day, a joint session met at noon. *Nordstjernen* reported, "The Capitol was full of people, hundreds stood outside and waited for the result, and the greatest excitement prevailed." Inside, the clerk called the roll of senators first. The break to Nelson came when the Senate president, Frank A. Day, rose to switch from Washburn to "Knute Nelson, the man of destiny." Many solons followed Day's lead until Nelson reached the 85th, and decisive, vote. His victory brought "a thunderstorm of applause from all parts of the great hall." A committee fetched the governor from his office. The "supremest applause" came when the short Nelson "became visible to all eyes" by mounting the speaker's stand.[100]

His acceptance speech was very brief, hardly more than two or three minutes. There was "a slight tremor in his voice as he began to speak"—perhaps he thought of Ingebjørg, Mary Dillon, the

218

long path that led to this moment. It had been a "notable" fight. In a considerable understatment he claimed, "I have never known of one less bitter." He praised Washburn as "an excellent and a good senator." He closed by looking to the future: "There is something elevating about a great office, and I hope that I may be influenced as some of my predecessors have been." After the speech, "in a very joyous frame of mind," the senator-elect "held an informal reception in the governor's rooms." He shook hands for two hours with friendly legislators and onlookers.[101]

The Minneapolis newspapers were certain Nelson needed some "elevating." The *Times* charged that, in stealing the Senate seat, "Nelson has displayed the piratical strain of his Viking ancestors." The *Tribune* thought it was time "for party, press and people to gently draw the curtain" on this three-act tragedy of treachery and corruption.[102] "Wond[er]ing what has hit us," Hale exclaimed to his diary, "Glad it's over." Reportedly very ill, the exhausted Washburn took to his bed at Fair Oaks.[103] Washburn supporters and newspapers called for the direct, popular election of United States senators.[104]

Outraged at talk of piratical Vikings, *Minneapolis Tidende* charged pro-Washburn Yankees with harboring anti-immigrant, anti-Norwegian prejudices. It reminded "the dear native-born" of immigrants' equal rights. "All citizens cannot come from Maine or bear a name with so aristocratic a ring to it as Washburn's." Those bitter "because a Washburn was beaten by a Scandinavian" must learn that "no one can obtain a high office in this state without Scandinavians' direct or indirect consent."[105]

Now, Norwegian-American pride could safely burst forth. A Senate seat was the highest office a foreign-born American could obtain, and Knute Nelson was the first Scandinavian American to reach the United States Senate. Moses had entered the political Promised Land. Even the Populist-leaning *Fergus Falls Ugeblad* could not hide its pride over the "little Norwegian."[106] Even the former Koshkonong minister, J.A. Ottesen, supporter of the 1860s slavery position Nelson hated, wrote the senator-elect, "I think

219

that was a splendid victory for us."[107] At strongly Norwegian-American Spring Grove, townspeople celebrated at a large public meeting held under a sign which read "godt gjort" (well done). Nelson's ethnic pride also soared. Writing to Rasmus B. Anderson two days after his election, he exulted, "It was indeed a great and glorious victory. The battle was a hard but short one against great odds, but the hot riotous Viking blood prevailed."[108]

It was Nelson's personal victory and a factional, anti-Washburn win, as much as an ethnic victory for hot Viking blood. Behind the scenes, ethnic support convinced some legislators. Yet, the anti-Washburn, anti-Minneapolis faction and Nelson's state employees gave him the initial strength which made his candidacy feasible. In the 1890s, Minnesotans' sensitivity to use of "the nationality issue" limited its usefulness as a *public* argument. Though individual legislators made the final decision, the Three-Week War was fought in public, in the press, with appeals to public opinion. Here, "the nationality issue" could not be raised without inviting a backlash. Nelson had to have other weapons: his 1892-1894 services to the party, his Civil War record, his residence in rural Minnesota, and his control of state patronage.

Speaking at a victory banquet given by Alexandria's Young Men's Republican Club at the Letson House, the senator-elect denied any desire to be elevated above his fellow townsmen: "He said he didn't feel a bit different than he did when he lived in a claim shanty. He felt as one of the boys and as he walked up from his home to town, he found it hard to realize that he had ever held public office; and conclud[ed], 'I don't want you to call me honorable, or governor, or senator, but Uncle Knute.'"[109] He could no longer be quite "one of the boys," but "Uncle Knute" was certain to be quite a different senator than the aristocratic Yankee from Fair Oaks.

Eleven

The Senator at Home and Abroad

Knute Nelson would yet have to prove himself a senator worthy of the elevation accorded him by the 1895 legislature. But not immediately. Congress would not meet until December, 1895. He could slacken his pace, relax, and enjoy his victory. In the spring he traveled to Deerfield for a banquet celebrating his elevation. He also spoke at Albion Academy. The first Norwegian-American senator was becoming a national, even international, celebrity. Tiny Evanger sent him greetings and praise for the honor he had brought to Norway.[1]

There was no question he would be a different kind of senator than the aristocratic Washburn. Journalists came to Alexandria and, later, to his home in Washington, D.C., to interview him and to introduce him to a national audience. A *St. Paul Globe* reporter wrote a human interest story about the senator at home. Saw in hand, he supervised a carpenter building a lean-to for his favorite horse, Lizzie. He showed the reporter his law office, where he was winding up legal cases, his 550-acre farm, and his favorite fishing spot ("He . . . was always ready to admit his fish were the smallest"). The self-described "drayhorse" could not completely relax. He was hard at work studying the currency question, yet would tell the reporter nothing about his views on it.[2]

221

Another visitor gave a rare description of Nicholina. "He has a true helpmeet in his most estimable wife" who was "a lady of refinement and tact." "She does not pretend to be fashionable," but she keeps house with "tact" and "grace."[3]

Seeing him in Washington, eastern reporters stressed other sides of the Nelson character. One was impressed by his "Joshua Whitcomb" beard: he looked like a "canny New Englander." "With his upper lip shaven, his mouth has a fair field to show its habitual smile." This New England newspaper emphasized his excellent, accent-free English, his reputed $10,000 annual income as a lawyer, and his "abstemious" habits. His manners were agrarian: comfortable, direct, with homey and rugged sentences. He abhorred "society," liked the theater and books, and told tales of the Vikings. He wore a slouch hat, was "fond of tobacco in the plug form," and ate his American pie with a knife, not a fork. Once the session began, they were impressed by his workmanlike attitude. At 7:00 A.M., he was first for breakfast at the Ebbitt House on Capitol Hill. He had a way of pumping people for information that would have made him "a first class reporter."[4]

Before this Norwegian Yankee strode into the Senate in December, he scored an important symbolic accomplishment. He translated Norway's amended 1814 Eidsvoll constitution into English. Apparently the first, his translation was printed in *Skandinaven* and in the *St. Paul Pioneer Press* in full, and published as a pamphlet. Especially gratifying was the *Pioneer Press*'s two-column editorial praising Norway's enlightened and liberal constitution. Nelson had proved his mother country's democratic credentials to old-stock Americans. The fact that his own mother was born in 1814 added to the personal symbolism. Yet he had brought Norway praise in a very lawyerly way, by translating a constitution, not by engaging in boastful demagoguery. Norway was praised for her resemblance to "the finest and best government on earth" (America's), not for antiquities of little practical use. And, this praise came soon after Norway's Storting backed away from its increasing demands for de facto independence

"THERE ARE MOM ENTS, ETC., ETC."
The Legislator Arrives Home to See What His Constituents Think of
the Senatori al Question.

"The Legislator arrives home." Cartoon in St. Paul Daily Pioneer Press, *January 13, 1895.*

from Sweden. Nelson may have sought a symbolic reassertion of Norway's self-rule after the humiliating retreat of spring and summer 1895; the threat of a Norwegian-Swedish war was eerily reminiscent of 1814.[5]

If he understood the symbolic importance the Eidsvoll constitution had for him, he failed to understand the symbolic importance the free silver issue had for Populists and Silver Democrats. The nation was bitterly divided over the unlimited ("free") coinage of silver, an inflationary proposal supported by debtors, farmers, and the silver-mining industry.

As he had promised, his first Senate speech, on December 31, 1895, was on this issue. It was scholarly, almost like a lecture. It convinced fellow senators that he spoke as a hard-working fact finder, not a demagogue. His approach was full of sound economic sense: most business was transacted with checks and drafts, not dollar bills or coins; a sound paper currency was more vital than limitless silver coins; the banking system must be modernized to create an elastic money supply, expanding with an expanding economy; retiring greenbacks from circulation would decrease the money supply and hurt the economy.[6]

Yet he did not address the broader issue of monopolistic concentration of economic power, for which "free silver" was the Populists' symbolic answer. He avoided conservative, "gold bug" extremism, but his practical tinkering with the monetary system would still leave economic concentration in place.

Refusing the luxury of a leisurely Senate apprenticeship, Nelson acted as if each year was the year he was up for reelection. He had reason to be concerned. Many Minnesota Republicans opposed Nelson's successor, Governor David Clough, in his bid for election to that office. Clough had to go first in asking voters to ratify the 1895 maneuver putting Nelson in the Senate and him in the governor's office. Nelson would have his turn in 1900-1901. Opposed to Clough was the "Committee of One Hundred" Minneapolis Republicans, the business elite, diamond stickpin types: Washburn, Major Hale, the flour-milling leaders—

Pillsburys, Peaveys, Bells—and others. On his copy of a petition they published in the *Minneapolis Journal* Nelson scrawled, "List of Hennepin Co. Raiders—on me and Clough."[7] His defeat of Washburn had rankled them and they were determined to beat Clough in 1896, then Nelson in 1901.

He walked a fine line, sufficiently anti-Populist to appeal to Republican regulars, but sympathetic to agrarian complaints to remind farmers that he differed from Washburn and the Minneapolitans.[8] In an April, 1896, Senate speech, he attacked a proposal to close smaller post offices and consolidate services in the larger ones. He claimed that this would result in "but one postmaster in a county, and that at the county seat, and he would be a sort of autocrat." That led to business consolidation and department stores: "the devil fish of modern society" these stores "injure the real business conditions of our cities."[9] This localistic message appealed to voters in the townships and to Main Street merchants worried about Sears, Ward's, and chain stores. He fought for dairy farmers with a speech attacking "filled cheese" (skim milk and leaf lard, which *Skandinaven* called *Humbug-Ost*) and proposing a tax on it. When a senator objected to the many costly pictures of cows in a government-printed book on dairy farming, he defended its usefulness to farmers.[10]

Not forgetting his roots, he delivered a lengthy speech on the Senate floor on immigration—on May 14, just in time for the Syttende Mai reports in Norwegian-language newspapers. He defended immigrants against criticisms from senators seeking to restrict immigration. Crammed full of statistics, his speech showed how few immigrants ended up in prison, and how much of America's success was due to their labors. Modestly omitting his own Scandinavians, he recited European history to prove that Germans, Italians, Russians, Poles, Hungarians, and Slavs had much to offer the United States, and that peoples of mixed ethnicity were more vigorous. He closed with one of his favorite homilies: "they bear a love for the country of their adoption . . . . Smoke her pipe in peace, bear her tomahawk in war." *Skandinaven*

225

printed the speech in full minus some statistical tables—in Norwegian.[11] Here he could appeal to Minnesota's many immigrant voters.

Nelson was laying a solid foundation for his reelection campaign four years later. Senators and voters learned that he spoke only when he was well prepared. Mary Dillon's prize pupil often turned in a ten-page speech when only a three-page one was expected. The intellectually lazy gave him a wide berth on the Senate floor, where he was a debater not to be taken lightly.

However, his Senate speeches were overshadowed by the most dramatic presidential campaign in American history. "Free silver" became the battle cry of the united Democrats and Populists (Demopops), and their barnstorming, eloquent young champion William Jennings Bryan. The dramatic "Battle of the Standards" (silver vs. gold) pitted Bryan against staid William McKinley of Ohio. In this political Armageddon, Nelson was again summoned to his battle station to fight Populism among the Scandinavian-American farmers of rural Minnesota.

With the fiery Demopop orator Mary Elizabeth Lease scheduled to give a Friday night speech in Alexandria, the Young Men's Republican Club hastily summoned Nelson to respond on Saturday night. The "Kansas Pythoness" of Populism could not go unanswered in Uncle Knute's home town. With her "raven black hair" and "remarkable voice," Lease was a "striking" and "effective" speaker. She was "a master of invective" who could "abuse to the queen's taste," according to one local newspaper report. Perhaps reluctant to pit his matter-of-fact speaking style too openly against Lease's stormy one, Nelson requested just "a quiet talk" to the club, but popular demand forced "a big mass meeting" in the opera house. He cited statistics, recited monetary history, and discussed the "free silver" issue in a dispassionate manner.[12] Who won this back-to-back duel was totally in the eye of the beholder.

Nelson then went on a grueling campaign tour: forty-eight speeches in Minnesota, three each in Wisconsin and South

Dakota, and two in North Dakota during a nine-week period. Clough survived the challenge of Demopop, represented by Swedish-American John Lind. Yet his 3,652-vote margin hardly reassured Nelson about *his* reelection chances. Lind won the Upper Country's Seventh District by nearly 8,000 votes, and the work of the Committee of One Hundred contributed to Clough's 3,000-vote defeat in Hennepin county.[13]

Upon his return to the Senate, Nelson hit upon an ingenious strategy to evade the wrath of Demopop farmers, who were often debtors. He wrote a federal bankruptcy law, which he offered as a substitute for a harsher Judiciary Committee version.[14] His bill emphasized voluntary bankruptcy declared by the debtor rather than forced bankruptcy demanded by creditors. Here, he could take a farmer-friendly stand on a subject in which he had expertise as a debt-collecting country lawyer. Here was the lawyer's answer to Demopop protest: "The country during the last four years has been in the midst of the hardest and most distressing times we have had in the memory of the oldest citizen. The people need help. [They] have been financially wrecked and stranded in the midst of hard times . . . and they ask a measure of relief at the present time . . . that those who are unable to pay their debts . . . shall have such legislation . . . as will give them a clearance and an opportunity to start in the world . . . instead of remaining inert under the shadows of [their] debts." Here was "a practical question," about which something could be done, unlike the "party questions" (currency and tariff) where opinions were hopelessly divided on party lines.[15] Here was even a chance to appeal to anti-lawyer sentiment, for Nelson's substitute drastically reduced the fees lawyers could extract from bankruptcy proceedings. Here Nelson spoke as a representative of the debtor West against the creditor East, many of whose senators favored the harsher, pro-creditor committee version. The issue was tailor-made for Knute Nelson.

Starting in late January, 1897, he painstakingly and patiently defended and amended his substitute bill when faced with other senators' objections. He compromised; he conceded minor points; he flattered and cajoled. In contrast to Populists' idealization of the producer, he praised the entrepreneur: "The men who create wealth and produce prosperity are the men who take their own means . . . [and] what they can borrow, and put it all into active employment . . . and furnish labor for other men." To these middle-class individualists, now paralyzed by debt, the Congress must say "in the language of the gospel, 'Take up thy bed and walk.'"[16] He secured Senate passage of his substitute in 1897, but the House passed the harsher Torrey bill. Nelson served on the conference committee in 1898 and obtained a conference report that leaned toward his recommendations. On June 24, 1898, the so-called Nelson Bankruptcy Act passed the Congress.[17] For years, filing bankruptcy was termed taking the "Nelson cure."

National excitement over the Spanish-American War almost completely overshadowed his impressive accomplishment. The Senate hurriedly debated the conference report, because its time was taken up with resolutions for the annexation of Hawaii. Passage of the report came as the country intently followed news reports of the American assault on Santiago, Cuba.[18] One week later, Theodore Roosevelt's Rough Riders charged up San Juan Hill. American expansion abroad and prosperity at home (not the "Nelson cure") would protect Nelson against the agrarian protest threatening his reelection.

The month before Congress declared war, Nelson predicted that result. Fearing war might damage "the agricultural and industrial interests of the Nation," James J. Hill cautioned Nelson and other senators against "ill advised haste." Nelson replied that "the demands of humanity and the national honor" outweighed "the prospective loss of a few dollars." For the anti-Populist Hill, he added a practical benefit of idealism: "A popular war might do more than anything else to relieve the country from the night mare of the free silver question. The success of Bryanism, Populism, and free silver would inflict infinitely more damage on this country than a short, sharp war with Spain."[19] Speaking during the Senate debate over the war resolution, he urged President McKinley to listen to "the sentiment of the American people" which favored intervention on behalf of the Cuban rebels.[20]

He enthusiastically supported the war effort. His nephew Henry Nelson of Deerfield was a volunteer serving, coincidentally, in the Fourth Wisconsin, Knute's old regiment. Writing to Søren Listoe after Admiral Dewey captured Manila, he now wanted more from the war than just a cure for Populism: "The conclusion of the war will find us in possession of Cuba, Porto Rico, and the Philippine Islands, and with a new inspiration never before known. Dewey's victory has put new ideas in our people, and I think the result will be that we will soon become one of the great powers of the world."[21]

The war lengthened the legislative session, complicated the 1898 campaign, and caused Nelson to postpone a planned visit to Norway, but it put new ideas in Americans' heads. It did not relieve the Minneapolitans' candidate for governor, William H. Eustis, of the nightmare of Populism. Running as a returned Spanish-American war veteran, John Lind soundly defeated Eustis, despite Nelson's regular campaign swing through the Populist Red River Valley.[22] Nelson worried that Eustis's defeat boded ill for him, but he had much greater rural popularity than the former Minneapolis mayor, Soo Line investor, and real-estate magnate.

To annex the Philippine and Hawaiian islands was the major new idea President McKinley laid before the Senate. The Hawaii decision was easy, but the Senate debate over ratification of the Treaty of Paris (involving acquisition of the Philippines) was a bitter and emotional one. Calling this a most unrepublican act of imperialism, anti-expansionists condemned the idea of the United States ruling a colony and denying it statehood or self-government. Philosopher William James charged that, in its greed for colonies, the old Republic of 1776 was ready to "puke up its ancient soul . . . in five minutes without a wink of squeamishness."[23]

On January 20, 1899, Nelson joined the Senate debate, and pro-

229

voked comments almost as disconcerting as James's metaphor. He began very decorously, as a constitutional lawyer defending the United States government's right to acquire territory by conquest, without intending to grant it statehood. Like a lawyer arguing corporations' right to marry and bear children, his argument drifted away from the concrete realities of the situation. It was another Nelson legal brief. He cited the Louisiana Purchase of 1803, the acquisition of Florida in 1819, and the conquest of California in 1848—but these lands were on the continent, contiguous to American territory, destined for statehood, and intended for settlement by American pioneer farmers. None of those conditions applied to the Philippines.[24]

Knute Nelson was a product of Civil War Republicanism. He was a nationalist who defended the national government's broad powers under the Constitution's "necessary and proper" clause (Article I, Section 8). He disputed anti-imperialists' argument that America could not rule colonies because the Declaration of Independence forbade taxation without representation and government without the consent of the governed. The Declaration "has never anywhere on the face of the earth been applied in its entirety." Women and minors could not vote, yet were taxed and governed anyway. To do the same to Filipinos was "no more unjust." Nelson traced opponents' squeamishness about acquiring territories back to Chief Justice Taney's opinion in the Dred Scott case. That ancestry was enough to condemn it in any Republican's eyes.[25]

Senator Mason of Illinois ended Nelson's soliloquy by asking if "he believes that outside of constitutional law . . . it is within the scope and policy of this Government to govern these people forever by force and without their consent."

Nelson objected, "That is not a practical question." "No one proposes to govern them in that way." Yet no one in the McKinley administration was setting a date for withdrawing American forces or for asking Filipinos' consent. Nelson turned to history to prove that England's rule over colonies had "served to increase

230

the liberties of Englishmen." It even increased Americans' liberties when they rebelled against it.

Mason interrupted to compare the acquisition of the Philippines to a hypothetical post-1783 French move to seize America "after she had helped us to our liberty." (America had enlisted the support of Filipinos rebelling against Spain to aid American forces fighting the Spanish in the islands.)

What exactly was the difference between the American patriots of 1776 and Filipino rebels in 1899? Here, Nelson began to slide into racial arguments about "people who are unfit for self-government . . . people like those of Egypt and India and other tropical countries." Self-government was not difficult "among people who have the intelligence of our own people." But among others—here he pointed with pride to England's patient work of teaching these others political skills. Was Mason arguing that American government was "so weak," or American institutions "so feeble," or Americans "so effeminate that we are incompetent to colonize, to develop, and to govern territorial possessions like England?"

"Pitchfork" Ben Tillman of South Carolina, a Populist but racist anti-imperialist, jumped in. Tillman had read of tension between Norway and Sweden over "the matter of self-government." "Norway had practically set up for herself in the matter of a flag even." He asked Nelson "why the Norwegians at home wish self-government and the Norwegians in the United States do not want to give it to the Philippines?"

Denying he "represented the people or Government of Norway," Nelson shot back: "the constitutional history and the liberties and rights of the Norwegians will bear comparison with those of the people of South Carolina." Tillman temporarily ignored this jibe at Jim Crow segregation and disenfranchisement of blacks, so Nelson went on to criticize the perfidy of the Filipino rebels and their commander, Emilio Aguinaldo. They were not fit to rule, so Americans must take over and prepare Filipinos for self-rule after 300 years of being the Spaniards' "serfs and slaves."

231

Tillman queried him on his use of the word "slaves." Nelson tried to qualify his description, but the slide backward toward Reconstruction issues proved irresistible. Comparing Reconstruction to military occupation of the Philippines, Tillman charged that Republicans had "forced on the white men of the South, at the point of the bayonet, the rule and domination of those ex-slaves."

Backtracking from Republicans' postwar idealism, Nelson insisted that "the negro question" was past. You Southerners "have the negroes in your midst; you have that problem to wrestle with. I am unwilling . . . to make your load or your burden heavier." He tried to escape Tillman's line of reasoning.

"Pitchfork" Ben had him pinned and would not let him go. He pressed the comparison: "You are undertaking to annex and make a component part of this Government islands inhabited by ten millions of the colored race, one-half or more of whom are barbarians of the lowest type." He objected to citizenship for "that vitiated blood, that debased and ignorant people."[26] Tillman's view of the subject merely represented the common view of white superiority at the time.

Nelson denied that annexation meant Filipinos became "voters, full citizens in every respect." No, someone could be a citizen and still be "entirely deprived of the right of suffrage." He again cited women and minors as examples, and ignored race as a rationale, but in fact race would be the reason Filipinos would not vote. Nelson was giving up Republican anti-slavery idealism "without a wink of squeamishness."

Continued invitations to repudiate Reconstruction came from an unexpected quarter—Senator George Hoar of Massachusetts, the seventy-four-year-old Republican anti-imperialist Yankee. Hoar pressed the point. What if some Filipinos moved to the continental United States? Wouldn't Reconstruction's 15th Amendment guarantee them "the right to become voters without regard to their race, color, or previous condition [of servitude]"?

"I do not think so," said Nelson, "That is a limitation upon

States, not upon the United States." This was a curious answer. States determined eligibility for voting, not the federal government. Yet it confirmed his de facto repudiation of Reconstruction. New inspirations and new ideas were very much entangled in old issues and ideals. Nelson denied the latter to embrace the former.

Using his Civil War lessons about Copperheads and stay-at-homes, Nelson pointed to the soldiers (some, Minnesotans, and "a dozen boys" from Alexandria) "maintaining the dignity and honor of our country and our flag" in the Philippines. For the anti-imperialists "to call them subjugating invaders" was "cruel and harsh" and served "to encourage . . . the enemies of this Government," namely, "Aguinaldo and his followers."[27]

When the Senate voted on the treaty on February 6, this final point counted, for, two days earlier, all-out warfare had started between Aguinaldo's troops and American soldiers. With one vote to spare, the Senate ratified the treaty by a vote of 57 to 27. Nelson voted to ratify as did Minnesota's other senator, Cushman K. Davis, the chairman of the Senate Foreign Relations Committee and a member of the commission that negotiated the treaty. The *St. Paul Pioneer Press* interpreted ratification as a personal triumph for Davis. After the vote, Davis's desk "was adorned with a handsome floral offering sent by admiring friends."[28] Nelson's support for the treaty healed his long-standing feud with Davis. It cemented his ties to the eastern leaders of the national Republican party. To accommodate his rural constituents and his own *bonde* sympathies, he had to distance himself from them on economic issues. Yet foreign policy was not a salient, determining issue in rural Minnesota. Here, he could walk hand in hand with his party. And the increasing importance of foreign policy freed him from the nightmare of Populism.

War's end and the treaty vote also freed him to take his postponed trip to Norway. In the spring, he had declined the offer of Sweden-Norway's King Oscar II to make him a Knight of the Order of St. Olaf. He claimed that the United States Constitution did not allow American senators to accept such honors from a foreign ruler—though it was permissible if the Senate gave its approval. However, in light of his exchange with Senator Tillman, he would certainly not have approached the Senate for such permission. Perhaps to avoid the appearance of rejecting the honor out of anti-Swedish animus, he tried to keep his rejection out of the Scandinavian-American press—to no avail.[29]

Though he had denied to Tillman that he "represented the people or government of Norway," he had greatly aided four Norwegian military officers who had come to the United States to observe the Spanish-American War. Their underlying purpose was to learn how to improve Norway's defenses against a possible future Swedish attack. The future Norwegian defense minister, Georg Stang, was greatly impressed by Nelson. Stang thought it "charming," when Nelson "spoke a pure parish dialect" (Vossing) of Norwegian. Nelson introduced Stang and the other officers to President McKinley and arranged for them to go with the 12th Minnesota regiment to Cuba. The Norwegian-American commander of the 14th Minnesota unsuccessfully tried to get them to accompany his regiment. When the Minnesotans were not sent to Cuba, Nelson again intervened with the army to get the officers to the theater of war.[30]

The senator left Washington for New York on July 24 to catch a boat for Europe.[31] Curiously, he traveled alone, without Nicholina, Henry, or Ida. One can only guess why his Norwegian-American family passed up a once-in-a-lifetime chance to visit the mother country. Nicholina may have felt duty-bound to take care of the home place. Henry owned a hardware store in Ashby. Whatever the reason, Knute's trip was an educational, political, quasi-diplomatic excursion, a working vacation—perhaps the only kind a "drayhorse" would allow himself. Newspaper reports stressed that he would visit Norway, Sweden, and Denmark.[32] Visiting all three Scandinavian countries had obvious political benefits for a Scandinavian-American politician. Yet he had a strong personal, sentimental desire to see the land of his birth. Reversing that 1849 voyage would bring back his fatherless years in Evanger and renew local whispers about the circumstances of his birth. But he was a toughened personality. By visiting Evanger as its most celebrated son, he may have settled some old scores for himself and for Ingebjørg. If so, he kept it to himself.

As the ship neared Norway's west coast, he saw "the Old Country emerge, the coast with its bare rock cliffs." His first thought was of Ivar Aasen's poem "Nordmannen," a popular song.[33] Like Frithjof the Bold, he was returning home after fighting many battles in exile.

Yet he knew that "dear Mother Norway" was split over many internal battles, some of them symbolic—political, religious, linguistic, diplomatic.[34] Three political parties dominated: Rene Venstre (the "Pure" Left), Moderate Venstre (the "Centrist" Left), and Høyre (the Conservatives). The socialist Arbeiderpartiet (social democratic Workers' Party) was a weak fourth. Geographical, religious, and socioeconomic divisions underlay partisan ones. Høyre flourished among Christiania's middle-class residents, large property owners, and High Church Lutherans. Haugean (Low Church) Lutherans from southern and western regions backed Moderate Venstre against what they saw as the unorthodox, atheistic, intellectual "Christiania-Liberalism" of Rene Venstre. The latter, though led by urbanites, enjoyed substantial support in eastern and northern regions.[35]

A country with two written languages—both of them Norwegian—Norway was divided, though not on class lines, between liberal supporters of rural *landsmål* and conservative supporters of the strongly Danish-influenced traditional language of Christiania, the larger cities, church, school, and government.[36]

As "Pitchfork" Ben Tillman knew, the greatest tension came from the Union of two countries, Sweden and Norway, under one king. Norway had its own parliament, the Storting, which managed internal affairs, but Swedish dominance of the Union's foreign affairs rankled Norwegian pride. In 1895, the Storting backed off from its demand for a separate Norwegian consular service. By 1899 the new symbolic issue was an 1898 Storting law removing the small Union emblem from the Norwegian flag. A more conciliatory Swedish foreign minister was abandoning Sweden's opposition to this law, but Swedish conservatives were still angered by it. The Rene Venstre government of Johannes Steen strongly pushed for the pure Norwegian flag. In 1899, it launched two armor-plated warships as part of its defense against Swedish attack. Høyre sought more compromise and less strife within the pragmatic Union.[37]

These sensitive issues of nationalism, religion, ideology, and language made Koshkonong's common-school quarrel seem a teapot tempest. Like Frithjof, Nelson would try to achieve reconciliation. The political situation may have convinced him to travel incognito and to avoid public "fuss and feathers."

Eager Vossings got the familiar Nelson silent treatment when he arrived in mid-August. In Vossevangen, the welcomers were unsure when he was coming to town, and whether by train, buggy, or horseback. His interest in Norwegian history saved them from surprise. Word came on Sunday, August 13, that he had stopped at an historic site on the way. They had time to decorate the streets with flags. Then, they saw "a short, stocky man coming, driving a buggy alone and coming down the street." Curious onlookers came to catch a glimpse of "the man about whom they have so often read in the newspapers." They saw an "American citizen in heart and mind," but still part Vossing and part Norwegian "at the bottom of his soul."[38]

The following Sunday, local officialdom held a banquet in his honor at 5 P.M. in "Madame Monsen's old-fashioned, cozy hotel" in Evanger. The village had changed greatly since he had left. Evanger was now a separate religious and political district—independent of Voss. It lay on the Bergen-Voss railroad built in 1883. Trains, not horsepower, now sped through Evanger "in nervous haste . . . without giving the traveler time to sink his senses in nature's beauty"—the deep river valley's scenery. Nelson did have time to appreciate the beautifully decorated dining hall, festooned like Balder's temple in the moving "Reconciliation"

236

scene. Spruce boughs hung on the wall, flowers decorated the tables, and his picture was featured in the "floral centerpiece."[39]

An Evanger official, Brynjulf Mugaas, gave the formal welcome as the banquet began. "Never has the *bygd* had such a guest! . . . An honored man, but not only honored, a beloved man" both in Norway and America. "Visibly moved, the Senator raised his glass in thanks" for this toast. He began what he confessed was his first speech in Norwegian, by which he probably meant a formal speech in *bokmål*, official Dano-Norwegian. He praised Norway's and Evanger's obvious modernization, and the Norwegian-American farmers' success in America. Modestly, he downplayed his political success ("Politics is a lottery for the most part and the best don't always come out on top"). He hadn't come as an official to be feasted. "I wanted just to visit old Mother [Norway] . . . and to go around here like a common American farmer."

Here was a strangely mixed situation, like the Swedish-Norwegian Union. Here were strangers, yet emotions of pride and love bound him to them. Here he seemed both distinguished senator and family member. The banquet was both family reunion and official reception for a visiting dignitary with a high place in the American government.

Succumbing to the family atmosphere, Knute switched into the Vossing dialect for a little confidential talk about the current tensions. Swedes and Norwegians lived together in America, and both voted for Nelson. "Try to live at peace at home here also! Keep the peace. . . . Don't separate with forts along the border!"

Quiet greeted his remarks. Then a local teacher rose to toast Norwegian Americans: "Tell them that no brave Norwegian wants conflict. But we are all agreed on one demand—a free fatherland."

Mugaas changed the subject by reminiscing about Ingebjørg's "considerable poetical talent and musical sense."

The local Lutheran minister praised Nelson's loyalty to the Norwegian-American Lutheran church. Cautiously, he replied

237

with facts about the Lutheran liturgy and the number of Norwegian Lutheran churches in America. "Although I have not always agreed with the Lutheran ministers," he confessed, "I have still had the idea that I will 'stick by the Lutheran church' as long as I could not find a better one." That was faint praise. In fact, he usually found the Congregational Church in Alexandria to be more to his liking. He returned to the facts: services were still conducted in Norwegian, but to accommodate the young that would have to change.

The formal banquet ended, the party adjourned to the hotel garden for punch, cigars, and coffee. In the lingering light of a moonlit Norwegian summer night, the informal conversation continued until nearly midnight. The Vossings switched to addressing him as "Du Knut." Approving, Nelson remarked that "when I come home from the train station [in Alexandria] all the small boys yell 'Hallo, Knute, any news from Washington?'" Showing his familiarity with the local dialect, he corrected someone who used the *bokmål* word *stedmoder* instead of the Vossing *stykmor* (stepmother).

Now that everyone had loosened up, the Vossings tried to "pump the statesman for diplomatic secrets," especially about American actions in Cuba and the Philippines. The Lutheran minister criticized the United States for "beginning the war in the name of freedom" then "acting as if it was a war of conquest." "Let me civilize you a little, you know," replied Nelson, looking at the minister. He switched to *bokmål* to correct this local authority, as if the man had been dispatched straight from Copenhagen. "There are many kinds of missionaries, as you know. Some use the catechism; others, the Krag-Jørgensen [rifle]." Anti-American jibes were unjustified. "Cuba and the Philippines will certainly get all the self-government they can manage." He switched back to Vossing for a proverb: "You know, you can't give children the same food as grownups."

A local Rene Venstre leader criticized him, a foreigner, for meddling in Norwegian politics with his call for a spirit of reconciliation toward Sweden. It was hard for a stranger to judge conditions rightly. It was equally hard for a leftist to understand a *Vossemål*-speaking, self-described *bonde* taking the conservatives' view on the Union and praising American imperialism. "Take the flag issue."

"As a matter of fact," replied 'Du Knut' in *bokmål*, "I had not intended to talk about your politics and I will not meddle in it, for it has nothing to do with me. But isn't it true that the Union emblem still appears on the Swedish flag?"

The "pure" leftist admitted that Swedes didn't insist on a "pure" flag.

"Then it appears to me that there can be no danger that foreigners will regard Norway as a province if on the same basis you both put each other's colors in your flags."

The Rene Venstre man replied that Swedish control of the Union's foreign affairs resulted in "the Swedish colors in our flag evoking the idea that Norway is a province [of Sweden]." Nelson thought it only "a question of taste."

The questions kept coming at Nelson. "Now and then, the Senator lightly [swung] his cape aside a bit to reveal some of his concealed opinions." From time to time a toast was given or a song sung.

He urged Norwegians not to be like Americans back home who walked into the saloon daring anyone to knock the chip off their shoulder. He asserted that, in America, "the Swedes were polite, more so than the Norwegians. When a Swede comes into my office and asks my clerk if I am available for a chat, he always says, 'Is the gentleman here?' A Norwegian comes and it's 'Is Knute around?'" Again, he urged reconciliation between Swedes and Norwegians.

As midnight approached, the Vossing senator took his leave, shook everyone's hand, gave one final, emotional salute to Norway, and asked *Kirkesanger* Mugaas to lead them in Ivar Aasen's song, "Nordmannen."

Leaving Evanger, Nelson traveled for the next month around

239

Norway, admiring the rich farmlands of his wife's native Toten, visiting her relatives there, and "making a little trip to Stockholm."[40] Apparently no journalist noticed him there, for no one described his Swedish visit. That was just as well—it might have offended Norwegian Americans. He had requested that his Evanger banquet remarks on Norway's politics "not be reported." Perhaps he thought making them in *Vossemål* underscored their private nature as opinions exchanged between friends. But a newspaper correspondent took down his remarks verbatim, in dining hall and hotel garden. Another summarized them.[41] They soon appeared in Norwegian newspapers and were reprinted in the Norwegian-American press, where they sparked a brief editorial conflict.

Helping to set it off was the Moderate Venstre organ *Vestlandsposten*'s use of them. "Let us take note of this wise and impartial Norwegian's pronouncements," it commented. "He sees our situation with the perceptiveness of a great statesman." Pressing the flag issue was not wise, for it "had annoyed and riled the Swedes." It hoped the Rene Venstre men in Voss would listen to his "pronouncements." Claiming neutrality on the flag issue, Rasmus B. Anderson of *Amerika* (Madison, Wisconsin) took Nelson to task for ignoring the common-sense rule that all Norwegian Americans visiting Norway stay out of Norway's politics. That especially applied to "Hon. Knute Nelson when he comes there as one of his country's highest officeholders." Anderson was also peeved that Nelson praised his rival, *Skandinaven*, to the skies in a Bergen interview. He grossly exaggerated *Skandinaven*'s circulation, yet the Chicago newspaper "reprinted such flattery of itself without a blush or a correction." A writer in *Superior Tidende* agreed that Nelson was no judge of newspaper circulation, but his views on the flag issue agreed with those of many Norwegian Americans. "There are many of us who think that the flag dispute borders on the childish." Probably few Norwegian Americans were Høyre supporters; many sympathized with the Haugean view of *Vestlandsposten*.[42]

Arriving in Christiania in mid-September, Nelson flatly ruled out any public banquet in his honor. "'I'm a common *bonde*, I am,' said the senator with a smile." He talked *Vossemål* "with amazing ease" and boasted that daughter Ida could read Norwegian. The Rene Venstre newspaper, *Verdens Gang*, was pleased to report that he was no Høyre man either, but an admirer of liberals' struggle for parliamentary rule and universal manhood suffrage. He worshipped at Vor Frelsers Kirke and visited a trade exhibition of Norwegian manufacturing. Clearly amending his fifty-year-old memory of "poor" Mother Norway, he praised her "rapid American-like progress." He offered to recommend these Norwegian manufactured goods to American firms when he returned to the United States. He explained his role back home on behalf of individuals. He "often received about 70-80 letters a day" asking his intervention. Toning down his advice on "the Union strife," he simply expressed a wish for as "good relations between the Norwegian and Swedish peoples" as there was in America. "'We certainly have no Great Swedes over there,' the Senator said with a charming smile."[43]

He attended two "private dinners" held in his honor by Rene Venstre leaders. Perhaps through the connections that Bjørnsterne Bjørnson and liberal Vossings had to Nelson, or because they were the governing party, the "pure" liberals took him under their wing despite his conservative views on Swedish-Norwegian relations. He met with Georg Stang and other military officers whom he had assisted during the Spanish-American War.[44] *Verdens Gang* editor Olav Thommessen hosted a Saturday soirée with Prime Minister Steen, cabinet ministers, Storting members, and cultural leaders, the "urban intelligentsia" of "Christiania-liberalism" that Haugean ministers distrusted.[45]

At this soirée, Knute Nelson bid "dear Mother Norway" goodbye "in a short, eloquent, fervent speech" that may have sounded too emotional, too Haugean to suit his listeners' tastes. He spoke on behalf of all Norwegian Americans, in Christiania's *bokmål*. "We did not leave you," he reassured them, "beloved countrymen, like emigrants from other countries, with hate or resentment. No, hard times, which were not our mother country's fault, and the Viking spirit drove us across the ocean." The fatherland, America, "received us with open doors and outstretched arms as if we had been its first-born." So, we have tried "to be good, useful, trustworthy fellow citizens" there—partly to bring honor to Norway. "Yes, dear Mother Norway, though we have settled in a distant land, we love you with a child's tender fervor." He used some of Ingebjørg's "poetical talents." Norwegian Americans were like stars in "the distant West." Joining with Norwegians to sing "Ja vi elsker," he recited the chorus in closing.

On Sunday morning he boarded the boat for Copenhagen. Here as elsewhere on the trip, he used "Nelson's separate consular service," the United States consuls and ministers who were his patronage appointees. He stayed with Minister to Denmark Laurits Swenson, a Minnesotan who spent some of his Copenhagen hours mending Nelson's political fences back home by mail. Other Nelson appointees included C.C. Andrews in Rio de Janeiro, Hans Mattson in Calcutta, Søren Listoe in Rotterdam, and John Goodnow (from the Nelson-Washburn campaign) in Shanghai.[46]

His one-week visit to Denmark was very polite and official—no emotional reunions, no political controversy. He evidently stayed with Swenson at the United States Minister's residence near Amalienborg palace—where he had an audience with His Majesty, King Christian IX. Swenson held an evening dinner attended by "their excellencies"—cabinet ministers, foreign diplomats, and the Court Hunting Master (*Hofjægermester*). The "common *bonde*" escaped Copenhagen officialdom to admire Danish dairy farms and milk cows. Interviewed by the newspaper *Dannebrog*, he praised Danish Americans, especially "in my state of Minnesota," where many had risen "to very high posts," especially in the dairy industry. It was due to their "initiative and enterprise that we now export butter from Minnesota to China" (not too much, though). Unlike American strikers, Danish workers facing a lockout behaved in a very orderly fashion, he noted.

From Copenhagen he traveled to Jutland for a politically important visit to Schleswig-Holstein. Danish Americans, and Scandinavians generally, were very concerned about the German government's attempts to eliminate Danish language and culture from that area, conquered from Denmark in 1864. Then, he went to Rotterdam to see Consul Listoe. They toured the Waterloo battlefield. And Nelson was off to England, which Mary Dillon had taught him to love. In his Evanger talk, he had ranked England with Norway and America as his three favorite countries.[47]

Unexpected excitement awaited him in London. In October, war broke out between British troops in South Africa and the Boers' (Afrikaners') self-proclaimed Transvaal republic. Queen Victoria called Parliament into an "extraordinary session" which began Tuesday, October 17, with Senator Knute Nelson sitting in the House of Commons gallery. Before the Queen's speech was read, guards undertook the "formality of searching the vaults under the houses of parliament for traces of treasonable conspiracy," a carryover from the Gunpowder Plot of 1605.[48] In an historic setting, Nelson viewed the main bulwark of the English liberties he had praised. In the prestigious *Times* of London, however, a United States senator did not rate any mention. He was simply an anonymous member of the American ambassador's "party" viewing the proceedings.[49]

Debate in the Commons offered interesting parallels to the Senate debate over the Treaty of Paris. Here, Britain was the imperialist power. Here, the Boers' President Paul Kruger played the role of Aguinaldo, a freedom fighter the imperialists had provoked into war—at least according to the anti-imperialist Liberals and Irish Nationalists. One Irish member blamed this "war between a giant and a dwarf" on the "stock jobbing rings." Here too, conservative imperialists regarded this wartime opposition as "disloyal," almost as treason. Here, however, longer experience in such debates resulted in greater tolerance for dissent

243

and more humor. When the Irish were accused of offering support to Kruger, a government leader recalled that they had offered similar support to all opponents of "her majesty's government, quite irrespective of race, creed or the theater of hostilities." "Such support was" never "regarded as important by those to whom it was proffered, and I advise the house to take the same view now. (Laughter)." Here the imperialists were less racist than their enemies, the Boers.[50]

Nelson returned to New York from his three-month European tour in late October, 1899. Coming up was 1900, not only a presidential election year but the year to elect the legislators who would continue or end his Senate career. Like Washburn in 1894, he would try to secure the nomination and election of Republican legislative candidates pledged to him.

During his entire political career, he had showed a keen interest in frontier issues of land law, Indian relations, and territorial government. Now, he served on the Senate's Committee on Territories and interested himself in issues concerning Alaska, where gold had recently been discovered.

In April, 1900, he locked horns with Republican Senator Henry Clay Hansbrough over the North Dakotan's amendment to a bill setting up civil government in Alaska. At the instigation of North Dakota Republican boss (and Alaska speculator) Alexander MacKenzie, Hansbrough sought to deny mining claims to Scandinavian immigrants at Cape Nome. Arguing that noncitizens should not own mining claims, MacKenzie and friends laid claim to them and received the title "claim-jumper" for their efforts. Outraged that Scandinavians encouraged to settle in Alaska were being robbed of their mining claims, Nelson helped to defeat Hansbrough's amendment. MacKenzie then persuaded President McKinley to appoint pro-MacKenzie men to the new judicial posts. They appointed the boss "receiver" of the mining claims with orders to "extract the gold therefrom."[51] Nelson fumed and the issue spilled over into the 1900 campaign.

No campaign year would find Nelson as politically active as in

244

Senator Nelson and lumber magnate Thomas H. Shevlin at the Milwaukee Depot on Minneapolis' Washington Avenue. Year unknown, probably 1905-1915.

1900, his de facto reelection year. Led by Simon Michelet and James A. Peterson, his supporters won an important endorsement for his reelection from the Republican convention in Hennepin county, the base of the vengeful Washburn men. His patronage appointees and his consular service worked hard, and, because of their reconciliation, so did Davis appointees, like United States Marshall William Grimshaw.[52]

Nelson began his fall campaign efforts at home on September 1, with a speech on the war in the Philippines before a crowd of about 250 Republicans in Alexandria's village hall. They listened as their former county attorney read a lengthy legal brief indicting Aguinaldo for "treachery" and a "premeditated" attack on American troops. The *St. Paul Pioneer Press* truthfully called it the most "exhaustive treatment" of the subject. It refuted "the anti-imperialist attorneys and allies of Aguinaldo," who compared him to George Washington. His local audience gave Nelson "deafening" applause at the start, according to the Republican *Pioneer Press*, but "many [left] the hall before he finished," reported the local Democratic paper.[53]

His strong pro-expansionist stance finally earned him the respect of his party's national leaders. Gone were the memories of his revolt against protectionism. His efforts to position himself between eastern Republicans and Populists no longer seemed so damaging in 1900, when foreign policy first became a major issue in a presidential campaign. After Nelson defended McKinley's expansionism in a mid-July speech to a "national convention of Republican league clubs," the national committee asked him to campaign with vice presidential candidate Theodore Roosevelt in mid-September.[54] The personal ties forged between the two on this campaign jaunt helped give Nelson ready access to the White House when Roosevelt later became president.

For the hero of San Juan Hill and current governor of New York, the 1900 campaign was a debut on the stage of national politics. "With pince-nez adorning a bulbous nose, toothy grin stretched in a near grimace, a full square face with its several chins resting on heavyset shoulders, a reedy voice, and pump-handle gestures, [Roosevelt] was a cartoonist's dream."[55] McKinley sent this dynamo on the campaign trail to match the barnstorming Bryan. The Great Commoner was about to be "Roosevelted."[56]

Nelson joined Roosevelt's party at LaCrosse, Wisconsin, on September 10. It included Robert M. LaFollette, a progressive Wisconsin Republican with Scandinavian-American support making his first successful campaign for governor. At the Empire Rink, before a capacity crowd, Nelson delivered a forty-five-minute address "on the issues of the day with great effect." He then introduced "THE HERO OF SAN JUAN" (the headline screamed). Bryan was then "Roosevelted" for backtracking on his pet "free silver issue" and daring to yell "militarism" in response to McKinley's Philippine Island war.[57]

With Nelson aboard, Roosevelt's special train, including his "private coach *Minnesota*," then sped through the night to South Dakota, to "Teddy"'s cowboy West. Here he received a more colorful reception than in staid Wisconsin. In four days, Roosevelt's party made over twenty campaign stops in South Dakota and two in Iowa—speaking in halls, opera houses, outdoors, or from the train. Torchlight processions, brass bands, a "mounted escort" of Dakotas, fireworks, Rough Riders, excursion trains from nearby towns, "broncho busters," and Dakota women "with papooses on their backs"—all greeted the party. Hammering away at Bryan's anti-imperialism, Roosevelt often managed to discover a local Spanish-American War veteran or regiment, then asked a delighted crowd if this hero was an "example of militarism." At Madison, he said, "South Dakotans [should] vote the way her men shot in the Philippines." At Flandreau, "when two dogs started a fight in the midst of the crowd," Roosevelt quipped, "Say, pull Aguinaldo off there." Jingoism drew applause wherever he spoke.[58]

Knute Nelson was clearly upstaged, but by steady work he managed to score some points. At Flandreau and Madison he "compar[ed] the Copperheads in the Civil War with those whose sympathy for the Filipinos now keeps alive the rebellion in Luzon." One reporter felt he was "more effective than Roosevelt ... where the population includes many Norwegians."

In Populist Brule county, a Norwegian-American woman "wearing a Bryan button" spoke to him in Norwegian.

"'Are you for Bryan?' asked the Senator."

"'No!' she said indignantly."

Nelson "pointed to the button." She quickly took it off.

"'I thought it was McKinley. I didn't have my specs on.'"

Nelson had a harder time communicating with the cowboys. They were Teddy's kind of people. When cowpunchers and bronco busters rode up to the platform at that same stop,

Roosevelt jumped down to shake their hands and to talk knowingly about local cattle brands. Nelson could only pun for them: all Westerners "were the locomotives of civilization" but "they were the cowcatchers." Still, by the time they reached Aberdeen, the crowds were crying "Nelson, Nelson."

From Aberdeen, the train headed into North Dakota, but Nelson refused the state party's requests that he speak there to appeal to the many Scandinavian-Americans voters. A month later, when he campaigned in East Grand Forks, they asked him to cross over to Grand Forks. He delivered a stinging rebuff. "Knute Is Hot," ran one headline. He would not help out in Hansbrough and Mackenzie's home state. They had tried to "deprive of their just rights in Alaska some of my countrymen who are citizens of this country," he explained. "Hansbrough called them Lap[p]s." One of these men was Dr. Kittleson of Wisconsin, son of a "one time member of the Wisconsin legislature." Hoping to use Nelson's anger to harvest votes, Populists distributed among Scandinavian Americans newspaper clippings quoting him.[59]

Nelson's speaking burden was increased by the sudden removal of Senator Davis from the campaign. After an August injury failed to heal, Davis's foot turned unbearably painful and badly infected. Ironically, he delivered his last address at Alexandria on September 24. Blood poisoning developed. He suffered kidney failure and died on November 27.[60]

On October 28, Nelson briefly stopped off at his Alexandria home "after an absence of 6 weeks, to rest for a few hours, get clean clothes and hastily run through my mail." He was confident of "a landslide for McKinley in the Upper Country." But he did not relax. "I am on the jump," he wrote as he headed off for the final week.[61] On November 5, the day before the election, he delivered four speeches in St. Paul in defense of Republicans' domestic and foreign policies.[62] The election results were a bountiful answer to Republicans' prayers. McKinley, Samuel Van Sant for governor, all their congressmen, and their state officeholders were triumphant. Nelson had the satisfaction of seeing his twenty-nine-year-old son Henry Knute Nelson elected to the state legislature.[63]

Thus, the son could vote to return his father to the Senate when the legislature met in January, 1901. Always a cautious worrier, the older Nelson approached the moment with some anxiety. "If the G.N. [Great Northern] is hostile and intends to use a lot of money," he warned a supporter, "of course they can make some trouble, but I am not sure they are going into that scheme."[64] They were not. Nelson's legislative reelection was a cut-and-dried certainty. Republicans held no caucus to debate the matter. The Democrats' token candidate, former federal judge R.R. Nelson, was easily outvoted on January 22. "I am so glad it is all over," a tired Nelson confessed.[65] He was safe for another six years.

He was certainly safe from agrarian protest and Populism, which were sputtering to an end because of McKinley-era prosperity and the unexpected salience of foreign policy in the 1900 campaign. However, the newer, more urban-oriented Progressive movement was starting to expand beyond city governments. La Follette's election as governor of Wisconsin established one state laboratory for Progressive experimentation. And, Progressivism was moving into national politics, especially after September, 1901.

While at Buffalo, New York, for the Pan American Exposition in early September, 1901, President McKinley was assassinated. Theodore Roosevelt took the oath of office on September 14. Senator Nelson's campaigning companion was now president. Nelson had been a close supporter of McKinley, who admired him in turn. John Goodnow wrote Nelson that the last time he saw McKinley, the President "spoke in the highest terms of you and in the most friendly way personally." Nelson praised McKinley: "He was the noblest type of American manhood . . . The memory of his life, his work & his death is sanctified to us forever more."[66] Nelson could not know that Roosevelt brought an urban, East Coast Progressivism that was to prove nearly as troublesome to him as Populism had been. When attention turned back to domestic policies, Progressives would attack the failure of pro-business, patronage politics, Nelson's kind, to solve problems of industrial concentration, environmental abuse, and political corruption.

Twelve

"On the Jump":
Insurgents, Territories, Hearings

Always "on the jump" in the fall of election years, Knute Nelson was touring northeastern Minnesota in mid-October, 1902.[1] From Duluth, he caught a train for Hibbing, where he spoke on Monday evening, October 13. The next morning he left Hibbing to make a speech in Two Harbors on Tuesday evening, and then to return to Duluth for a talk on Wednesday night.

His plans were disrupted by a train wreck blocking the track east of Hibbing. He commandeered a handcar and a helper and set out for Wolf Junction five miles away. "His body undulating with the motion of the handles," the senator "worked his end of the lever" and his helper the other. They were making about 10 m.p.h., but "as his long coat flopped back and forth, one of the rapidly moving handles caught in one of the pockets and tore the cloth." Perspiring freely, he discarded his coat and continued in shirt sleeves. At Wolf Junction, a small crowd admired the incoming "senator with disheveled hair and semi-undress" aboard his "unique campaign special." They asked for "a rear platform speech," but Nelson rested, "fanned himself, donned his coat," and "asked to be excused." He made it to Duluth and to Two Harbors, which welcomed this hardworking politician of distribution who had secured an initial federal appropriation for the city's harbor.[2]

He would have to work just as hard to survive in the new Progressive era as he had to reach Wolf Junction. The end of Populism brought him little respite. He still seemed to be struggling against the wind, though that adverse wind was now coming from a different direction. Easterners were now the reformers, more than Westerners; urban experts, more than farmers and the small-town elite. Expertise came from social scientists as much as from lawyers; political leadership, from the executive branch as much as the legislature; political mobilization, from interest groups more than from the partisan armies of the Gilded Age. Small-town editors increasingly cast off partisan allegiance and claimed independence from patronage and politicians' subsidies. Popular magazines gave muckraking journalists a national audience for their political exposés. They popularized the anti-patronage, anti-machine views of the old Mugwump reformers who had convinced *Budstikken* in 1876 and harassed Congressman Nelson in 1883 over civil service reform.[3] They exposed the sins of the old politics of settlement and development which Nelson knew from frontier days. Too much had been promised to encourage corporations' work of economic development. New "producer groups," development's offspring, were so divided against each other that distributing a little something to each group seemed utterly self-contradictory.[4]

These changes rendered obsolete Knute Nelson's role as the Upper Country farmer-politician who barnstormed against Populism in the Red River Valley in even-numbered years and distributed political favors in the odd-numbered years. Being a western farmer no longer blunted reformers' charges. His legal and legislative expertise counted for less. Running as a Republican no longer guaranteed an army of campaign workers or small-town editorial support. Distributing federal jobs and favors still worked, but was subject to increasing criticism.

To survive these changes, Nelson modified his former tactics to fit the new situation.

First, he attempted to strike a moderate course. Four discernible, though overlapping ideological groupings characterized Minnesota politics. Laissez-faire conservatives resisted government's regulatory interference in the economy, apart from tariff protection and improvements to infrastructure (roads, river and harbor improvements). Moderate Progressives approved anti-trust actions, if not too intrusive, but opposed government ownership as a tool of reform and thought the American political system basically sound. They were usually middle-class Americans: lawyers, successful farmers, shop owners, small businessmen. More anti-capitalist Progressives followed Insurgent leaders, who saw basic flaws in the political system and sought procedural reforms to remedy them. They were strongly anti-trust and anti-corporate. The fourth, and smallest, group were the radicals or socialists who voted for Eugene Debs and later supported the Industrial Workers of the World (IWW). Nelson could never tolerate their harsh criticisms of America. He was a moderate Progressive on most issues, though he could briefly ally with conservatives or Insurgents on specific issue.[5] In light of Minnesotans' strong Progressivism, he tried to avoid any perception that he was a laissez-faire, "stand-pat" conservative.

Secondly, he continued to play the role of intercessor so essential to American legislators' political longevity. Jobs, pensions, widows' benefits, promotions and pay raises in federal service, patronage jobs everywhere—he was besieged with hundreds upon hundreds of appeals. He usually made a conscientious effort to help. Much of his political popularity can be traced to this indefatigable "drayhorse's" use of "pull" on behalf of his constituents. Such legwork never became obsolete.

Finally, he continued to follow his instinct that the frontier was his safety valve to escape divisive issues—or, at least, issues that were divisive in Minnesota. By concentrating on territorial matters as a member of the Senate Committee on the Territories, he could continue in the politics of settlement and development. Those were still major issues in the territories, long after the nation had moved on to the politics of regulation and reform. Also, his views on the territories nicely dovetailed with those of Progressives.

In August, 1902, Senator Albert J. Beveridge, chairman of the Senate Committee on Territories, wrote to ask Nelson's advice on territorial matters. Four territories sought statehood: Arizona, New Mexico, Oklahoma, and Indian Territories. Myriads of controversies swarmed around their search, and Beveridge mentioned several.[6]

Should they be admitted as two states, three states, or four? Were they ready for statehood? New Mexico had been a territory since the dramatic year of the Compromise of 1850, and had almost 200,000 inhabitants in 1900, but many argued that it was not yet ready. The Spanish-American War had left many Americans with negative perceptions of Hispanic peoples, and New Mexico's population was largely Spanish American.[7] The Indians in Oklahoma and Indian Territories were also judged by some to be unready for statehood. Beveridge asked Nelson if he could "think of a method" of including the Indian Territory within a state of Oklahoma while "excluding the inhabitants of Indian Territory from participation in the state government for the present."[8] The chaotic factionalism of territorial politics was proof to many observers that none of the four was yet ready. Further hurting their chances was the nationalist Republican party's post-1860 policy of having the federal government run "the territories as . . . a passive group of colonial mandates, taking the protests and demands of the western citizens with a casualness that would have provoked serious rebellion in the Old Northwest."[9]

Progressivism complicated matters. As Howard Lamar notes, "statehood symbolized that a satisfactory 'Americanization' had been achieved" in a given geographical area.[10] Progressives held to higher standards than other mortals on most subjects, includ-

254

ing Americanization and who made a proper American citizen. Their effort to delay statehood for the four territories resembled their drive for immigration restriction.

They held state governments to a higher standard, and feared statehood would bring a wasteful exploitation of natural resources. Under the leadership of Forest Service chief Gifford Pinchot, the Roosevelt administration was acting to protect forests, grazing lands, and mineral deposits by restricting or licensing private users of these resources. An Easterner, an aristocrat who acquired his expert's credentials in European forestry schools, Pinchot had a zealot's eyes set "over a truculent nose that hovered above ferocious muleskinner moustachios." Sometimes expressing contempt for Congress, Pinchot used his direct access to Roosevelt (the "Tennis Cabinet") to promote conservation by executive decree—possible because of government ownership of many forests, grazing lands, and mineral deposits.[11] And, many were in the territories. In the early twentieth century, fifteen percent of Arizona and twelve percent of New Mexico was "set aside as national forests." Territorial residents protested these limitations on development, and Pinchot opposed statehood as a threat to his conservation policies.[12]

Conservation and good citizenship were not the Progressives' only reasons for opposing statehood. Their anti-trust stance made them suspicious that corporate interests were behind the drive for statehood. Finally, they feared statehood was a "standpatter" plot to increase the number of conservative senators.[13]

Here, the Progressives' point man was Senator Beveridge of Indiana. For November, 1902, he arranged a quick tour of Arizona and New Mexico to gather information damaging to both territories' cause. Skillful at publicity like his friend Pinchot, Beveridge enlisted the support of eastern journals before his trip, which was a kind of "muckraking" search for signs of frontier disorder, Spanish-language use, and corporate influence. Pleading tiredness from the campaign, Nelson turned down Beveridge's invitation to go along, but he was assigned a

255

leading role in the chairman's filibuster against the statehood bill the following January.[14]

For several days, Nelson took up the time assigned for debate on the Omnibus Statehood Bill with a lengthy historical and cultural survey of the territories. Occasionally Beveridge lobbed easy questions at him to consume more time. Nelson criticized the high illiteracy rate and arid climate in Arizona, but saved his harshest attacks for the "Spanish aroma" of New Mexico. It failed to demonstrate that essential American quality: growth. Its agriculture was "feeble." Worse, its legislature was dominated by Hispanic members from a few leading families, who conducted the sessions "in the Spanish language." Illiteracy was too high, public schools too few, and where they existed, "the Spanish language was taught side by side on an equality with English" (as Norwegian could be taught in Koshkonong schools under Nelson's 1869 bill). He favored statehood for a combined Oklahoma-Indian Territory, where many of "our own kith and kin" were "in a political strait-jacket" under Indian governments.[15] Clearly, for Knute Nelson, Americanization, agriculture, and education were prerequisites for statehood and good citizenship.

Supporters of statehood for Arizona and New Mexico reacted with scorn and ridicule. The *Arizona Republican* joked that "the verbatim notes of the Senate stenographer represented" Nelson "as saying: 'Ay tank does fellairs en Arizona not beene enofe Amaracaines. To bay goot seetyzain, a fellair moost bay Amaracaine.'"[16] As they sat listening to Nelson read "the early Spanish history in New Mexico," that territory's governor and delegate were amused at "the way he toiled around the names . . . giving every letter its full English sound."[17]

Countering Nelson's argument, Senator Foraker of Ohio pointed to Minnesota's large foreign-born population as proof that "the foreign element is sometimes a very valuable mixture." Indignantly defending Minnesota's progressive Scandinavian Americans, in particular, Nelson asserted, "They are Americanized; and that is my objection to the Mexican people [of

New Mexico]; that although they are natives of this country, they have not become Americanized as the great mass and body of our people have." Minnesota's Scandinavian Americans and German Americans, by contrast, were "to all intents and purposes an English-speaking people."[18] Nelson's remarks might be controversial to residents of the territories, but not to his Minnesota constituents, as these words of praise demonstrate.

Nelson's exhaustive speeches and Beveridge's parliamentary tactics appeared likely to fail in avoiding a statehood vote, despite President Roosevelt's support for the filibusters' cause. Taking advantage of a senatorial courtesy (no voting when the committee chairman was absent), Beveridge hid for a week in the third floor den of "Gifford Pinchot's home at 1615 Rhode Island Avenue." That and other delaying tactics killed the Omnibus Bill in the Fifty-Seventh Congress.[19] None of the four territories attained statehood that year.

Many Progressives' opposition to statehood revealed an elitist, Anglocentric, undemocratic, culturally condescending side to their thinking. They thought they knew the correct policy outcomes better than did voters. Where government ownership was a fact (not a radical idea), where presidential discretion ruled rather than legislative compromise, where the federal government ruled subordinate territorial authorities—there they were quite willing to dispense with democracy's messy processes. Though not unequivocally a Progressive, Knute Nelson agreed with them here, primarily because he doubted that Spanish Americans and Indians, illiterate and poor farmers, made suitable American citizens. Certainly they were right that territorial democracy was exceedingly messy, with corrupt "rings," fraudulent elections, bribery, and profit-seeking public officials.[20] Yet Nelson's own Upper Country in the Kindred-Nelson year 1882 provided just as good an example as did Arizona or New Mexico.

Nelson also stood with Roosevelt and the Progressives in their opposition to the attempted merger of the Northern Pacific, Great Northern, and Chicago, Burlington & Quincy (CB&Q) railroads.

257

After battling for several months for control of the CB&Q, James J. Hill and Edward Harriman, together with J. Pierpont Morgan and Kuhn, Loeb and Company, had formed the Northern Securities Company, a holding company, to control all three roads. Progressives reacted predictably to this anti-competitive merger that formed a near-monopoly in the Northwest and Upper Midwest. Pragmatic conservatives, too, saw a window of opportunity, for here the trust-makers had clearly gone too far. The GN and NP were the major competing lines in Minnesota. Minnesota's Governor Samuel Van Sant seized the political high ground, called a conference of western governors, and ordered his attorney general to bring suit to break up the merger.[21]

As he had in the 1894 Great Northern strike, Nelson largely played the cautious lawyer in the Northern Securities case. He exchanged letters with Minnesota's attorney general, W.B. Douglas, in which "with great diffidence" he expressed opinions about complicated questions of court jurisdiction and constitutionality. He delivered no anti-merger rhetoric, but simply had the Senate print up his correspondence with Douglas as a self-explanatory document.[22] His past association with Hill and Hill's ability to bankroll a Senate opponent meant that Nelson could not either favor or stridently oppose the merger. Douglas filed suit before the United States Supreme Court to block the merger, but the Court ruled that it lacked jurisdiction. Filing a separate suit against the merger, Roosevelt's attorney general claimed it violated the Sherman Anti-Trust Act. That federal suit prevailed, and the Court ruled against the merger on March 14, 1904.[23]

In the 1902 campaign, Nelson praised Roosevelt and Van Sant for their anti-merger zeal, but assured Republicans that his zeal was not motivated "by any feeling of ill will or hostility to our railroad or their able and public-spirited managers." Quite the contrary. It was because "our great railroad men of Minnesota" (here, obviously referring to Hill) were getting "well along in years" and might shortly "pass from our midst." That would leave Minnesotans "at the mercy . . . of an army of non-resident stockholders." When he hand-pumped his way through north-eastern Minnesota, he largely criticized the non-resident corporations, especially the coal-mine owners of the East.[24]

He was only too willing to sponsor a bill establishing a Department of Commerce, with a Bureau of Corporations that Roosevelt could use to investigate these largely non-resident corporations. It became law in February, 1903, and represented Nelson's most important contribution to Rooseveltian Progressivism.[25]

In the summer of 1903 Nelson had the opportunity to move away from the touchy question of the railroads and return to territorial issues that were less controversial, at least in Minnesota. Beveridge requested that he be on a Senate subcommittee assigned to visit Alaska and investigate conditions there. Nelson initially resisted, but Beveridge insisted, "it [was] of almost supreme importance" that his good friend from Minnesota accompany senators William P. Dillingham (Vermont), Henry E. Burnham (New Hampshire), and Thomas M. Patterson (Colorado).[26] An expert in land law, Nelson was a member of the Senate Committee on Public Lands. His presence was of supreme importance because the subcommittee "must formulate laws for the settlement of the agricultural portion of Alaska." Other senators, congressmen, and their committees had visited Alaska but this was to be the definitive visit, "the first thorough and serious congressional investigation."[27]

Nelson reluctantly agreed to go on the time-consuming, two-month trip. He wanted one more member quietly added to the senatorial party: editor John S. McLain of the *Minneapolis Journal*. Nelson was adept at winning over one-time political opponents. McLain had bitterly opposed his dumping of Washburn in 1895 and had been cool toward him for a number of years. Here was a chance to mollify McLain, who would write a series of newspaper articles and a book based on the trip.[28]

Although it proved to be one of Nelson's most enjoyable trips, the Alaska journey was no senatorial junket. Travel would be diffi-

259

cult. The subcommittee would head into the Alaskan interior, which no previous committee had done. The group left Seattle on June 28 on the packet steamer *Dolphin*, sailing the Inland Passage off British Columbia. McLain compared this island-sprinkled path past inlets and mountains to the fjords of Norway's west coast.[29]

Nelson probably suggested that comparison to him. It was not the only link between the two Lands of the Midnight Sun. Nelson had already intervened on behalf of Scandinavian-American settlers near Nome. From the beginning, Knute Nelson was disposed to look favorably upon Alaska's claims, unlike those of Arizona and New Mexico. As he later told the Senate, "the white people in Alaska are our own people, of our own kith and kin."[30] They were not asking for statehood, but for territorial status or a delegate to Congress—depending on whom you asked. The District of Alaska had no elections except for municipal posts. Outside incorporated towns, appointed commissioners ruled. Everywhere, appointed judges dispensed justice. Alaska was Seattle's Upper Country, needing roads, railroads, and land offices, as the Twin Cities' Upper Country had in 1871. These Nelson was prepared to approve. Like the Bloody Fifth in 1882, Alaska was divided into two main regions, a coastal southeastern region and an interior region along the Yukon River.[31] But it did not need to satisfy Progressives' high standards, since its requests were relatively modest.

The *Dolphin* soon brought them to the southeastern region: Ketchikan, Wrangell, Juneau, and Skagway. Here, a Citizens League had been organized "to get progressive Alaskans" to "present a united front" to the senators—in favor of a territory, with an elected legislature and governor. The mayor of Ketchikan objected that there was talk of "self-government for the Philippines, for Hawaii, and Puerto Rico," but not "a word about it for Alaska." Yet Alaskans were "Americans" who "should be treated the same as" residents of the forty-five states.[32] Alaskans were not united. Large corporations with mining and fishing interests in Alaska opposed territorial status for fear a legislature would levy taxes. Some of their local representatives were personally acquainted with the visiting senators, "and found them quick of comprehension as to their point of view." In his questions, Nelson indicated his skepticism about the feasibility of conducting elections over such a large area. One witness responded that southeastern Alaska could be "created into a Territory" by itself.[33]

On July 3, they arrived at Skagway, whence they would head into the Canadian Klondike and Alaska's interior, where there was little pro-territorial sentiment. Skagway was "swathed in bunting" for the Fourth of July, which "these disenfranchised Americans" celebrated with gusto. On the 6th they boarded a train on the narrow-gauge White Pass and Yukon Railway, which carried them over the mountains to the Yukon River. A British company built it and seemed to operate it so as to discriminate in favor of Canadian ports. There was only one nine-mile American-built railroad in Alaska.[34]

At Whitehorse, they took a river steamer for the 275-mile trip downriver to Dawson (still in Canada), the heart of the Klondike gold-mining area. Here they made the embarrassing discovery that the Canadian government was better at building roads and governing a frontier—far better than an American government which prided itself on over 100 years of experience in both. They were even better at the land office business. "The contrast between the [Canadians'] business-like methods . . . and the miserable tangle" of confusion over mining claims in Alaska "is no credit to our American statesmanship."[35] As the land-law expert, Nelson's job was to clear up this confusion.

In and around Dawson, Nelson attended a banquet, visited several gold mines, listened to Eva Booth preach at the Presbyterian church on Sunday, and attended the Dawson Theatre on Monday. The senators departed Dawson on Tuesday, July 14, on a river steamer going downriver to Eagle, Alaska. They arrived at this military post and customs office at 1:30 A.M., still twilight in mid-July. Exploring the area, Nelson one day rode "on horse back on [a] pack trail" about fifteen miles to Mission Creek, a mining

261

Nelson's Viking sea legs were occasionally tested during the Senate committee's trip to Alaska in the summer of 1903.

Cigar-smoking Senator Nelson heads out on an inspection tour from Eagle, Alaska, on July 17, 1903, probably to eye potential routes for the Valdez-to-Eagle road he would recommend to Congress.

camp. McLain reported that Eagle's "feminine population affords some fine examples of enterprise and pluck." That included Miss Thomson, a former schoolteacher on the "outside" (the States) at whose hotel they stayed.[36]

They boarded the *Jefferson C. Davis* to proceed down the Yukon to Rampart, where Judge James Wickersham was holding his circuit court. With Alaskans gathered from a distance, it was an excellent chance to hold a hearing. Rampart was crowded, like an Upper Country county seat during court week. "Beds in severalty, so to speak, are hard to get," joked McLain. Rampart exuded the very masculine atmosphere characteristic of frontier law and politics. While there, the senators were inducted into the Arctic Brotherhood, a secret fraternity, attended a "smoker," and were admitted to the Alaska bar.[37]

Unfortunately, the subcommittee had chosen the wrong season to hold hearings in the interior. In the summer, small prospectors were too busy mining to attend a hearing, whereas the large mine owners "with the biggest investments had the largest amount of time to spend at the hearings."[38] One of Nelson's questions at the Rampart hearing indicated that he felt that mining was primarily useful to "open up a market for agricultural products." As they traveled down the Yukon, he tried to fit Alaska into his Minnesota preconceptions about a territory's development. Alaska seemed to fit them better than New Mexico. Alaskans were not "a sort of disorganized mob" in the mining camps. Conditions were "orderly" and "peaceful." In "many sections of Alaska" there seemed "as much show to make a permanent agricultural settlement" as there was "in the northern part of Sweden and Norway." Stopping at a Jesuit mission, he carefully noted the livestock, garden, and hay. Questioning an Eskimo, he wondered at their failure to grow gardens. He seemed to assume that the Eskimo would eventually be removed to reservations.[39] This Upper Country should develop as his had in the 1870s.

By Monday, July 27, they had reached the mouth of the Yukon after a nearly 2,000-mile trip downriver. The following day, the United States revenue cutter *McCulloch,* their home for the remainder of the trip, ferried them across Norton Sound to the then booming town of Nome. A dangerous ship-to-shore transfer at harborless Nome convinced three drenched senators (including Nelson) that harbor improvements there were no pork-barrel superfluity. A supply point for the interior gold-mining district, Nome counted over 12,000 residents in the 1900 census but that number was falling off. The local women's club treated them to a ball, with Nelson and "Miss Major Moore" leading the grand march. Nelson met local Norwegian Americans and received "a great gold nugget" as a souvenir. They held more hearings on Alaska's needs.[40]

On August 1, the *McCulloch* left Nome for St. Paul Island in the Pribilofs, 500 miles west in the Bering Sea. Here they watched a commercial seal kill, a grisly business which McLain blamed on "milady," who "must have the furs which these pretty creatures wear."[41] Then they departed for Unalaska and Dutch Harbor in the Aleutian Islands, where they saw the North Pacific fleet of Roosevelt's beloved navy. Passing through the Aleutians, they stopped briefly at the salmon-fishing villages of Kodiak Island.[42]

From there, they sailed up Prince William Sound to Valdez, the proposed terminus of a 400-mile road to Eagle that they were planning to recommend. Accompanied by two military officers, Nelson "rode on horseback twenty-five miles up the Government trail to Thompson's Pass" to verify the feasibility of the route. On August 16 they left for some sightseeing and souvenir buying at Sitka, then they were off to Juneau and so back to Seattle, where they arrived on August 26. They had covered some 6,600 miles in two months.[43]

Nelson caught the eastbound Great Northern train and arrived in Alexandria on August 30 after seventy days on the road. "It was a great trip," he told the *Alexandria Post–News*. Alaska "possesses much greater resources than any of our people at home imagine." But, he added, "What Alaska needs more than anything else to develop it are good wagon roads in the country."[44] There was no doubt in his mind that development was the proper goal. After Pinchot and Roosevelt later created the Chugach National Forest in southern Alaska, Nelson remarked, "I look upon the making of that forest reserve as a great folly."[45]

Yet Nelson adopted a moderate position on what type of development and government to recommend. He was no preservationist, but neither did he blindly acquiesce in corporate control of development. Though cautious about the feasibility of elections and legislatures in a huge area, he did not share Progressives' elitist disdain for frontier politics.

Back at the Capitol, the subcommittee members "assumed the role of Alaska patriarchs, . . . authorities on all subsequent legislation." Nelson became Alaska's *de facto* senator. They disappointed the Citizens League by recommending against territorial status

265

and by failing to recommend an elected delegate. Some Alaskans believed that the subcommittee or corporate lobbyists had convinced Roosevelt that Alaska was a corrupt, ring-dominated district like New Mexico, "in which none but a corporation man could be elected delegate." Nelson had a "marked sympathy" for the small prospector, and helped to keep the subcommittee's report somewhat balanced. In early 1904, he "braved the disapproval" of his subcommittee colleagues by fighting — in vain — for an elected delegate. He passed the "Nelson bill" establishing an "Alaska Fund" for road-building, education, and welfare expenses. Given the United States government's shrunken capacities and Alaska's swollen size, his road-building legislation created only primitive trails and patronage positions for "broken down lawyers and politicians." Still, he became popular in Alaska.[46] And, his proposed Alaska legislation did not threaten his popularity with his Minnesota constituents.

The growing tension between Norway and Sweden, still unequally yoked together in the Union, did pose risks to his popularity in Minnesota. The old controversy about a separate consular service for Norway flared up again in February, 1905, when negotiations over implementation collapsed. On May 27, the Norwegians presented to King Oscar II a unilateral bill establishing the separate consular service. The King promptly vetoed it.[47]

On May 29, Knute Nelson spoke at a banquet held at Minneapolis' Swedish-Norwegian Odin Club in honor of a touring group of Norwegian singers. Speaking at a recent Syttende Mai celebration, Governor John A. Johnson, a Swedish American, had gently touched on the tension by expressing the lofty hope that the hostile boundary between Sweden and Norway be erased—just as there were none between states in the United States. Learning little from his experience at the Evanger banquet, Nelson, by contrast, descended into the specifics. As at Evanger, he urged that Norway remain in the Union, and even wished it extended to unite all three Scandinavian countries — the ideal solution for a Scandinavian-American politician! The audience applauded, except for the Norwegian students. Their leader, Dr. Thompson, politely responded that his group "could not agree with their hospitable American countrymen in that regard."[48]

The criticism aimed at Nelson's remarks extended to the Norwegian newspapers, and it was not all so polite. A local critic called it "tactless advice" that showed that Nelson "pleads his own cause rather than Norway's." Normally quite supportive of Nelson, *Minneapolis Tidende* called his comments "unfortunate" and "opposed to what the whole Norwegian people unanimously insist on." A critical article also appeared in Christiania's *Aftenposten.*[49]

At Evanger, he had to defend himself without help from his patronage appointees and political allies. Now, in Minnesota and in Christiania, the Nelson "machine" and the Nelson consular service sprang to his defense. His longtime ally, *Nordvesten*, gave excuses: he had been misunderstood; it was a "nonpolitical" talk; "a literal translation into Norwegian" gave his "innocent English expressions . . . a completely different meaning." The editorial suggested that the plainspoken Nelson had delivered an American-style "after dinner talk," in which "the speaker with a little wit and humor tries to put the audience in a convivial mood." In Christiania, American Consul Henry Bordewich protested to *Aftenposten*'s editor. The consul and a Norwegian businessman arranged for the editor to interview Laurits Swenson, former American minister to Denmark and close Nelson ally, who defended the senator. Right then, Nelson was seeking to find a consular post for Swenson. Consul Søren Listoe, in turn, sent the *Aftenposten* "defense" to *Nordvesten* for its use.[50]

Meanwhile, the Union was breaking up. The King's veto caused the Norwegian cabinet to submit its resignation, but the King refused to accept the resignation. On June 7 the Storting declared that King Oscar II "had ceased to function as the King of Norway." The Storting authorized the cabinet to function as a provisional government of an independent Norway. Norway embarked on a campaign to persuade foreign governments, especially Great

Britain and the United States, to recognize its independence. Norwegian Americans embarked on a letter-writing campaign to persuade Knute Nelson to use his influence with the Roosevelt administration to that end. Here was the critical hour. Norway's future hung in the balance. War was a serious possibility, depending on Sweden's response. As the "most prominent" Norwegian American, Nelson could "prepare the ground" for American recognition, which "might even prevent war."[51]

Nelson would have none of it. He swiftly distanced himself from the issue. He prepared a form letter ("Dear sir") to send to the letter writers. It was "premature" to press for recognition. Sweden had not yet responded. Norway's government was "at present only a temporary" one. The cautious lawyer would wait until others had molded the fluid situation into hard legalities that he could acknowledge as facts. More importantly, he insisted, "I am a Senator of the United States" and cannot "take any other action in this matter than would become and be proper for a United States Senator. In other words I have not as free a hand in this matter as an outsider would have."[52] Writing to Consul Listoe, he discussed farming and patronage matters at length before ending with a brief, passive comment on the "awful snarl in Norway and Sweden. . . The good Lord only knows what the outcome may be."[53]

Coming from a man who had privately intervened and lobbied on behalf of hundreds of pension, job, and favor seekers, that was an evasive excuse. He had informally used his insider's influence before, why not now for "dear Mother Norway"? Why stand on the formality of presidential conduct of foreign affairs? Roosevelt could accept or ignore his advice.

Those who thought Nelson was a fellow countryman who could use his political pull to give Norway "a great lift" did not understand his political career or American political culture.[54] They saw appearances, not realities. Though of Norwegian birth, he was Americanized. Though he received ethnic votes at the polls, he could never have reached his high position without the

268

support of old-stock American leaders in the Republican party. In winning their support, he had been socialized into Gilded Age political culture. It sanctioned the distribution of patronage plums to ethnic groups but expected them to become Americanized. That was especially true of the nationalistic Republicans, somewhat less so of the more pluralist, localist Democrats. It was especially true in foreign affairs. Nelson had insisted (*had* to insist) to "Pitchfork" Ben Tillman that he did not represent the Norwegian people.

Ethnicity, like territorial issues, worked to insulate Nelson from ideological attacks within Minnesota. Given his Americanization, Republican nationalism, and Minnesota's ethnic diversity, it could not work to cause him openly to advocate an American foreign policy tilt toward his homeland. Norwegian Americans' very emotional involvement in the crisis of 1905 threatened his role as a political broker. It indicated that they were not as Americanized as he had boasted to the Senate that they were in contrast to New Mexicans. His broker role depended on their remaining sufficiently ethnic to regard him with uncritical ethnic pride. But the 1905 crisis, if it led to war, threatened to spark such ethnic loyalty as to cause them to look for leadership to advocates of cultural preservation, not to brokers. It threatened to cause ethnic conflict between his Swedish and Norwegian constituents. To demand he back Norway was to draw a line in the sand which he had to cross to prove his ethnicity—something his birth had been sufficient proof of before.

The 1905 crisis revealed how fully Knute Nelson was a product of Gilded Age patronage politics. His high position made him automatically a leader in the Norwegian-American community; but he was not a Norwegian-American *cultural* leader. When he found defenders of his Norwegian-American credentials, they were his patronage appointees, not the cultural leaders, the prominent intellectuals, Lutheran clerics, and *bygdelag* chiefs.

1906 kept him "on the jump" as new attacks came from an ideological, not ethnic, direction. 1906 was his year to campaign for

269

reelection. By supporting—and in part sponsoring—Roosevelt's legislative proposals and talking tariff reduction, Nelson had tried to identify himself with TR's moderate Progressivism. Yet times had changed. The moderate position that partly shielded him from agrarian protest in the 1880s and 1890s would not protect him from the new urban, expert reformers, the administrators and muckraking journalists and independent editors. They set higher standards for him, and for themselves—they claimed independence from partisan loyalties and patronage.

1906 was the year Wisconsin's fiery Progressive, "Battling Bob" La Follette, brought Insurgency to the Senate. His background was uncannily similar to Nelson's: a pious, widowed mother, a stepfather he did not respect, youth on a farm in a Norwegian area of Dane county, an ability to speak a Norwegian dialect, although he was not Norwegian American, rebellion against parental piety, legal training in Madison, three terms as a Republican congressman in the 1880s, service as governor, and election to the Senate. However, he was the skilled orator Nelson could never be—one of those grandstanding politicians whom the matter-of-fact Nelson could not abide. In the 1890s, he turned against the patronage, machine politics he had played a decade earlier.[55] Nelson likely saw his switch and his moralistic, anti-machine rhetoric as hypocrisy, not repentance. Thirteen years younger than Nelson, he had not been shaped by the Civil War, but spoke to a second and third generation of Norwegian immigrants who wanted to move beyond Civil War party loyalties.[56]

This younger man spoke to Nelson's natural constituency, sometimes in a Sogning dialect, but with a very different message. He appeared only too willing to battle the Senate itself and his fellow senators—to secure their defeat.[57] He symbolized the new political style, often called Insurgency, which Nelson found annoying. Primarily western Republicans, the Insurgents rebelled against the patronage, machine tactics of the established Republican leaders—especially after Taft became president.

La Follette's timing was excellent, for the Senate, the institution, was under increasing attack by 1906. Respected national journals like the *Atlantic Monthly* and the *North American Review* published critical articles. Because it was not apportioned according to population, it was undemocratic. It was not directly elected by the people. Senatorial courtesy and limitless debate enabled filibusters like Beveridge and Nelson to block legislation and thus hold the democratic House hostage to their pet ideas. The seniority system of allocating committee chairmanships produced an oligarchy.[58] In *The Election of Senators* (1906), political scientist George H. Haynes calculated that some twenty-six senators owed their election to their own wealth, their representation of "corporate wealth," or "political manipulation." Only seventeen owed it to their "statesmanship." Nelson he ranked with the twelve "men of the rank and file" — "Men of fair ability, but of no proved capacity for leadership."[59]

Personally, Nelson escaped unscathed from criticisms of the Senate as an aristocratic "House of Lords." It was impossible to portray Nelson as an arrogant nabob when he lived in a nine-room farmhouse and ate cornmeal mush as his dietary staple. Rural Minnesotans hearing him on the county-fair circuit would never believe that. At the Lyon county fair, "the Senator casually remarked that he had put up 250 loads of hay himself. 'Yes,' said the farmer, 'in your life-time, I suppose.' 'No sir, I have done that this summer,' emphatically replied the Senator-farmer, opening the eyes of many who were listening."[60] Constituents would never listen to the journalist who attacked Nelson as an aristocrat. Yet what weakened the institution also damaged his credibility. When critics emphasized "machine" politics and close ties to Big Business, Nelson was vulnerable.

In 1906 the first such critic was Joel Heatwole, editor of the *Northfield News* and former Republican congressman. The son of a Quaker abolitionist, Joel made a likely Progressive, but an unlikely prophet of Insurgency. In the 1890s he had built up quite a patronage-based "machine," which he maintained after retiring from Congress in 1903. He became a typical small-town

271

Progressive editor, albeit one with a strong ambition for the United States Senate. In 1904 Heatwole hoped to defeat Senator Moses Clapp's bid for reelection.[61] Nelson's men accused him of planning a "dump Nelson" maneuver for 1906-1907. He wrote to Nelson to deny it and to promise his support. However, Nelson dumped Heatwole's man, William Verity, as secretary of the 1904 Republican state central committee.[62]

To Nelson it seemed hypocrisy, spite, and bad faith when in 1906 Heatwole blasted him in a summer series of articles and editorials. The editor accused Nelson of deliberately inserting an "immunity clause" in his bill creating the Department of Commerce. This so-called "immunity bath" allowed a federal judge to dismiss indictments against Chicago meat packers. Heatwole also criticized Nelson's "Federal Machine" of patronage appointees for manipulating legislative nominations to ensure Nelson's reelection.[63] It took a machine builder to know one, but the Northfield editor was correct here. The "immunity bath" charge was doubtful.

The "wily Alexandrian" asked the President to defend him against this "bitter personal enemy." He had worked closely with Roosevelt on the Department of Commerce bill. They had asked Attorney General Philander Knox to draw up the amendment with the "immunity clause." They intended it to strengthen the Bureau of Corporations' investigative powers and regarded the judge's interpretation of it as unwarranted.[64] Roosevelt wrote back to support Nelson: "My memory of that matter is just the same as yours . . . . if it had not been for your action the Bureau of Corporations would have been a very ineffective bureau indeed . . . No one of us had the slightest reason for supposing that under [the amendment] such a decision as that of Judge Humphrey was possible." Using Roosevelt's reply, Nelson and John McLain composed an anti-Heatwole editorial ("Another Heatwole Nightmare") for the *Minneapolis Journal*. It became a Nelson campaign pamphlet.[65]

On November 1, the senator came to the editor's own town to

refute the "immunity bath" charge. Appearing at the Armory before an audience "composed largely" of St. Olaf and Carleton college students, he tactfully praised both institutions. Yet he admitted that he had especially come there to make his first visit to Norwegian-American St. Olaf. In fact, muckrakers and Insurgents found an audience in the growing number of high school and college graduates, who increasingly rejected the old patronage politics. This was not the place for Nelson to defend his "Federal Machine," nor did he try.[66] That same week, Heatwole responded by reprinting muckraker David Graham Phillips' attack on Nelson from his inflammatory *Cosmopolitan* series, "The Treason of the Senate."[67]

Heatwole had the honor of getting Knute Nelson's name into Phillips' series, which ran from March to November, 1906. It created a nationwide sensation. It "implied that most Senators were guilty of great public wrongdoing." It went far beyond previous criticisms. Small country weeklies reprinted parts of it and it was the talk of many small towns. In October, Nelson appeared in the senatorial rogues' gallery, as "Jim Hill's contribution to" a corporate-dominated Senate. Almost all of Phillips' portrait of "Jim Hill's Nelson" was derived from the *Northfield News*. (Phillips gave proper credit, though Heatwole may have been inspired by Phillips' "Treason" series when he first attacked Nelson back in June.) Of course, the "Jim Hill" charge was twenty-five years old and the "immunity bath" charge was greatly exaggerated. But this was the year many Americans made the discovery that "business corrupts politics," so both seemed convincing.[68]

Just as the October *Cosmopolitan* hit the newsstands, Senator La Follette arrived in Minnesota on "a five-month speaking campaign" to spread Insurgency in the West. He hoped his lecture fees would help pay for his new $30,000 farm near Madison. Hutchinson's public library board invited him to address that town's civic-minded citizens. For over three hours—past midnight, the audience "eagerly drank in the astonishing story" he so dramatically told: the American people had lost control of their

273

government. As elsewhere on his tour, when La Follette told of his railroad-valuation amendment, the audience demanded to know how their senators voted on it. "I've got the record here," La Follette replied. La Follette "didn't abuse" his fellow senators: "I read the roll call." Nelson had voted against it. This reading was his stock dramatic gesture. In this new nonpartisan age of experts and social scientists, it was the perfect "objective" act.[69]

This nonpartisan, Insurgent spirit invaded the Norwegian-American press. The *Ugeblad* ridiculed Nelson's mid-October speech in Fergus Falls. A "crowd of women and college students" heard "our very famous Senator," who had lost popularity. The affectionate nickname "the little Vossing" was no longer used. *Ugeblad* even dared make light of the familiar "poor immigrant" story repeated by the Park Region College professor who introduced Nelson. The "little Vossing's glory was tied" to that far-distant rags-to-fame story. Now, he "is twenty years behind the times," for he "preaches only party loyalty." "Our Norwegian immigrants' first Big Brother" was famous, but the political corruption so recently exposed in his party made his fame of little consolation to his countrymen.[70]

Had Norwegian Americans already become so Americanized that Nelson could no longer count on ethnic pride to shield him from ideological criticism? Some had, but the *Ugeblad* was not typical. That year, La Follette found ethnic pride still a formidable factor when he tried to run an Insurgent Swedish American, Irvine L. Lenroot, for governor against a more conservative Norwegian American, James O. Davidson. Many of La Follette's Norwegian-American supporters deserted to Davidson, who defeated Lenroot.[71]

In Minnesota, the Insurgents lacked a strong candidate to run against Nelson. And most Progressives were still united behind Roosevelt. Also when the October *Cosmopolitan* appeared, Senator Beveridge came to Minnesota and praised Nelson: his "offical life has been as pure as the falling snow."[72] Heatwole proved no match for Nelson, though the senator unwittingly reinforced the percep-

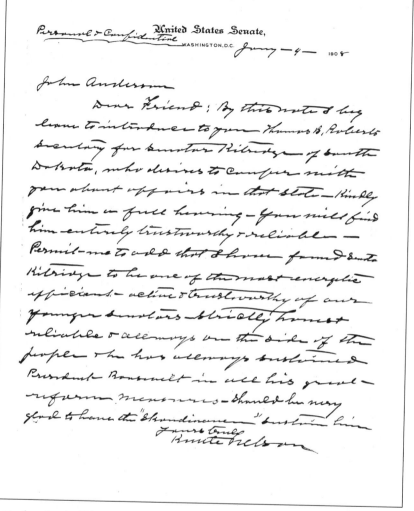

Letter from Senator Nelson to John Anderson, publisher of Skandinaven *in Chicago soliciting his support for a political candidate, January 4, 1908.*

tion he was behind the times when he refused to ride in an automobile on a last-minute campaign swing around Minneapolis. United States Marshall William Grimshaw, Nelson's patronage appointee, was to drive him in his car, "but the Senator balked" at

275

being carried by this federal machine. Dutifully, Grimshaw defended his chief: "It makes me nervous to ride in those machines myself." Nelson took a horse-drawn carriage.[73]

On January 22, 1907, the state legislature overwhelmingly elected Knute Nelson to a third term. Ole Sageng of Dalton, "the lone Populist" in the State Senate, had to nominate a Democrat as the Populist candidate. "His party, he admitted, is about dead." Prohibitionists also nominated a candidate. They had a future, especially in Alexandria. Nelson had six more years in the Senate.[74]

Nelson's personal life also revealed that time was passing him by. He had no grandchildren, and no prospect of any. Ida remained unmarried, stayed at home, and stayed in bed too late in the morning, in her father's opinion. His greatest trials were with his maverick bachelor son Henry Knute Nelson. He had provided Henry with the capital to start a hardware and implement business and a farm in Grant county. A convivial man in his thirties, Henry lacked his father's work ethic but not his temper. Folks around Alexandria thought he was unable "to overcome the stature of his father's reputation." Henry became a drinker "and neglected his business." All sorts of "bums and drinkers hung around him as he had money to spend," Knute recalled. Others remembered, "Many is the time his father dragged him out of a saloon by the ear." After still another bitter father-son confrontation in 1905, Henry moved to Everett and then Tacoma, Washington. Here he worked for a lumber and sawmill firm under the protective eye of David Clough, his father's former lieutenant governor.[75]

He contracted tuberculosis ("consumption") in 1906. Knute had him hospitalized at a sanitorium in Colorado Springs. His condition slowly worsened. Knute visited him in mid-August 1907, and Nicholina spent over two months with him.[76] In early February, 1908, Knute made a "final visit" to the dying Henry. He did not remain until Henry died, for the doctor was uncertain how long Henry would last, and Knute "was obliged to return" to Washington. Undoubtedly, his political career had called him away many times when his family needed him. While in the House, the governor's office,and the Senate, he had never brought his entire family to live in St. Paul or Washington. Politics meant separation. Henry died on March 17. "You can imagine how sad it makes me feel to give up my only son," he wrote to Consul Listoe. "He was only a baby when we went to Alexandria, in August, 1871." He was buried in Alexandria on March 20, 1908. Grimshaw, Nelson aide Simon Michelet, and State Senator Ole O. Canestorp were among those from out of town who attended.[77]

That was another result of a long political career. Were these men friends or just hangers-on dependent on Nelson for patronage? How could one tell the difference? Friends were likely to ask for a job at some point, and jobholders like Listoe tried to be friendly. The lines blurred. Nelson's lack of grandchildren, his lengthy absences, his hardworking preoccupation with his role as Minnesota's senior senator—all meant he gradually ceased to have a private life. Senator became almost his first name. Voluntary retirement became increasingly unlikely.

Voluntary retirement is just what Theodore Roosevelt chose— or rather, he chose to honor the traditional two-term limit on presidents. Roosevelt picked Secretary of War William Howard Taft as his choice for the Republican nomination, which Taft won. On a cold, snowy, late-September morning, Taft pulled into Alexandria's Great Northern depot on his 1908 campaign train. It "had hardly stopped when Senator Nelson was lifted on board by members of the party and in a few words introduced Mr. Taft." Nelson spoke for two minutes, and Taft for eight, and then the "Presidential Special" was off to Fergus Falls and up the old St. Vincent extension to Ada and Crookston. Nelson left it at Crookston, but Taft continued west and on into the White House with a victory over Bryan.[78]

Roosevelt departed on an extended African safari and European tour, and left Taft to continue Roosevelt's policies. Taft tried, but within a few months he was in trouble over allegations that he was sabotaging Roosevelt's conservation policy. The re-

277

sulting controversy brought Knute Nelson his most dramatic, most extended role on the national stage.

Developed in close cooperation with Gifford Pinchot, Roosevelt's conservation policy was his darling, his greatest legacy. Pinchot's professional, public-spirited Forest Rangers were a symbol of Roosevelt's administration, as John F. Kennedy's Peace Corps volunteers were of his. Relatively free of congressional interference, relying on presidential control of the public domain, Roosevelt had withdrawn millions of acres of western lands from the Land Office and eventual sale. He created national forests and forest reserves. Enjoying almost unlimited access to Roosevelt, Pinchot raided other agencies' turf and became the conservation "czar." An advocate of resource planning, he convinced the president in 1908 to create a national planning body, the National Conservation Commission, not authorized by Congress. Because of his expertise in land law, Nelson was picked to head its Lands Section and to be on its Executive Committee. Pinchot pestered Nelson ("Do not think me too insistent") to attend its meetings regularly.[79]

Pinchot was no preservationist. Disgusted at the wanton waste under Gilded Age politics of settlement and development, he simply wanted rational, sustainable use of natural resources—leased, not sold, by the federal government. He knew of Nelson's ties to the old politics. One of his many journalist friends wrote to warn him that Nelson was "a treacherous, dishonest, time-serving politician" who "has joined in stabbing the Forestry movement, so far as it concerns Minnesota."[80] Pinchot held the Land Office in particular contempt as "a haven of inefficiency and archaic procedure . . . a lawyers' agency" which "habitually took what Pinchot believed to be a narrowly legalistic approach to resource policy." Roosevelt brought in a lawyer, a Progressive and former reform mayor of Seattle, Richard A. Ballinger, to reform the Land Office. He did so, but Pinchot disliked the new, efficient Land Office that fought his poaching on its turf. Until Ballinger returned to Seattle in March, 1908, bureaucratic in-fighting raged

between the agencies, between an easterner courting corporations and a westerner sympathizing with small prospectors,
ranchers, and entrepreneurs.[81]

Pinchot lost his virtual cabinet status when Taft took over.
Worse, Taft chose Ballinger as his Secretary of the Interior:
Pinchot's Forest Service was in the Department of Agriculture;
the Land Office, in Interior. Lawyers Taft and Ballinger felt that
Roosevelt's land withdrawals exceeded statutory authority and
began to reverse them. Convinced Taft was undoing TR's conservation policy, Pinchot fumed, but the public would not understand an attack over disputable interpretations. On July 16, 1909,
a young, idealistic Land Office agent, Louis R. Glavis, informed
the Forest Service of his investigation into claims filed by businessman Clarence Cunningham and his associates in coal fields
in Alaska's Chugach National Forest. Over the next month,
Glavis informed Pinchot and his subordinates that he had evidence that Ballinger was moving to approve these fraudulent
"Cunningham claims." They helped him gather evidence, inter-
pret it, and, later, publicize it in national magazines such as
Collier's Weekly. Here was proof that would down Ballinger.[82]

Or so they thought. Actually, the Land Office was preparing to
disallow, not allow, the claims. While out of office, Lawyer
Ballinger had represented Cunningham before his old department, but when he became secretary he recused himself from involvement in the case. Not a large corporation, the Cunningham
claimants were small investors who had run afoul of the land
law's unrealistic maximum 160-acre plots, far too small for prof-
itable coal mining. Alaska desperately needed locally mined coal
for railroad development. Glavis's charges were "a fantastic per-
version of the record" based on a skewed "selection of evidence."
They were aimed at an old, corrupt Land Office that no longer existed. After Pinchot sent Glavis to tell his story to Taft, the president heard Interior's version, exonerated Ballinger, and fired
Glavis. The whistleblower published his muckraking exposé in
the November 13th issue of *Collier's Weekly.* After Pinchot pub-

licly questioned Taft's handling of the matter, he was fired too. With public opinion aroused, Congress established a joint House-Senate investigating committee, headed by that Alaska and land-law expert, Senator Knute Nelson.

The Ballinger-Pinchot hearings were a national cause célèbre, an "American Dreyfus case," a long-running soap opera of bureaucracy, and an Insurgent indictment of old-style politics. To domesticate the soap opera, Glavis's "attractive blond" estranged wife stayed in Washington during the hearings. She promised "a big sensation," presumably to discredit the key anti-Ballinger witness.[83]

From January to May, 1910, and then briefly in September, Knute Nelson watched his career pass before his eyes: the Land Office and land-office lawyers, claimants' frauds, Alaska, patronage. At sixty-eight, he had finally risen in the seniority system to chair the Senate Committee on Public Lands, then to chair the Ballinger-Pinchot committee, the center of national attention. By the time he arrived, though, he was behind the times. The night before the committee held its first meeting, Senator La Follette hosted a soirée for Insurgent solons and journalists at his Washington home. Miss Emily Bishop, a Chautauqua performer, gave a monologue featuring satiric impersonations of mossback senators. She "waded into the conservatives" in the Senate, "cut them into frying sizes, and put them in the pan." She may not have impersonated Nelson, but the hearings put him in the frying pan.[84] No longer a safe haven, land law for territories was now a very divisive issue.

Public hearings began on Wednesday, January 26, 1910, in Room 210 of the Senate Office Building. Knute Nelson sat at the head of a long table, with senators on his left, congressmen on his right, stenographers further down, and the first witness, Louis Glavis, at the foot "in a raised chair . . . flanked by" attorneys. Nearby was the press table. The room was full of spectators, most of them women, on this and succeeding days. Though denied the vote, women read the muckraking journals. While they demanded the vote, here was a chance to participate. The audience became "two camps of partisans," taking sides and debating right in Room 210.[85]

Days earlier, the chair of the forestry committee of the Detroit Federation of Women's Clubs wrote to inform Nelson that their 3,000 members "stand for Pinchot and the Pinchot Policies." With words sure to rile Nelson, she quoted a Michigan professor: "The land office always had a bad name." When women in Detroit cared about land claims in Alaska, the politics of distribution was in trouble: conflicting views were sure to collide. The males-only politics which Nelson was comfortable with was also in trouble. These same 3,000 women warned Representative Edwin Denby of Michigan, a committee member, that if he failed to support Pinchot he would not be reelected. The *Washington Post* doubted "if one woman in the whole lot is familiar with the facts" in the Ballinger-Pinchot case. But many probably were, for the press was airing them. Many would find out the facts firsthand in Room 210.

The male protagonists were an assortment of American regional types: Pinchot, the wealthy eastern expert and arrogant bureaucrat; Ballinger, the self-made, moralistic westerner sure the white-hats must win and the little guys defeat "Federal land-lordism"; George Wharton Pepper, the polite, aristocratic Philadelphia lawyer representing Pinchot; Louis D. Brandeis, the brilliant, aggressive Jewish lawyer from Boston, representing Glavis and *Collier's Weekly*; and John J. Vertrees, the drawling, slow-thinking Nashville lawyer, "prone to epithet," accustomed to haranguing a rural jury in Tennessee. Finally, Knute Nelson, Norwegian-American farmer, career politician, and country lawyer, "not unaware of the flavor of a quid of tobacco." In Room 210, over five months, under a national spotlight, these men grated on each other's stereotypes. Pinchot later described Nelson as "a hardboiled, tobacco-chewing, short and powerful squarehead Norwegian." Nelson thought Pinchot "very bitter and vindictive," and Brandeis, "very bright" but "one of the worst and most unscrupulous pettifoggers I have ever seen."[86]

281

The stakes were very high, for Pinchot aimed to prove that Taft was destroying Roosevelt's policy. "Both newspaper men and spectators were eager to have the proceeding develop into a sensational controversy between President Taft and his predecessor." Rejecting a proposal to focus the hearings on shaping future legislation, Nelson erred by making their scope almost unlimited. Taking advantage of that, Brandeis angered the committee by refusing to give specific charges against Ballinger and by ultimately prosecuting the whole system of patronage, influence-peddling politics. To protect Taft, Republican leaders in Congress tried to ensure that the committee's 7-to-5 Republican majority was solidly for the president. The day after the hearings began, Knute and Nicholina dined at the White House. As chairman, he was responsible for protecting Taft's interests.[87]

He tried, but reading law in Madison with William Vilas was no preparation for Brandeis, Harvard Law School graduate, corporate lawyer, and "people's attorney." When Brandeis requested more documents to support his broad case, Nelson resisted. In mid-February, reported Brandeis, "I had a private tussle with Senator Nelson, Chairman, about withholding documents of the Interior Dept. we had called for, but won my point & relations are diplomatically friendly."[88]

Not friendly for long, for on April 1, Nelson grew frustrated during a long fencing match over a letter Glavis had written but apparently not sent—but which Brandeis used as evidence. Nelson erupted: "There is evidence that it never was sent. You knew that. Now, why did you not tell the committee that."

Brandeis said, "I did not know it. I do not know it now."

Nelson insisted, "That is Mr. Glavis's testimony. Why did you conceal that fact when you offered that [letter]?"

"Mr. Chairman!" shouted Brandeis angrily, "as he fairly leaped toward the Senator, his face livid. 'I object strenuously . . . that statement is absolutely improper and ought to be withdrawn.'" Two Democratic congressmen insisted Nelson withdraw his statement.

"'I won't withdraw it,' said Chairman Nelson stubbornly. His face was crimson." After much parliamentary maneuvering, committee members backed away from a move to force Nelson to repent, but the incident weakened his leadership. Though chairman, they agreed, he was no different than the others. His word counted for no more.[89]

On April 30, the committee denied Brandeis's request to subpoena records of Attorney General George W. Wickersham. (Taft had asked Wickersham to write a report on Glavis's charges and Ballinger's denials.) Brandeis wanted to prosecute Taft's politics: "I think Wickersham and his acts are a fair sample & product of our special interest activities." Also, Brandeis became convinced that the attorney general had pre-dated his report—and, later, that Taft's letter exonerating Ballinger was based on a memorandum drafted by one of Ballinger's subordinates, Oscar Lawler. The committee did not want the "circus atmosphere of the hearing" prolonged. The administration denied that the report was pre-dated or that the exonerating letter was based on any Lawler memorandum.[90]

Meanwhile Ballinger had taken the stand, and Brandeis grilled him relentlessly. On May 10, the pro-Ballinger chairman could take it no longer. He felt that the Boston attorney was browbeating Ballinger. When Brandeis insisted upon his way of cross-examining the witness, Nelson angrily pounded the table, "You have insulted the witnesses, but you can not insult this committee."

"Then, to the astonishment of the committee and the crowd of spectators, a woman came to the rescue of the discomfited counsel." From the rear of the room a middle-aged woman yelled, "Your committee can't insult him either." The audience burst into laughter. "The woman was Miss Margaret Hamilton, a lawyer, . . . a spectator at the hearings and . . . a pronounced anti-Ballinger partisan." Her comment broke the tension caused by the Nelson-Brandeis standoff.[91]

The real tension was still to come. Brandeis kept demanding to see the supposed Lawler memorandum. Under the ground rules,

Nelson felt "utterly helpless" to cut short Brandeis's endless cross-examination of Ballinger. On Saturday, May 14, Frederick M. Kerby, Ballinger's private secretary, spilled the truth. In a statement published in the Washington newspapers, he asserted that Lawler had dictated to him a letter "substantially the same" as the President's letter. From the golf course that afternoon, Taft issued a denial of Kerby's charges. He, Taft, dictated the letter, and did not base it on Lawler's memorandum. That same day, Wickersham sent the committee "a carbon copy of the original Lawler letter, which he said had just been found." It proved Taft wrong and made him look like "a liar and forger." On Sunday Republican leaders, including Nelson, held an emergency meeting at the White House. The President's mood "was black and pathetic." That day he wrote a letter to Nelson explaining the pre-dating and the use of the Lawler memorandum.[92]

On Tuesday, Brandeis presented Kerby as a witness, to Nelson's surprise ("Is he in the room?"). The chairman acted as prosecuting attorney, cross-examining the twenty-four-year-old Kerby "to confuse and entangle him." Nelson especially pressed him on what job he had been promised to induce him to testify, since Ballinger had fired him. Journalists had promised him a job, which they delivered. He did not break. Lawler wildly charged that Pinchot and Brandeis had paid Kerby money to make up the story. "The spectators who crowded the room, most of them women, hissed [Lawler] loudly and the custodian . . . summoned the police to preserve order."[93]

Brandeis's case against the Taft administration held. The Cunningham claims were largely forgotten in the outrage caused by Taft's bumbling of the Lawler memorandum. It happened that "Halley's Comet was making another appearance on its seventy-six-year circuit"; the evening of May 18, earth was to pass through the comet's tail. People were alarmed about possible damage. It was a bad omen for Taft, for he was seriously damaged by the Ballinger-Pinchot case. The following month Roosevelt returned and soon began sounding like a presidential candidate for 1912.

The Ballinger-Pinchot hearings enjoyed a brief fall run—as farce. The committee met at the West Hotel in Minneapolis in early September, because a National Conservation Congress was then in session in St. Paul. With several Republicans absent from the Twin Cities, the Democratic minority "was temporarily in the majority." The Democrats tried to pass a committee report harshly critical of Ballinger. To prevent that, two Republicans left the meeting and hid in Room 222, directly above the committee's room, to deny the Democrats a quorum. The sergeant-at-arms went to fetch the absent members. When he found them, they refused to come down and Nelson had refused to authorize him to arrest them. Thereupon, the Democrats passed their anti-Ballinger (anti-Taft) report. To stop this, "Senator Nelson announced that he was going to the washroom for a few minutes." After a half hour he had not returned. Now suspicious, the Democrats found a Nelson note calling the committee to meet in Chicago the following Tuesday, when the Republicans could reassemble their majority. A Minneapolis reporter discovered Nelson up in Bill Grimshaw's room. "The old senator was sitting there, chuckling."[94]

In December Nelson was "able to gather enough of his truant committee under one roof to constitute a quorum" and pass the Republican, pro-Ballinger report. But the country had long since found Taft and Ballinger guilty. And Nelson they found unfairly biased, stubborn, hot-tempered, and guilty of leading a whitewash of Ballinger. La Follette and Brandeis became good friends as Ballinger-Pinchot invigorated Insurgents. Yet it presaged their failure. By fragmenting power, American politics forced reformers to seize all power bases for long periods lest one block or undo their efforts. Bypassing Congress, Pinchot's reform by executive order only interrupted government's "incorrigible bungl[ing]" in Alaska. Inertia and patronage politics ultimately proved too much for reformers. Hearings were soon forgotten.

Nelson also failed. Even the White House seemed ungrateful for his effort. A year later, an informal party, including the president, heard Senator Robert Taylor of Tennessee tell his stories. One was on old Senator Knute Nelson. "Taylor said whenever he heard him speak he always thought of an old clock they had at home. When the hands of the clock pointed to twelve and it struck six, he felt certain that it was twenty minutes to two." Taft, not Nelson, had sounded uncertain, inaccurate notes during the hearings, but his cronies forgot that fact.[95]

Thirteen

Serving the Fatherland: Reprise

After Taft's bungling of the Ballinger-Pinchot affair, Knute Nelson distanced himself from the president. In September, 1911, he told a Minnesota editor visiting Washington that, if Taft ran for reelection in 1912, he had "a farm near Alexandria, which would need a lot of looking after." He knew that Minnesota voters had not applauded his own performance at the hearings. While bass fishing, he insisted to friends that he was prepared to lose his own reelection bid in 1912: "I won't shed any tears if I am beaten. I had rather be boss on my farm here than be a servant of any man or set of men in the Senate. . . . No man or set of men can boss me against my own will and judgment, and I will stand by my friends, down or up, when they are in the right."[1] That was mostly bluster, a pair of false choices. He hoped to be neither beaten nor bossed. His canny instincts usually allowed him to escape such traps. And his officeholding friends were rarely in the right, in the eyes of Insurgents, yet he had little choice but to stand by them, for they ran his "Federal Machine" back in Minnesota.

In 1911, Nelson pursued a cautious and quasi-Progressive course to forestall any serious opposition. In the Senate he spoke in favor of direct election of United States senators, but with

Congress retaining its constitutional authority to regulate such elections. A nationalist, he insisted on that power lest urban socialists and workers disrupt elections or intimidate voters. Southern senators interpreted it as a threat to southern laws denying the vote to African Americans.

Nelson denied that this authority was aimed at the South. Senator Bacon of Georgia denied using the word "South." "The Senator will pardon me if I did refer to the South." After the Georgian pardoned him, Nelson added, "I did not do it in an un-Christian sense."

Bacon objected to northerners' reassurances containing the word "South" and implying that southerners had improper election procedures that they needed to be reassured about. Covering his eyes and ears, Nelson would see and hear no evil: "The laws are enforced North and South . . . . there is no occasion for Federal interference."[2]

Nelson also followed a Progressive course on Taft's reciprocity agreement lowering tariffs on Canadian exports to the United States. He joined about a dozen Insurgents, including Moses Clapp and La Follette, in dogged resistance to reciprocity. It would allow Canadian grain into the country duty-free and harm Minnesota farmers. "I shall under no circumstances go back on the farmers," he wrote. Taft's proposal was defeated.[3]

Nelson skillfully distributed patronage, worked both sides of the political street, and served his constituents as they needed him. He placed Nicolay Grevstad of *Skandinaven* as Minister to Uruguay and Paraguay and defeated conservative congressman James Tawney on the International Joint Commission regulating use of international waters between the United States and Canada. Tawney and Congressman Andrew J. Volstead sent him lists of voters in their districts so he could mail them seeds, farm bulletins, and copies of his speeches.[4]

That failed to impress Insurgents or their clientele, the growing number of civic good-government groups concerned about corruption of politics by business. Minnesota had many: the

United States Senator Moses E. Clapp points with pride or views with alarm at the Grant county fair in Herman in 1911.

Municipal Voters' League (Minneapolis), Minnesota Citizens' League, Saturday Lunch Club. They now had better means of communicating with ordinary citizens: magazines and newspapers now more accessible through rural free delivery, new public library systems, and the telephone.[5] Louis Brandeis came to Minneapolis in early January, 1912, to address the Saturday Lunch Club and a local La Follette-for-President group. He pointedly praised Senator Clapp, but not Nelson. Reportedly, the La Follette forces had decided "a fight will be made on Senator Knute Nelson" and Brandeis would later return to give anti-Nelson speeches. A Minneapolis attorney, La Follette supporter, former state legislator, and Norwegian American, James A. Peterson, announced his candidacy for Nelson's seat.[6]

As usual, Nelson waited before announcing his intentions. Rather than allow La Follette to claim Insurgents' sole allegiance in the fight against Taft, Roosevelt entered the race for the Republican nomination in February. Still Nelson waited. After the June Republican convention nominated Taft, and Roosevelt bolted to form the Progressive ("Bull Moose") Party, Nelson worriedly wrote to Michelet: "How does the result affect us politically in Minnesota? How are the papers lining up on T[aft] and R[oosevelt]?" To him, the tri-cornered presidential race, with Democrats nominating New Jersey's progressive governor, Woodrow Wilson, looked "very chaotic." Michelet advised a short campaign that kept political operatives and "bosses in the background." Adding to the uncertainty was Nelson's need, under a new state law, to campaign for a popular election, not a legislative ballot.[7]

Avoiding presidential commitments and even the appearance of pushing his own candidacy, Nelson worked through surrogates to survive the chaos of 1912. For months, he refused to take sides in the Taft-Roosevelt-Wilson triangle. He refused to announce his candidacy, until correspondents by the score wrote to urge him not to retire. Nelson was Minnesota's all-time master at creating the illusion of a political draft. By the time his affidavit of candidacy was filed — for him — on July 31, his "Federal Machine" had lined up editorial endorsements by the *St. Paul Pioneer Press*, the *St. Paul Dispatch*, the *Minneapolis Tribune*, and the *Duluth News Tribune*. Editor H.V. Jones of the *Minneapolis Journal* was more hesitant. He warned Nelson, "The Ballinger matter hurt you in the State." Others repeated the warning. Yet, by making a deal with the Roosevelt campaign — Nelson would not "injure Roosevelt" if the Roosevelt men did not oppose him — he neutralized much of the pro-Pinchot sentiment against him.[8]

La Follette's Minnesota supporters still strongly opposed him. On August 31, less than three weeks before the Republican primary, *La Follette's Weekly* harshly attacked him as a servant of the "trusts." "Minnesota's System Senator: Nelson's Service to Plutocracy" was widely distributed as a campaign tract. On his speaking tour, Peterson repeated La Follette's 1906 "roll call" tactic and the old 1906 charges ("immunity bath," etc.). The *St. Paul Daily News* hammered him with front-page cartoons: Nelson mopping Ballinger with whitewash and poking Justice in the eye

KING KNUTE
(After Thackeray.)

Old King Knute was weary-hearted; he had reigned for
  years a score,
Battling for the wealthy interests on the stand-pat senate floor,
And he thought upon his actions walking by the wild
  seashore.

On that day a something vexed him; that was clear to
  old and young,
Thrice he yawned in dull vexation at the jibes Jim Tawney sprung,
Once Ed Smith would have consoled him, but he bade
  him hold his tongue.

"Something ails my gracious master," cried the steel
  trust with a roar.
"Sure, my lord, it is the whitewash on thy hand that
  makes thee sore?"
"Pshaw!" exclaimed the angry monarch, "whitewash is
  an awful bore."

Up spake little Jakey Preus, Adolph Olson's comforter,
"Taft will heal thee of thy aching—cling to Taft and
  Ballinger!"
Old King Knute, with blazing eyeballs, made a lunge for
  Jakey's fur.

Wheelock, brave and lusty keeper of the drawbridge
  and the moat,
Up and cried, "Cheer up, great chieftain — hang to
  Adolph Olson's coat."
"Wretch!" shrieked good old Knute, "your scheming
  seeks to rob me of my goat!"

"Might I stay this dire revision, good Sir Edward," old
  Knute cried.
"Could I bid trust prosecutions stop for good their on-
  ward ride
I might still make folks forget the barbed trust arrows
  in their hide.

"But the voters are uprising like a mighty troubled sea,
And I greatly fear the rushing waves will soon rush
  over me—

I hate to think that folks will say 'Where in the world
  is he?'

"Will the advancing waves obey me, if I make the old
  con sign?"
Said Ed Smith, "O lord and master, land and sea alike
  are thine."
"Still I can't forget," said old Knute, "that Jim Tawney's in the brine."

Then Knute turned toward the ocean—"Back," he cried,
  "turn in retreat,
Venture not, thou stormy rebel, to approach the master's
  seat—
Ocean, be thou still! I bid thee come not nearer than
  my feet."

But the sullen ocean chortled, "Little man, you are a
  bun—— ——
Think not you can stay my progress on the havoc I've
  begun—
And as for your feet, well Knute, you'll never need
  them more to run."

Then a curious interloper jostled up and said "Before
You go back to camp, please tell me are you strong for
  Theodore?"
But a wad of silence walloped him and left him lame
  and sore.   —LARRY HO.

"King Knute." Cartoon in St. Paul Daily News, *September 13, 1912.*

with the mop handle; "a perspiring Knute Nelson wearing a Taft button and being pushed by lumber, steel, and liquor interests" and being pulled "by Jim Hill and a dog" whose face looked much like Bill Grimshaw's.[9]

Nelson did not deliver a single speech or attend a single political meeting. Campaign work was done by old friends, officeholders, and friendly editors. He closeted himself in Alexandria, composed a fourteen-page campaign booklet and had 50,000 copies of it mailed out, often with a personal note, and wrote numerous letters.[10] His campaign was more a mass mailing inviting Minnesotans to an all-state reunion than a discussion of Insurgents' issues. Inertia is a powerful force in politics. Peterson represented the new style; Nelson, the old memories. Direct election of United States senators gave voters their choice, but not the information on which to base it. With the Republican newspapers peddling the myth that the "Grand Old Man," indifferent to politics, was "attending to his farm work," the politics of nostalgia was strong.[11] With Nelson secluded, Peterson shadow-boxed and landed no blows. Also relying on speeches and friendly editors, the Insurgent did not have much greater contact with voters than the regular Republican.

On September 17, Nelson won nomination with 58 percent of the vote to Peterson's 42 percent. For a forty-year veteran supported by both Roosevelt and Taft Republicans, that was less than impressive. Grimshaw expected a two-to-one margin and all eighty-six counties. Peterson carried six counties, primarily ones with large Swedish-American populations.[12]

Nelson continued his direct-mail campaign against his general election foe, Democrat Daniel Lawler, his 1892 gubernatorial opponent. Rarely did he venture far from Alexandria. He stubbornly resisted requests to join the Republican state campaign train or to endorse Taft. After Archbishop John Ireland's desperate appeal in late October, he relented, drove to Osakis, boarded the campaign special, and ever so slightly supported Taft. "I filed as a Republican . . . and it is my intention now to support the

Republican ticket from top to bottom." He did not mention Taft by name. The train made twenty-four whistle-stops that day. Nelson left it at Hallock, lest he be too closely identified with the unpopular president.[13]

The election confirmed his pessimism about Taft, who received less than 20 percent of the state's vote and failed to carry a single Minnesota county. The Socialist Eugene V. Debs carried two counties, received almost 50 percent of Taft's total, and outpolled him in fifteen counties. Bull-Mooser Roosevelt defeated runner-up Wilson in Minnesota, although Wilson won the national election. Nelson received the highest vote total of anyone (173,072) and handily beat Lawler (102,541), but the election showed that political revolt was just beginning, not ending.[14] Insurgency had stirred up voters and made them too unpredictable to suit an old-style politician like Nelson.

Nationally, the 1912 election made the Congress too Democratic to suit a veteran of Gilded Age Republican supremacy. The Democrats won a comfortable 51-to-44 margin in the Senate and an overwhelming 291-to-127 majority in the House—plus control of the White House by a former political science professor who believed in a strong presidency and a strong party control of government. In January, 1913, the Minnesota legislature formally ratified voters' decision to send Nelson into this new political alignment. In a "first," matching the first popular election of a United States senator, "a movie picture machine planted in the house chamber took the members in the act" of unanimously selecting Nelson.[15]

The senator was not in St. Paul for the pro forma vote, but he returned in early February to address the legislature and to attend a seventieth-birthday banquet in his honor. Enroute to St. Paul, he gave an interview which revealed his secrets of success: hard work, temperate habits, spartan tastes, lack of greed, and "careful study of law and politics, constitutional history and general history." His "sympathy with modern progressive ideas" showed a realization that times had changed. Yet his was a lawyer's

293

Nelson around the time of his reelection to the Senate in 1912.

Progressivism, looking to the courts, dependent on a jury's willingness to convict.[16]

The bipartisan banquet was a high-water mark of his popularity, still intact despite Ballinger-Pinchot, Peterson's charges, and a congressional report highly critical of Michelet's conduct as Indian agent at White Earth Reservation. James J. Hill sat on

294

Nelson's right at the speakers' table. The senator reminisced about Hill bringing the St. Paul and Pacific railroad to Alexandria. Governor Adolph Eberhart, Hill, and former university president Cyrus Northrop all praised "Minnesota's Grand Old Man." Nelson's speech to the legislative joint session was also a summing-up of the important legislation passed since he went to the Senate in 1895.[17]

Beginning a month later, Wilson's administration was not like anything he had heretofore experienced. Wilson led a revitalized Democratic party, including over a hundred freshman representatives eager to undo their party's reputation as "the organized incompetence of the country." From the start, Wilson seized the initiative. He called a special session and addressed Congress in person, the first president to do so in 112 years. He kept Congress in almost continuous session for nearly two years—which tired the aging Nelson. He achieved tariff reduction in only five months; Nelson thought it was biased toward southern interests. He used the Democratic caucus to hurry the Senate's slow consensus-building, "senatorial-courtesy" style. Nelson hated being in an ignored minority: "when it comes to a Democratic caucus we Republicans are ignored and are outside of the breastworks."[18] To make matters worse, Brandeis was Wilson's major adviser on domestic reform.

The 1913 debate over banking and currency reform illustrated how powerless Nelson was serving under Wilson compared to his service under Roosevelt. Reform had been demanded for years by Populists and Insurgents railing at the "Money Trust." The Panic of 1907 increased demands for the somewhat contradictory goals of "sound money," "easy credit," safe banks, and local control. City bankers sought a dominant role in a centralized system to forestall popular pressures for inflation. Headed by conservative Senator Nelson W. Aldrich, the National Monetary Commission recommended what the American Bankers' Association sought. Bryan Democrats and some Insurgents favored government control of a decentralized system. Country bankers like Marcus Lauritsen of Tyler, Minnesota, also thought "there is no way possible to keep a central bank free from Wall St.," and stressed small banks' interests. With the Democratic party triumphant, anything from the conservative Republican Aldrich was suspect. With his large majorities, Wilson was positioned to broker a compromise.[19]

Knute Nelson seemed positioned to affect the outcome. He was the highest-ranking Republican on the Committee on Banking and Currency. He made his usual thorough study of the problem, which impressed impartial observers. He understood both the theory and the mechanics of the system of money and banking. From his rural midwestern perspective, he argued that the 1907 panic was caused by midwestern bankers depositing reserves in New York City banks, which used them to make call loans for stock market speculation. Safety and security were his bywords: high reserve requirements, gold reserves not paper assets, reserves kept at home not sent to New York, government control of banking. He demanded that banks grant more farm loans, which he probably regarded as the most secure.[20]

Yet the key players squaring off were large eastern and midwestern bankers against small country bankers, and conservative Democrats against radical Bryan Democrats. They argued centralization against decentralization, and government control against bankers' control. The Republican plan was likely only a bankers' bargaining chip to force changes in the Democrats' Glass-Owen bill. The Republicans were pawns, not players. Democrats and bankers compromised on a decentralized system with twelve regional Federal Reserve banks run by bankers but supervised by a government-dominated central board in Washington. Though Nelson on December 8 delivered a major address defending the Republican plan, time had run out. A week later, caucus rule prevailed. While Nelson sat on the conference committee, Republicans were not permitted to play any substantive role. Four days after the Federal Reserve Act passed, he delivered an angry and sarcastic attack on caucus rule. He warned Democrats that "it

296

is a long road that has no turning." He abhorred caucus rule as a violation of the traditional process of reasoned debate and compromise.[21]

The Federal Reserve Act gave Wilson a trophy that historians call his greatest legislative achievement, but it met few other goals. Decentralization was meaningless. The New York Federal Reserve bank and the Washington board dominated. A national financial market undercut efforts to set regional interest rates and credit terms. The "Fed's" reliance on short-term commercial notes as the basis of its "elastic currency" exacerbated the business cycle. Government control was not effectively utilized to moderate these upswings and downswings until after the 1929 Crash revealed the necessity of it. Nelson was likely pleased at the greater credits for agriculture and continued independence for the many small country banks, but both factors led to numerous rural bank failures in the 1920s. The Act hardly achieved Nelson's main goal: safety for depositors. It did, however, insulate banking and currency issues from political debate by placing them in the hands of experts.[22]

That came too late to benefit Nelson, who had already suffered through the "free silver" storm of 1896. Yet he certainly welcomed the change. Likewise, his favorite issue of territorial expansion had been removed by the 1912 admission of Arizona and New Mexico.

Still very much alive, the anti-trust issue became Wilson's next goal. Advised by Brandeis, he recommended anti-trust prohibitions (the Clayton Act) more specific than those in the Sherman Act (1890), and a regulatory Federal Trade Commission (FTC).[23] Here, Nelson played both sides of the issue. At times, he called Wilson's proposals anti-business, and, at other times, weak and ineffective in combating trusts. He called the FTC a "Pooh-Bah Commission" that would only nibble at trusts' behavior while leaving their monopolies intact. He claimed that the Clayton Act offered little or no remedy for small operators swallowed up by giants like Standard Oil. He offered alternative bills strengthen-

297

ing existing regulation through the Commerce and Justice departments. The Democratic Congress rejected them. He ended up voting against the Clayton Act and the FTC bill. Both passed despite his opposition.[24]

More personal battles followed, with his old antagonists, La Follette and Brandeis. The Norwegian-American Andrew Furuseth, a Seamen's Union leader, sought federal legislation to improve sailors' working conditions and shipboard safety. In April, 1912, the *Titanic* disaster strengthened his case. He found an ally in La Follette. Nelson fought them and proposed alternatives more acceptable to shipowners. With Wilson's help, La Follette prevailed in February, 1915.[25]

A year later, Wilson nominated La Follette's friend Brandeis to the Supreme Court. A tough confirmation fight ensued. With "covert, even perhaps unconscious anti-Semitism," and overt disdain for Brandeis' Insurgent views, opponents blocked confirmation for four months. Grevstad wrote Nelson to complain that the choice of Brandeis was "a strong bid for the vote of a financially very prominent element of the population." Nelson worked behind the scenes to defeat him, but did not publicly attack him in such terms. The battle split Boston and Harvard, not Scandinavian Minnesota, and centered (in the Senate) on the conservative Democrats. Wilson lined up three Republicans, including La Follette, and all but one Democrat to win the fight. The Twin Cities' *American Jewish World* wondered why "our own Senator Nelson voted against Brandeis," but Nelson was not long on explanations.[26]

But that occurred after the long recess from March 5 to December 7, 1915. By March 5th, Nelson was exhausted from twenty-three months of almost continuous session. Wilson had ridden Congress to the point of breaking its will to work. The *New York Times* called Nelson one of the Senate's "wheelhorses" (he preferred the term "drayhorse"), but even a "horse" feels its advancing years.[27] Needing to recuperate, he headed home to spend his first summer in seven years on his farm. He oversaw work on

The Grand Old Man comes home from a Senate session, ca. 1915.

a four-room addition to his house: a dining room and pantry downstairs, and two bedrooms upstairs.[28] It remained modest by senatorial standards. The year-old war in Europe was raising crop prices, and it was a good time to build.

He declined many speaking invitations, but accepted a few. At a St. Paul dinner, he speculated that he might resign, "if the Governor would appoint [former Republican congressman] Stevens in my place." Appointment and resignation were both unlikely, but he insisted he meant it. "When a man gets to be 72, it's time for him to quit (No!No!) and prepare for the next world. I feel sure my good friend [Archbishop Ireland] will agree to that."[29]

In fact, he had reached the end of his political agenda. Wilson had completed, though not to Nelson's liking, the reforms in banking, anti-trust laws, and the tariff that Nelson had sought in order to blunt radical criticism of democratic capitalism. The territories were safely admitted as states; Scandinavian Americans were admitted to full participation in Minnesota politics; and Minnesota's Scandinavian-American farmers seemed committed

299

"Uncle Knute" drives his wagon down Broadway, Alexandria's main street, on a rainy day in 1915.

to the Republican party. From now on, he would play the negative role of opposing others' agendas. Or Republican conservatives would use him to achieve their goals.

The day after the dinner the world was shocked when a German submarine sank the British passenger ship *Lusitania*, with the loss of 1,200 lives. In the following weeks, New York newspapers repeatedly asked for his views on submarine warfare and neutrals' rights, but he kept silent. Strict neutrality was Wilson's policy and the one preferred by the majority of Minnesotans in the war's first year. When Nelson addressed a G.A.R. encampment at Luverne in early July, the crowd hoped for a Nelson stand on submarine warfare, but they "were doomed to disappointment." He stuck to the safe topic of Civil War history.[30] Speaking at an "Americanization Day" rally (July 4, 1915), he praised America's hospitality to immigrants and urged 4,000 newly-naturalized citizens to reciprocate with patriotism. He said nothing about the war convulsing their countries of origin.[31]

The morning of the rally, Farmer Nelson rose early, and was walking the streets of Minneapolis by 7 A.M. "'Let's talk about crops,' the senator said, smiling." To reporters in front of the Radisson Hotel, he insisted, "No, I would not say anything about Washington . . . Nothing about politics."

A man with a movie camera quickly "moved from hiding and a tripod was set up on the sidewalk."

"The crops—," he continued, to the accompaniment of the camera's whirring. He "looked up. 'My goodness!' he said." While the camera distracted the reporters, he vanished "like a shadow darting across a wheat field." Some thought "they saw his coattails swish through the [Radisson's] revolving entrance door."[32] No admirer of new technologies, he remained unaware of the major changes they were making in American society.

He could not so easily escape the new phemonenon of American entanglement in a European war after more than a century of isolation. By the time Congress met on December 7, 1915, internationalists had formed the curiously-named League to Enforce the Peace, which had a Minnesota branch. In his message to Congress, Wilson sounded an oddly warlike note to a nation at peace. He called for a larger standing army and attacked "disloyal" elements. ("Such creatures of passion, disloyalty, and anarchy must be crushed out.")[33]

Nelson responded to this rhetoric with the patriotism of his Civil War years. In early January, he attacked advocates of strict neutrality for abandoning American rights on the high seas. He stressed German submarine attacks on merchant ships of smaller neutral nations, especially Norway. He defended American rights to German-American constituents who wrote to protest his increasingly critical stance toward Germany. "I think you German-Americans are doing yourselves an injustice in this matter," he wrote to one. "I have no particular love for the English," he added. In fact he *did* admire the English and that inclined him toward the Allied cause.[34]

In February, 1916, isolationist Bryan Democrats forced the issue

301

with their Gore-McLemore resolutions warning Americans not to travel on ships of belligerent nations. Opposing the resolutions, Wilson demanded freedom to conduct foreign policy. Also opposed were eastern, internationalist Republicans like former president Roosevelt and Massachusetts Senator Henry Cabot Lodge. When Congress voted in early March, Nelson was the only Minnesotan to vote to table (kill) the Gore-McLemore resolutions, which were tabled. Senator Clapp and all ten congressmen voted against tabling—"a vote generally interpreted as being for" Gore-McLemore. Eastern Republicans were dismayed that a majority of House Republicans and twelve Republican senators had voted against tabling—and *with* Bryan Democrats! The *New York Times* attacked Minnesota's delegation, which, it claimed, "consists of eleven Kaiserists and one American, and a mighty fine one, Senator Knute Nelson, born in Norway. . . . The German-American Alliance of Minnesota urged or bullied these eleven weaklings to the course they followed." Many "weaklings" were Insurgents like Clapp and La Follette.[35]

Here was conservative Republicans' chance to hit Insurgency and to hit it hard. Here was Nelson's chance to stand again as the lone voice of reason in the West as he had during the Populist 1890s. And patriotism had wider appeal to Minnesota voters than had the gold standard. He received some initial criticism. The *Bemidji Herald*'s editorial called him "a British boot-black" and "a narrow-minded sycophant."[36] Augsburg Seminary professor John O. Evjen, president of the American Neutrality Society, questioned Nelson's list of torpedoed Norwegian ships, and argued cogently for American non-involvement in the war. Yet many Minnesota newspapers supported his stand, including Scandinavian-American ones like *Minneapolis Tidende* that had usually backed him.[37]

Here was a switch to foreign-policy issues similar to the Spanish-American War and the Filipino guerrilla war. It could hardly hurt Nelson. The stand-pat conservatism of a Nelson Aldrich had never been popular in Minnesota, and he had shied away from it. More popular were attacks on German torpedoes and defenses of American rights on the high seas, and he made them repeatedly. He criticized Clapp as "crazy for embargo legislation" (embargo on American arms sales to the Allies), which "would make him strong with the German-Americans."[38]

Dumping Clapp, who in 1916 faced his first reelection by popular vote, became the priority for Minnesota's newly resurgent conservative Republicans. Their candidate was "highly successful corporation lawyer" Frank B. Kellogg, onetime junior partner in the late Cushman Davis's St. Paul law firm. By prosecuting several trusts and quietly supporting Roosevelt in 1912, he became sufficiently Progressive to be electable in Minnesota. A wealthy man who hated to campaign and loved to winter at California resorts, Kellogg withdrew from the race, but his backers later arranged a Nelson-style draft. They used all the techniques that the popular Nelson never needed: press manipulation, corporate donations to newspapers, Easterners' influence with national media, and Twin Cities salesmen's "pull" with small-town customers. They tried to get Nelson to come out for Kellogg. The canny old veteran never obliged until after Kellogg won the Republican primary over Clapp, Charles A. Lindbergh, Sr., and former Governor Eberhart. Yet Nelson preferred Kellogg to Clapp.[39]

He lent a hand in the fall campaign by delivering the Republicans' keynote speech on Saturday, September 30, 1916. The Republicans chose the tiny hamlet of Sunburg in Kandiyohi county as the site — to show their concern for farmers and small towns. A Norwegian-American crossroads community with "a store, creamery, postoffice and hotel," Sunburg was stranded fourteen miles from the nearest railroad. The automobile was quietly making such small trade centers obsolete, though their fate was not yet unmistakable. The "Twin City and state capitol politicians" disembarked from their campaign train at Brooten. "Members of the Brooten and Sunburg automobile clubs" drove them to the "show tent" in Sunburg where Nelson was to speak.

303

Autos brought hundreds of farmers and townspeople to hear him. An automobile also brought the speaker. Now willing to ride in cars, the tobacco-chewing senator preferred convertibles ("I want to ride where I can spit").[40]

His two-hour speech made no concessions to a speeded-up age. It was as long as a buggy ride into town. He read his lengthy manuscript, "which evoked but little enthusiasm" among Willmar folks, according to the Democratic *Willmar Tribune*. He ridiculed Wilson's domestic legislation. He criticized Wilson's assertive style of initiating legislation, using caucus rule to pass it, addressing Congress in person, and keeping it in session so long. The Democrats' campaign slogan—"He Kept Us Out of War"—was "far-fetched and ludicrous." A wide ocean, American military weakness, and Europeans' preoccupation with fighting each other meant "that none of the belligerents could well get at us, nor we at them." Thousands of copies of the speech were sent out as campaign pamphlets.

The last week of October, Nelson traveled on the Great Northern from Minot to Grand Forks, making whistle-stop speeches for Republican Senator Porter J. McCumber. Republicans worried that the new Non-Partisan League (NPL) sweeping the state would somehow swamp McCumber, though the League was not running a candidate against him.[41]

To conservative Republicans, the NPL was an alarming movement using new technologies and methods to threaten their uncertain political rule. The NPL was started in North Dakota in 1915 by an Alexandria High School graduate, Arthur C. Townley, a failed flax farmer and recent Socialist party organizer. A superb salesman, Townley perfected a system of mobilization more focused, efficient, and modern than the Alliance's horse-and-buggy lecturers and Saturday schoolhouse meetings. To overcome rural distances, Townley provided a Ford for each organizer. He taught them "salesmanship and applied psychology." Rather than form democratic suballiances, the NPL organizer sold individual memberships for $16 (a post-dated check was acceptable) in an

Evidently, a Non-Partisan League organizer here explains the NPL to two farmers standing by his car with the NPL banner—"We'll Stick" was the NPL slogan.

interest-group organization led by others. Townley was the un-elected NPL president. "The League was less a movement *of* the people than *for* the people." Thus, the new NPL avoided the factionalism which afflicted the Alliance. The NPL was free to focus on its program.[42]

That program was similar to the moderate North Dakota Socialist platform: state-owned grain elevators, state grain inspection, state hail insurance, rural credit banks. Instead of forming a third party to achieve these goals, the NPL creatively used that most Progressive innovation, the direct primary. Its disdain for party fit the Progressive era's anti-partyism. Guided by the leaders, NPL members chose candidates to run, almost always, in the Republican primary; if they won, they became the Republican candidates in the fall election. They pledged to uphold NPL principles once in office. Using this method in 1916 in North Dakota, the NPL won the governorship, all but one statewide office, control of the House, and a sizeable minority of the Senate. When the legislature met in January, 1917, it was caucus rule with a vengeance: nightly caucus meetings at which League leaders advised neophyte legislators, who then voted as a bloc.[43]

In February, 1917, the NPL *Nonpartisan Leader* announced, "The United States is on the verge of one of those great political and economic revolutions that periodically shake nations to their foundations . . . a peaceful revolution by means of the ballot." In the early fall of 1916, from eighty to ninety organizers drove their Fords into Minnesota to begin "an intensive farm-to-farm canvass, with the objective of capturing the state" in the 1918 election.[44]

Conservatives had reason to be concerned. Here was a true political machine: dues, members, voting pledges, preselected candidates, bloc voting, caucus rule, a tight legislative agenda. Compared to this, their alliance of county-seat elites, friendly editors, and government jobholders was a fragile gossamer web. They lacked confidence that their tenuous hierarchical linkage could hold at its weakest point—where the county-seat editor or small-town leader had to persuade the farmer. Also, the NPL's socialist origins were clear. It was alarming that this popularized socialism could appeal to farmers, whom conservatives increasingly needed as bulwarks against urban working-class radicalism and unionism. The twenty-five-year-old work of Nelson and others in convincing farmers that Republicans could best accomplish pragmatic reforms seemed about to be torn up by the roots.

Conservatives had other events to view with alarm. The farmers' Equity Cooperative Exchange was battling the grain dealers' Minneapolis Grain Exchange for a stake in grain marketing. A violent strike led by organizers from the Industrial Workers of the World (IWW) rocked the Iron Range in the summer of 1916. IWW-led lumber workers struck northern Minnesota sawmills that winter. Socialist Thomas Van Lear won election as mayor of Minneapolis that fall. Longtime legislators lost, including Nelson's friend, Charles Gilman.[45]

In an immigrants' state like Minnesota, the growing debate over the loyalty of "hyphenated" Americans (for example, Norwegian-Americans) further worried conservatives. Could the United States absorb recent waves of immigrants, Americanize them, and count on their loyalty in the event of war against their European

A Non-Partisan League rally at Fort Ridgely, ca. 1918, with United States flag conspicuously draped over the chair behind the speaker.

countries of origin? Many doubted it could, unless the laissez-faire approach to Americanization was replaced by a more aggressive one. In 1915 Theodore Roosevelt made this concern about "those evil enemies of America, the hyphenated Americans," a national issue.[46] Concern about radicalism fed concern about hyphenism: "new" immigrants from eastern and southern Europe were more supportive of the IWW and socialism.

Upper-midwestern Norwegian Americans sought refuge from anti-hyphenism by distinguishing between political loyalty to the United States and cultural loyalty to their Norwegian heritage. The two loyalties could co-exist. In normal times, that distinction posed no problem. When wartime fears of radicalism caused a drastic narrowing of the definition of political loyalty, the distinction evaporated. Some met the issue by recalling the Civil War era: anti-hyphenists resembled Know-Nothings and Norwegian Americans' support for the Union had proved loyalty and dis-

307

proved Know-Nothingism.[47] Yet radicalism complicated matters and fifty-year-old loyalty counted for little during World War I.

Into this volatile mix came a series of momentous events: German resumption of unlimited submarine warfare (January 31), the cutting off of diplomatic relations with Germany (February 3), release of the Zimmermann Telegram proposing an alliance between Germany and Mexico in case of war between Germany and the United States (February 28), and finally, Wilson's request for a declaration of war (April 2). The ideological gulf widened. Van Lear held a peace rally in Minneapolis, and socialists blamed capitalism, the military, the churches, munition makers, and profiteers for the move toward war. Supporters of intervention held a "counter rally" the next day and hailed the newly-formed Minneapolis Loyalty League. There was no doubt where Nelson stood. A month before the key vote, he met Wilson at the Capitol, grasped his hand, and declared, "I want you to understand that you can count on me."[48]

True to his word, he voted for the declaration of war (La Follette voted against it), which involved him in a name-calling contest with A.G. Johnson, publisher of *Svenska Folkets Tidning*. He called Johnson "unpatriotic and cowardly" for opposing American intervention. Johnson warned him: "You are getting too old and cross. You are worse than the czar of Russia used to be before he was forced to abdicate and if you are not careful God Almighty will force you to abdicate."[49]

Nelson's age was a factor — not that it made him irascible, but it gave him memories of Civil War experiences that virtually programmed his stance in 1917. When he "stood by" the president, he saw the shade of Abraham Lincoln over Wilson's shoulder. In a September, 1917, parade down Pennsylvania Avenue to honor the capital's draftees, Nelson, dressed in a Union-blue suit, walked right behind Wilson.[50] In a Senate speech on the Espionage Act, he commented, "Oh, Mr. [Senate] President, a spirit of old times comes over me. I can not help it." He reminisced about Civil War soldiers "sitting around the camp fires singing our songs," one of which went

"Tell the traitors all around you
That their cruel words, we know,
In every battle kill our soldiers
By the aid they give the foe."

Defending the Act's strict control of defense-related information, he recalled how northern newspapers aided the Confederacy by publicizing the movements of Union armies. His argument "that when the safety of the country is at stake the rights of the individual must be subrogated" echoed Lincoln's arguments for suppression of press freedoms and civil liberties to preserve the Union.[51]

Civil War memories returned when he observed the Norwegian-American community debating American involvement. He questioned their commitment to the war: Lutheran ministers showed "a strong pro-German sentiment." "The poison came . . . from the Missouri Synod, like the poison of the Slavery Question in the sixties." He strongly desired "to show our American fellow citizens that the Norwegians are as patriotic and loyal as any class in the community."[52] He "deplored what he considered to be a strong pro-German tilt on the part of Norwegian- and Swedish-language editors." He had his friend Grevstad hired by the Minnesota Commission of Public Safety (MCPS) as its hyphenated-press watchdog. Grevstad produced numerous articles for Scandinavian-American newspapers. He praised the results. His suspicions of pro-Germanism were exaggerated, as his view of pro-southernism back home during the Civil War had been. Yet from the political front, the hyperpatriotic atmosphere of wartime Washington, cautious supporters looked like slackers.[53]

The same superpatriotism reigned at the State Capitol in St. Paul. Alarmed at reports of attempted sabotage in the Twin Cities —and concerned over the NPL, IWW strikes, growing unionism, and pro-German sentiment, the Minnesota legislature created the MCPS in April, 1917. Dominated by the xenophobic Judge John F.

McGee, it used its near-dictatorial powers to intimidate the NPL, suppress criticism of the war, interfere in a Twin Cities streetcar strike, and coordinate war mobilization.[54] The MCPS permitted local county-seat elites to vent their hostility against the NPL. Local vigilantes were the worst offenders against civil liberties.[55] To stop its move into Minnesota, conservatives charged the NPL with disloyalty and, in many areas, outlawed NPL meetings. The methods used to defeat Clapp and Insurgency were clearly inadequate to defeat Townley. More were needed—and used.

That is what happened in Douglas county in the late summer of 1917, when Nelson returned home.

Norwegian-American editor Carl A. Wold's *Park Region Echo* supported the NPL, while the *Post News* and the *Citizen* were pro-Republican and pro-Democrat, respectively. Nelson's former law partner Constant Larson and his political ally George Treat, both county-seat leaders, led the local America First Association. America Firsters pledged to help "the Government in putting down sedition and disloyalty"—and the NPL.[56]

In late July, the *Echo* criticized a pro-war speech made by Larson, who then asked Nelson to intercede with the Post Office to have the *Echo*'s second-class mailing privilege revoked under the Espionage Act. "If the government will not act, we will have to take steps ourselves here to put a stop to this treasonable sheet." Nelson then wrote to the postmaster general. Earlier, he had written to McGee to request MCPS action against the *Echo*. Neither move succeeded. The MCPS lacked authority to suppress newspapers, and, after Wold presented his side, the Post Office refused to act.[57]

On Labor Day, September 3, 1917, Alexandria High School's most notorious graduate, Arthur C. Townley, came to town to address a large patriotic NPL rally. Automobiles brought farmers by the thousands from neighboring counties. Some 400 autos participated in the parade. "The city was literally invaded by farmers from all sides"—a metaphor conservatives may not have appreciated. Townley defended the NPL record and his right to speak

Non-Partisan League members in Alexandria for the Labor Day rally, September 3, 1917. The sign on the car reads, "Carlos [Township] Our Rights Must Be Preserved."

in Minnesota. He had as much right as did Nelson. "The only difference between Senator Nelson and me," said Townley none too tactfully, "is that the Senator is about thru and I have just commenced."[58]

The day after that *Echo* report on the NPL rally, the *Echo* office was broken into, "the linotype ruined," and the press damaged. Attorneys Larson and Treat may have been shrewd enough to avoid direct participation in this vandalism. Yet it was almost certainly committed by the local organization they had formed "to handle the situation in this county." It was the latest in a series of "threats of loss of business, withdrawal of advertising, bluffs," and buy-out attempts. Its purpose was to prevent Wold from mailing the newspaper out on time, which would result in loss of the mailing privilege.[59]

Six days after the break-in, a returned Senator Nelson spoke at a banquet honoring Alexandria's draftees before their departure for training camp. Larson spoke before Nelson, who was introduced as "Uncle Knute." He reminisced about his Civil War sol-

311

diering and gave some practical advice. He warned that there would be dissenters ("back fires") at home: "We had it in the War of the Rebellion. They were called 'copper heads.' We have copper heads today in this war." He assured the draftees, "we will do our best to protect you against them."[60]

The next night Wold's enemies raided the *Echo* offices again, doing more damage to linotype and press, taking his files, and scattering job-work, "bills, receipts, and letters" on the floor. NPL backers came to his rescue with financial contributions and advance subscription payments. They vowed: "The battle is on. It is a fight to the finish. The Echo will be published as usual and continue the same policy as in the past." Wold suggested that "the gang" who had tried to secure postal suspension of his mailing privileges had carried out the raid. That was almost certainly true.[61]

In late December, a week after an America First rally in town, Wold was assaulted in downtown Alexandria by a man angered at his editorial criticism of the president of the State America First Association. In July, 1918, after being convicted on a charge of discouraging enlistments, he was found to have inoperable cancer of the stomach. He died in late October, shortly before the election, "a circumstance that cast him in a Nonpartisan League martyr's role."[62]

Nelson did not condone vigilante harrassment of Wold, but he did nothing to stop it. His harsh attacks on the NPL, Wold, disloyalty, and Copperheads encouraged the "rough element" to settle local scores violently.[63] Private Nelson could grouse about slackers and Copperheads back home without any harmful effects. Senator Nelson's grousing brought results. However, his donation of over a dozen pro-war books (for example, *To Neutral Peace Lovers)* to the Alexandria Public Library apparently persuaded few hometown opponents.[64]

He also got results far beyond Alexandria. He helped secure the arrest and internment of Frederick Bergmeier, editor of *Volkszeitung* (St. Paul). Nelson accused the *Volkszeitung* of "throwing cold water on the war [effort]." He "suggested to the Department of Justice" that if the newspaper "supports the war in a proper spirit, he might be let out on parole on the condition that the paper behaves"—unusual parole terms![65] He urged the MCPS to go after James A. Peterson for writing a critical article for the *Echo*. When a Gaylord civil engineer wrote him a bombastic anti-war letter, Nelson reported him to State Auditor J.A.O. Preus, the MCPS, and the Justice Department. Preus promised "to do my best to have this man interned." Judge McGee reported that a Justice agent would "give him the scare of his life."[66]

Old Civil War attitudes alone cannot account for this vindictive drive to stamp out dissent. Nor can a fear of political defeat have scared the seventy-five-year-old veteran who had never lost an election and who planned to retire soon. The prospect of an NPL tide engulfing their political futures motivated Preus and his other Minnesota cronies, but not Nelson. The NPL exposed the thinness of their political support. Years of campaigning had left Republicans with very tenuous ties to voters. Campaigns had been superficial: a few county-seat wire-pullers manipulating perfunctory conventions, a few officeholders planting favorable stories in compliant newspapers, a few Grimshaws and Michelets mailing out pamphlets. Political activists' control depended on voter passivity, which the NPL dramatically altered. Minnesota's "Grand Old Man" commanded enough residual support to defeat any NPL challenger, but, if he retired, he might be succeeded by an NPL senator. That would amount to a repudiation of the course he had followed ever since the Populist-fighting 1890s.

As 1918 approached, he indicated that he would retire. This time he may have meant it. He had been in politics since 1867, fifty years now, and had been a senator for nearly twenty-five years. To Grevstad, he wrote, "I begin to feel the burden of advancing years, and I have a dread of moping about the Senate Chamber as a shadow of my former self." Privately, he told associates this was his final term.[67]

Others were not so sure. The mercurial McGee was determined

313

that Nelson should take a fifth term. So was Daniel Lawler, his onetime Democratic opponent. Minnesota Democrats were pleased at his loyal support of Wilson's wartime administration. Lawler hinted at a Democratic endorsement of Nelson.[68] In December, 1917, someone (probably Republican) leaked a letter supposedly written by Wilson. It praised Nelson's knowledge of international affairs. His services were "invaluable" to a nation at war. Even if he had only "one more year to live," the letter stated, "he owes that year to his country." It led Nelson to expect support from a bi-partisan coalition. In Washington that winter, John Lind protested to the Wilson administration. Such a reactionary coalition would destroy Minnesota's Democratic party and force Progressives over to the NPL. He failed to obtain a public denial of the letter. In a private denial, Wilson explained, "I have not [publicly] denied its authenticity because of my warm feeling for the Senator himself, whom I greatly esteem."[69]

Many joined the chorus demanding reelection. Maria Sanford told him, "We can't spare you." The Populist-turned-Republican farmer-legislator Ole Sageng wrote to warn Nelson, "With the headway which the Non-Partisan League has made among our farmers—even a very large part of our really substantial and or-dinarily cautious Scandinavian farmers have been carried away by this wholly unsound movement— . . . there is some chance, I fear, that a candidate of the Townley-Manahan type may be nom-inated in the Republican primary in case you are not a candidate for re-election."[70] Herschel V. Jones of the *Minneapolis Journal* added a new dimension: John Lind. According to Jones, Lind was promising to lobby for defense contracts for the lumber industry in order to win support for a Senate bid.[71] True or not, that report set Nelson's competitive juices stirring. He did not wish to be su-perceded by a Swede, especially Lind—or an NPL man, as Sageng predicted.

A week after Jones's letter, the ever-secretive senator sent his in-structions to Grevstad. When political supporters asked about Nelson's plans, Grevstad was to tell them that "while you don't

314

Blue-suited Senator Nelson and gray-suited Confederate veteran, Senator Bankhead of Alabama, marched down Pennsylvania Avenue behind President Wilson in a September 1917 parade honoring draftees. Wilson set such a fast pace that the senators had trouble keeping up.

know as to what my plans . . . are . . . it looks to you as though public opinion would force me into the field." When he finally announced on April 15, 1918, he cast his decision in patriotic terms. People had "insisted" that his wartime Senate services were "needed" and "that it would be unpatriotic" to retire now. That is what "affected me most of all," he claimed. "I was not a slacker in 1861 and I do not want to be a slacker in this far greater war."[72]

Two days before Nelson announced, his sole Republican opponent was convicted of violating the Espionage Act. James A. Peterson was found guilty of "discouraging recruiting and enlistments." In February-March, 1918, Peterson wrote two newspaper articles. One criticized the United States Senate for its failure to oppose the Allies' war aim of seizing territory. That article brought the conviction; the jury acquitted him on the article,

315

"Stand By the President." Accurately claiming infringement of his right of free speech, Peterson pointed to his son's enlistment as proof of his innocence — to no avail. A friend had warned that "if I filed as a candidate for United States senator I would be indicted." Actually, the MCPS asked for a prosecution before Peterson filed. Nelson's role is unclear. Ten months earlier, he had asked the MCPS to prosecute Peterson for an earlier article. If he didn't cause the 1918 prosecution, he certainly approved of it. His longtime friend, Judge Page Morris, sentenced Peterson to four years. His allies schemed to remove Peterson's name from the ballot. Peterson stayed on the ballot and out of prison. The United States Supreme Court later reversed the conviction.[73]

Peterson's hope for NPL support never materialized. The League would not antagonize pro-Nelson voters who might be persuaded to vote for Charles A. Lindbergh, Sr., its candidate for governor. As in North Dakota, the NPL targeted state offices. Counterattacking, anti-NPL forces used the MCPS and county safety commissions as de facto campaign organizations more efficient and extensive than the old Republican county-seat "rings." (Both often relied on the same local leaders.) With their Liberty bond rallies, food conservation drives, Red Cross campaigns, and Home Guards, MCPS local units were in much closer contact with ordinary citizens than rings had ever been. At the state level, the MCPS had a ready publicity apparatus. Grevstad targeted Scandinavian-American newspapers with the messsage that a near-unanimous vote for Nelson was needed to prove Scandinavian Americans' wartime loyalty.[74]

"Without leaving Washington or making a speech," his campaign handled by Grevstad and others, Nelson swamped Peterson (229,923 votes to 89,464). More vulnerable, Governor J.A.A. Burnquist defeated Lindbergh by almost 50,000 votes. The NPL found Minnesota a harder state to crack than North Dakota. Nelson lost only three counties, including his own Douglas, where the NPL was aggressively effective and where the attacks on Wold produced "back fires" against him.[75]

Alexandria's county-seat wire-pullers' failure illustrated conservatives' weakness. They mailed pamphlets, sample ballots, and announcements, "but no matter how much a meeting was advertised it was impossible to get a crowd." Their township chairmen could accomplish little. One of his patronage appointees blamed "the rat Wold;" Nelson realized the vote showed that prosecuting Wold was a mistake.[76]

The NPL ran an ad-hoc "Farmer-Labor" ticket in the general election, but still ran no candidate against Nelson. Democrats also ran no one against him, though Lind obtained a last-minute Democratic endorsement for Prohibitionist Willis G. Calderwood, candidate of the National Party, a "temporary amalgam of prowar Socialists, a Bull Moose Progressive remnant, and the left wing of a fragmented Prohibitionist party." Lind tried to save Minnesota Democrats from oblivion and to reduce Nelson's margin. Nelson was angry: Lind was "hostile" because "he has always felt that I have had the place that he ought to have."[77] Still, Nelson said nothing publicly. He would win or lose on his reputation.

He won in "the last all-male general election in Minnesota." His margin was smaller than predicted: 206,428 votes to Calderwood's 137,334. Calderwood carried ten counties, a strange mix of German-American, ex-Populist, prohibitionist counties—and Douglas. Given his prestige and Democratic support, Nelson's victory was less than overwhelming. The "Farmer-Labor" ticket elected no statewide candidates, but the NPL elected 33 legislators. It was still very much alive.[78]

Six days later, the war was over. Yet the Armistice did not end the campaign against what the *Minneapolis Tribune* earlier called "pro-German, Bolsheviki, I.W.W. and uncatalogued flotsam and jetsam."[79] As a member of the Overman Judiciary Subcommittee, Senator Nelson was already pursuing pro-German propaganda supposedly sponsored by the brewing industry. Organized after widely publicized charges by A. Mitchell Palmer, the Overman Subcommittee had been holding hearings for almost two months.

History buff Nelson soon had the chance to question noted

317

(allegedly pro-German) historian Albert Bushnell Hart: "Did you ever do any dueling while you were a student in a German university? . . . Did you give any attention to [Henrich von] Treitschke on history?"

Hart thought Treitschke "a good deal of a prig" for refusing to correct "27 mistakes" Hart detected "in his lectures on English history." He assured Nelson he had supported the war.

"I am glad to hear it," said the senator.[80]

In early February, 1919, the subcommittee was abruptly side-tracked from its investigation of pro-German brewers by alarming news from Seattle. After management refused to meet with negotiators for 35,000 striking shipyard workers, the Central Labor Council called a general strike for February 6—the nation's first. Though not controlled by the IWW, the Council and its leader, James Duncan, were sympathetic to the Wobblies and to the Russian Bolsheviks. The November, 1917, Bolshevik Revolution had electrified the American left and even moderate socialists hailed the Bolsheviks. The strikers' *Union Record* closed its editorial announcing the general strike with a shout: "we are starting on a road that leads—NO ONE KNOWS WHERE!" Panic spread. Seattle's citizens rushed to purchase goods to hoard. Seattle's Norwegian-American Mayor Ole Hanson requested federal troops.[81]

Many Americans thought they knew where this road led—to a Bolshevik revolution in America. After all, one Wobbly slogan was "every strike is a small revolution and a dress rehearsal for the big one."[82] They paid no attention to the fact that Wobblies were not ideologically communist, and that the left was already beginning to split over the Bolshevik experiment.

On February 8, Nelson spoke in the Senate on the danger of Bolshevism and anarchism. Here was "a greater danger than that which we faced during the war." He entered into the record the text of "Hunger-The International Revolutionist," a pro-Bolshevik, pro-IWW pamphlet issued in Minneapolis a week earlier. Along with stark proletarian prose, "Hunger" included many drawings—one showed a rooster sitting on a gallows dated July 4, 1919, and crowing "Awake Ye Slaves." One poem praised Russia's supposed abolition of marriage. Nelson was outraged at these attempts "to poison and demoralize the American people." Such propagandists were "outside the pale of constitutional" protection. Attempts to extend it to them he dismissed as "academic constitutional discussion." Insurgent William E. Borah extended it to them and criticized Nelson, for whom he expressed a "very tender regard."[83]

Shocked at the Seattle general strike and at a recent pro-Bolshevik meeting in Washington, D.C., the Senate unanimously instructed Overman's subcommittee to investigate Bolsheviks as well as brewers.[84] The strike soon failed.

After calling several anti-Bolsheviks as witnesses, the Overman Subcommittee heard their first pro-Bolshevik witness on February 20. At her own request, Louise Bryant, writer, speaker, and activist, testified. She and her husband John Reed, the noted journalist and radical, had visited Russia from September, 1917, to February, 1918. They witnessed the Revolution. Reed had recently completed an account, *Ten Days That Shook The World*.[85]

The committee room was "packed with men and women" when Bryant began. An "extremely beautiful woman" in her thirties, she "appeared nervous as she faced the committee." Perhaps more nervous, "Reed paced . . . up and down the room" as the Senators questioned her. They were hostile from the start. They pointedly questioned her on her religious beliefs, her failure to use her husband's name, and her divorce from a Portland, Oregon, dentist—all to discredit her testimony.

When Nelson told her to "not be so impertinent" in responding to questions about Reed's activities in Russia, the anti-Bolsheviks applauded and the others hissed. A moment later, Bryant insisted, "I expect to be treated with the same courtesy as former witnesses, and I have not gotten it so far." "The Bolshevik adherents—the majority of them women—started to applaud and the pro-Americans countered with a storm of hisses." The women were probably friends from the National Women's Party, and not necessarily pro-Bolshevik. After more applause, Overman ordered the audience to leave; Reed and the reporters stayed.[86]

Knute Nelson handled much of the questioning. Here was an utter contrast of personalities, backgrounds, and beliefs. The 77-year-old Vossing-American war veteran, farmer, lawyer, and crusty, tobacco-chewing politician could hardly comprehend this young woman, a radical suffragist, poet, and lifelong urbanite— or Reed. Nor they, him. Both had left well-to-do Portland homes to rebel against the America that nurtured them. The poor immigrant boy grateful for America's open arms could never understand that. Also incomprehensible was the Reeds' sexually liberated life in Greenwich Village.

Fortunately, they did not discuss Life, but the Bolsheviks. No ignorant provincial, Nelson had delivered a lengthy, detailed speech on Russia and the Revolution a month earlier.[87] He questioned her assertions that there were few signs of food shortages and that the Russians had not betrayed the Allies by making peace with Germany. He opposed violent revolution. She called it a "transitory stage," like the harrassment of Tories during the American Revolution, an example of popular "self-determination."[88]

"Self-determination at the point of a gun?," he asked.

"All governments have had to be self-determined at the point of a gun." (She later called Yakov Peters, Cheka leader and reputed executioner, "a very aesthetic young man.")

Nelson denied it. "Have you studied this league of nations? [Laughter.]"

She could "understand" the Bolsheviks' execution of Russian army officers. He asked if she thought they had "to pass through a Bolshevik purgatory in order to land on terra firma in Russia?" She claimed no right to judge what Russians should do. Her relativism could not condemn such executions.

Most reprehensible for the land-hungry son of a landless "widow" was the Bolsheviks' land confiscation. "You believe that

. . . the Government should possess all the land, and that the tillers of the land should be nothing but tenants?"

"I believe that; yes. That is socialism."

Nelson was not present the next day to hear Reed's definition of socialism and denial of Bolshevik atrocities. Senators grilling witnesses and threatening coercive measures inevitably look heavy-handed, while witnesses look brave. Yet, viewed as individual not senator (could one still separate Nelson and the office?), Nelson was wiser, less naive, more durable than Bryant or Reed. Over the years he had lost faith in the appeal of his oft-repeated Castle Garden immigrant's story. Now he would use coercion to insure that his story prevailed over Reed and Bryant's self-dramatizing rebellion.

Nelson erred in denying dissenters their civil liberties. He no longer believed in America's ability to retain citizens' loyalty if they heard anti-capitalist, anti-democratic ideas. Politicians like Nelson had manipulated the political system so long that they had lost confidence that the public supported it. Raised in a political age, they worried that radicals like Bryant and Reed were persuasive enough to sway public opinion. Because he only worked, read, chewed, ate cornmeal mush, slept, and avoided movie cameras, Nelson underestimated the power of consumerism, which would bind Americans to capitalism. Autos, movies, radios, and refrigerators would recruit Republican votes more effectively than Grimshaw or Michelet ever could. By 1920 entrepreneurs, mostly immigrants, were fashioning American popular culture in films, magazines, vaudeville. Rebellion would become cultural, not political. A Louise Bryant would give way to the flapper. A John Reed, to the expatriate literati. Finnish Americans attending socialist picnics would stand around debating "the virtues of the Buick and the shortcomings of the Ford."[89] But Nelson knew he would not live to see the final outcome of the struggle against radicalism.

Fourteen

Closing Arguments

The main priority in February, 1919, was not ascertaining Louise Bryant's views on Bolshevism, but ending the war with a suitable peace treaty. The fighting had ended on November 11, 1918, with an armistice only. Breaking precedent again, the president had traveled to Paris to head the American delegation to the peace conference, which began on January 18, 1919. Six days before Bryant testified, Wilson announced to the conference his plan for a League of Nations to maintain peace through a written "covenant" of collective security.[1] A sort of global constitution, the covenant would be part of the peace treaty. Nations would ratify this "constitution." Senate debate on the League Covenant would be the last major one for Knute Nelson.

Support for the League appeared overwhelming in the United States. "A survey conducted in December 1918 showed that of 833 editorials, only 20 were hostile to the League idea." Republican internationalists such as Taft and Insurgents' allies like civic good-government groups generally favored it. The appalling casualties (nearly 25 million total, including 300,000 Americans) became powerful silent arguments for an international organization to prevent a recurrence. By going to Paris, Wilson staked his reputation on the success of such a body. The world's people demanded it, he said. "A war in which they had been bled white to beat the terror that lay concealed in every balance of power must not end in a mere victory of arms and a new balance."[2]

There were obstacles. Though broken by American entry into the war, the 130-year-old tradition of non-involvement in European power politics was still powerful. Inertia kept isolationism a strong force. The League went even beyond the thirty-year-old, largely Republican tradition of internationalism, which emphasized international law and arbitration. Satisfying Americans' insistence on written constitutions, the covenant at the same time aroused their traditional suspicion about the fine print, the constitutional minutiae.

Nelson compared opponents' worries to Anti-Federalists' concerns: then, "most dire results" were predicted "if the Constitution were ratified."[3] Now, the anti-ratification campaign was worse. Republicans had a deeper partisan stake in the outcome than had the loose, ad-hoc Anti-Federalist coalition. Republicans feared Wilson might seek a third term based on a League win.[4] The Senate had an institutional stake in protecting its constitutional role in foreign policy from presidential or League usurpations. The Constitution's checks and balances—here, the required two-thirds Senate vote to approve the covenant—did not lend themselves to bold ventures or global agreements.

Typically, Senator Nelson cautiously studied Wilson's proposals and the final covenant. He delayed taking a stand. On March 3 Republican Senate leader Henry Cabot Lodge presented his "round robin," a resolution opposing the treaty and covenant in their current form. Nelson refused to sign it. Lodge obtained thirty-seven Republican signatures—enough to block ratification.[5] Returning to Paris, Wilson secured further concessions for the covenant's critics. On May 7, Nelson speculated that the Senate would probably ratify the amended treaty after examining it "most carefully" and extracting "concessions," although none requiring its renegotiation.[6]

324

A Democratic Senate leader advised Wilson that Nelson "could be influenced" by a Wilson speech to his constituents. Instead, Wilson met with Nelson at the White House on July 17, in one of a series of one-on-one meetings with senators. Afterward, Nelson indicated that he supported certain "reservations," binding interpretive concessions that the Senate would insert in its resolution of ratification. He was one of the so-called "mild reservationists," ten Republican senators who wanted a few mildly worded reservations to secure approval and avoid renegotiation or offended Allies. Yet he did not participate in their early strategy meetings or even outline his position until July 29. By contrast, Senator Kellogg quickly assumed a leadership role in the mild reservationist camp.[7]

Using strange-sounding categories, journalists and politicians counted votes. Some thirty-five Democratic senators supported the treaty without reservations. Sixteen senators (fourteen Republicans and two Democrats) opposed the treaty with or without reservations. They were called the "irreconcilables,"—more picturesquely, the "battalion of death" or "bitter-enders." About twenty-five Republicans led by Lodge stood between the irreconcilables and the mild reservationists. They supported the treaty only if strong reservations were attached—probably offending the Allies and leading to renegotiation. (Hence, they were called "strong reservationists.") Some hoped for reservations so strong that Wilson would reject his own altered League. Using this group as his nucleus, Lodge tried to keep his divided Republican flock together. He had enough votes to defeat the treaty if Wilson refused to compromise. Wilson needed sixty-four votes and had only forty-seven Democrats (only forty-four of them pro-treaty), so he needed Republican votes to secure approval.[8]

In a July 29th speech in the Senate that aroused "special interest," Nelson demonstrated that he was no backward-looking isolationist. "We can no longer isolate ourselves in our relations with other countries," because "modern science has made distant nations our near neighbors." As for George Washington's warning against foreign alliances in his Farewell Address, Nelson could not "take much stock in the [no] 'entangling alliance' argument." In April, 1917, "we jumped that fence." Now, "why should we not entangle ourselves to secure the results of our victory and avoid being entangled in another war?" He favored reservations concerning Article 10 (which appeared to commit the United States to deter aggression regardless of Congress's war-making power), withdrawal from the League, the Monroe Doctrine, and domestic matters such as immigration. The Treaty's demand for high reparations and German disarmament was justified. Disarmed Germans should rejoice that their taxes would be lower! Finally, ratification would help defeat Bolshevism and anarchy, because a secure peace would produce "a full revival" of commerce and industry.[9]

The longer the debate continued, the more strongly pro-League he became. He supported mild reservations mainly for tactical reasons, to win enough Republican votes for passage and to maintain Republican unity. "The emotions of wartime remained strong" for him, and he saw irreconcilables as the same group who supported Gore-McLemore and opposed the war effort. "A voracious reader of history, he was convinced that the old order had failed." This immigrant who had toured Europe in 1899 could not turn his back on European affairs. He sharply criticized irreconcilables who "conjure and bring up all kinds of ghosts and goblins in Europe" and want to "cut loose from everything and get back into our shell again." This Norwegian American sympathized with nationless ethnic groups, Poles and Czechs and Slovaks, to whom the Versailles settlement granted statehood. Polish independence was "one of the grand results of the war that we can not help but rejoice in."[10] Unlikely to run again, he was less interested in the politics of the treaty fight.

"Pretty busy as Chairman of the Judiciary Committee," his strength declining, he did not assume a leadership role during the crucial days of mid-August. He deferred to Kellogg and to the scholarly, distinguished Lodge, who he assumed was working to secure a qualified ratification. Democrats and mild reservation-ists began to work out a deal, but Wilson refused to compromise, forcing the latter group to negotiate with Lodge. It was a fatal error. A Wilson-hater, Lodge delayed action in his Foreign Relations Committee by reading "the entire Treaty aloud for two full weeks," even though all members had copies. The erudite Lodge slowed matters with "his linguistic proficiency by compar-ing supposedly subtle differences" in the French and English texts of the treaty. Unaware that time was short, Nelson played little role in behind-the-scenes talks.[11]

His temper ended his passivity. On August 27, Senator Albert Fall (Republican-New Mexico), a "bitter-ender," admitted the "nervous strain" of protracted debate and yet criticized pro-treaty senators for their "impatience."[12]

His patience at an end, Nelson demanded to know just what Fall found "objectionable" in the treaty. "There is no use of at-tempting to chop up this treaty into mincemeat."

Feeling reprimanded like a schoolboy, Fall protested that Nelson "was taking advantage of his age."

"The Senator need not pay any attention to my age; he may consider me the youngest man in the Senate." Fall said he consid-ered Nelson to be in his "second childhood." The 77-year-old Senator demanded and received an apology.

Three days later, Nelson met with four other mild reservation-ists. He began to play a leading role in this group of ten senators, who held a swing position. Both Lodge and the Democrats needed their votes. He was angry at Lodge's "dilatory tactics": "while Senator Lodge is a great scholar and a fine orator, he is a poor political leader and manager." Nelson mistakenly assumed that Lodge's goal was to ratify with reservations and he was fail-ing at that. Lodge's real goal was to keep Republicans united for the 1920 campaign and to prevent Wilson from scoring an unre-stricted victory on the League issue. He was succeeding bril-liantly at that. Lodge's implacable hatred for Wilson blocked Wilson's foreign policy ambition.[13]

327

On September 3, Wilson aided Lodge's cause by leaving on a speaking tour designed to persuade Americans to pressure their senators into supporting the League. His decision to go over their heads angered some senators. "There is no way the people can vote on the treaty," one solon huffed. "Only the Senate can do that." Senate prerogatives clashed with presidential oratory, as Lodge did with Wilson. Speaking where Wilson had spoken, attacking Wilson's League, several senators went on their own tours. Two parts of the same government were at loggerheads.

Nelson naively thought ratification would come within a month or so. Yet he blamed Lodge, not Wilson, for the ill-advised "campaign tour." In a September 19th Senate speech, he disputed opponents' comparison of the Allies' League to the autocratic Holy Alliance of 1814. The League would defend the new European democracies, not fight democracy to preserve a monarchical status quo, as the Holy Alliance had done. *Minneapolis Tidende* sided with Nelson against "irreconcilable" Hiram Johnson, who spoke in Minneapolis. Johnson could be eloquent but Minnesotans listened to "their own Senator, who for so many years has talked to them . . . from the heart."[14]

Also speaking from the heart, Wilson called critical senators "contemptible quitters." Though he had secretly drafted some "mild" reservations and left them with the Democrats' Senate leader, he presented an either-or case to his audiences. Either approve the treaty as it stood, or reject it. Confidentially given a less "mild," Lodge-backed compromise reservation on Article 10, he publicly denounced it. Mild reservationists were outraged. Two days later, an exhausted Wilson collapsed at Pueblo, Colorado, and was rushed back to the White House, where he suffered a near-fatal stroke. Paralyzed on his left side, he became even more resistant to reservations. Public support for the treaty declined. Strong reservationists demanded more stringent limits on American membership in the League. To retain a chance of ratification, "mild" leaders like Nelson had to accommodate their demands.[15]

Increasingly frustrated, Nelson delivered another Senate speech on October 9, not as Minnesota's senator, but in "the spirit of old Corp[ora]l Nelson, of the Fourth Wisconsin." Now that "Americanism" and its "'holier than thou' cry of patriotism" was turned against the League, he was skeptical of them. When used to attack the League, it was "counterfeit 'Americanism.'" Opponents of the war effort, especially anti-English ones, were now anti-League. Taught by Mary Dillon to admire England, Nelson could not tolerate Anglophobia. The League would safeguard eastern European democracies as bulwarks against Bolshevism.[16]

Nelson voted against all amendments that would disable the treaty. Wilson's illness and intransigence again forced the "mild" senators to deal with Lodge. Instead of final strings tying up Wilson's treaty, they became the tail to Lodge's kite. In late October the "Lodge reservations" (actually written and negotiated by the mild reservationists) were placed before the Senate.[17]

On November 8, Nelson tried unsuccessfully to amend a "strong" one denying the president a voice in any future withdrawal from the League. "A dramatic plea for the President, lying upon his sick bed, was made by Senator Nelson." The "aged Minnesotan" was ready to break with Lodge. It was a slight to Wilson, argued Nelson, to cut him off from withdrawal decisions. He did not approve of the "intense partisanship" behind the treaty wrangle. He was appalled at "the utter lack of elasticity" in the American system as compared to the parliamentary system of Great Britain. The British never saw "the spectacle" Americans "witnessed of a branch of the Congress [the Senate] being in apparent hostility to the executive head of this Government." He closed by saying he would not continue "prolonging the debate unless somebody assaults me [Laughter on floor and in the galleries.]"[18]

By November 18, the Republicans pushed through the "Lodge reservations," which required and received a majority vote to be added to the treaty ratification resolution. The key vote was set for November 19. It would take a two-thirds vote to ratify. Republicans would need Democratic votes to ratify the "Lodged" treaty. Democrats would need about twenty Republican votes to ratify Wilson's treaty without reservations. Both sides refused to budge, and expected the other to back down.

The *Washington Post* called the Senate session of November 19 "one of the most dramatic and spectacular sessions in the nation's history." The Senate first voted on a motion to ratify *with* the "Lodge reservations." The motion lost, 39 yeas to 55 nays. Loyal Democrats (at Wilson's request) and irreconcilables voted no. Nelson and Kellogg voted to ratify. A senator moved to reconsider, which was done. Democratic leaders implored "mild" senators to soften the reservations. The latter pleaded with Democrats to ratify it with the present ones. Neither side backed down. The Senate again voted against ratification by a 41-to-51 margin. Nelson did not vote. He had apparently left the chamber in disgust at the outcome of the first vote. Lodge permitted one vote on the treaty *without* reservations. With irreconcilables now joining all but one other Republican in voting No, this motion lost also, 38-to-53. Nelson was absent.[19]

Though further efforts were made in early 1920 to pass the treaty, American participation in the League was effectively dead. No isolationist or militarist, Nelson was genuinely and deeply disappointed. He made no dramatic prophecies, but he knew that a grand opportunity had been fatally squandered in partisan, personal, and institutional squabbling.

Life consists of the momentous and the mundane. An event with small beginnings was to hurt Nelson nearly as much as the treaty defeat. While he was in Washington debating the League, Ida was getting acquainted with a new hired man at home. Anders Gustaf Nelson, a Swedish American in his early fifties, was hired in June, 1919. He first came to Alexandria in 1886, but soon returned to Sweden, where he served in the army and managed timber lands for an English firm. He traveled widely in

Europe. He worked in the Swedish legation in New York City after returning to America in 1916. At Christmas, 1918, he came to Alexandria, where his mother lived. The well-traveled Ida, now fifty-one and accustomed to Washington society, saw something in Gustaf she had never seen in Alexandria's young men. They were married on September 23.[20]

Her father did not share her fascination. He called Gustaf "Sweet Tramp" and was not pleased with her Swedish roustabout who acted like nobility. He had his career partly to blame; he was preoccupied with the League during the three-month courtship. Rather than work, Gustaf hunted with his ten hunting dogs. Driving down main street (Broadway), some dogs inside and some running alongside his Model T, he made "quite a commotion," which did not endear him to the local citizens.[21]

The newlyweds lived in the Nelson house that winter of 1919-1920. With Knute and Nicholina away in Washington, Gustaf swaggered around the farm like a Swedish estate manager. Nicholina's nephew, Oscar Jacobson, was renting land, farm buildings, and tenant house. It was an informal arrangement: no cash rent; Oscar supplied dairy products and firewood to the Nelson house; Knute kept some livestock and machinery on the farm. As a senator's son-in-law and a former estate overseer who had kept peasants from hunting in the Englishmen's forest, Gustaf lorded it over the Jacobsons. Treating them like peasants, he "claimed authority" from Knute "to look after the farm," walked around with a shotgun, and terrified Oscar. Threatening and cursing, he demanded daily milk deliveries, though Nicholina had only ordered deliveries every other day.[22]

In March, 1920, while the League was again up for debate in the Senate, Nelson sold his farm, to a local Republican—all but the house and fifty acres. Trouble between Gustaf and the Jacobsons may have caused him to sell.[23]

On Wednesday, March 10, Oscar, his son Herbert, and a helper, Joe Middleton, were preparing to move from the farm. While they worked, Jacobson's horses and cows grazed in a straw pile and rye field. That annoyed the shotgun-toting Gustaf, who drove the animals into a fenced area. Gustaf and Joe argued over that. Gustaf stuck his shotgun in Joe's chest. "Middleton grabbed the gun near the muzzle and during the struggle that ensued the gun went off." Pellets hit Middleton in the right arm. Within seven hours, he died from loss of blood.[24]

This tragedy had a great emotional impact on a community still deeply divided over the Nonpartisan League, wartime loyalty crusades, and attacks on Wold and the *Echo*. County Attorney Walter H. Jacke had won in 1918 on the NPL ticket. Local Republicans like Constant Larson felt that Knute Nelson's son-in-law could not get a fair hearing before Jacke's grand jury. A Republican Justice of the Peace, Edward P. Wright, scheduled a hearing to determine if Gustaf should be held in custody on first-degree murder charges. Wright had questioned Middleton before he died, possibly to obtain exculpatory evidence at Larson's request.

The hearing was held the next day in Wright's office at the telephone exchange building. Constant Larson represented Gustaf, Jacke presented evidence, and witnesses testified, while a girl tried "to take down the evidence on a typewriter." Wright ruled that the evidence did not warrant jailing Gustaf, and he released him. Yet, in Alexandria's charged, partisan atmosphere, NPL'ers and Gustaf-haters interpreted this hearing as a trial—his decision as a not-guilty verdict.[25]

A large mob had gathered during the hearing—NPL farmers and local residents. They filled the office and lobby, and blocked the sidewalk outside. Feeling was running high over this preferential treatment for Nelson's unpopular son-in-law. His release sparked "a general riot" and threats of hanging. As Gustaf walked out, someone in the crowd dealt him a blow in the face which knocked him to the ground. He retreated inside to the safety of the sheriff's custody. The Republican mayor had to promise that he would be tried on another charge before the crowd would disperse.[26]

Here was the chance for the *Echo* and local NPL farmers to wreak vengeance on Nelson and company for the harrassment and trial of Wold, for the vandalism at the *Echo* office. Roles were neatly reversed. While deploring mob action, the *Echo* protested the absurdity of "a petty justice of the peace . . . try[ing] a murder case." "Would Wright have acted as he did if the accused had been a Nonpartisan League farmer instead of the son-in-law of Knute Nelson?"[27]

Gustaf's trial for first-degree murder was scheduled for September 20, in the midst of the important 1920 campaign. While not a Bolshevik-style "show trial," it was a trial of Knute Nelson's politics as much as of his son-in-law. To aid their campaign, local NPL'ers hired the NPL candidate for state attorney general, Thomas V. Sullivan, as acting Douglas county attorney to prosecute Gustaf. To embarrass Nelson and the Republicans, Sullivan called Knute to testify, although his testimony was hardly needed.[28] Sullivan had reason for revenge. He had defended Townley in a 1918 "conspiracy" trial and may have been fraudulently denied a victory in the 1918 Republican primary race for attorney general. The 1918 Nelson coalition countered with their own Sullivan, State Senator John D. Sullivan, reputedly "the best criminal lawyer in the state," to defend Gustaf. A Democrat, John Sullivan had opposed a 1919 bill to abolish the Minnesota Council of Public Safety.[29]

While the trial was pending, Nelson turned down most speaking invitations and a chance to appear with Republican presidential candidate Warren G. Harding at the Minnesota State Fair.[30] He did help his protégé "Jake" Preus win the Republican endorsement for governor over several rivals, and the nomination over the NPL'er Henrik Shipstead. Preus battled "to save the state from the menace of socialism" — NPL socialism.[31]

The trial began on Monday, September 20, in the Douglas county courthouse. The courtroom was packed with vocal spectators eager for scandal, inside details about Nelson's family, or revenge for 1918. Jury selection took three days. The NPL'ers won the advantage: nine farmers, two village laborers, and the manager of a farmers' elevator were chosen. No merchants or county-seat elites sat on the all-male jury.

In his lengthy cross-examination of Gustaf, the NPL Sullivan ranged far beyond the March 10th tragedy. Going back to events of 1887 and to gamekeeper Gustaf's alleged murder of two men in Sweden, Sullivan crafted a portrait of threatening arrogance sure to anger Scandinavian-American farmers who recalled Old World oppressive elites. Sullivan played to courtroom spectators' passions and they responded by applauding him and deriding the defense attorney. The judge tried to keep order and to confine testimony to 1920 events.

Sullivan's portrayal was dramatized when tenant Oscar Jacobson, "in deadly terror" of Gustaf, suffered a nervous breakdown the morning he was scheduled to testify. He was found hiding in the haymow of his barn. On Monday, Knute Nelson testified that he had given Gustaf permission to gather wood from his tenant's land. NPL'ers used his testimony—largely irrelevant to the charge—and the trial to exploit tensions over farm tenancy, which had doubled, from 15 percent to 30 percent, in parts of west-central Minnesota. Businessmen worried that Old-World tenancy might replace American ownership. Later, an NPL attorney appealed to class antagonisms by calling Nelson's house the "Manor" and stressing that "the tenant [did] the actual farm work on the place." Oscar's terror emphasized the point of owner mistreatment of tenants.

The *Echo* trumpeted the trial in a spectacular front-page story. A week later its front page announced that "the son-in-law of United States Senator Knute Nelson had been found guilty of murder in the first degree." "Nelson Draws Life Sentence," blared the headline. The *Echo* reported the eruption that occurred when sheriff's deputies came for Gustaf. As he fought them, "Knute Nelson's daughter demanded that she be taken in with him" and "screamed at the top of her voice" and "complained bitterly that the deputies handled Nelson as a 'common man.'"[32]

Gustaf's trial affected the 1920 campaign. The pro-NPL *Minneapolis Daily Star* reported it in detail. "Following his victory in the Nelson murder trial," the *Star* exclaimed, "Thomas V. Sullivan . . . addressed several hundred farmers . . . in opening his campaign" for attorney general. Sullivan polled a higher percentage than other NPL or Farmer-Labor statewide candidates except Shipstead. Still, Preus was elected governor, and Harding, president. Before the election, Nelson told one of his patronage appointees, "John, I want to live until we have a Republican administration." Now he had one. Yet the NPL's nascent Farmer-Labor party had displaced the Democrats as the chief opposition party in Minnesota. Despite Nelson's three decades of work, agrarian protest still thrived among Scandinavian-American farmers flocking to a new party.[33]

Unfortunately, Nelson continued to be represented before the public by "Sweet Tramp," a surrogate he had surely not chosen. In early March, the Minnesota Supreme Court overturned the jury's verdict and ordered a new trial. Associate Justice Homer B. Dibell, a Republican who had defeated an NPL'er in 1920, wrote the opinion: the evidence did not support the first-degree murder conviction and the trial court had allowed the NPL-led prosecution "to discredit the defendant by 'sneers and innuendo'" and by the introduction of unrelated matters. The *Echo* accused the court of Republican partisanship and noted that two of Alexandria's "leading capitalists" were sureties for Gustaf's release on bond. Defense attorneys demanded a change of venue to escape "the anarchists of Douglas County" (per the *Echo*). In June, 1921, the NPL's county attorney tried Gustaf in Fergus Falls on a lesser charge (first-degree manslaughter). Gustaf of the "Manor" was convicted and sentenced to twenty years in Stillwater prison.[34]

By then the return to "normalcy" under Warren G. Harding was well under way. Abundant new consumer goods affordable to increasing numbers of Americans were winning voters over to Republicanism and the "New Era." As Judiciary Committee chairman, Nelson presided over confirmation hearings. Harding appointed four Supreme Court justices (including Minnesotan Pierce Butler) and "Republicanized the federal bench" with sixty new federal judges. By pushing the appointment of John McGee to a federal judgeship, Nelson rekindled bitter wartime antagonisms over the MCPS. He succeeded in gaining McGee's confirmation but at the expense of strengthening the Farmer-Labor party, which was largely an anti-MCPS coalition.[35]

Behind the scenes, trouble was brewing in the Harding White House. Though married, Harding carried on illicit affairs worthy of a promiscuous Greenwich Villager in Reed and Bryant's day. He called for enforcing nationwide prohibition while he drank freely in the White House. His Secretary of the Interior was Nelson's debating foe, Albert Fall of New Mexico, who opposed the conservation movement. In an affair superficially similar to Ballinger-Pinchot, Fall secretly leased oil reserves to friends in exchange for bribes. Nelson was not around when these scandals were ultimately exposed.[36]

On August 8, 1922, his wife of fifty-four years, Nicholina (Jacobson) Nelson, died in Washington, D.C. "after a lingering illness." She was seventy-five years old. *Minneapolis Tidende* gave an accurate eulogy: "Like her husband, Mrs. Nelson was a woman of simple habits; she did not take part very much in high social life, for which she as a Senator's wife was eligible. She preferred domestic pursuits." The Norwegian Lutheran church in Alexandria was too small to hold the crowd that came to her funeral. The *Citizen News* reported that she "had endeared herself to many . . . on account of her unselfish acts of goodness and helpfulness."[37]

Saddened, reminded of his own mortality, Knute was talking with friends (including Governor Preus) at his home after the funeral. Then, "he went up into the attic of his home and got out from an old chest the corporal's uniform that he wore in the civil war." Surprisingly, he put it on and "regaled his friends" with war stories. Preus suggested he donate it to the Minnesota Historical Society. Knute held on to it: "No one can have this until after I am dead and gone." Later that month Nelson visited Mary Dillon's grave in Whitewater, Wisconsin, for another nostalgic moment.[38]

That fall Preus ran against Swedish-American "dirt farmer" and Farmer-Laborite Magnus Johnson. Kellogg faced an even tougher challenge from Henrik Shipstead. Both men sought the campaign services of the "Grand Old Man." Nelson was too old to "stump" the state. He did speak briefly at a rally in Alexandria in mid-October. Showing his age, he recalled that two Republican candidates, including Preus, had served him in Washington as young clerks. Other speakers made Nelson out to be popular in his home area. The main speaker, Senator Irvine L. Lenroot, was more accurate when "he wondered if we of Alexandria realized [Nelson's] true greatness" and quoted the proverb about the prophet without honor at home.[39]

Appropriately, he gave his last campaign speech in Detroit Lakes on October 21. He began by recalling the 1882 "circus tent" nomination and noting the great changes since then: "After I was nominated a large share of my campaigning was done in buckboards and buggies," for "at that time we had neither the telephone, rural free delivery or the automobile." He praised Kellogg, improbably, as a "big man for the [pro-] farmer legislation" which only the Republicans could pass. As in the 1890s, he ridiculed radicals: "those visionary people who live in Utopias; who engage in nothing but pulling down and destroying. . . . None of them has any remedy for anything; no legitimate program to offer." He presented the patented Nelson list of statistics — this time, to prove Democrats were spendthrifts. He closed by reminiscing: "We have had in Minnesota all kinds of parties, most of them political sideshows. We have had the Grange and the Greenback party, the Farmers Alliance and Populists. Now we have what they call the Nonpartisan League. Now all these parties have been like local showers. The national government has gone on under the republican or democratic parties. These sideshows have cut no figure. . . .

"I feel tonight like I am parting with old friends and I have one

337

favor to ask of you. If you believe I have attempted to serve you faithfully and well, all I ask in return is that you vote the republican ticket on election day."[40]

They did not. Farmer-Laborites Johnson, Shipstead, and Knud Wefald carried Becker county by overwhelming margins. Wefald defeated Knute's old friend Halvor Steenerson for Congress. Shipstead became the first Farmer-Labor United States senator by trouncing Kellogg.[41] Nelson could not bequeath his popularity as he would his farm. It began to seem unlikely he would have a Republican successor (Preus) as he hoped.

In his last important Senate speech, on January 6, 1923, he mourned another failure: "This may be a sort of a funeral oration on the days of the past, and yet I felt then, and I feel now, that we made the greatest mistake in the world when we did not adopt the treaty of Versailles . . . . If we had done that, conditions in the world to-day would have been much better than they are now." He ridiculed as "peanut politics" Republicans' demand that the few remaining American troops in Germany be withdrawn.[42]

On February 2nd and 3rd, the Senate celebrated Knute Nelson's 80th birthday (actually, his 81st)—to the extent that the modest Viking would permit. He refused to be photographed with the vice-president "because he as usual wanted to avoid anything that looked like self-glorification." Congratulations poured in anyway—from Harding, ex-President Taft, Governor Preus, the Norwegian ambassador, and dozens of other dignitaries. King Haakon of Norway sent his "best wishes with thanks for your never-failing sympathy for old Norway." Pleased to be honored, Nelson still tried to put in a day's work. He beamed as he displayed soon-to-be-indicted Attorney General Harry Daugherty's gift: a box of his favorite chewing tobacco. "Now I have enough tobacco to last me for a long time to come." When senators praised him on the Senate floor the next day, he was visibly moved. "His voice quivered with emotion as he thanked his colleagues in a few words."[43]

He was suffering from a heart condition, from bronchial infections and influenza. In February, 1923, he wrote his will. He planned to go home to Alexandria in early April, but delayed his departure until Saturday, April 28. On Friday evening, he had a mild heart attack. He "insisted" it was "an attack of indigestion," but his doctor suspected the truth. Vainly urging him to postpone the trip, the doctor stayed with him until past midnight.

Before leaving on Saturday evening, he said goodbye to several senators, to Simon Michelet, and to Republican boss Edward E. Smith of Minneapolis. His housekeeper, Mrs. Edith Truscott, Nicholina's niece, also boarded the train for home. Ida awaited him in Alexandria. Coincidentally, and appropriately, two state patronage appointees, Minnesota's insurance commissioner and his deputy, sat by him in the train. He told the commissioner, "I'm feeling fine because I'm going home."[44]

Shortly after 8 P.M. the train passed through the town of Timonium, eleven miles from Baltimore and only a few miles from camps Dix and Randall, where the Fourth Wisconsin had bivouacked. Riding over the same Pennsylvania Railroad track that brought Private Nelson into Baltimore in late July, 1861, he died of a heart attack at 8:15. Somehow he would have liked that coincidence.[45]

In Christiania, *Dagbladet* reported the news. "Knute Nelson was one of the most prominent Norwegians to play a role in American politics . . . . A bit of fairy-tale radiance has surrounded Knute Nelson, the Norwegian peasant boy who won such a great name for himself in America."[46]

Knute Nelson had no grandchildren to mourn him, no living son to eulogize him. He had proved a better political parent, and his finest "son" was Preus, who, deeply moved, confessed, "It is hard for me to speak of our personal relations; he was like a father to me." Michelet became the eulogizing son, recalling Nelson's private life: "The Senator had a certain gruffness of manner" that misled people into "believ[ing] that he was careless of the feelings of men . . . . he could be as tender-hearted as a woman and many times was."[47] The fatherless boy who found mentors in the mas-

339

After having lain in state in the Capitol, Nelson's body is taken to St. Paul's Union Depot on May 1 for the train ride to Alexandria and burial the following day.

culine world of politics died without a son, except these political ones he had mentored.

Accompanied by Preus, the body traveled from Harrisburg, Pennsylvania, to St. Paul. Preus asked Lee Willcutts, a Nelson patronage appointee, and John F. McGee, a judicial appointee, to make memorial arrangements. The body lay in state in the Capitol rotunda on Tuesday, May 1. Thousands of Minnesotans paid their last respects. That evening it was taken by train to Alexandria, where Constant Larson planned a public funeral for the armory on Wednesday afternoon, May 2. Preus declared May 2nd a public day of mourning.[48]

On Wednesday morning "simple services" were held at the Nelson home. Officiating were the local Norwegian Lutheran minister, A.T. Tjornholm, and the president of the Norwegian Lutheran Church in America, Hans G. Stub. Before over 1,200 mourners at the armory, Dr. Stub preached on a text from II

Samuel (3:38): "Know ye not that there is a prince and a great man fallen this day in Israel." The 3rd Infantry band led a military honor guard marching the "simple bronze casket" to Kinkead Cemetery. Right behind the members of the immediate family came an automobile carrying "seven men, all of whom had been former employees of the senator," including Preus and Michelet. Numerous senators and state officials also came to Alexandria for the funeral of the Grand Old Party's "Grand Old Man."[49]

The headline to the *Baltimore Sun*'s discussion of his death read "Heavy Blow to GOP." It "eliminated the only remaining dominating regular Republican figure in the Northwestern States." It aided La Follette's 1924 presidential campaign, expected to be endorsed by Minnesota's Farmer-Labor party. The main barrier to La Follette Insurgency and Farmer-Laborites had been Nelson, "whose influence was widespread, especially among the large Scandinavian populations in his own and the surrounding States."[50] He could never outlive the Castle Garden and Civil War stories. Nor could he escape, except by death, his longtime duty to defend the farm states from advancing agrarian radicalism.

His last campaign failed. His "son" Preus lost the special election to choose a new United States senator. Farmer-Laborite Magnus Johnson won in a landslide. Preus's career was finished. Nelson's successor came to Washington calling attention to himself as a "dirt farmer" in a way the dignified Nelson would have abhorred.[51]

Already, time and the political tides had seemingly erased much of Knute Nelson's legacy. The trail he pioneered for Scandinavian-American candidates could not be erased. Numerous Scandinavian-American governors and senators followed Nelson into Minnesota history. Still, Nelson did not see trailblazing as his primary task. And he could blaze that trail only because of his Americanization, his Civil War service, and the opportunities a frontier region offered. The politics of patronage, unregulated development, distributive government, unquestioned patriotism—the politics that gave him his chance and that he remained loyal to—by the 1920s these were judged a failure.

Notes

Chapter One

[1] Lars Schjærven and Johannes Gjerdåker, *Evanger-boka. Gards- og ættesoga,* 2 vols. (Voss, Norway, 1984), 1:184. Here, and below, see the information on Kvilekval on pp. 184-197. The spelling of the name varied—other variants were Kvilekvaal, Quillequall (1611), and Quilequal (1723). For a brief explanation of the name and its likely meaning, see Amund Helland, *Norges land og folk topografisk-statistisk beskrevet. Bind XII, Søndre Bergenhus Amt* (Christiania, 1921), 925. The title of this chapter comes from Knute Nelson, undated handwritten manuscript, in Knute Nelson Papers, Minnesota Historical Society, St. Paul. Quoted in Millard L. Gieske, "The Politics of Knute Nelson, 1912-1920" (Ph.D. dissertation, University of Minnesota, 1965), 4.

[2] Millard Gieske, interview with Johannes Gjerdåker, 6 October 1988. Gjerdåker is a Voss historian.

[3] For an excellent description of mid-nineteenth century Voss, see Odd S. Lovoll, "A Pioneer Chicago Colony from Voss, Norway: Its Impact on Overseas Migration, 1836-60," in Rudolph J. Vecoli and Suzanne M. Sinke, eds., *A Century of European Migrations, 1830-1930* (Urbana, Illinois, 1991), 182-199.

[4] "Lars Kindem Collection of Voss Traditions," at the Library, Voss, Norway. The source for this particular account was Torstein G. Haukenes. See also Brynjulf N. Mugaas' toast to Knute Nelson at a banquet in Evanger in August, 1899, in Knute Nelson Papers.

[5] "Kyrkjebok for presten," Voss parish, A 13 (1836-1851), entry 72, 62-63, in Statsarkivet, Bergen, Norway.

[6] Schjærven and Gjerdåker, *Evanger-boka,*2:16-20; Gieske, interview with Gjerdåker, 4 October 1988. Schjaerven and Gjerdåker list Helge as Knute Nelson's father. For a description of Styve *gård,* see Schjærven and Gjerdåker, *Evanger-Boka,* 2, 9-44, especially 19. By the 1840s, the *gård* Styve had been sub-

NOTES

divided into four separate farms (*bruk*). As the oldest son, Helge inherited *bruk* number two in 1832.

[7] Leiv Slinde, *Knute Nelson. Frå fattiggut til verdskjent statsmann* (Oslo, 1950), 9.

[8] Voss *Kyrkjebok*, "People who left the Parish," in Voss archives, Voss, Norway; undated, handwritten note in Box 1, Correspondence 1861-1864 Folder, Knute Nelson Papers; Schjærven and Gjerdåker, *Evanger-boka*, 2:19. Brynjulf N. Mugaas, an Evanger contemporary of Nelson and one who knew both the Styve and the Kvilekval families, claimed that Helge, though a "man of good ability" was a person of "bad habits" and "not a highly regarded personality." See Mugaas to Minister to Oslo (Ambassador) Lauritz B. Swenson, 25 December 1924 (translated by Theodore C. Blegen in 1964), in Knute Nelson Papers. In the "Lars Kindem Collection of Voss Traditions," one informant claims that Helge died after becoming intoxicated, passing out, and freezing.

[9] K.A. Rene, *Historie om udvandringen fra Voss og Vossingerne i Amerika* (Madison, Wisconsin, 1930), 503.

[10] George Rudolph Bjorgan, "The Success Story of an Immigrant" (Ph.D. dissertation, University of Minnesota, 1967), 7; Wollert Keithau, "Baardsen, Gjest," in *Norsk Biografisk Leksikon* (Kristiania, 1923), 1:335.

[11] Rene, in *Udvandringen fra Voss* (502-503), gives the correct birthdate and some details about his birth and childhood, but does not venture a guess as to the father.

[12] Rene, *Udvandringen fra Voss*, 258-259; Schjærven and Gjerdåker, *Evanger-boka*, 188.

[13] Mugaas to Swenson, 25 December 1924, in Nelson Papers.

[14] Lovoll, *The Promise of America: A History of the Norwegian-American People* (Minneapolis, 1984), 4-11; Blegen, *Norwegian Migration to America, 1825-1860* (Northfield, Minnesota, 1931), 42-48.

[15] Lovoll, "Pioneer Chicago Colony," 183-184.

[16] Gjerdåker, "Life and development in Voss 1836-1986. A Survey," in *Gamalt frå Voss: Utvandring frå Voss til Amerika, Eit 150-årsminne* (Voss, 1985), 61-66.

[17] Gjerdåker, "Life and development," 61-66; Blegen, *Norwegian Migration, 1825-1860*, 136.

[18] Translated and quoted in Blegen, *Norwegian Migration 1825-1860*, 201-202. The letter from "John Haldorson Qvilequal to his relatives" was dated 22 December 1843, and originally appeared in *Vossingen*, 5:1, 8-10.

[19] Blegen, "The Norwegian Government and the Early Norwegian Emigration," in *Minnesota History*, 6(1925), 115-140.

[20] Blegen, *Norwegian Migration, 1825-1860*, 211-212.

[21] Lars Fletre, "The Vossing Correspondence Society of 1848 and the Report of Adam Løvenskjold," in *Norwegian-American Studies*, 28 (1979), 248-249, 266. See also, Albert O. Barton, "Norwegian-American Emigration Societies in the Forties and Fifties," in *Norwegian-American Studies and Records*, 3 (1928), 26-34.

[22] *Kyrkjebok for presten, Voss*, A15 (1845-1855), no. 41-42, in Statsarkivet, Bergen, Norway.

[23] Recollections dated 12 and 23 September 1919, as told to Simon Michelet,

Knute Nelson's personal secretary, in Simon Michelet Papers, MHS. The pocket Bible is in the Nelson papers.

²⁴ New York Evening Post, 5 July 1849. Repeated inquiries to the National Archives have failed to turn up Knute and Ingebjørg's names in ship passenger arrival records.

²⁵ J.A.O. Preus to Martin W. Odland, 28 January 1926, in Odland Papers, MHS. Preus interviewed Ingebjørg in Deerfield, Wisconsin, about 1908. See Odland, The Life of Knute Nelson (Minneapolis, 1926), 7. Nelson appears to have been the original source for the story. Preus asked Ingebjørg about it in the 1908 interview and her answer was that the incident happened at Castle Garden.

Chapter Two

¹ The fullest account of the Vossing colony in Chicago during this period is in Lovoll, A Century of Urban Life: The Norwegians in Chicago before 1930 (Northfield, 1988), 12-14, 44-54.

² Pearl Keating, "Senator Knute Nelson Got Start Peddling Newspapers in Chicago" (interview with Nelson), 25 September 1922, newspaper clipping in Simon Michelet Papers, MHS.

³ For information on Jon's family, see Rene, Udvandringen fra Voss, 258-259.

⁴ Blegen refers to the 1849 cholera epidemic and other incidences of fatal disease among the immigrants in his Norwegian Migration to America: The American Transition (Northfield, Minnesota, 1940), 59. See also Lovoll, A Century of Urban Life, 38-42, 60-61.

⁵ Knute Nelson to Emilie Smith, 1 January 1915, letter in possession of Inger Heiberg, Emilie Smith's niece, Oslo, Norway. A copy is in the University of Oslo Library.

⁶ Keating, "Senator Knute Nelson Got Start Peddling Newspapers in Chicago."

⁷ Nelson to Emilie Smith, 1 January 1915.

⁸ Blegen, Norwegian Migration: The American Transition, 151.

⁹ For more information on the Norwegian colony in Chicago, see Lovoll, A Century of Urban Life, cited in n.1. In his Promise of America, 173, Lovoll writes that "Organizational life among Norwegian Americans commenced in earnest in the 1880s." He was referring to "charitable institutions," but the same could be said for cultural, social, and other institutions.

¹⁰ Lovoll, Promise of America, 153; Carlton C. Qualey and Jon A. Gjerde, "The Norwegians," in June Drenning Holmquist, ed., They Chose Minnesota: A Survey of the State's Ethnic Groups (St. Paul, 1981), 230.

¹¹ Samuel Eliot Morrison and Henry Steele Commager, The Growth of the American Republic (New York, 1962), 643-644. See also Richard N. Current, The History of Wisconsin: The Civil War Era, 1848-1873 (Madison, 1976), 377, 380, 456-457. Current dates the advent of mechanization in Wisconsin to the Civil War and postwar years.

¹² Kindem, Vossaboki, 2 (Voss, 1981), 457-461.

¹³ Barton, "Norwegian Emigration Societies," 25 (especially n. 10); Fletre, "Vossing Correspondence Society," 249.

¹⁴ For Grotland's life in Chicago and Skoponong, see Rene, *Udvandringen fra Voss*, 275, 325; and Nelson to Smith. Rene describes the Skoponong colony on 218-220. Other spellings of Nils' name were Grodtland and Grjotland. He was also known as Nils Tangen, after his Dane county farm, and Nils O. Nilson. See also Odland, *Knute Nelson*, 12-13.

¹⁵ Blegen, *Norwegian Migration: The American Transition*, 75.

¹⁶ Rene reports that Nils settled on a 40-acre plot belonging to a man named Holly, who sold it to Nils' nephew Ivar in 1852 — thus, Nils never owned it. The man's name was undoubtedly Hylle, for two Hylle families lived next to Nils. Knute Nelson's version was that nephew Ivar let them have it if they would pay the taxes. Ivar Grotland owned up to 140 acres at Skoponong, but also worked in Chicago. See Rene, *Udvandringen fra Voss*, 275, 325, and the map on 219; Nelson to Smith.

¹⁷ See map in Rene, *Udvandringen fra Voss*, 220.

¹⁸ Rene, *Udvandringen fra Voss*, 220; J. Magnus Rohne, *Norwegian American Lutheranism up to 1872* (New York, 1926), 71, 93.

¹⁹ The term "Norwegian Indian" appears in C.A. Clausen, ed., "A Norwegian Schoolmaster Looks at America," in *Norwegian-American Studies and Records*, 13 (1943), 79; and in Consul General Løvenskjold's report, quoted in Fletre, "Vossing Correspondance Society," 256. The Vossings claimed this was "a great distortion of the truth." See Fletre, 264. Though he quotes one American as comparing Norwegian newcomers' clothes with Indian clothes, Ole Munch Ræder presented a more positive account of Americans' attitude toward Norwegians. See Gunnar J. Malmin, *America in the Forties: The Letters of Ole Munch Ræder* (Northfield, Minnesota, 1929), 37-46. For other examples of anti-Norwegian prejudices, see Blegen, *Norwegian Migration: The American Transition*, 282.

²⁰ Bjorn Holland, "A sketch of the late Senator Nelson's Boyhood Days," undated, in Nelson Papers. Odland altered this version to suit his editorial taste. See Odland, *Knute Nelson*, 15-16. Mary Blackwell Dillon to Nelson, 18 September 1881; Odland, *Knute Nelson*, 12-13; Holland, *History of the Town of Moscow from 1849 to 1919* (Hollandale, Wisconsin, 1919), 161-162.

²¹ Nels Holman to Odland, 2 February 1926, in Odland Papers. Odland tells the story in his *Knute Nelson*, 23.

²² Dillon to Holland, 15 October 1882, noted in Holland reminiscences, in Nelson Papers.

²³ Holland, *History of the Town of Moscow*, 164.

²⁴ For the debate, see Blegen, *Norwegian Migration: The American Transition*, 248-262; and Lovoll, *Promise of America*, 67-69. The quotations are from Blegen, 250, 255.

²⁵ Holland, "A Sketch of the late Senator Knute Nelson's Boyhood Days."

²⁶ Dillon to Nelson, 6 May 1878, 18 February 1878, 29 September 1879, and 22 April 1881, all in Nelson Papers.

²⁷ Gieske, "The Politics of Knute Nelson," 46-47. As sources, Gieske cites two articles which appeared following Nelson's death: *Minneapolis Tribune*, 30 April 1923 and *Minneapolis Journal*, 29 April 1923. See also Odland, *Knute Nelson*, 319-320.

²⁸ Blegen, *Norwegian Migration, 1825-1860*, 141; Lovoll, *Promise of America*, 39.
²⁹ Blegen, *Norwegian Migration, 1825-1860*, 142-143.
³⁰ Quoted in Fletre, "Vossing Correspondence Society," 251. Perhaps the best description of Koshkonong is that given by Odland, who had been a school superintendent there, in his *Knute Nelson*, 18. For a description of Deerfield township, see *Madison, Dane County and Surrounding Towns; Being a History and Guide* (Madison, 1877), 437-439.
³¹ Rene, *Udvandringen fra Voss*, 502. See also the map after 240 for the location of the farm of Nils O. Grotland.
³² But see Nelson to G. Thompson, 24 June 1861, in which he signs off as "your friend K. Tangen."
³³ Nelson to Smith.
³⁴ This interpretation is based on several Civil War letters from Knute to his parents: Nelson to "Kjære Foreldre", 6 February 1862; Nelson to "dear parents", 10 June 1862, and Nelson to William Nelson, 25 March 1864, all in Nelson Papers. See also, Mother to Knute Nelson, 8 March 1864. During his Civil War absence from home, Nelson wrote many letters to his parents, and these provide the best glimpse of their relationship. See also Gieske, ed., "Some Civil War Letters of Knute Nelson," in *Norwegian-American Studies*, 23 (1967), 17-50.
³⁵ Rene, *Udvandringen fra Voss*, 250-251.
³⁶ Nelson to "Kjære Foreldre," 24 October 1863, in Nelson Papers. Thompson later gave $300,000 to the University of Wisconsin "as an endowment of the Scandinavian department." See Odland, *Knute Nelson*, 19. Knute was schooled by the Lutheran minister—perhaps in confirmation class—for he tells his brother William that William's teacher "has recited many les[s]ons with me before our former Lutheran minister." See Nelson to brother William, 15 May 1864, in Nelson Papers.
³⁷ Nelson to "Kjære Foreldre," 30 March 1864, in Nelson Papers. Nils and Ingebjørg were not prominent in Vossing America, whose journal *Wossingen* (1857-1860) does not mention them. Ivar Grotland, however, was an agent for *Wossingen*. See *Wossingen*, vols. 1 and 2, State Historical Society of Wisconsin.
³⁸ Undated (1919) manuscript in Simon Michelet Papers, MHS; S. Michelet to Martin Michelet, 25 September 1919, in Michelet Papers. As Nelson's congressional assistant, Michelet took down Nelson's stories by dictation, but often did not date them.
³⁹ Blegen, *Norwegian Migration: The American Transition*, 517-520. Blegen reports that "the first of the Norwegian-American colleges was established in 1861." That was Luther College in Decorah, Iowa. Rev. Bernt J. Muus established an academy at Holden, Goodhue county, Minnesota, in 1869. See *Norwegian Migration: The American Transition*, 263.
⁴⁰ Nelson to Smith.
⁴¹ A.R. Cornwall, "Albion," in *Madison, Dane County and Surrounding Towns*, 283-287; J.Q. Emery, "Albion Academy," in *The Wisconsin Magazine of History*, 7:3 (March, 1924), 301-321; Odland, *Knute Nelson*, 20-21.
⁴² Cornwall, "Albion," 284; Nelson to Smith.

[43] Odland, *Knute Nelson*, 21. Head told the story to Odland around 1903-1905, though Odland gives no exact date.

[44] Emery, "Albion Academy," 310-311.

[45] For a description and picture of the *kubberulle*, see Lovoll, *Promise of America*, 46, 48. The description of the noise it made is Odland's. See his *Knute Nelson*, 23.

[46] *Alexandria Post*, 4 December 1874. See also Odland, *Knute Nelson*, 22.

[47] Emery, "Albion Academy," 305, 310-313. In its original form, Albion Academy operated from 1854 to 1892 (with a three-year hiatus from 1880-1883). It reopened under private ownership from 1894 to 1901, and the Norwegian Lutherans ran H.A. Preus Lutheran Academy in the same buildings from 1901 to 1917. Emery is the best single source on the original Albion Academy.

[48] Nelson to Smith.

[49] Nelson to Smith.

[50] Lovoll, *Promise of America*, 50.

[51] Nelson anecdote, dictated 29 September 1919, in Michelet Papers.

[52] C. J. Melaas to Odland, 18 January 1926, in Odland Papers; Odland, *Knute Nelson*, 32-33; *Stoughton Courier-Hub*, 7 January 1926. Melaas said that Nelson gave "Republican" speeches denouncing Democrats, but the evidence indicates that Nelson was a Douglas Democrat in 1860.

[53] Lovoll, *Promise of America*, 71; Arlow William Andersen, *The Immigrant Takes His Stand:The Norwegian-American Press and Public Affairs, 1847-1872* (Northfield, Minnesota, 1953), 12-13, 16-17, 20, 24-25, 30-31, 65.

[54] Nelson Holman to Odland, 2 February 1926, in Odland Papers. Quoted in Odland, *Knute Nelson*, 30. Holman was a classmate of Nelson's at Albion.

Chapter Three

[1] Bernard Bailyn *et al.*, *The Great Republic: A History of the American People*, 1 (4th ed., Lexington, Massachusetts, 1992), 595; George B. Tindall with David E. Shi, *America: A Narrative History*, 1 (3rd ed., New York, 1992), 638.

[2] Nelson to General F. C. Ainsworth, 12 December 1911, in Nelson Papers. See also Nelson to "Gode Foreldre," 8 September 1861, in Nelson Papers.

[3] Out of the 76 names listed for Company B, only four were possibly Scandinavian. See Newton Chittenden, "History and Catalogue of the Fourth Regiment Wisconsin Volunteers" (Baton Rouge, Louisiana, 1864), 26. Nelson's copy of this short pamphlet is in the MHS Research Center.

[4] For accounts of the 15th Wisconsin, see Blegen, *Norwegian Migration: The American Transition*, 390-395; Lovoll, *Promise of America*, 75; Andersen, *Immigrant Takes His Stand*, 85-89, 92-95, 97, and "Lincoln and the Union: A Study of the Editorials of *Emigranten* and *Fædrelandet*," in *Norwegian-American Studies and Records*, 15 (1949), 95-99. For Nelson's increasingly embittered feelings, see below.

[5] Blegen, *Norwegian Migration: The American Transition*, 388.

[6] Nelson to "dear parents," 10 June 1862, in Nelson Papers. See also, Gieske, "Some Civil War Letters," 28.

[7] Nelson preserved fifty-seven Civil War letters, fifty-four of which he wrote —mostly to his parents and to his half-brother William. He must have written double or triple that number to other correspondents, but these have not been

saved. Twenty-four are written in Norwegian, although he expressed some discomfort over having to reply in Norwegian to his parents' letters ("Jeg vil pröve og besvare eders paa Naarsk da I begjere det.") His parents evidently had a neighbor translate his English-language letters, and he had a Dane from a New York regiment translate one of his mother's letters, which must have been written in old script. He did write in English to his brother William, and those letters tended to be much more flowery in style. To his mother, he admitted, "I always show the best side I can in my letters to you." That bias must be kept in mind when analyzing these Civil War letters. In addition, nine personal anecdotes and essays have survived, which reveal much about his personality and political views during the war. See Nelson to "Kjære Foreldre," 8 October 1863; Nelson to "Kjære Moder," 11 September 1862; and Nelson to "Dear brother," 15 January 1863, all in Nelson Papers. For a complete treatment of the letters, see Gieske, "Some Civil War Letters."

[8] Nelson to "Gode og velsindede foreldre," 9 July 1861; Nelson to G[ullick] Thompson, 24 June 1861, both in Nelson Papers. For a translation of the June 24 letter, see Gieske, "Some Civil War Letters," 21-22.

[9] Nelson to "Gode Foreldre," 28 July 1861. In Norwegian, "Dampvognen var vor hest og en rask hest var den." Nelson's description of the trip is taken entirely from this letter, which is translated in Gieske, "Some Civil War Letters," 22-24.

[10] *Chicago Tribune*, 16 July 1861.

[11] For the Fourth Wisconsin's arrival, and the departure of the three-month volunteers, see *Baltimore Sun*, 24 and 25 July 1861.

[12] Gieske, "Some Civil War Letters," 24, 26.

[13] See, for example, Nelson to "Kjære Foreldre," 8 July 1862; Nelson to "Kjære Foreldre," 6 February 1862, both in Nelson Papers. In one letter, he expressed concern that his mother had to "cradle and work so hard at harvest." See Nelson to "Kjære Foreldre," 20 September 1862. According to the itemized statement filed with the Civil War letters, Nelson received $494.13 in regular soldier's pay and three bounty payments of $110 each—one on July 2, 1861, the second on July 28, 1866, and the last on February 6, 1868.

[14] Nelson to William [Nelson], 25 March 1864; Nelson to "Kjære Foreldre," 8 July 1862; Nelson to "Dear parents," 29 July 1862, all in Nelson Papers.

[15] Nelson to "Kjære Foreldre," 20 September 1862; Nelson to "dear parents," 10 June 1862, both in Nelson Papers.

[16] Gieske, "Some Civil War Letters," 25. A translation of Nelson to "Langt bortfjernede foreldre," 12 September 1861, in Nelson Papers.

[17] Nelson to "Kjære Foreldre," 8 October 1863; Nelson to Kjære Moder, 11 September 1862; and Nelson to William [Nelson], 3 February 1864, all in Nelson Papers.

[18] Nelson to "Kjære Foreldre," 16 December 1863, in Nelson Papers. See also Gieske, "Some Civil War Letters," 43.

[19] Nelson to "Kjære Foreldre," 8 October 1863, in Nelson Papers.

[20] Nelson to "Kjære Moder," 11 September 1862; Nelson to "Kjære Foreldre," 8 October 1863, both in Nelson Papers.

[21] Lovoll, *Promise of America*, 79-80; Blegen, *Norwegian Migration: The American*

Transition, 420, 422, 425-428. Blegen has a complete account of the controversy on pages 418-453. This statement was not accepted by the lay delegates to the Synod meeting, but was merely a resolution signed by the clergy.

[22] Nelson to "Kjære Foreldre," 8 October 1863, in Nelson Papers.

[23] Nelson to "Kjære Moder," 11 September 1862, in Nelson Papers.

[24] Nelson to "Kjære Foreldre," 24 October 1863, in Nelson Papers.

[25] Nelson to "Kjære Foreldre," 24 October 1863, in Nelson Papers.

[26] Nelson to "Dear Parents," 13 November 1861, in Nelson Papers.

[27] Nelson to "Kjere Father og Moder," 3 September 1863, in Nelson Papers.

[28] Nelson to William [Nelson], 23 April 1864, in Nelson Papers.

[29] Nelson to "Kjære Father og Moder," 3 September 1863, in Nelson Papers; Gieske, "Some Civil War Letters," 40.

[30] Nelson to "Kjære Moder," 18 February 1863, in Nelson Papers; Gieske, "Some Civil War Letters," 34.

[31] Nelson to "Gode og velsindede foreldre," 9 July 1861, in Nelson Papers.

[32] Nelson to "Langt fraverende foreldre," 9 October 1861; Nelson to "Dear Parents," 13 November 1861, both in Nelson Papers.

[33] [Knute Nelson], "Thoughts and observations scribbled 'down' as they have occured or suggested themselves," undated handwritten notes [1862?], in Nelson Papers.

[34] Nelson to "Gode Foreldre," 12 November 1862; Nelson to "Dear brother"[William], 15 January 1863; and Nelson to "Dear brother William," 25 January 1863, all in Nelson Papers.

[35] Esaias Tegnér, *Frithjofs saga af Esaias Tegnér, oversat fra svensk* (Chicago, 1894); Clement B. Shaw, translator, *Frithiof's Saga: A Legend of Ancient Norway* (Chicago, 1908). I have relied on Shaw's helpful plot summaries. A historian with a bent for Freudian psychoanalysis might stress the Oedipus complex which could be inferred from Knute's fascination with this story. Of course, Ingebjørg and Helge were the names of Knute's mother and (supposed) father. However, the poem's general popularity, literary merit, and applicability to Knute's wartime odyssey are sufficient to explain his fascination with it, in my opinion.

[36] See "Explanatory Letter of Frithiof's Saga By Esaias Tegner" (1839), in Shaw, *Legend of Ancient Norway*, 339-343, especially 340. Shaw explains the poem's "peculiar form of stanza, rhyme and measure," xvii-xxii.

[37] Nelson to William [Nelson], 23 April 1864, in Nelson Papers.

[38] *Frithjofs saga . . . oversat fra svensk*, 20. In his letter to William, dated 20 October 1862, Knute does not quote the first line, nor does he quote accurately. For the full sense, the complete stanza is given here. The translation is Keillor's.

[39] Nelson to "Dear brother"[William], 20 October 1862, in Nelson Papers. Here, Nelson was apparently quoting, in English, from the above stanza.

[40] Nelson to "Langt fraverende og bekömrede foreldre," 22 August 1861; Nelson to "Dear parents," 13 November 1861, both in Nelson Papers. Nelson's letters do not mention a duty assignment in Washington. J.A.O. Preus reported that Nelson was stationed there, near the Washington Monument, then under construction, and seven blocks from the Capitol. Preus reported that President

Lincoln once came to briefly review the troops. Nelson, however, says nothing about this in his letters—a strange omission if Preus's account is correct. See J.A.O. Preus to Martin Odland, 28 January 1926, in Odland Papers. Chittenden, in "History and Catalogue," 4, notes that 22 men were detached to cavalry duty in Washington on January 9, 1862, but it is not known if Nelson was part of this group. One explanation may be the hiatus in Nelson's correspondence between November 13, 1861, and January 28, 1862.

[41] Nelson to Anfin Johnson, 28 January 1862, in Nelson Papers. Here, and below, for details of the Fourth Wisconsin's movements, see Chittenden, "History and Catalogue."

[42] Nelson to "Dear Parents," 31 March 1862, in Nelson Papers; Shaw, *A Legend of Ancient Norway*, 154-167. In his trip, Frithjof encountered great difficulties, but seasickness was not one of them.

[43] In retaliation, Jefferson Davis ordered that if Butler was ever captured, he should immediately be hanged. J.G. Randall and David Donald, *The Civil War and Reconstruction* (Lexington, Massachusetts, 1961), 334-335, 444-446.

[44] All of these actions are as reported in Nelson's letters home. See Nelson to "dear parents," 10 June 1862; and Nelson to "Dear brother" [William], 20 October 1862, both in Nelson Papers.

[45] Chittenden, "History and Catalogue," 7; Nelson to "dear parents," 10 June 1862, in Nelson Papers.

[46] Nelson to "Dear brother"[William], 20 October 1862, in Nelson Papers.

[47] Nelson to "dear parents," 10 June 1862; Nelson to "Kjære Foreldre," 8 July 1862, both in Nelson Papers; Gieske, "Some Civil War Letters," 32.

[48] Nelson to William Nelson, 8 July 1862, in Nelson Papers.

[49] Nelson to "Kjære Foreldre," 8 July 1862, in Nelson Papers; Gieske, "Some Civil War Letters," 33-34.

[50] Nelson to "Dear Parents," 20 September 1862, in Nelson Papers.

[51] Nelson to "Dear brother" [William], 12 April 1863, in Nelson Papers.

[52] Nelson to "Dear parents." 30 April 1863, in Nelson Papers.

[53] Nelson to "Dear brother"[William], 22 May and 3 June 1863, in Nelson Papers; Gieske, "Some Civil War Letters," 35-39.

[54] Nelson to "Kjære Fader og Moder," 3 September 1863, in Nelson Papers; Gieske, "Some Civil War Letters," 40-41.

[55] Here, and below, see "Reminiscence of the 14th June 1863," undated [ca. September 1863] handwritten notes, in Nelson Papers.

[56] Nelson to William [Nelson], undated fragment, July, 1863, in Nelson Papers; Gieske, "Some Civil War Letters," 39-40.

[57] Nelson anecdotes, 6 September 1919, in Michelet Papers.

[58] Nelson to "Kjære Foreldre," 16 December 1863, in Nelson Papers; Gieske, "Some Civil War Letters," 42-43.

[59] Reid Mitchell, *Civil War Soldiers* (New York, 1988), 121. Mitchell's book also provides an excellent account of other topics covered in this chapter: for example, Union soldiers' desire to punish the South and Union soldiers' attitudes toward Confederates,

[60] Gieske, "Some Civil War Letters," 44-45.

[61] Nelson to William [Nelson], undated fragment, July, 1863?, in Nelson Papers; Gieske, "Some Civil War Letters," 39-40.

[62] [Knute Nelson], "Baton Rouge Sept. 2nd 1863," handwritten memorandum, Nelson Papers.

[63] [Knute Nelson], "The present War—its nature and consequences," handwritten memorandum, undated, in Nelson Papers.

[64] Nelson to "dear parents," 10 June 1862, in Nelson Papers.

[65] Richard Franklin Bensel, *Yankee Leviathan: The Origins of Central State Authority in America, 1859-1877* (New York, 1990), 414-415, 421-436.

Chapter Four

[1] *Alexandria Post*, 4 December 1874. For the new beard, see Odland's article on his early life in the *Minneapolis Journal*, 18 March 1906.

[2] Nelson, "Manuscript of Remarks on Lincoln," seven-page undated manuscript; also his "Memoranda on the life of Abraham Lincoln," two-page undated manuscript, both in Nelson Papers. These speeches were not delivered at Albion, but are typical of Nelson's early Lincoln addresses, and, thus, indicative of the content of his 1864 speech.

[3] H.L. Gordon, "An Address to the Voters of the Fifth Congressional District" (1882), 6, pamphlet in Nelson Papers. Gordon says that Nelson graduated in 1865, and in the fall of 1865 started reading law under William F. Vilas. Martin Odland does not give a year of graduation, but two contemporary (1860s) biographical summaries, probably based on information furnished by Nelson himself, indicate that he graduated in 1865. See *Wisconsin State Journal*, 17 October 1867; and *Emigranten*, 23 September 1867.

[4] *Emigranten*, 14 October 1867.

[5] For Anderson's trials as seen from his own perspective, see Rasmus B. Anderson, *Life Story of Rasmus B. Anderson Written by Himself* (Madison, Wisconsin, 1915).

[6] Current, *Wisconsin: Civil War Era*, 7, 77, 169, 495. For a picture of the state capitol, ca. 1868, see the photograph facing 128.

[7] *Emigranten*, 23 September 1867.

[8] Anton-Hermann Chroust, *The Rise of the Legal Profession in America*, 2 (Norman, Oklahoma, 1965), 105-108, 174-175. Chroust briefly notes the existence of the University of Indiana law school (207), and, in his survey of early law schools (176-219) he mentions none closer to Wisconsin.

[9] Horace Samuel Merrill, *William Freeman Vilas: Doctrinaire Democrat* (Madison, Wisconsin, 1954), 11, 16-19. Vilas served as counselor to Grover Cleveland, postmaster general (1885-1888), secretary of the interior (1888-1889), and United States senator (1891-1897). Nelson's decision to "read law" with a Democrat does not necessarily indicate a return to the Democratic party. See also Vilas to Gordon, 4 September 1882, in Gordon, "Address to the Voters," 6-7.

[10] For typical apprenticeship practices, see Chroust, *Rise of the Legal Profession*, 174-175. For Vilas's practices and counsel, see Merrill, *William Freeman Vilas*, 16.

[11] Vilas to Gordon, 4 September 1882, in Gordon "Address to the Voters," 6-7.

Nelson's personal payment record, including bonuses, is found in Box 1 of the Nelson Papers.

[12] *Emigranten*, 2, 23, September 1882, in Gordon "Address to the voters," 6-7. Nelson's first advertisement for his legal business appeared in *Emigranten* on September 2, 1867.

[13] *Emigranten*, 23 September 1867.

[14] *Emigranten*, 16 March 1868.

[15] Story quoted in Merrill D. Peterson, *The Great Triumvirate: Webster, Clay, and Calhoun* (New York, 1987), 98.

[16] For a brief biography of Spencer, see *History of Dane County*, (Chicago, 1880), 1139.

[17] Odland, *Knute Nelson*, 52-53. Though Odland provides no specific source to support Spencer's influence, the Democrats' charge that Spencer pushed for Nelson tends to confirm his account. See *Wisconsin Daily Union*, 16 October 1867. See also Bjorgan, "Success Story of an Immigrant," 49-50.

[18] Nelson to "Friend Erdall," 29 August 1867, in Nelson Papers. The "only Norwegian among the delegates," Nelson did support Johnson at the convention, held in early September—but Ole Johnson received only four votes. See *Emigranten*, 9 September 1867.

[19] Odland, *Knute Nelson*, 51; *Biographical Review of Dane County, Wisconsin. Containing Biographical Sketches of Pioneers and Leading Citizens* (Chicago, 1893), 518-520. For a brief note on Lars J. Erdall, see *Biographical Review*, 565.

[20] Odland, *Knute Nelson*, 51, 53; *St. Paul Pioneer Press*, 9 September 1900; *Minneapolis Journal*, 18 March 1906. Though Odland's account is based on Nelson's later recollection, the convention report in the *Wisconsin State Journal* tends to confirm the story, which has the ring of authenticity to it.

[21] *Wisconsin Daily Union*, 16 October 1867. See also *Emigranten*, 9 September 1867, which credited Nelson's selection as a delegate to the Republican state convention to "the Americans who elected him" and not to "his countrymen."

[22] *Wisconsin State Journal*, 17 October 1867.

[23] *Emigranten*, 21 October 1867.

[24] *Wisconsin State Journal*, 22 October 1867.

[25] For the editorial support, see *Wisconsin State Journal*, 7 and 20 October 1867, and *Emigranten*, 14 and 21 October 1867. For the election results, see *Emigranten*, 11 November 1867. Nelson owed over 20 percent of his majority to his home township of Deerfield, heavily populated by Norwegian Americans.

[26] *Emigranten*, 14 October 1867, and 16 March 1868.

[27] *Emigranten*, 14 October 1867.

[28] *Emigranten*, 16 March 1868; Evans, "Early Political Career," 9-11; Odland, *Knute Nelson*, 54; Bjorgan, "Success Story of an Immigrant," 55. Odland reported that Madison's political boss, Elisha W. Keyes, became upset when Nelson refused to support "certain legislation" which "the big lumbering interests" desired. However, there does not appear to be any written evidence behind that account—only verbal reminiscences recorded by Odland in the early twentieth century. See Odland, *Knute Nelson*, 57-58.

[29] Odland, *Knute Nelson*, 54-56; Evans, "Early Political Career," 10; Bjorgan, "Success Story of an Immigrant," 55-58.

[30] See the marriage certificate, dated 22 January 1868, and signed by Erdall, in the Nelson Papers. Odland, *Knute Nelson*, 40. Though he correctly reported the year as 1868 in his 1900 article on Nelson's boyhood, Odland (deliberately?) changed this to 1867 in the biography. See *St. Paul Pioneer Press*, 9 September 1900.

[31] Odland, *Knute Nelson*, 40.

[32] R. P. Ronne to Nelson, 30 October 1866, 12 March 1867, and 28 March 1868, all in Nelson Papers. Ronne had lived in Elk Point since 1860.

[33] Nelson to Erdall, 3 July 1867, in Nelson Papers.

[34] Nelson to William Nelson, 30 August 1867, in Nelson Papers. Nelson's office was at 13 King Street.

[35] P.L. Spooner to Nelson, 6 September 1871; Spooner to Nelson, 25 March 1871, both in Nelson Papers. Though the September, 1871, letter was written after Nelson moved to Alexandria, it accurately indicates Spooner's dependence on Nelson for work with Norwegian-American clients *while Nelson was still in Dane county*. For a request that Nelson collect legal fees from a client in eastern Dane county, see John C. Spooner to Nelson, 4 August 1870, in Nelson Papers.

[36] Nelson to "Brother William," 30 August 1867, in Nelson Papers.

[37] *Emigranten*, 9 September 1867.

[38] Current, *Wisconsin: The Civil War Era*, 452-455.

[39] Odland, *Knute Nelson*, 51.

[40] *Fædrelandet og Emigranten*, 4 February 1869.

[41] Odland, *Knute Nelson*, 58; Evans, "Early Political Career," 11; Bjorgan, "Success Story of an Immigrant," 61-62.

[42] Evans, "Early Political Career," 11. According to *Fædrelandet og Emigranten*, A.J. Turner was one of three main candidates for Assembly Speaker at the Republican caucus; he lost. See *Fædrelandet og Emigranten*, 28 January 1869.

[43] *Fædrelandet og Emigranten*, 4 February 1869; Evans, "Early Political Career," 12; Bjorgan, "Success Story of an Immigrant," 63.

[44] *Wisconsin State Journal*, 26 January 1869.

[45] *Wisconsin State Journal*, 26 January 1869; Ray Allen Billington, *The Genesis of the Frontier Thesis: A Study in Historical Creativity* (San Marino, California, 1971), 9-11.

[46] Frederick Jackson Turner, "The Significance of the Frontier in American History," in *Annual Report of the American Historical Association for the Year 1893*, 200.

[47] Blegen, *Norwegian Migration: The American Transition*, 250-251, 253-256; Andersen, *Immigrant Takes His Stand*, 111-113; Arthur C. Paulson and Kenneth Bjørk, "A School and Language Controversy in 1858: A Documentary Study," in *Norwegian-American Studies and Records*, 10 (1938), 76-106.

[48] Blegen, *Norwegian Migration: The American Transition*, 249-250, 257-258.

[49] For a discussion of underlying causes, see Blegen, *Norwegian Migration: The American Transition*, 243-244. For the class antagonisms, see Lowell J. Soike, *Norwegian Americans and the Politics of Dissent 1880-1924* (Northfield, Minnesota, 1991), 15-16, 20-23.

[50] Rasmus Anderson offered this as one of his resolutions at the 1868 Synod meeting in Chicago, but it was not adopted. See Blegen, *Norwegian Migration: The American Transition*, 257-258, and R.B. Anderson, *My Life Story*, 98-99. For Nelson's actions, see *Fremad* (Milwaukee), 22 April 1869, and Bjorgan, "Success Story of an Immigrant," 65. For an account of the Wisconsin Senate's debate over the 1868 bill, see *Emigranten*, 17 February 1868.

[51] *Fædrelandet og Emigranten*, 11 February 1869.

[52] *Fædrelandet og Emigranten*, 16 September 1869.

[53] Blegen, *Norwegian Migration: The American Transition*, 258-259; Lovoll, *Promise of America*, 107; *Nordisk Folkeblad*, 31 March 1869. There is an excellent treatment of this meeting, the preparatory planning for it, and the outcome, in Lloyd Hustvedt, *Rasmus Bjørn Anderson: Pioneer Scholar* (Northfield, Minnesota, 1966), 66-72.

[54] *Fremad*, 22 April 1869; *Skandinaven*, 14 April 1869.

[55] *Fremad*, 22 April 1869; *Skandinaven*, 14 April 1869.

[56] Odland, *Knute Nelson*, 60-62; R.B. Anderson, *My Life Story*, 125-127; Bjorgan, "Success Story of an Immigrant," 67-69; Evans, "Early Political Career," 13-14.

[57] *Fædrelandet og Emigranten*, 9 September 1869; *Fremad* (Milwaukee), 9 September 1869; *Nordisk Folkeblad*, 8 September 1869.

[58] *Fædrelandet og Emigranten*, 19 September 1869; *Wisconsin State Journal*, 2 September 1869; *Madison Daily Democrat*, 2 September 1869.

[59] *Wisconsin State Journal*, 2 September 1869; *Madison Daily Democrat*, 2 September 1869.

[60] For the Spencer story, see Sam Ross, *The Empty Sleeve: A Biography of Lucius Fairchild* (Madison, Wisconsin, 1964), 119-120; *Wisconsin State Journal*, 9 October 1869; *Madison Daily Democrat*, 11, 25 October 1869; and *Fædrelandet og Emigranten*, 14, 21 October 1869.

[61] For an expression of this growing sense of capability, see J.A. Johnson, "Et Akademi for norske Børn," in *Emigranten*, 2 October 1865. Johnson called Koshkonong "the largest Norwegian settlement in Wisconsin, perhaps in America, as well as the oldest." Here, Norwegian-American farmers were "among the most prosperous in the state."

[62] Turner, "Significance of the Frontier," 216.

[63] For Turner's pioneering ancestry, see Billington, *Genesis of the Frontier Thesis*, 216.

[64] For "Norwegianization" in Koshkonong, see, for example, Lovoll, *Promise of America*, 50; and Clausen, *Chronicler of Immigrant Life*, 132. For Portage's ethnic diversity, see Billington, *Genesis of the Frontier Thesis*, 215.

Chapter Five

[1] Lars K. Aaker to Nelson, 29 March 1870, in Nelson Papers.

[2] Odland, *Knute Nelson*, 64. The former register, Lewis Lewiston, complained bitterly that Aaker was appointed because Lewiston had supported Ignatius Donnelly against Senator Alexander Ramsey's candidate, Christopher C. Andrews, in the 1868 congressional race. See *Nordisk Folkeblad*, 21 July 1869, and Blegen, *Minnesota: A History*, 290-291.

³ *Nordisk Folkeblad*, 14, 21 July 1869. For the importance of Hjelm-Hansen's report in encouraging Norwegian-American immigration to the Red River Valley, see Lovoll, *Promise of America*, 92.

⁴ Aaker to Nelson, 29 March 1870, in Nelson Papers. Aaker referred to the main Northern Pacific line from Duluth to Moorhead. For the Northern Pacific's later abortive attempt to extend the St. Paul & Pacific line, see Ralph W. Hidy *et al.*, *The Great Northern Railway* (Boston, 1988), 19-23. In 1870, plans still called for the St. Paul & Pacific track to pass well to the east of Alexandria on its way to a junction with the Northern Pacific line west of Brainerd. See Hidy *et al.*, *Great Northern Railway*, 22.

⁵ For the political and speculative uses of land-office posts, see Malcolm J. Rohrbough, *The Land Office Business: The Settlement and Administration of American Public Lands 1789-1837* (Belmont, California, 1990).

⁶ For Alexandria's attempt to secure a place in the NP's plans, see *Alexandria Post*, 6 May 1871, especially the reprinted letter of 21 April 1871 from Geo. L. Becker to Aaker. From the fact that Becker wrote to Aaker directly and referred to the earlier lobbying effort, it may be inferred that Aaker was a leader in that effort.

⁷ L.K. Aarhus to Nelson, 10 December 1870, in Nelson Papers.

⁸ Hidy *et al.*, *Great Northern Railway*, 22; 1 February and 22 March 1871 board of directors' meetings, Series A, Reel 1, Great Northern Railroad Records, MHS; *Alexandria Post*, 25 March 1871. For the congressional legislation, see *Grants of Land, &c., by Congress, and Charter of the St. Paul & Pacific and of the First Division of the St. Paul & Pacific Railroad Companies. General Railroad Laws of Minnesota and of the Territory of Dakota* (St. Paul, 1879), 23-24.

⁹ *Alexandria Post*, 6 May 1871.

¹⁰ *Alexandria Post*, 6 May 1871.

¹¹ *Alexandria Post*, 10 June, 22 July 1871. Editor Joseph Gilpin charged that the "Aaker clique" had started the legal case against the eight and had persuaded local Norwegian Americans that "this was a question of nationality" in order to increase their political and business influence. "Their great effort is to get up a feeling of national enmity between Norwegians and Americans, for their own political ends." Apparently, there is no extant account of the "Aaker clique"'s side of the story. A search of the *Post* in the succeeding months failed to turn up any outcome for this case. It may have been dropped.

¹² *Alexandria Post*, 24 June 1871.

¹³ Recorded in Activity Book, 15 August 1871, in Nelson Papers.

¹⁴ *Alexandria Post*, 24 June, 1 July 1871; Aaker to Nelson, 13 July 1871, in Nelson Papers. Nelson guessed right about the St. Paul & Pacific's decision. On August 8, the First Division's board of directors voted to "abandon the survey via Long Prairie and put Engineer force on line from St. Cloud via Alexandria." See First Division Minute Book, 132, Reel 1, Series A, Great Northern Records.

¹⁵ Recorded in Activity Book, 15 August 1871, in Nelson Papers. See also Odland, *Knute Nelson*, 64-65.

¹⁶ *Alexandria Post*, 10 June 1871.

¹⁷ Odland, *Knute Nelson*, 65, quoting Nelson, and 74, quoting the *Alexandria Post*.

¹⁸ Odland, *Knute Nelson*, 67-68, quoting a 13 September 1882 letter from Soren Listoe, register of the Fergus Falls Land Office, to the *Minneapolis Journal*. See *Minneapolis Journal*, 1, 15 September 1882. This charge was used against Nelson in both the 1882 congressional campaign (for example, the *Journal* articles) and the 1892 gubernatorial campaign (see *Great West*, 4 November 1892). The account in the *Great West* is wildly exaggerated.

¹⁹ J.H. Van Dyke and Aaker to Commissioner, General Land Office (GLO), 31 May 1869, "Letters Sent by Register," Alexandria Land Office, U.S. Land Office Papers, MHS, St. Paul; *Minneapolis Journal*, 15 September 1882.

²⁰ Commissioner, GLO, to Register and Receiver, 1 November 1871, and 13 January 1872, both in "Letters Received by Register and Receiver," U.S. Land Office Papers; Aaker to Commissioner, GLO, 6 December 1871, "Letters Sent by Register," U.S. Land Office Papers; Odland, *Knute Nelson*, 65-66.

²¹ *Douglas County News*, 28 September 1882; *Alexandria Post*, 8 September 1882. The Washington law firm was Chipman, Hosmer and Company. See Nelson Papers, 1871-1873, for the legal correspondence. For more extensive treatment, see Bjorgan, "Success Story of an Immigrant," 75-80; Odland, *Knute Nelson*, 64-68.

²² *Minneapolis Journal*, 1, 15 September 1882; Eugene Roth to June D. Holmquist, 9 December 1969, in Knute Nelson Biographical Papers (P939), MHS. Whether from remorse or with regard to his upcoming congressional attempt, Nelson interceded with the GLO Commissioner to obtain for Kilbourn a refund of his $150 payment for the property. See N.J. Baxter to Nelson, 8 May 1876.

²³ Quoted in Odland, *Knute Nelson*, 66.

²⁴ For Norwegian farmers' distrust of the *embedsstanden* (official class), see, for example, Soike, *Politics of Dissent*, 15.

²⁵ *Alexandria Post*, 2 November 1872. Coming at the end of a political campaign, this charge may be exaggerated, but certainly Aaker himself had stressed to Nelson the advantages of practicing law near a Land Office. See Aaker to Nelson, 29 March 1870, in Nelson Papers. For another attack on the collusion between land offices and lawyers, see an Otter Tail county resident's letter in the *Anti-Monopolist*, 22 October 1874.

²⁶ "Record of Cases," notebook in Box 76, Nelson Papers; "Daybook," 59-70, vol. 15 in Box 79, Nelson Papers. Of 93 cases during 1873, about 29 cases (31 percent) were handled for clients with Scandinavian last names. Of course, judging by last names is somewhat inaccurate because of errors in spelling, Anglicized names, similarities between some old-stock and some Scandinavian last names.

²⁷ *Minneapolis Daglig Tidende*, 25 January 1923. From Nelson's records, it appears that in 1870 alone clients (and others?) gave him $1,530 in notes payable. See "Record of Cases," Box 76, Nelson Papers.

²⁸ Odland, *Knute Nelson*, 76. For a newspaper notice of a district court session and the attorneys (including Nelson) in town for the event, see *Glenwood Eagle*, 18 October 1873.

²⁹ John C. Sawbridge to Nelson, 15 February 1875, in Nelson Papers.

³⁰ "Daybook," 67, vol. 15, Box 79, Nelson Papers; Nelson reminiscences, 12

September 1919, in Simon Michelet Papers; Odland, *Knute Nelson*, 77-78; "K.Nelson in a/c with Douglas County," handwritten ms., Box 76, Nelson Papers. Actually, Nelson took the county attorney's job before the election, when his predecessor resigned. See *Alexandria Post*, 2 November 1872.

[31] "Daybook," 59-70, vol. 15, Box 79, Nelson Papers. See also the numerous letters from implement dealers and other businesses to Nelson in the Nelson Papers for the 1870s. Nelson also earned fees as an agent for the Minnesota Farmers Mutual Fire Insurance Association of Minneapolis and the (Scandinavian-American) Hekla Insurance Company of Madison, Wisconsin. See, for example, W.A. Nimocks to Nelson, 18 November 1874, in Nelson Papers; and Nelson to J.A. Johnson, 30 November 1878, in J.A. Johnson Papers, NAHA.

[32] The Nelson home is now an historical site operated by the Douglas County Historical Society (DCHS). Information on the house is based on a tour given to the author (Keillor) by DCHS Executive Director Barbara Grover on September 28, 1993.

[33] For the 1872 campaign in Douglas and Pope counties, see *Alexandria Post*, 5, 26 October 1872; *Glenwood Eagle*, 30 October 1872; *Alexandria Post*, 2 November 1872. See also a letter from H.L. Gordon (the Register of the St. Cloud Land Office) to Nelson, 29 December 1871, in Nelson Papers.

[34] *Glenwood Eagle*, 26 September 1874; Peder Engebretson to Nelson, 8 October 1874; L. Lewiston (Duluth Land Office Receiver) to Nelson, 7 September 1874; A.A. Brown (Receiver of New Ulm Land Office) to Nelson, 10 October 1874, all in Nelson Papers. See also, *Alexandria Post*, 2, 30 October 1874.

[35] *Nordisk Folkeblad*, 28 October 1874. Not sympathetic to the Anti-Monopoly party, *Nordisk Folkeblad* argued that Van Hoesen, the regular Republican candidate, was the "true and real" Anti-Monopolist.

[36] For the Anti-Monopoly party, see Martin Ridge, "Ignatius Donnelly and the Granger Movement in Minnesota," in *Mississippi Valley Historical Review*, 42(March, 1956), 693-709; and Thomas A. Woods, *Knights of the Plow: Oliver H. Kelley and the Origins of the Grange in Republican Ideology* (Ames, Iowa, 1991), 155-159. Beginning in July 1874, Ignatius Donnelly and friends published the party organ, the *Anti-Monopolist*.

[37] See the Democratic *St. Paul Dispatch*, 10 November 1874.

[38] *Nordisk Folkeblad*, 3 September 1873. Of course, the *Folkeblad* was a staunchly Republican newspaper. See Lovoll, *Promise of America*, 121. For a detailed analysis of why the Grange failed to appeal to Scandinavian Americans, see Steven J. Keillor, "Democratic Coordination in the Marketplace: Minnesota's Rural Cooperatives, 1865-1917" (Ph.D. Dissertation, University of Minnesota, 1992), 157-166. Douglas county's first (possibly Scandinavian-American) granges were not formed until December, 1873, and Pope county's five earliest granges were formed between June, 1873 and February, 1874. "Subordinate Granges in Minnesota," folder in Minnesota State Grange Papers, MHS; *Glenwood Eagle*, 20 December 1873.

[39] *Alexandria Post*, 30 October, 6, 20 November 1874. The county vote was as follows:

County	Van Hoesen	Nelson
Douglas	509	642
Big Stone	29	0
Grant	23	173
Pope	292	409
Stevens	53	63
Totals	906 (41%)	1287 (59%)

The 29-0 margin in unsettled Big Stone county looks a bit suspicious—a not uncommon feature of frontier vote totals.

[40] A.R. Cornwall to Nelson, 19, 22 November 1874, in Nelson Papers.

[41] Blegen, *Minnesota: A History*, 294; Odland, *Knute Nelson*, 84.

[42] *Minneapolis Tribune*, 20 January 1875; Odland, *Knute Nelson*, 83-84.

[43] *Alexandria Post*, 5 February 1875. Nelson denied bribery had "been attempted"—"unless you call promise of place or patronage bribery, and in this all candidates indulge more or less." For more of Nelson's comments on the long senatorial "agony," see his legislative letter in the *Post*, 19, 26 February 1875. For a specific charge of an attempt at bribery, see *Minneapolis Tribune*, 23 January 1875. In December, 1875, Nelson delivered a lengthy speech titled "Official Corruption" to the Alexandria Library Association. In it he denounced bribery and public officials profiting from their offices, but he did not attack the patronage system or come out for civil-service reform. See *Alexandria Post*, 10 December 1875.

[44] In 1881, Gordon later told Folwell, speculator Selah Chamberlain offered him thousands to vote for a state bill to buy out defunct railroad bonds (Chamberlain owned 967 of them). He responded with a "thundering" oration in the legislature. Gordon to William W. Folwell, 10 March 1908, and Folwell to Gordon, 16 March 1908; and Gordon autobiography, all in Hanford L. Gordon Papers, MHS.

[45] *Alexandria Post*, 12 February 1875.

[46] Hidy *et al.*, *Great Northern Railway*, 20, 22-23; *St. Cloud Journal*, 15 April 1875. The *St. Cloud Journal* ran a series of seven lengthy, informative, yet biased articles on the problems of the St. Paul & Pacific, from 15 April to 27 May 1875.

[47] For some of the financial details, see J.P. Farley, "Petition of the Receiver of the St. Paul & Pacific Railroad to the Legislature of Minnesota," January, 1874, pamphlet at MHS.

[48] Hidy *et al.*, *Great Northern Railway*, 25; *Alexandria Post*, 8 April 1871.

[49] *St. Cloud Journal*, 13 May 1875. See also *Journal*, 22 April 1875. For constituents' expectations of Nelson, see, for example, Theresa J. Hicks *et al.*, [1875] petition to Nelson; W.S. Moles to Nelson, 18 January, 3 February 1875; John C. Sawbridge to Nelson, 15 February 1875; and James Chambers to Nelson, 18 February 1875, all in Nelson Papers.

[50] *Minneapolis Tribune*, 14 January 1875; *St. Paul Daily Pioneer*, 14 January 1875; *Alexandria Post*, 12 February 1875.

[51] *Alexandria Post*, 12 February 1875 (emphasis in original).

[52] *Alexandria Post*, 5 February 1875 (emphasis in original).

[53] For a description of the 1873 campaign and the 1874 legislation, see George

H. Miller, *Railroads and the Granger Laws* (Madison, Wisconsin, 1971), 133-137. Miller downplays the role of the Grange outside of Wisconsin, and emphasizes that the "Granger laws were prepared by lawyers, usually with the help of merchants and shippers, and sometimes with the aid of railroad officials. Their agrarianism was an invention of their enemies," 167-168.

[54] The 1874 rates established by the commissioners were both maximum and *minimum* rates—occasionally *higher* than previous ones, so that some localities actually experienced an increase in freight and passenger rates. The best single source on Minnesota's Granger-era legislation is Rasmus S. Saby, "Railroad Legislation in Minnesota, 1849 to 1875," in *Minnesota Historical Society Collections*, 15 (1915), 1-188. For the conflict between promotional and regulatory functions, see Miller, *Granger Laws*, x, 42-49, 117, 139. According to Miller, "Minnesota's tardiness in obtaining adequate railroad facilities" compromised and eventually scuttled attempts at regulation, because the need for promotion outweighed the perceived need for regulation. For a strong pro-promotion and anti-regulation editorial, see *St. Paul Daily Pioneer*, 26 February 1875.

[55] Hidy *et al.*, *Great Northern Railway*, 25-26; *St. Cloud Journal*, 15, 22 April 1875.

[56] *Alexandria Post*, 19 February 1875.

[57] *Alexandria Post*, 12 February 1875; *Fergus Falls Journal*, 4 March 1875.

[58] For editorial comments on the St.Paul-NP group's "Delano bill," see *St. Paul Pioneer*, 10 March 1875; *Fergus Falls Journal*, 11 March 1875; *Duluth Minnesotian*, 13 March 1875; and *Sauk Rapids Sentinel*, 23 March 1875. In addition, "North West"'s series of articles in the *St. Cloud Journal* (April- May 1875) defended the Delano bill.

[59] *Alexandria Post*, 26 February 1875; *St. Cloud Journal*, 25 February 1875; *Anti-Monopolist*, 25 February 1875. For a complete copy of the original Nelson bill, see *Alexandria Post*, 5 March 1875.

[60] For criticism of Nelson's bill, see *Great West*, 30 September 1892, Supplement; *St. Cloud Journal*, 13, 20 May 1875; *Anti-Monopolist*, 11 March 1875; *St. Paul Daily Pioneer*, 4 March 1875. For a vigorous debate in the House over the rights of actual settlers, see *Anti-Monopolist*, 25 February 1875.

[61] *Anti-Monopolist*, 4 March 1875.

[62] *St. Paul Daily Pioneer*, 4 March 1875; *Anti-Monopolist*, 11 March 1875.

[63] *St. Paul Daily Pioneer*, 4 March 1875; *Fergus Falls Weekly Journal*, 11 March 1875. For the five-man committee, see the defense (seventeen years later) of Nelson's conduct in the 1875 legislature, in *Alexandria Post*, 7 October 1892.

[64] The quotation is taken from *Duluth Minnesotian*, 13 March 1875.

[65] *Alexandria Post*, 12 March 1875; *Fergus Falls Weekly Journal*, 11 March 1875; Austin to Nelson, 23 March 1875, in Nelson Papers.

[66] *Perham News*, 10 April 1875; *Fergus Falls Weekly Journal*, April, 1875.

[67] J.P. Farley to Nelson, 5 April 1875, in Nelson Papers; Hidy *et al.*, *Great Northern Railway*, 25, 29.

[68] "North West" in *St. Cloud Journal*, 20 May 1875. Editor Mitchell of the *Journal* offered Nelson space in his columns to rebut "North West"'s arguments, but it does not appear that he took Mitchell up on the offer. However, a rebuttal did appear in the rival *St. Cloud Press*, most likely written by Nelson ally C.A.

360

Gilman. See W.B. Mitchell to Nelson, 22 April 1875, and Gilman to Nelson, 16, 19 April 1875, all in Nelson Papers; *St. Cloud Press*, 3 June 1875.

[69] *Abstract of Lands*, Book 1, 105, Douglas County Recorder's Office, Alexandria. This transaction was recorded March 24, 1875. It is unclear if Nelson was benefitting from "inside information" in making the purchase.

[70] Peter Ohlsen to Nelson, 13 March 1875, in Nelson Papers. Similarly, his vote for the Morse bill, which emasculated the 1874 railroad regulation law, caused no damage in the Upper Country or among his Scandinavian-American constituents. The provisions of the Morse bill are given in *St. Paul Daily Pioneer*, 4 March 1875, and *St. Cloud Times*, 3 March 1875. For the final vote (with Nelson voting Aye), see *St. Paul Daily Pioneer*, 4 March 1875.

[71] Nicholina to "Dear husband," 9 January 1875; William Nelson to Nelson, 21 January 1875; Nicholina to Nelson, 7 February 1875, all in Nelson Papers.

[72] For Nelson's few cases, which usually involved settlers who had accidentally settled on SP&P land thinking it was government land, see Herman Trott to Nelson, 16 November 1874, 22 October 1874, and 31 March 1875, all in Nelson Papers. Trott was the SP&P's land commissioner. See Hidy *et al.*, *Great Northern Railway*, 21.

[73] Here and below, the description of the Fourth is given in the *Alexandria Post*, 7 July 1876, while the speech is reprinted in full in the *Post*, 14 July 1876.

[74] George B. Wright to Nelson, 30 April 1876, in Nelson Papers.

[75] *Budstikken*, 25 April 1876. See also *Fergus Falls Weekly Journal*, 6 April 1876, and *Budstikken*, 9 May 1876.

[76] *Budstikken*, 1 August 1876.

[77] Levi Butler to Nelson, 1 May 1876, in Nelson Papers.

[78] Originally Detroit, the name was changed to Detroit Lakes in 1926 at the request of the Post Office Department. *Moorhead Red River Star*, 17 June 1876; *Budstikken*, 1 August 1876; Thomas Torgesen to Nelson, 2 May and 16 July 1876; W.F. Ball to Nelson, 7 August 1876, all in Nelson Papers.

[79] Nelson to Andrew R. McGill, 27 August 1881, in Andrew R. McGill Papers, MHS.

[80] *St. Paul Daily Pioneer*, 19, 20 July 1876; *Minneapolis Tribune*, 20 July 1876; *Budstikken*, 25 July and 1 August 1876.

[81] *Minneapolis Tribune*, 20 July 1876.

[82] *Budstikken*, 1, 8, 22, and 29 August 1876.

[83] *Budstikken*, 22 August 1876. The *Alexandria Post* strongly denied *Budstikken*'s charge that Warren Adley, Land Office Receiver at Alexandria, was removed for supporting Nelson and opposing Stewart. The *Post* asserted that Adley "has been a supporter of Dr. Stewart from first to last"—which tended to confirm *Budstikken*'s broader point about federal officeholders. See *Alexandria Post*, 15 September 1876.

[84] *Budstikken*, 5, 19 September, and 29 August 1876.

[85] *Budstikken*, 5, 12, 26 September 1876.

[86] *Budstikken*, 12 September 1876.

[87] H. Sahlgaard to Nelson, 7 August 1876; S.J.R. McMillan to Nelson, 23 August 1876; W.D. Washburn to Nelson, 24 August 1876; J.H. Stewart to Nelson,

24, 26 August 1876; Sahlgaard to Nelson, 29 August 1876, all in Nelson Papers. Nelson did write to at least one supporter on Stewart's behalf. See Ole A. Boe to Nelson, 26 September 1876, in Nelson Papers.

[88] *Alexandria Post*, 13 October 1876.

[89] Nelson to George H. Reynolds, 11 September 1876; H. Sahlgaard to Nelson, 29 August 1876, both in Nelson Papers. If Nelson was faking illness, he did not tell his close friend from Wisconsin days, L.J. Erdall. See Erdall to Nelson, 24 September 1876, in Nelson Papers.

[90] Thomas Torgerson to Nelson, 6 August 1876, in Nelson Papers; *Alexandria Post*, 15 September 1876. Gudmond Johnson of *Budstikken* strongly denied that he had claimed Nelson's support for the bolt to McNair. See *Budstikken*, 19 September 1876. Very likely, Nelson encouraged Johnson to bolt, but insisted that Johnson not make this encouragement known publicly.

[91] *Alexandria Post*, 20 October 1876.

[92] "Budstikkens Udgivere" to Nelson, 19 October 1876, in Nelson Papers. The editors were reacting to an October 16 Nelson letter to Hans Mattson, not to Nelson's October 16th letter to the *Post*, which did not appear until the October 20th edition.

[93] Stewart to Nelson, 21 October 1876, in Nelson Papers. Stewart wrote "that certain parties laughed at my beautiful faith as they called it, for you . . ." but "I am more than proud that I stuck to my 'beautiful faith.'"

[94] Ole A. Boe to Nelson, 14 November 1876, in Nelson Papers.

[95] *Alexandria Post*, 17 November 1876; J.H. Stewart to Nelson, 20 November 1876, and John C. Sawbridge to Nelson & Reynolds, 20 December 1876, both in Nelson Papers.

[96] *Alexandria Post*, 24 November 1876.

[97] Hidy *et al.*, *Great Northern Railway*, 29; Evans, "Early Political Career," 46-48; Bjorgan, "Success Story of an Immigrant," 160-162.

[98] Hidy *et al.*, *Great Northern Railway*, 29-30; Albro Martin, *James J. Hill and the Opening of the Northwest* (New York, 1976), 126-129, 134-135. During the 1878 legislative session, Nelson complained in one of his legislative letters that he had not been informed about the negotiations until Hill told him in January 1878. See *Alexandria Post*, 1 February 1878.

[99] Here and below, Nelson to Emilie Smith, 1 January 1915, 8, copy in University of Oslo Library. See also, *Alexandria Post*, 18 May 1877.

[100] *Alexandria Post*, 25 May 1877; obituary, May 1877, in Nelson Papers.

[101] Ingebjørg Nelson to Knute Nelson, 12 November 1877, in Nelson Papers. Another indication that he was depressed comes in his complaint to his former teacher, Mary Blackwell Dillon, that some of his new friends had let him down. He expressed a nostalgic wish to visit Dillon again. See Dillon to Nelson, 18 February, 6 May 1878, both in Nelson Papers.

[102] *Minneapolis Journal*, 1 September 1882.

[103] *Alexandria Post*, 1, 15 February, 8 March 1878; *St. Paul Pioneer Press*, 5, 6, 7 March 1878; Hidy *et al.*, *Great Northern Railway*, 30. A mass meeting at Moe (Douglas county) on January 10 passed a resolution stating that Douglas county's legislators should "do their best to get the railroad up through here as

fast as possible." See John Arntson to Nelson and J.B. Cowing, 15 January 1878, in Nelson Papers.

[104] *Alexandria Post*, 15 February, 8 March 1878; *St. Paul Pioneer Press*, 5 March 1878.

[105] Sam H. Nichols to Nelson, 6 April 1878, in Nelson Papers.

[106] On June 4, Nelson sounded convinced at last that the ordeal was ending: "They inform me they will be at work on our road within 2 or 3 weeks — At all events I am satisfied we shall have the road this season." Nelson to Geo. H. Reynolds, 4 June 1878, in Nelson Papers.

[107] J.P. Farley to Nelson, 24 August 1878, in Nelson Papers.

[108] *Douglas County News*, 7 November 1878; *Alexandria Post*, 15 November 1878.

[109] Henry Nelson to K. Nelson, 6, 11, 16 September, 28 October 1878, all in Nelson Papers.

[110] *Alexandria Post*, 19, 26 April 1878. For politicians' suggestions that he seek the post of lieutenant governor, see C.A. Gilman to Nelson, 23 January 1879; Nelson Williams to Nelson, 14 January 1879; J.B. Wakefield to Nelson, 12 February 1879, all in Nelson Papers. For Nelson's lackluster "campaign," see *Alexandria Post*, 5 September 1879; *St. Peter Tribune*, 13 August 1879; and *St. Paul Dispatch*, 3 September 1879.

[111] E.H. Shaw to Nelson, 17 October 1879, in Nelson Papers. For a good, brief summary of Hill's career in Minnesota, see Blegen, *Minnesota: A History*, 299-304. The definitive biography is Martin's *James J. Hill and the Opening of the Northwest*.

[112] *Alexandria Post*, 11 July 1879, clipping at Douglas County Historical Society.

[113] *Alexandria Post*, 14 June 1878.

[114] J.J. Hill to Nelson, 17 September 1879, in Nelson Papers; N.Q. Puntches to Nelson, 29 September 1879; Nelson to Hill, 24 July, 22 September, 24 October 1879, all in James J. Hill Correspondence, President's Office, Great Northern Records, MHS.

[115] Nelson to Hill, 24 October 1879; H.A. Langlie to Nelson, 6 August 1880; Nelson to Hill, 11 August 1880, all in Hill Correspondence.

[116] Nelson to Hill, 21 July 1879, in Hill Correspondence.

[117] At the "crowded" Land Office, the *Fergus Falls Advocate* reported (tongue in cheek), "a casual inspection leads one to imagine an earnest bible class of truth-seeking men is assembled." *Fergus Falls Advocate*, 9, 23, 30 May 1879. "Proving up" notices from the Land Office took up two full columns of the *Fergus Falls Journal* in early July, 1879. See *Fergus Falls Weekly Journal*, 4 July 1879. Pillsbury & Co. was planning to build a grain elevator in Fergus Falls. See *Fergus Falls Weekly Journal*, 1 August 1879.

[118] Nelson to Hill, 20 June 1879, in Hill Correspondence. For Nelson's legal notice regarding the appointment of the commissioners, see *Fergus Falls Weekly Journal*, 4 July 1879. Here Knute Nelson is listed as "Attorney for said company" (the St. Paul, Minneapolis & Manitoba).

[119] *Fergus Falls Weekly Journal*, 8, 15 August 1879.

[120] Hill to Nelson, 13 June 1881, St. Paul, Minneapolis and Manitoba

Letterbook, Volume #5, 253-254, Microfilm, in J.J. Hill Papers, James J. Hill Reference Library, St. Paul.

[121] *Sauk Centre Herald*, 15 August, 5 September 1879; Nelson to Hill, 11 September 1879, in Hill Correspondence. In January 1881, Nelson apparently assisted Hill by mailing to prominent Otter Tail county leaders fifty copies of a *St. Paul Pioneer Press* editorial "against voting bonds for Railroad aid." Hill was trying to defeat a local effort to build a competing line. See Hill to Nelson, 26 January 1881, St. Paul, Minneapolis and Manitoba Letterbook, Volume 4, 600, in Hill Papers.

[122] Nelson to Hill, 30 December 1879, in Hill Correspondence.

[123] Nelson to Hill, 8, 11 August, 29 September, 26 October 1879, 10 February, 30 March 1880; and E.B. Wakeman to Nelson, 26 July 1880, all in President's Correspondence, Great Northern Records; Hill to Nelson, 28 June 1879, and 15 July 1879, both in Microfilm R1, Railroad Series, Hill Papers.

[124] SPM&M payments to Knute Nelson are listed in the Abstract of Vouchers, Microfilm 551, Great Northern Records, MHS. It was assumed that vouchers paid in January were for work done in the preceding year. Subtracted were all vouchers which evidence indicates were merely reimbursements for Nelson's travel and other expenses. That is difficult to determine exactly, for the Abstract does not seem to distinguish between legal fees and travel reimbursements. For the obvious reimbursements, see "K.Nelson a/c Edward Sawyer on Right of way fund," handwritten account, in Box 76, Nelson Papers. This account reveals that Nelson handled large sums of money for the SPM&M and that he personally paid farmers with funds from the SPM&M.

[125] See vol. 16, 231-267, in Box 79 of the Nelson Papers. These totals include some reimbursements for postage and other expenses. By contrast, the average annual earnings of a non-farm employee were $386 that year (1880). Skilled workers, for example, engineers and machinists, earned $2.17 and $2.45 respectively, *per day*, or about $670 and $760 *per year*. U.S. Bureau of the Census, *Historical Statistics of the United States: Colonial Times to 1970* (Washington, 1975), 165, 211.

[126] He paid, in total, $1,542.40 for the property and sold it off in segments for $2,805.00. The profit would be reduced by $950 if he shared ownership with Louis Peterson. The record is unclear on that point. See *Abstract of Lands*, Book 1, 105, and Book 2, 235. For the townsite plat, dated 3 December 1892, see *Townsite Abstract*, Book 3, 148, and Plat-Townsite of Nelson, both in Douglas County Recorder's Office, Alexandria.

[127] Nelson to Hill, [March 1883?], in President's Correspondence, Knute Nelson File, Great Northern Railway Records.

Chapter Six

[1] Richard L. McCormick, *The Party Period and Public Policy: American Politics from the Age of Jackson to the Progressive Era* (New York, 1986), 204-212. The essay cited here, "The Party Period and Public Policy: An Exploratory Hypothesis," was first published in the *Journal of American History*, 66 (September, 1979), 279-298.

NOTES

² Because of its increased population, Minnesota gained two additional congressional seats following the 1880 census, to bring its total to five seats.

³ See Nelson's 1882 Account Book, Box 76, Nelson Papers.

⁴ Nelson to Luth. Jaeger, 24 November 1881, in Nelson Papers.

⁵ Nelson to Jaeger, 10 December 1881, in Nelson Papers.

⁶ *Budstikken,* 27 December 1881.

⁷ See *Budstikken,* 14, 21, and 28 March, and 4, 18, and 25 April, 1882. For the appointment as regent, see Odland, *Knute Nelson,* 134. By May, *Budstikken* began to worry that Kindred was "buying" Scandinavian votes. See *Budstikken,* 2 May 1882.

⁸ See Nelson to Jaeger, 2 and 14 April, 1882, in Nelson Papers.

⁹ Other candidates were Ozora P. Stearns and former Governor Horace A. Austin. In June 1882, the *Duluth Tribune* reported a "very general feeling among the people here . . . that we ought to have a Duluth man for congress" and "the business men and taxpayers were . . . heartily united" in pursuing that goal. *Duluth Tribune,* 23 June 1882.

¹⁰ See Elmer E. Adams, "The Nelson-Kindred Campaign of 1882," in *Minnesota History Bulletin,* 5(May, 1923), 87-107; Adams, "The Nelson-Kindred campaign," *Fergus Falls Journal,* 17, 20, 25, and 31 January 1923; Odland, *Knute Nelson,* 98-131; Bjorgan, "Success Story of an Immigrant," 181-220; Harlan P. Hall, *H.P. Hall's Observations: Being More or Less a History of Political Contests in Minnesota, from 1849 to 1904* (St. Paul, 1904), 285-295; W.W. Folwell, *History of Minnesota,* 3: 147-149. Nelson's personal papers have been "weeded out" for the year 1882. For forty years Nelson kept his 1882 campaign papers in the safe in his Alexandria office. In 1922, he lent some of them to Elmer E. Adams for use in his account. Adams recommended that they be placed in the state archives; this was never done. By their own admission, Simon Michelet and J.A.O. Preus culled documents and correspondance, primarily from 1882 and 1894-1895, to protect the deceased senator's good name. As a result, Nelson's 1882 file contains only 29 letters instead of the several hundred it would have contained had the papers been left intact. For instance, there are no letters from prominent state politicians and no replies from Luth. Jaeger. See Ida G. Nelson to Elmer E. Adams, 10(?) May 1923, in Elmer E. Adams Papers, MHS; and Simon Michelet to Martin Odland. This "weeding out" is especially regrettable, since the highly charged nature of the 1882 campaign renders the numerous newspaper accounts somewhat suspect.

¹¹ For an account of the occasional chicanery and fraud in Gilded Age politics, see Robert D. Marcus, *Grand Old Party: Political Structure in the Gilded Age 1880-1896* (New York, 1971), 13-14.

¹² Reprinted in *Perham Journal,* 26 October 1882.

¹³ *Duluth Tribune,* 4 August 1882. A local historian claims that Kindred came to Brainerd in 1874, but gives no evidence for that. See Carl Zapffe, *Brainerd, Minnesota 1871-1946* (Brainerd, Minnesota, 1946), 24.

¹⁴ Stanley N. Murray, "Railroads and the Agricultural Development of the Red River Valley of the North, 1870-1890," in *Agricultural History,* 31 (October, 1957), 59-62; Hidy *et al., Great Northern Railway,* 25. For an example of Kindred's

365

speculation in Dakota lands and his use of his NP influence for private gain, see 30 October 1879 agreement; Kindred to F.D. Hager, 27 January 1880; James B. Power to Kindred, 26 January 1880; Hager Bros. to Kindred, 30 March 1880; and Cancellation of Agreement (n.d.), all in Fred D. Hager Papers, MHS. Hager Bros. was an Iowa firm which formed a partnership with Kindred to operate "a general banking and land agency" in Jamestown, Dakota Territory. The division of labor was for Fred Hager "to devote *his* time" to the business "to be offset by the influence and business which said Kindred shall bring to the firm and the said Kindred is to use every legitimate influence and information" to benefit the partnership. Kindred's "influence and information" came from his NP clerkship. To keep his participation secret, the firm was deceptively called Hager Bros.

[15] Here, and below, see *Duluth Tribune*, 4 August 1882, a reprint from the *St. Paul Pioneer Press* of 2 August 1882. This is a verbatim reprint of the report of the NP's land committee to its board of directors, dated 17 February 1881. Murray terms this charge by the land committee "a misunderstanding concerning his [Power's] purchase and use of depreciated Northern Pacific stock." Murray, "Development of the Red River Valley," 63.

[16] Adams, "Nelson-Kindred Campaign," 88-89. Adams also gives a good description of the Power-Kindred *modus operandi*.

[17] For land office chicanery, see Rohrbough, *Land Office Business*, 18, 28-29, 66, 79. For a Minnesota example, see William J. Stewart, "Settler, Politician, and Speculator in the Sale of the Sioux Reserve," in *Minnesota History*, 39 (Fall, 1964), 85-92.

[18] *Verndale Journal*, 13 October 1882.

[19] Adams, "Nelson-Kindred Campaign," 90.

[20] Adams, "Nelson-Kindred Campaign," 95; *St. Paul Pioneer Press*, 11 July 1882; *Duluth Tribune*, 23 June 1882.

[21] *St. Paul Pioneer Press*, 11 July 1882.

[22] Kenneth N. Owens, "Pattern and Structure in Western Territorial Politics," in *Western Historical Quarterly*, 1 (October, 1970), 377.

[23] Adams, "Nelson-Kindred Campaign," 92-93; *St. Paul Pioneer Press*, 11 July 1882.

[24] *St. Paul Pioneer Press*, 11 July 1882.

[25] Owens outlines the "common reasons for chaotic factionalism" in his essay, "Pattern and Structure," 378-379.

[26] According to one political geographer, Richard Hartshorne, a political area (or state) functions best if it is "a *region*" characterized by "1. contiguity of settled population; 2. homogeneity . . . of the population; 3. historical continuity . . . ; [and] 4. coherent unity of the area." The Fifth District lacked all four of these factors to a large degree. See Hartshorne, "Morphology of the State Area: Significance for the State," in Charles A. Fisher, ed., *Essays in Political Geography* (London, 1968), 27-32.

[27] *Duluth Tribune*, 23 June 1882.

[28] Adams, "Nelson-Kindred Campaign," 92; *Perham Journal*, 26 October 1882. Of course, many settlers along the NP owed Kindred money, and others had been given favors by him. Many regarded him as a great promoter of their region.

NOTES

²⁹ *Duluth Tribune*, 21 July 1882.

³⁰ In mid-May, Nelson requested passes for three or four men for pre-convention campaigning. In late September, he requested a pass for Albert Scheffer who "intends to assist me on the stump" for the remainder of the campaign. Thanking Hill for "past favors," he also reported to Hill that the SPM&M agent in St. Vincent "is very friendly and a word from you to him will put him actively to work." Nelson ally Solomon Comstock also requested Hill to encourage SPM&M workers to vote for him. See Nelson to Hill, 15 May, 13 October, and 30 September 1882; C.A. Gilman to Hill, 2 November 1882; and Comstock to Hill, 2 November 1882, all in James J. Hill Correspondence, President's Office, Great Northern Records.

³¹ For Frederick Jackson Turner's discussion of the different frontiers, see his "Significance of the Frontier in American History," 206-212.

³² *St. Paul Pioneer Press*, 11 July 1882.

³³ *Moorhead Enterprise*, 11 October 1882.

³⁴ Owens, "Pattern and Structure," 378-379.

³⁵ Adams, "Nelson-Kindred Campaign," 90-91; *St. Paul Pioneer Press*, 12 July 1882. Nelson proposed that the difficult matter of the contested delegations should be submitted to the state central committee for decision, but Kindred refused this offer. See *St. Paul Pioneer Press*, 11, 12 July 1882.

³⁶ *St. Paul Pioneer Press*, 11 July 1882. Somewhat improbably, the *Pioneer Press* worried that Republicans would lose the Fifth, and, with it, control of the United States House of Representatives.

³⁷ *Duluth Tribune*, 14 July 1882. Editor R.C. Mitchell of the *Tribune* was at Detroit Lakes for the convention, and sent back an eyewitness account, as did the editor of the *Fergus Falls Independent* and numerous reporters. Thus, the convention details were reported in great detail by the local, regional, and Twin Cities press, and the curious can still peruse the pages of the *Fergus Falls Journal*, *St. Paul Pioneer Press*, *Minneapolis Tribune*, *Minneapolis Journal*, *St. Paul Globe*, and numerous other papers. See, for example, *Fergus Falls Independent*, 19 July 1882.

³⁸ *Fargo Daily Republican*, 13 July 1882.

³⁹ Here, and below, see *St. Paul Pioneer Press*, 8, 11, 12, 13 July, 1882; *Duluth Tribune*, 21 July 1882; *Minneapolis Journal*, 12, 18 July, 1882; *St. Cloud Journal Press*, 13 July 1882; *Fargo Daily Republican*, 15 July 1882; Adams, "Nelson-Kindred Campaign," 97; Hall, "Observations," 287; Nelson's 1882 Account Book, Box 76, Nelson Papers

⁴⁰ *St. Paul Pioneer Press*, 13 July 1882; *Duluth Tribune*, 14 July 1882; Adams, "Nelson-Kindred Campaign," 97-98; Hall, "Observations," 287. Writing three days after the convention, Johnston complained to Comstock "that if you believed I had sold out to Kindred" they should have communicated that to him instead of simply removing him as chair. See George H. Johnston to S.G. Comstock, 15 July 1882, in Solomon G. Comstock Papers, Northwest Minnesota Historical Center, Moorhead.

⁴¹ This account is largely based on the *St. Paul Pioneer Press*, 13 July 1882. See also the sources listed in footnote 39 above, and *Svenska Folkets Tidning*, 19 July 1882.

367

⁴² *St. Paul Pioneer Press*, 13 July 1882.

⁴³ *St. Paul Pioneer Press*, 13 July 1882.

⁴⁴ H.G. Stordock to Comstock, 25 September 1882; Nelson to "Friend Comstock," 24 July 1882, both in Comstock Papers. Comstock ran for the State Senate as a Nelson ally. Several additional letters in his papers reveal how the Nelson-Kindred battle spilled over to the legislative races. See J.R. Harris to Comstock, 17 June 1882; Stordock to Comstock, 28 July, 9 September 1882; M.S. Converse to Comstock, 12, 28 September 1882; and Nelson to Comstock, 11 September 1882.

⁴⁵ For Nelson's speech, see *Alexandria Post*, 10 December 1875.

⁴⁶ *Polk County Journal* (Crookston), 20 July 1882; Hanford L. Gordon, *An Address to the Voters of the Fifth Congressional District*, 24-25, copy in Nelson Papers.

⁴⁷ Begun in mid-September, during the campaign, the *Daily Telegram* announced in mid-October that it would be delivered to Fergus Falls residents "without consultation with them" for only 75 cents a month. *Fergus Falls Telegram*, 1, 14 October 1882; *Duluth Tribune*, 21 July 1882; *Moorhead Enterprise*, 10 October 1882. The Moorhead newspaper was begun in early October, 1882. For a denial of the charge that Kindred's men had fomented a strike at the rival (pro-Nelson) *Moorhead News*, see *Moorhead Enterprise*, 11 October 1882. For the *News* editorial, see *Duluth Tribune*, 21 July 1882.

⁴⁸ *Duluth Tribune*, 28 July 1882; *Perham Journal*, 26 October 1882; (Ortonville) *Big Stone County Herald*, 19 October 1882; *Morris Journal*, 28 October, 4 November 1882. Changing hands in the midst of the campaign, the *Big Stone County Herald* was pro-Nelson on October 12 under editor J.H. Sheets, and pro-Kindred on October 19, under the ostensible control of L.C. Lane, an Ortonville doctor. Announcing that he was not abandoning his medical practice, Lane boasted that he had "an able corps of men to assist me" at the newspaper. These, no doubt, were Kindred publicists. See *Big Stone County Herald*, 19 October 1882. For the *Herman Herald*'s vigorous denial of a Nelson newspaper's charge that its publisher had "taken a contract to support Kindred in Grant county," see *Fergus Falls Telegram*, 14 October 1882.

⁴⁹ Among NP-line newspapers supporting Kindred were *Moorhead Enterprise*, *Perham Journal*, *Verndale Journal*, *Brainerd Dispatch*, and *Duluth Daily Bee*. Of course, there were exceptions. The *Northern Pacific Farmer* (Wadena) remained neutral and merely urged citizens to get out and vote. See *Northern Pacific Farmer*, 2 November 1882; *Verndale Journal*, 3 November 1882.

⁵⁰ Marcus, *Grand Old Party*, 14. For the highly partisan nature of Minnesota newspapers during the territorial period, see George S. Hage, *Newspapers on the Minnesota Frontier 1849-1860* (St. Paul, 1967), especially the second and third chapters.

⁵¹ The pro-Kindred *Pope County Press* charged that at least one new paper, the *Evansville Enterprise*, was "started by the Nelson barrel." See *Pope County Press* (Glenwood), 13 October 1882.

⁵² Nelson to Jaeger, 11 May 1882, in Nelson Papers.

⁵³ *Budstikken*, 26 July, 2, 9, 30 August, 1, 8 November, all 1882. On October 27, Johnson and Gjedde signed a letter denying the Kindred charges.

⁵⁴ *Polk County Journal* (Crookston), 20 July 1882; *Sauk Centre Herald and Melrose Record*, 26 October 1882; *Fergus Falls Independent*, 19 July 1882; *Fergus Falls Journal*, 12 October 1882; *Moorhead News*, 12 October 1882. Of course, both the *Alexandria Post* and the *Douglas County News* (Alexandria) supported Nelson partly because he was a local favorite son. Two SPM&M papers which supported Kindred were the *St. Vincent Herald* and *Fergus Falls Daily Telegram*.

⁵⁵ *St. Paul Pioneer Press*, 2 August 1882; *Duluth Tribune*, 4 August 1882. See also "Minutes of the Board of Directors," 17 February 1881 meeting, Vol. 5: 305-306, in Northern Pacific Papers, MHS; E.V. Smalley, compiler, *Northern Pacific Railroad Book of Reference, For the Use of the Directors and Officers of the Company* (New York, 1883), 211. For confirmation of Kindred's winter 1880-1881 trip to New York City, see *Brainerd Tribune*, 25 December 1880. However, the *Tribune* covered up the Kindred-Power affair, claiming that Kindred resigned because the NP land office was moved to St. Paul, and that Power resigned in a policy dispute over "raising the price of the company's lands in Dakota." This cover-up in Brainerd, which continued during the 1882 campaign, testifies to the possibility that many Brainerd leaders were implicated with Kindred in the frauds. See *Brainerd Tribune*, 25 December 1880, 26 February 1881.

⁵⁶ Gordon, *An Address to the Voters of the Fifth Congressional District*. Only two copies have survived, and both are at MHS (both came from Nelson). When measured against this extensive distribution of literature, Nelson's claim to have spent only $5,000 on the campaign seems far too low. However, he may have been referring to his own personal funds.

⁵⁷ See, for example, *Morris Journal*, 4 November 1882.

⁵⁸ The quotation is from the *Duluth Tribune*, 4 August 1882.

⁵⁹ For defenses of Kindred's business dealings, see *Verndale Journal*, 13 October 1882; *Perham Journal*, 2 November 1882; *Pope County Press*, 27 October 1882; and *Big Stone County Herald*, 2 November 1882.

⁶⁰ *St. Paul Daily Globe*, 5 September 1882; *Minneapolis Journal*, 1 September 1882; *Fergus Falls Journal*, 7 September 1882. For defenses of Nelson on this point, see *Alexandria Post*, 8 September 1882; and *Duluth Tribune*, 29 September 1882. Many of the attacks on him are brought together in the *Moorhead Enterprise*, 18 October 1882. Nelson did have his daughter Katherine Louise baptized at the Norwegian Evangelical Church in Alexandria in 1876. See "Ministrialbog for Alexandria og anneterede norsk-evang. lutersk menigheder begyndt den 11 januar 1876," at First Lutheran Church, Alexandria.

⁶¹ *Fergus Falls Telegram*, 17 October 1882; (Ortonville) *North Star*, 31 October 1882.

⁶² *Minneapolis Journal*, 1, 15 September 1882; *Fergus Falls Telegram*, 8 October 1882; *Alexandria Post*, 8 September 1882; *Douglas County News*, 28 September 1882; *Duluth Tribune*, 29 September 1882.

⁶³ (Ortonville) *North Star*, 31 October 1882; *Alexandria Post*, 8 September 1882. The *Pope County Press* correctly charged that State Senator Nelson had opposed the "railroad interests" of Glenwood and Pope county in favor of "the interests of Douglas county and the Manitoba Railroad Company." *Pope County Press*, 3 November 1882.

[64] (Crookston) *Polk County Journal*, 2 November 1882; *Big Stone County Herald*, 2 November 1882; *Perham Journal*, 2 November 1882. For Nelson's $250 (?) fee from the Association, see his "Day Book," 3, 4, at Douglas County Historical Society, Alexandria.

[65] *Moorhead Enterprise*, 13 October 1882; *Perham Journal*, 2 November 1882; *St. Paul Daily Globe*, 20 October 1882.

[66] Adams, "Nelson-Kindred Campaign," 103, 105; *St. Paul Daily Globe*, 20 October 1882; *Perham Journal*, 26 October 1882.

[67] See *Fergus Falls Journal*, 31 August 1882, for a reprint of the damaging article.

[68] *Douglas County News*, 21 September 1882, supplement; *Morris Journal*, 7 October 1882; Adams, "Nelson-Kindred Campaign," 104-105. The *Journal* piece, written by Nelson's campaign committee, contained details that could have come only from his Civil War letters.

[69] *Fergus Falls Journal*, 12 October 1882.

[70] Nelson to Alexander Running, 26, 29 July 1882, in Nelson Papers.

[71] For an example of Joseph Wheelock's attempts to gather information from both sides, see J.A. Wheelock to "My Dear Sir," 8 August 1882, in Comstock Papers.

[72] Quoted in *Fergus Falls Telegram*, 14 October 1882.

[73] *Morris Journal*, 18 August 1882; *Duluth Tribune*, 6 October 1882. According to the *Tribune*, a Kindred supporter in Northern Pacific Junction (Carlton county) rented the only hall in that small community in late September in order to prevent the Nelson campaign from holding any meetings there. *Duluth Tribune*, 29 September 1882.

[74] For the story, in the *Brainerd Dispatch*, and a denial that the oxen's wanderings were politically motivated, see *Alexandria Post*, 8 September 1882.

[75] *Duluth Tribune*, 6 October 1882; Adams, "Nelson-Kindred Campaign," 104; Nelson, "Memorandum" 11 March 1921, in Michelet Papers. Elmer Adams told a great story about a Kindred trap door on the platform from which Nelson spoke in Verndale (Wadena county): "when Nelson stepped upon that particular spot he would disappear underneath the platform." But a Norwegian lumberjack stopped this scheme by threatening to "thrash" the Kindred operative, who then told Nelson about the spot "and the meeting was conducted without disturbance." See Adams, "Nelson-Kindred Campaign," 104. However, this story varies greatly from the 1882 account in the *Fergus Falls Journal*, and that charge was hotly denied by the *Verndale Journal* (and by one "B. Zevely") and seemingly retracted by the pro-Nelson *Duluth Tribune*. See *Fergus Falls Journal*, 5 and 12 October 1882; *Fergus Falls Telegram*, 11 October 1882; *Verndale Journal*, 6, 13, 27 October, 1882.

[76] Marcus, *Grand Old Party*, 15. For the drunkenness and fighting at frontier elections, and the masculine character of public life there, see John Mack Faragher, *Sugar Creek: Life on the Illinois Prairie* (New Haven, Connecticut, 1986), 151-153.

[77] Marcus, *Grand Old Party*, 12.

[78] Nelson's 1882 Account Book, in Box 76, Nelson Papers.

[79] Nelson to Alexander Running, 26, 29 July 1882, in Nelson Papers.

[80] Marcus, *Grand Old Party*, 11-12.

[81] (Ortonville) *Big Stone County Herald*, 12 October 1882.

[82] *Fergus Falls Journal*, 8 November 1882; *Fergus Falls Independent*, 8 November 1882.

[83] Folwell, *History of Minnesota*, 3: 147.

[84] Nelson to Elmer E. Adams, 27 May 1922; Adams to Nelson, 22 May 1922, both in Adams Papers, MHS. For his historical account, Adams interviewed E.G. Holmes, Kindred's campaign manager, who admitted that at least $150,000 was spent, but said that $75,000 of that was borrowed money.

[85] For a report of vote fraud by Kindred workers at St. Vincent in the northwestern corner of the state, see *Fergus Falls Journal*, 9 November 1882. For national coverage of the vote fraud, see *New York Times*, 6, 7 November 1882.

[86] Cushman K. Davis to Lucius F. Hubbard, 30 August 1882; C.F. Kindred to Hubbard, 2 September 1882; Nelson to Hubbard, 11 September 1882; Davis, petition filed 25 September 1882 with Governor Hubbard; Nelson, Gilman, Barto, and Aaker to Hubbard, telegram dated 25 September 1882; H.L. Gordon to Hubbard, 6 October 1882, all in Governor's Office Papers, Lucius F. Hubbard, State Archives, MHS. See also, *Duluth Tribune*, 29 September 1882; and Gordon to S.G. Comstock and L.O. Storla, telegram dated 24 September 1882, in Comstock Papers.

[87] *Minneapolis Journal*, 9, 10, 11, and 13 November, 1882; *Detroit Record*, 11 November 1882. As late as November 17, the pro-Kindred *Pope County Press* was still claiming that Kindred's "election is now certain." *Pope County Press*, 17 November 1882.

[88] *Duluth Daily Tribune*, 15 November 1882, quoting the *St. Paul Pioneer Press* dispatches of 12 November 1882.

[89] *Minneapolis Tribune*, 10, 14, 15 November 1882; *New York Times*, 7 November 1882.

[90] *Minnesota Legislative Manual - 1883*, 310. Nelson carried Clay, Otter Tail, and Todd counties, which had both the NP and SPM&M within their borders.

[91] The estimate of fraudulent votes is based on the following data:

County	1880 Popul.	1885 Popul.	1880 Males Over 21	1885 Males Over 21	1882 Votes Cast	Est. Fraud Votes
Carlton	1,239	3,189	478	1,422	1,179	500
Cass	486	1,135	191	432	573	500
Crow Wing	2,318	8,743	94	2,962	2,379	1000
Itasca	124	237	52	181	643	500

[92] Of the some 57 anti-Kindred delegates, 15 or 16 had Scandinavian last names. Of course, this is only a crude measure of ethnicity. For the list of delegates, see *St. Paul Pioneer Press*, 12 July 1882.

[93] L.S. Reque to Nelson, 9 April 1883, in Nelson Papers.

Chapter Seven

[1] *Budstikken*, 15 November 1882.

[2] Some newspaper publishers attempted to collect on Nelson's alleged cam-

paign promises of financial aid. The publisher of the *Fergus Falls Independent* had asked for $500 in September, 1882, to stay in business, but was turned down. In February, 1883, the publisher of the *Norman County Banner* (Ada) pleaded: "The $100 now would be worth more to me than $500 six months from now . . . I dislike to say a word to you about this, it was your suggestion, and nothing earned by me, but I am placed where I either got to pay or give up." See Peter Clare to Nelson, 7 September 1882, and Bronson Strain to Nelson, February, 1883, both in Nelson Papers. On the other hand, John Anderson of *Skandinaven* (Chicago) complained bitterly that some Scandinavian-American newspapers spread the rumor that he had "bled" Nelson in 1882 to secure financial support. Anderson denied it to Nelson: "You know that I did not bleed you when you ran for Congress . . ." See Anderson to Nelson, 2 November 1883, in Nelson Papers.

³ Odland, *Knute Nelson*, 142.

⁴ Gilman to Nelson, 4 August 1883; W.W. Hartley to Nelson, 15 December 1883; Kindred to Nelson, 29 November 1883; Gilman to Nelson, 6, 11, 17 December, 1883; A.K. Teisberg to Nelson, 9 August 1883; A.J. Underwood to Nelson, 11 August 1883; J. Henry Sonef to Nelson, 6 August 1883, all in Nelson Papers.

⁵ Leonard D. White, *The Republican Era: 1869-1901: A Study in Administrative History* (New York, 1958), 288, 301-302; *St. Paul Pioneer Press*, 13 July 1882.

⁶ Paul C. Sletten to Nelson, 4 January 1883; Charles Kittelson to Nelson, 15 January 1883; Gilman to Nelson, 30 January, 1 February (telegram), 16, 24 February, 1883; and Nelson O. Foss to Nelson, 23 February 1883, all in Nelson Papers. Despite the urgings of William D. Washburn, Sletten, and others, that he come to Windom's assistance, Nelson cagily avoided direct involvement. He was determined not to be caught on the losing side. Washburn was especially indignant over Sabin's election: "Minnesota Republicans should feel proud in having Dunnell, Kindred and the Democrats elect their U.S. Senator for them." See Washburn to Nelson, 4 February 1883, in Nelson Papers.

⁷ Ethan Allen to Nelson, 26 February 1883, in Nelson Papers. See also, Ole Bolsta to Nelson, 17 February 1883, in Nelson Papers.

⁸ George W. Boyington to Nelson, January 1883; H.G. Stordock to Nelson, 17 January 1883; Amund Levorson to Nelson, 4 February 1883; Underwood to Nelson, 15 February 1883, all in Nelson Papers. For a discussion of senators' and representatives' power over federal patronage in their states and districts, see White, *Republican Era*, 31-35.

⁹ *St. Paul Daily Globe*, 23 March 1883. For an article correcting the *Globe's* account in several particulars, see *Fergus Falls Weekly Journal*, 29 March 1883. See also *Fergus Falls Independent*, 28 March 1883.

¹⁰ *St. Paul Pioneer Press*, 24 March 1883.

¹¹ *St. Paul Pioneer Press*, 26 March 1883. Listoe responded that pro-Nelson jobholders had also neglected their duties to campaign in 1882. See *Fergus Falls Weekly Journal*, 5 April 1883.

¹² *Budstikken*, 11 April, 28 March 1883.

¹³ H.G. Stordock to Nelson, 3 March 1883, in Nelson Papers. Stordock had been recommended by others for the land office post, and was offended when

Nelson bypassed him. See Henry C. Page to Nelson, 19 February 1883; Underwood to Nelson, 15 February 1883; Levorsen to Nelson, 4 February 1883; and Stordock to Nelson, 21 February 1883, all in Nelson Papers. For a private letter criticizing the appointment of a non-Scandinavian, see Chr. Brandt to Nelson, 4 April 1883, in Nelson Papers.

[14] Quoted in Stordock to Nelson, 3 March 1883, in Nelson Papers.

[15] On April 2, Boyington informed Nelson of his decision to decline. This was not publicly announced in the *Fergus Falls Journal* until April 19. See Boyington to Nelson, 2 April 1883, in Nelson Papers; *Fergus Falls Journal*, 19 April 1883; and Underwood to Nelson, 9 April 1883, in Nelson Papers. As late as March 30, Boyington had been inquiring about the official papers confirming his appointment. The reason for his declining is unclear. See Boyington to Nelson, 30 March 1883, in Nelson Papers.

[16] A.K. Teisberg to Nelson, 3 April 1883; B.N. Johnson to Nelson, 3 April 1883; John Schroeder to Nelson, 9 April 1883; Henry C. Page to Nelson, 9 April 1883; Underwood to Nelson, 9 April 1883; and J. Austin to Nelson, 10 April 1883, all in Nelson Papers. For B.N. Johnson's appointment, which he accepted, see *Fergus Falls Weekly Journal*, 3 May 1883; and Johnson to Nelson, 5 May 1883, in Nelson Papers.

[17] As early as the summer of 1879, Nelson had asked Governor John S. Pillsbury for the appointment as regent. Governor Lucius Hubbard appointed him to the post in January 1882. Nelson to Luth. Jaeger, 30 April 1880, in Nelson Papers; Odland, *Knute Nelson*, 100, 134.

[18] *Board of Regents Minutes, 1868-1887*, 226-232, 238, 254-277, University of Minnesota Archives, Minneapolis.

[19] For letters from candidates, see Peter Hendrickson to Nelson, 3 March 1883; and Luth. Jaeger to Nelson, 24 March 1883, both in Nelson Papers. For the editorials, see the clippings attached to Jaeger's March 24th letter to Nelson, especially the ones from *Skaffaren och Minnesotas Stats Tidning, Folkebladet,* and *Svenska Folkets Tidning.* A number of editorials were reprinted in *Budstikken,* 28 March and 2 May 1883. At the Regents' meeting on June 2, 1882, Nelson offered a resolution to appoint a professor of Scandinavian Languages, but this was referred to the Executive Committee. See *Board of Regents Minutes,* 232.

[20] These clippings are attached to Luth. Jaeger to Nelson, 24 March 1883, in Nelson Papers.

[21] Quoted in *Budstikken,* 28 March 1883, which also makes clear that *Fædrelandet og Emigranten* opposed Jaeger for the same reason.

[22] T.K. Torgerson to Nelson, 20 April 1883; John Peterson to Nelson, 1 May 1883; M. Holmstrom to Nelson, 2 May 1883, all in Nelson Papers.

[23] John W. Arctander to Nelson, 26 March 1883, in Nelson Papers. For other expressions of support for Jaeger, see Rasmus B. Anderson to Nelson, 1 March 1883; Jaeger to Nelson, 18 April 1883 (enclosing a recommendation from Bjørnson himself); Anders A. Sörengen to Nelson, 30 March 1883, all in Nelson Papers.

[24] Nelson to Anderson, 29 December 1880, 4, 15 January 1881, all in Rasmus B. Anderson Papers, Wisconsin State Historical Society, Madison; Anderson to

Nelson, 2 and 19 January 1881, both in Nelson Papers. The *Alexandria Post,* 11 March 1881, reported that Bjørnson "delivered an instructive and eloquent lecture," which apparently did not touch any religious subjects.

²⁵ Einar and Eva Lund Haugen, eds. and trans., *Land of the Free: Bjørnstjerne Bjørnson's America Letters, 1880-1881* (Northfield, Minnesota, 1978), 196, 223. This was high praise, especially when compared with Bjørnson's disparaging remarks about the "stupid," "ignorant," "ill-bred people" (217-218) whom he met on his 1880-1881 tour.

²⁶ For his tour, see Haugen and Haugen, *Land of the Free;* Arthur C. Paulson, "Bjørnson and the Norwegian-Americans, 1880-1881," in *Norwegian-American Studies and Records,* 5 (1930), 84-109; and Lovoll, *Promise of America,* 104-105. Arctander and Jaeger had also hosted the Norwegian author on this tour. For *Budstikken's* (Jaeger's) criticism of the clerical view of Bjørnson, see issue of 8 March 1881.

²⁷ Nelson to Bjørnson, undated [1882], in University of Oslo Library Archives, Oslo, Norway. See also Nelson to Rasmus B. Anderson, 9 February 1882, in Anderson Papers.

²⁸ *Budstikken,* 2 May 1883.

²⁹ Jaeger to Nelson, 24 March 1883, in Nelson Papers; *Board of Regents Minutes,* 258-259, 260, 262; Lovoll, *Promise of America,* 207. The "committee to fill vacancies" was also searching for a new University president to succeed William Watts Folwell. Born in Norway, Breda had studied philology at the University of Christiania and theology at Concordia Seminary in St. Louis. After serving as pastor of a Lutheran church in St. Paul for two years, he taught at Luther College and in Norway before accepting the University's offer. See E.B. Johnson, *Dictionary of the University of Minnesota* (Minneapolis, 1908), 42; and [University of Minnesota] *Alumni Weekly,* 16: 17 (29 January 1917), clipping in University of Minnesota Archives.

³⁰ Mark Flower to Nelson, 8 September 1883, in Nelson Papers.

³¹ Lucius F. Hubbard to Nelson, 1 October 1883, in Nelson Papers.

³² Luth. Jaeger to Nelson, 26 September 1883, in Nelson Papers.

³³ For one such request, see Peter Anderson to Nelson, 24 September 1883, in Nelson Papers. Anderson warned Nelson to remember what had happened to Carl Schurz, who had loyally supported the Republicans in the face of German-American opposition to the GOP.

³⁴ *St. Paul Pioneer Press,* 24 October 1883; *St. Paul Dispatch,* 24 October 1883. For a rebuttal, see *Budstikken,* 30 October 1883. For another report of Nelson's speech, see *Fergus Falls Journal,* 24 October 1883.

³⁵ Flower to Nelson, 29 October 1883, in Nelson Papers. Overjoyed, candidate Hubbard wrote to Nelson that he was under lasting obligation to Nelson and would reciprocate "when I have an opportunity." See Hubbard to Nelson, 27 October 1883, in Nelson Papers.

³⁶ *St. Paul Dispatch,* 6 November 1883; *Budstikken,* 7 November 1883; W.D. Washburn to Nelson, 25 October 1883; J.A. Wolverton to Nelson, 21 November 1883, both in Nelson Papers.

³⁷ A.J. Underwood to Nelson, 8 November 1883, in Nelson Papers. With 58,521

votes (44.6 percent), Biermann carried nineteen counties, including such German-American strongholds as Carver, Brown, and Stearns. Receiving 72,462 votes (55.4 percent), Hubbard saw his 1881 victory margin cut in half. Despite Nelson's efforts, more Scandinavian Americans defected to Biermann's Norwegian appeal than Republican leaders had hoped.

[38] Odland, *Knute Nelson*, 147, 233.

[39] For the ways in which a protectionist policy "allowed the Republican party to reaffirm its claims as the party of national unity" during and after the Civil War, see Tom E. Terrill, *The Tariff, Politics, and American Foreign Policy 1874-1901* (Westport, Connecticut, 1973), 26-27.

[40] Edward McPherson, *Hand-Book of Politics: III 1884-1888, Being a Record of Important Political Action, National and State, July 31, 1882-August 31, 1888,* (reprint New York, 1972), 1884 section, 225, 227.

[41] Richard Franklin Bensel, *Sectionalism and American Political Development 1880-1980* (Madison, Wisconsin, 1984), 62-63. By 1885-1889, pensions accounted for 27 percent of total federal expenditures; by 1890-1894, pensions were greater than any other category of expenditure, and accounted for 37.3 percent of the total. See Bensel, 67.

[42] See Map 3.1 in Bensel, *Sectionalism*, 68.

[43] McPherson, *Hand-Book of Politics*, 1884 section, 129.

[44] Edward Stanwood, *American Tariff Controversies in the Nineteenth Century*, 2 (New York, 1903), 220-221; *St. Paul Pioneer Press*, 7 May 1884. The four congressmen were Milo White, J.B. Wakefield, H.B. Strait, and Nelson,

[45] *St. Paul Pioneer Press*, 7 May 1884. For Washburn's explanation of his vote, see the May 7th *Pioneer Press*.

[46] Stanwood, *American Tariff Controversies*, 226-234, 239-242; Terrill, *Tariff, Politics, and Foreign Policy*, 109-140. For the partisan breakdown in the House (Democrats-169, Republicans-152) and the Senate (Democrats-37, Republicans-39), and for Cleveland's message, see McPherson, *Hand-Book of Politics*, 1888 section, 89-96, For Nelson's mild praise of Cleveland's message, see *St. Cloud Times*, 9 December 1887.

[47] *Minneapolis Tribune*, 30 March 1888. For the headlines, see the *Tribune* of March 30, and *St. Paul Pioneer Press*, 30 March 1888. For the speech itself, see *Congressional Record*, 19:3:2504-2509. The "Great Debate" began on April 17; Nelson spoke on March 29. According to Stanwood, the congressional speechmaking was primarily designed for election purposes: "these speeches, circulated by their authors, would impress voters with a sense of the fitness of sitting members." Stanwood, *American Tariff Controversies*, 234. For a brief summary of Nelson's speech, see *Skandinaven*, 4 April 1888.

[48] For the argument about cost of production and the difficulties of calculating American costs and European costs, see Joseph F. Kenkel, *Progressives and Protection: The Search for a Tariff Policy 1866-1936* (Lanham, Maryland, 1983), 27-31.

[49] Terrill, *Tariff, Politics, and Foreign Policy*, 57; Bensel, *Sectionalism*, 70.

[50] *Washington Post*, 30 March 1888. The *Post* called Nelson an "enlightened Republican," and indicated that his speech was frequently applauded by the Democrats. *Budstikken* briefly summarized Nelson's speech on 4 April 1888.

[51] *New York Times*, 20, 28 February 1888, and 13 June 1888. The *Times* was partly relying on a survey of country editors' opinions in *Minneapolis Journal*, 18 February 1888. In an editorial, the *Minneapolis Journal* reported that the national Republican policy of protectionism was "producing a feeling of restlessness everywhere among Western Republicans that threatens party disintegration." It cited C.A. Pillsbury's letter to Nelson, which Nelson had read during his tariff speech. See *Minneapolis Journal*, 31 March 1888.

[52] Lovoll, *Promise of America*, 71-72.

[53] Terrill, *Tariff, Politics, and Foreign Policy*, 105-108; Bensel, *Sectionalism*, 63-64.

[54] White, *Republican Era*, 220; Bensel, *Sectionalism*, 66. White has an excellent overview of the operations of the Pension Office (208-221).

[55] Here, and below, see *Congressional Record*, 19:5:4836-4844.

[56] See, for example, McPherson, *Hand-Book of Politics*, 1886 section, 186-187, 192-193, 229-231, and 1888 section, 17-18, 29, 181-182. For Nelson's briefer comments on another Minnesota pension case, see *Congressional Record*, 20:2:1417-1418.

[57] For GAR lobbying for more generous pensions, and for the GAR's influence with the Republican party and the Pension Office, see Bensel, *Sectionalism*, 63; and White, *Republican Era*, 218-220.

[58] *Congressional Record*, 19:7:6275-6277. For a complimentary summary of the speech, see *Budstikken*, 18 July 1888. For the role of shipping subsidies in the wider congressional debate over the surplus, see Terrill, *Tariff, Politics, and Foreign Policy*, 107. For a summary of the debate on shipping subsidies, see *Washington Post*, 14 July 1888.

[59] Reprinted in *St. Paul Daily Globe*, 25 August 1888. Also quoted, in part, in Odland, *Knute Nelson*, 146. The *Globe* termed the *New York Marine Journal* "a Radical, Protection, Subsidized Journal"—presumably meaning it was Republican and protectionist in its politics. For the debate between the Democratic *Budstikken* and the Republican *Skandinaven* over the *Journal* attack, see *Budstikken*, 5 September 1888.

[60] *St. Paul Daily Globe*, 25 August 1888.

[61] *Congressional Record*, 19:7:6277. The steamship subsidy bill was defeated by a vote of 55 in favor and 135 opposed. All but one of the votes for the bill was cast by Republicans. Robert La Follette and fellow Norwegian-American Nils P. Haugen, both of Wisconsin, joined Nelson, John Lind, 27 other Republicans, and most Democrats in voting against it. See McPherson, *Hand-Book of Politics*, 1888 section, 170-171.

[62] The sheriff was Canute R. Matson. See Lovoll, *A Century of Urban Life*, 181-182. *Congressional Record*, 19:3:2460. The Swedish-American congressman John Lind of Minnesota also opposed Felton's idea. Of course, Nelson was in error about his age and his mother's widowhood.

[63] *Congressional Record*, 20:1:397. See also the first section of Nelson's 1884 Red Lake bill, *Congressional Record*, 15:3:2739. Population estimates for Red Lake and White Earth are taken from Folwell, *History of Minnesota*, 4:198, 220.

[64] *Congressional Record*, 15:3:2740, and 15:5:4992.

[65] Folwell, *History of Minnesota*, 4:199.

[66] For the text of the order, see *Douglas County News*, 9 August 1883.

[67] Nelson to Sletten, 6 August 1883, in Nelson Papers. Nelson even tried to convince his youngest brother, Henry Nelson of Deerfield, to file a homestead claim in the thirteen townships, but Henry remained in Wisconsin. See Henry Nelson to Knute Nelson, 19 August 1883, in Nelson Papers.

[68] *Douglas County News*, 9, 16 August 1883.

[69] For perceptive analyses of the national "Friends of the Indian" movement, see Francis Paul Prucha, *The Great Father: The United States Government and the American Indians*, 2 (Lincoln, Nebraska, 1984), 611-630; and Christine Bolt, *American Indian Policy and American Reform: Case Studies of the Campaign to Assimilate the American Indians* (London, 1987), especially 86-102. For the Indian Rights Association, see William T. Hagan, *The Indian Rights Association: The Herbert Welsh Years, 1882-1904* (Tucson, Arizona, 1985).

[70] Folwell, *History of Minnesota*, 4:193-194, 195-202.

[71] Evans, "Early Political Career," 69-70; Bjorgan, *Success Story of an Immigrant*, 252-258; Folwell, *History of Minnesota*, 4:219, n.28.

[72] Nelson to Johnson, 7 January 1884, in Nelson Papers.

[73] *Congressional Record*, 15:5:4993-4994. For the Red Lake bill's original provisions as amended by the Committee on Indian Affairs, see *Congressional Record*, 15:3:2739. To secure passage, Nelson stressed the similarity between his bill and Senator Henry Dawes' bill for the Sioux Reservation (Sioux Bill), which was an early allotment measure strongly supported by the IRA and other reformers. See Prucha, *Great White Father*, 636-637.

[74] *St. Paul Daily Globe*, 14 January 1888; Nelson to James J. Hill, 13 October 1884, in Great Northern Records, MHS; Hagan, *Indian Rights Association*, 50-51.

[75] *Congressional Record*, 15:5:4988-4992.

[76] *Congressional Record*, 15:5:4993-4994.

[77] Wallace Farnham, "'The Weakened Spring of Government': A Study in Nineteenth-Century American History," in *American Historical Review*, 8:3 (April, 1963), 676.

[78] *Congressional Record*, 19:2:1886-1888.

[79] *White Earth Progress*, 18 February, 10 March 1888.

[80] *White Earth Progress*, 14 April 1888. The *Progress* also battled the *Red Lake Falls Gazette*'s charge that the Beaulieus were trying to scuttle the Northwest Indian Commission agreements and the Crookston chamber of commerce's criticism of the Nelson bill. However, it did not criticize Nelson himself until February, 1889. See *White Earth Progress*, 25 February, 24 March, 1888.

[81] *St. Paul Pioneer Press*, 30, 31 March, 1 April 1888; *Minneapolis Tribune*, 31 March 1888.

[82] *Congressional Record*, 20:1:396-400. For the sorry tale of how the Ojibway were defrauded, see Folwell, *History of Minnesota*, 4:235-243, 261-283; Rev. J.A. Gilfillan, *Causes of the Late Chippewa Outbreak in Minnesota. An Address to the Mohonk Conference*, pamphlet in MHS. Shortly after the Nelson Act was passed, Nelson explained its provisions for *Skandinaven*'s readers and the readers of the other Scandinavian-American papers which reprinted the article. See *Fergus*

Falls Ugeblad, 8 May 1889. Melissa L. Meyer, *The White Earth Tragedy* (Lincoln, Nebraska, 1994).

[83] *Congressional Record*, 15:3:2740.

[84] *White Earth Progress*, 16 February 1889; *Congressional Record*, 20:3:2367.

[85] *Congressional Record*, 19:9:8084.

[86] Quoted in Odland, *Knute Nelson*, 138. For another statement by Nelson on his decision to retire, see *Fergus Falls Daily Journal*, 2 January 1888. In this interview, he stated, "I am anxious to get out of politics and into private business," because the "career of a politician is not congenial to me."

[87] *Douglas County News*, 14 October 1886; *St. Paul Pioneer Press*, 12, 13 October 1886; Eugene Roth to June D. Holmquist, 9 December 1969, in Knute Nelson Biographical Papers, P939, MHS; Dr. Daniel L. Johnson to Steven Keillor, 21 March 1993, letter in author's possession.

Chapter Eight

[1] Nelson to A. Solem, 22 February 1892, in Nelson Papers. For the pieces in question see *Fergus Falls Ugeblad*, 9 September 1891, and 3 February 1892. Nelson wrote in response to a letter from Solem, whose friendly tone had "somewhat surprised" Nelson and had shown his suspicions to be baseless. A. Solem to Nelson, 19 February 1892, in Nelson Papers.

[2] Nelson to Solem, 22 February 1892, in Nelson Papers. For the *Ugeblad*'s early support for Nelson, see A.K. Teisberg to Nelson, 3 April 1883, in Nelson Papers.

[3] Solem to Nelson, 27 February, 10 March 1892, both in Nelson Papers; *Fergus Falls Ugeblad*, 9 March 1892. Of course, Nelson *had* been an attorney for Hill's SPM&M in 1878-1881. It is unclear whether Nelson assured Solem he had *never* been a railroad attorney or told the editor he was not one *then*—and Solem assumed he had never been one. For Solem's politics in 1892, see Soike, *Politics of Dissent*, 92, 102-104.

[4] Nelson to Emilie Smith, 1 January 1915, University of Oslo Archives.

[5] Nelson to Søren Listoe, 16 November 1888; Lind to Nelson, 28 May 1892, both in Nelson Papers; *St. Paul Daily Globe*, 14 January 1888. Bjorgan argues that he had no thoughts of the Senate in 1888-1889. A closer examination reveals otherwise. See Bjorgan, "Success Story of an Immigrant," 246-247.

[6] His old friend Hanford L. Gordon, now living in San Jose, even wanted him to handle a case in California. Nelson to Gordon, 5 May 1890, in Gordon Papers, MHS. Nelson declined because of his heavy legal work load.

[7] *Fergus Falls Ugeblad*, 13 November 1889, quoting the *Douglas County News*; *Douglas County News*, 31 October 1889 and 7 November 1889. For charges that Nelson was an attorney for Hill, see Solem to Nelson, 10 March 1892, in Nelson Papers; *Fergus Falls Ugeblad*, 3, 10 and 17 August 1892; and *Great West*, 25 July 1890. For Nelson's clearest clarification of his 1878-1881 SPM&M role, see *Alexandria Post*, 26 August 1892 and *Mower County Transcript*, 7 September 1892, both quoting from the *Minneapolis Journal*.

[8] The speech was printed in full in three successive issues of *Fædrelandet og Emigranten*, undated [late September-early October 1889] clippings in Nelson Papers.

⁹ Blegen, *Minnesota: A History*, 339-408; Edward Van Dyke Robinson, *Early Economic Conditions and the Development of Agriculture in Minnesota* (Minneapolis, 1915); Merrill E. Jarchow, *The Earth Brought Forth: A History of Minnesota Agriculture to 1885* (St. Paul, 1949). Anne Mayhew argues that farmers protested against dependence on an impersonal market which forced them to borrow and to grow cash crops—and not only against low prices or high costs. Mayhew, "A Reappraisal of the Causes of Farm Protest in the United States, 1870-1900," in *Journal of Economic History*, 32(July 1972), 464-475.

¹⁰ James Turner, "Understanding the Populists," in *Journal of American History*, 67(September 1980), 354-373, especially, 358, 372. For an elaboration of this argument, see Keillor, "Minnesota's Rural Cooperatives, 1865-1917," 297-301. Farmers' grievances are outlined in John D. Hicks, *The Populist Revolt: A History of the Farmers' Alliance and the People's Party* (Minneapolis, 1931), 54-95.

¹¹ Folwell, *History of Minnesota*, 3:169; *Great West*, 14 February, 9 May, and 25 July, 1890.

¹² For a description of the sub-alliances, see Keillor, "Minnesota's Rural Cooperatives, 1865-1917," 274-337.

¹³ *St. Paul Daily Globe*, 16, 17 July 1890; *Great West*, 25 July 1890.

¹⁴ *St. Paul Daily Globe*, 17, 18 July 1890; *Great West*, 25 July 1890; *St. Paul Pioneer Press*, 18 July 1890.

¹⁵ *St. Paul Daily Globe*, 18 July 1890.

¹⁶ *St. Paul Daily Globe*, 18 July 1890; *St. Paul Pioneer Press*, 18 July 1890. Nelson's Papers do not contain the Alliance telegrams, pre-convention letters from Everett Fish and Sidney M. Owen asking Nelson to run as an Alliance candidate, or any Nelson letters on the 1890 Alliance nomination. These items may have been culled out by Simon Michelet and J.A.O. Preus. For the Fish and Owen letters, see Odland, *Knute Nelson*, 152; *Fergus Falls Ugeblad*, 7 September 1892; and *Spring Valley Sun*, 9 September 1892.

¹⁷ Odland, *Knute Nelson*, 153-156; *Fergus Falls Ugeblad*, 30 July 1890; Chrislock, "Politics of Protest in Minnesota," 35-36, 103, 115-116. Chrislock relates William H. Eustis' story: he and two other "anti-Merriam Republicans" went to Alexandria in the spring of 1890 to ask Nelson to run against Merriam. Nelson consulted Merriam's St. Paul backers, who promised him the 1892 nomination if he stayed out in 1890. So the story goes. No evidence confirms it—or disproves it.

¹⁸ For a good analysis of the election returns, see Chrislock, "Politics of Protest in Minnesota," 120-126.

¹⁹ For an analysis of the varying appeal of Populism to Norwegian Americans of different areas in Minnesota, see Soike, *Politics of Dissent*, 44-47, 75-78.

²⁰ For example, William B. Dean, a critic of Nelson's speech at an 1887 Mankato convention, wrote to apologize more than four and one-half years later. Dean to Nelson, 24 December 1891, in Nelson Papers.

²¹ Quoted in Odland, *Knute Nelson*, 160.

²² *Fergus Falls Ugeblad*, 3 February 1892. Nelson did not repudiate Bondy's letter when he mentioned it to Solem. He likely had encouraged him to write the letter. See Nelson to Solem, 22 February 1892, in Nelson Papers. Governor Nelson appointed Bondy to a state position in 1894.

[23] *Minneapolis Journal*, 26 March 1892; R.C. Dunn to Nelson, 8 March 1892; H.B. Strait to Nelson, 27 June 1892; and Søren Listoe to Nelson, 14 May 1892, all in Nelson Papers.

[24] John Shely to Nelson, 27 June 1892; Charles M. Reese to Nelson, 2 and 6 July 1892; D.C. Lightbourn to Nelson, 8 July 1892; C.H. Smith to Nelson, 9 July 1892; A.C. Clausen to Nelson, 15 July 1892; and P.W. Wildt to Nelson, 15 July 1892, all in Nelson Papers.

[25] Reese to Nelson, 6 July 1892, in Nelson Papers.

[26] Patrick Fox to Governor Knute Nelson, 11 January 1893, File 631, Governor's Records—Knute Nelson, State Archives, MHS. Upping the ante, Fox offered to contribute $5,000 to the 1894 Republican campaign, if Nelson appointed him surveyor general for the Stillwater district.

[27] Reese to Nelson, 2 July 1892; and H.F. Brown to Nelson, 30 July 1892, both in Nelson Papers. For biographical details on Brown, see *Minneapolis Journal*, 15 December 1912, clipping in MHS Scrapbook, 72:36, microfilm, MHS.

[28] *Anoka County Union*, 22 June 1892. See *Anoka County Union*, 6, 13, 20 and 27 July 1892; and S. A. Langum to Friend [Charles] Kittleson, 9 July 1892, in Nelson Papers. Patronage considerations and fears of the Alliance, not ethnic pride, may even have motivated some urban Scandinavian Americans to favor Nelson. Senator Washburn wrote, "I am somewhat surprised to find that the Norwegians in Minneapolis, many of whom have not been especially friendly to Mr. Nelson in the past two or three years, now strongly favor his nomination." Washburn to Major W.D. Hale, 4 April 1892, in William D. Hale Papers, MHS.

[29] *Anoka County Union*, 22 June 1892. Pease was responding to a *St. Paul News* interview of a Nelson backer who argued that Republicans needed a Norwegian-American candidate to recover Norwegian-American votes lost to the Alliance. Former state representative Allen G. Greer later denied having made the statements. See *Anoka County Union*, 22, 29 June 1892; and *Princeton Union*, 30 June 1892.

[30] Quoted in *Anoka County Union*, 6 July 1892.

[31] *Minneapolis Journal*, 26 March 1892; *St. Paul Pioneer Press*, 26 March 1893.

[32] Washburn to Nelson, 10 April 1892, in Nelson Papers; *St. Paul Pioneer Press*, 30 March 1892.

[33] Actually, a Davis supporter joked about or disparaged reports of the near-drowning, while seconding Davis's nomination in the Republican legislators' caucus in 1887. Davis denied encouraging such jokes, and insisted that he had always argued for the authenticity of Nelson's accident. See C.K. Davis to Marcus Johnson, 17 July 1892; and Charles A. Pillsbury to Nelson, 6 May 1892, both in Nelson Papers. For McGill's argument for its authenticity, see *Princeton Union*, 26 May 1892, quoting the *Minneapolis Tribune*.

[34] Charles A. Pillsbury to Nelson, 6, 12 May 1892, both in Nelson Papers; *Anoka County Union*, 18 May 1892.

[35] See, for example, *St. Paul Dispatch*, 6 April 1892; *Anoka County Union*, 18, 25 May, 1 June, 13 July, 1892.

[36] Pillsbury to Nelson, 12 May 1892, in Nelson Papers.

[37] *St. Paul Pioneer Press*, 27 March 1892.

[38] Senator William D. Washburn to Major W.D. Hale, 7, 21, 28 February, 30 March, 4, 10 April, 1892, all in William D. Hale Papers, MHS.

[39] *Anoka County Union*, 20 July 1892; *Duluth Tribune*, 13 May 1892; *Northfield News*, quoted in *Princeton Union*, 12 May 1892; Editor Bob Dunn of the *Princeton Union* ridiculed such "ultra-straights" for their dogmatism.

[40] *St. Paul Pioneer Press*, 26 March, 4 July,1892; *Duluth Herald*, 11, 19 July 1892.

[41] *St. Paul Dispatch*, 28 July 1892; *St. Paul Pioneer Press*, 29 July 1892.

[42] *St. Paul Pioneer Press*, 29 July 1892; *St. Paul Dispatch*, 29 July 1892.

[43] *St. Paul Pioneer Press*, 29 July 1892. For Donnelly's authorship of the preamble, see Martin Ridge, *Ignatius Donnelly: Portrait of a Politician* (Chicago, 1962), 295-296, 302.

[44] Under the plan, farmers could only "borrow up to 80 per cent of the local market price" of the stored crop. Lawrence Goodwyn, *The Populist Moment: A Short History of the Agrarian Revolt in America* (New York, 1978), 109-110.

[45] Washburn to Major W.D. Hale, 21 July 1892, in Hale Papers; Ridge, *Ignatius Donnelly*, 283-288, 294-302; Chrislock, "Politics of Protest in Minnesota," 144-151. A few Alliance leaders in the "old Fifth" (especially Otter Tail) resisted the change.

[46] Ridge, *Ignatius Donnelly*, 264, 266. For the American Protective Association's use of anti-Catholic prejudice among Scandinavian Americans, see Soike, *Politics of Dissent*, 56-62. From Soike's description, it appears that the APA was not yet sufficiently organized to have a significant impact on the 1892 campaign. Its greater influence came in 1894. Clearly, there was unorganized anti-Catholic sentiment. "We will not need to worry about having Catholic schoolteachers if Knute Nelson is elected," wrote one Scandinavian American just before the vote. *Skandinaven*, 2 November 1892.

[47] John Lind to Nelson, 29 July 1892; Gideon S. Ives to Nelson, 29 July 1892; Cushman K. Davis to Nelson, 29 July 1892; William D. Washburn to Nelson, 29 July and 10 August 1892; Gilman to Nelson, 10 August 1892; Elmer E. Adams to Nelson, 1 August 1892, all in Nelson Papers. Nelson put a McGill representative on the Republican state central committee to help ensure that group's support.

[48] There is no unbiased account of this dinner, but the basic facts were not in dispute. See *Great West*, 30 September 1892, Supplement; *St. Cloud Daily Times*, 27 August 1892; *Red Wing Daily Republican*, 2 September 1892.

[49] *Great West*, 30 September 1892, Supplement, also quoting the *St. Paul Daily Globe*'s account of the dinner. Fish's attack was an attempt to replay Democratic tactics in the 1884 presidential campaign, when James Blaine's banquet with New York millionaires was called "Belshazzar's Feast." Along with other last-minute mistakes, it cost Blaine the election. See Bailyn *et al.*, *Great Republic*, 2:152-154.

[50] *St. Cloud Daily Times*, 27 August 1892.

[51] D.B. Searle to Nelson, 29 August 1892, in Nelson Papers; *Red Wing Daily Republican*, 2 September 1892.

[52] In its issue of 31 August 1892, *Skandinaven* translates in full the *St. Paul Daily Globe*'s account of Seeley's speech — and adds its criticisms to the *Globe*'s.

[53] *St. Cloud Daily Times*, 27 August 1892. Before the Republican convention,

Nicolay Grevstad told Nelson that the Democrats were mainly responsible for spreading anti-immigrant attacks on Nelson. One old-stock voter wrote directly to tell Nelson that *"America must be run by Americans."* Grevstad to Nelson, 18 July 1892; Charles Whitney to Nelson, 9 June 1892 (emphasis in original), both in Nelson Papers.

[54] *Rush City Post*, 5, 19 August 1892.

[55] *Princeton Union*, 9, 30 June, 1892; *Douglas County News*, 3 November 1892. Grevstad reported "the Grand Army and the Anti-Catholics" would help persuade old-stock voters. Grevstad to Nelson, 18 July 1892, in Nelson Papers.

[56] Thomas Lajord to Nelson, 16, 18, 19, 20, 21 August 1892; and Tams Bixby to Nelson, 16 August 1892, all in Nelson Papers. For Lajord's ongoing debate with "M.A." see *Fergus Falls Ugeblad*, 3, 10, 17, 24 August 1892.

[57] *Fergus Falls Ugeblad*, 3, 10 August, 1892.

[58] *Skandinaven*, 2 November 1892. The translation is the author's (Keillor's). The songwriter was Alfred Leifson.

[59] *Spring Valley Sun*, 9 September 1892; *Fergus Falls Ugeblad*, 7 September 1892, citing the *Fergus Falls Journal*. The *Journal* had published the Fish letter.

[60] For reprints of the *Journal* interview, see *Alexandria Post*, 26 August 1892; and *Mower County Transcript*, 7 September 1892. For the Populist accusations against Nelson, see *Great West*, 30 September 1892, Supplement, and 14 October 1892.

[61] *Alexandria Post*, 7 October 1892. For another defense of Nelson's railroad stance in the State Senate in the 1870s, see *St. Paul Pioneer Press*, 5 November 1892.

[62] *St. Paul Pioneer Press*, 27 August 1892; *Minneapolis Tribune*, 27 August 1892; *Skandinaven*, 31 August 1892.

[63] For his stops in La Crescent, Caledonia, Spring Valley, and Austin, see *St. Paul Pioneer Press*, 2, 3, 4, 5 September 1892; *Spring Valley Sun*, 2 and 9 September 1892; and *Austin Register*, 8 September 1892.

[64] Frank B. Fobes to Nelson, 20 August 1892, in Nelson Papers. Nelson promised to come but had to cancel because of illness. See *Freeborn County Standard*, 5 October 1892. Merriam owed part of his political success to his position as president of the State Agricultural Society, which sponsored the State Fair. See Folwell, *History of Minnesota*, 3:184.

[65] *Grant County Herald*, 27 Thursday 1892. The following account is based on a number of often conflicting and usually biased sources. See *Grant County Herald*, 27 October 1892; *St. Paul Pioneer Press*, 28, 29 October 1892; *Grant County Herald*, 3 November 1892; *Alexandria Post*, 4 November 1892; *Fergus Falls Ugeblad*, 2 November 1892; *Skandinaven*, 9 November 1892; *Battle Lake Review*, 3 November 1892; *Grant County Farmer* (Ashby), 3 November 1892; and *Great West*, 4 November 1892. The *Great West* reprints the *St. Paul Daily Globe*'s account, and the *Battle Lake Review* reprints the report of the *Fergus Falls Journal*.

[66] *St. Paul Pioneer Press*, 29 October 1892; *Great West*, 4 November 1892; *Fergus Falls Globe*, 29 October 1892; *Battle Lake Review*, 3 November 1892. For other editorial reactions, see *Norman County Index* (Ada), 4 November 1892; *Warren Sheaf*, 3 November 1892, 4; *Alliance Advocate* (Henning), 3 November 1892; and *Polk County Journal* (Crookston), 3 November 1892.

[67] *Skandinaven*, 9 November 1892. For some Grant county Populists' anti-county-officer (anti-incumbent) attitude, see *Fergus Falls Ugeblad*, 2 November 1892.

[68] *Fergus Falls Daily Journal*, 28 October 1892; *Alliance Advocate* (Henning), 3 November 1892.

[69] *Alliance Advocate* (Henning), 27 October, 3 November 1892. Though pro-Alliance, the *Advocate* supported an anti-Donnelly faction led by John B. Hompe.

[70] *Polk County Journal* (Crookston), 10 November 1892.

[71] *Polk County Journal*, 10 November 1892; *Fertile Journal*, 10 November 1892. The *Journal* supported the Populist ticket. *Fertile Journal*, 3 November 1892.

[72] *Moorhead Daily News*, 1 November 1892; *Polk County Journal*, 10 November 1892; *Norman County Index* (Ada), 4 November 1892.

[73] *Moorhead Daily News*, 4 November 1892.

[74] *Norman County Herald*, 11 November 1892.

[75] A.O. Serum speech, n.d. [1890s], 6, handwritten manuscript, in A.O. Serum Papers, NAHA.

[76] *St. Paul Pioneer Press*, 8 November 1892.

[77] *St. Paul Pioneer Press*, 7 November 1892.

[78] *St. Paul Pioneer Press*, 7 November 1892. The 1891 legislature had extended to the entire state the Australian ballot system of state-printed ballots cast secretly in booths. Voting thus became more individualistic and less subject to group pressure.

[79] See, for example, *Fergus Falls Daily Journal*, 27 October 1892; *Warren Sheaf*, 3 November 1892; and *Norman County Index*, 4 November 1892.

[80] Quoted in Ridge, *Ignatius Donnelly*, 309.

[81] For ethnic concentrations (per the 1880 census), see Holmquist, *They Chose Minnesota*, 226. For vote totals, see 1893 *Legislative Manual*, 376-483. The seven townships were Hendrum, Halstad, Anthony, Shelly, Strand, Fossum, and Waukon.

[82] Holmquist, *They Chose Minnesota*, 257. The townships were Swede Grove (Meeker), and Mamre, Fahlun, Kandiyohi, Gennessee, Lake Elizabeth, and Whitefield (all Kandiyohi),

[83] *Alexandria Post*, 18 November 1892; *Douglas County News*, 17 November 1892.

[84] *St. Paul Pioneer Press*, 13 November 1892.

Chapter Nine

[1] Hill to Nelson, 15 December 1892, in Nelson Papers.

[2] Quoted in Martin, *James J. Hill*, 408-409. Nelson appointed Ira B. Mills to the Commission. See *Legislative Manual* (1893), 319.

[3] James Bryce, *The American Commonwealth*, 1 (2nd ed., London, 1891), 509. For a brief historical overview, see Larry Sabato, *Goodbye to Good-time Charlie: The American Governorship Transformed* (2nd ed., Washington, D.C., 1983), 1-11. For a description of the governorship after the Progressive changes, see John M. Mathews, "The New Role of the Governor," in *American Political Science Review*, 6 (May, 1912), 216-228.

⁴ Bryce, *American Commonwealth*, 507.

⁵ *Legislative Manual* (1893), 225-296, 317-340b. In addition, the state oil inspector may have hired deputy oil inspectors, but these are not listed in the *Legislative Manual*.

⁶ Bryce, *American Commonwealth*, 509.

⁷ A.F. Edman to Knute Nelson, 17 December 1892, in Governor's Records—Knute Nelson, State Archives, MHS. Edman was an informant, not the would-be assassin. Nelson received another death threat in the spring of 1893. See *Douglas County News*, 11 May 1893.

⁸ *Douglas County News*, 5 January 1893.

⁹ *Alexandria Post*, 6 January 1893.

¹⁰ *Polk County Journal* (Crookston), 12 January 1893.

¹¹ "Inaugural Address of Governor Knute Nelson to the Legislature of 1893," 4 January 1893, manuscript in Nelson Papers. The entire text is in *St. Paul Pioneer Press*, 5 January 1893. For abuses and railroads' interference in wheat marketing, see Keillor, "Minnesota's Rural Cooperatives, 1865-1917," 547-555, 560-565. "Country" elevators were local elevators, not the large grain elevators in terminal markets like Duluth and Minneapolis.

¹² *St. Paul Pioneer Press*, 5 January 1893.

¹³ Chrislock, "Politics of Protest," 190-191.

¹⁴ *St. Paul Pioneer Press*, 24 March 1893. See also *Minneapolis Tribune*, 31 January 1893.

¹⁵ *Minneapolis Tribune*, 17 February 1893.

¹⁶ *Minneapolis Tribune*, 1 and 24 March 1893; *Legislative Manual* (1893), 111, 113, 568, 583.

¹⁷ *St. Paul Pioneer Press*, 3 March 1893; *Legislative Manual* (1893), 114, 594.

¹⁸ *Minneapolis Tribune*, 24 March 1893; *St. Paul Pioneer Press*, 24 March 1893.

¹⁹ *Minneapolis Tribune*, 24 March 1893; *St. Paul Daily Globe*, 24 March 1893.

²⁰ Namely, Chief Grain Inspector A.C. Clausen, Chief Deputy Inspector (Minneapolis) John Shely, and State Weighmaster (Minneapolis) Charles M. Reese. See Shely to Nelson, 27 June 1892; Reese to Nelson, 2 and 6 July 1892; and Clausen to Nelson, 15 July 1892, all in Nelson Papers.

²¹ *St. Paul Pioneer Press*, 30 January 1893. Clausen had worked for Nelson in 1892. See Clausen to Nelson, 15 July 1892, in Nelson Papers. For the alleged incompetence and inactivity of the Republican appointees in the State Dairy Commission, see C.H. Higgs to Nelson, 1 December 1892; T.L. Haecker to Nelson, 20 December 1892; and H.C. Howard to Nelson, 28 December 1892, all in Governor's Records—Knute Nelson, State Archives, MHS.

²² *Minneapolis Journal*, 17 April 1899. This is the investigation referred to in Stephenson, *John Lind*, 170-171.

²³ Chrislock, "Politics of Protest in Minnesota," 194-195, especially n.8; Bjorgan, "Success Story of an Immigrant," 318. Though three Alliance senators defected to help the Republicans organize the Senate, there was no guarantee they would support the Governor's Grain Bill.

²⁴ For the vote, see *Minneapolis Tribune*, 24 March 1893; *St. Paul Daily Globe*, 24 March 1893. For the partisan affiliation of state senators, see *Legislative Manual*

(1891), 560-571; and *Legislative Manual* (1893), 566-596. For legislators' sensitivity, see, for example, *St. Paul Globe*, 6 April 1893.

[25] Quoted in Chrislock, "Politics of Protest in Minnesota," 190. See Nelson to O.O. Canestorp, 9 March 1911, in Nelson Papers.

[26] The maneuverings are described in the *St. Paul Pioneer Press*, 8 April 1893. Democrat P.H. Kelly of St. Paul denied that Nelson used the veto threat, but the vote of all six St. Paul Democrats is hard to explain otherwise.

[27] Bjorgan, "Success Story of an Immigrant," 317-322; Chrislock, "Politics of Protest in Minnesota," 201-205.

[28] *St. Paul Pioneer Press*, 11 April 1893; Folwell, *History of Minnesota*, 3:207.

[29] Charles M. Reese to Nelson, 2 July 1892, in Nelson Papers; Tams Bixby to Nelson, 16 June 1892, in Nelson Papers; H.F. Brown to Nelson, 27 February 1892, in Nelson Papers; Patrick Fox to Nelson, 11 January 1893, in File #631, Governor's Records—Knute Nelson, State Archives, MHS. The *Mississippi Valley Lumberman* estimated that the Republican "campaign fund" had gained $5,000-$8,000 "each election" in contributions from the surveyors general. See *Mississippi Valley Lumberman*, 17 February 1893. One close Nelson associate complained that S.S. Brown had not worked hard enough in 1892 to organize Itasca county for the Republicans! D.B. Searle to Nelson, 7 December 1892, in File #631, Governor's Records—Knute Nelson.

[30] Brown to Nelson, 30 July 1892, in Nelson Papers; Nelson's handwritten note on C.A. Gilman to Nelson, 15 January 1893, in File #631, Governor's Records; *Legislative Manual* (1893), 339. For lobbying letters on behalf of Stephen B. Lovejoy for surveyor general, see A.R. McGill to Nelson, 25 November 1892; S.E. Olson to Nelson, 21 November 1892; and S.B. Lovejoy to Nelson, 3 December 1892, all in File #631. Lovejoy claimed to have supported Nelson before the 1892 Republican convention.

[31] *Minneapolis Tribune*, 4 February 1893. Under the proposed bill, "the surplus earnings" of the surveyor general above the $5,000 salary would "go back to the lumbermen who pay the scaling fee."

[32] Folwell, *History of Minnesota*, 3:509.

[33] *Mississippi Valley Lumberman*, 17 February 1893.

[34] *Mississippi Valley Lumberman*, 9 December 1892, and 17 March 1893.

[35] *Mississippi Valley Lumberman*, 2 December 1892; 10, 24 February 1893; 3, 10, 17, 24 March 1893. For charges (and denials) that bribes were offered by the Browns, and that one legislator tried to extort money from the lumbermen in exchange for the bill's passage, see *Mississippi Valley Lumberman*, 17 March 1893.

[36] *Mississippi Valley Lumberman*, 24 March 1893; Chrislock, "Politics of Protest in Minnesota," 205-206; Folwell, *History of Minnesota*, 206-207, 504. While factually accurate, both Chrislock's and Folwell's accounts miss the connection between the "pine land" investigations and the lumbermen's battle with the surveyor general over the latter's fees. The link is apparent in reading the *Mississippi Valley Lumberman* for December, 1892 through April, 1893.

[37] *St. Paul Pioneer Press*, 11 April 1893.

[38] Folwell, *History of Minnesota*, 3:506.

[39] Ridge, *Ignatius Donnelly*, 312-313; Chrislock, "Politics of Protest in Minnesota," 211-214; *St. Paul Pioneer Press*, 15, 16, and 23 March, 1893.

[40] *St. Paul Pioneer Press*, 24 March 1893; Chrislock, "Politics of Protest in Minnesota," 214-215; Ridge, *Ignatius Donnelly*, 313.

[41] Ridge, *Ignatius Donnelly*, 313; Chrislock, "Politics of Protest in Minnesota," 217.

[42] Nelson's speech was printed in its entirety in *St. Paul Pioneer Press*, 6 June 1893. For the problems with the Sherman Act and the argument that it only codified common-law prohibitions on restraint of trade and monopoly, see Martin J. Sklar, *The Corporate Reconstruction of American Capitalism, 1890-1916: The Market, Law, and Politics* (New York, 1988), 105-120.

[43] For the corporatization of the legal profession, see Morton Keller, *Affairs of State: Public Life in Late 19th Century America* (Cambridge, Massachusetts, 1977), especially chapter three, "The Province of the Law."

[44] *St. Paul Pioneer Press*, 7 June 1893; *Chicago Tribune*, 6 and 7 June 1893.

[45] *St. Paul Pioneer Press*, 7 June 1893.

[46] Ridge, *Ignatius Donnelly*, 315.

[47] *St. Paul Pioneer Press*, 7 June 1893.

[48] *St. Paul Representative*, 14 June 1893.

[49] For the Sunday visits, see *Douglas County News*, 30 March, 27 April, 11, 25 May, 15 June, 10 August, 21 September, 12 October, and 2 November, all 1893.

[50] *Douglas County News*, 22 June 1893, and 10 August 1893.

[51] *Douglas County News*, 31 August 1893.

[52] Nelson filed several obituaries of Cornwall's death in his personal papers. See, for example, *Aberdeen Sun*, 18 May 1893, clipping in Nelson Papers. Cornwall died on May 14.

[53] *Whitewater Register*, 10 August 1893, clipping in Nelson Papers.

[54] Francis Dillon to Nelson, 18 August 1893, in Nelson Papers, spelling errors corrected. Census records show Mary Dillon as being either 62 or 65 years of age when she died.

[55] He visited the Fair on May 17, October 13, and sometime shortly after September 23 on a private visit with Nicholina. For this last trip, see *Douglas County News*, 28 September 1893. He may have also visited the Fair during a break in the Anti-Trust Conference in June.

[56] *Minneapolis Tribune*, 18 May 1893; *Minneapolis Journal*, 18 May 1893; *St. Peter Herald*, 2 June 1893. John A. Johnson was president of the Minnesota Editorial Association. He absolved the governor of any blame. Nelson could have attended both the Minnesota celebration in the morning and the Norwegian-American ceremony in the afternoon.

[57] *Chicago Tribune*, 18 May 1893; *Skandinaven*, 24 May 1893; *Minneapolis Tribune*, 18 May 1893.

[58] The entire speech was translated into Norwegian and printed in *Skandinaven*, 31 May 1893. See also *Chicago Tribune*, 18 May 1893.

[59] *Skandinaven*, 24 May 1893.

[60] *Minneapolis Tribune*, 18 May 1893; *Minneapolis Journal*, 18 and 19 May 1893; *North-Western Chronicle*, 26 May 1893; *Minneapolis Journal*, 20 May 1893; *Svenska*

Amerikanska Posten, 13 June 1893. *Scandia* called the governor's action "thought-less." See *Scandia* (Duluth), 2 June 1893.

[61] *Minneapolis Journal*, 19 May 1893; *Chicago Tribune*, 18 May 1893; Winifred G. Helmes, *John A. Johnson: The People's Governor* (Minneapolis, 1949), 45-47.

[62] *Redwood Gazette*, 28 September 1893.

[63] *St. Paul Globe*, 14 October 1893; *Minnesota Day at the World's Columbian Exposition, Friday, October Thirteenth, 1893* (Minneapolis, 1893), 6-9, 17. For criticisms of the exhibits and seating in Minnesota's state building, see *St. Paul Representative*, 14 June 1893; and *Freeborn County Standard*, 30 August 1893.

[64] *Minnesota Day*, 14.

[65] Martin, *James J. Hill*, 411, 415; Nick Salvatore, *Eugene V. Debs: Citizen and Socialist* (Urbana, Illinois, 1982), 119-120.

[66] Salvatore, *Eugene V. Debs*, 120.

[67] Bryce, *American Commonwealth*, 509.

[68] A.B. Robbins to Governor Nelson, 28 April 1894, in Governor's Records—Knute Nelson.

[69] *Willmar Republican Gazette*, 26 April 1894; *St. Paul Pioneer Press*, 24 April 1894.

[70] *St. Cloud Daily Times*, 19 April 1894; *St. Paul Pioneer Press*, 21 April 1894.

[71] *St. Paul Pioneer Press*, 24 April 1894; Governor Knute Nelson to Eugene V. Debs, 23 April 1894, in Nelson Papers. For Hill's reply, see James J. Hill to Knute Nelson, 23 April 1894, in Great Northern Records, MHS.

[72] *St. Cloud Daily Times*, 20 April 1894.

[73] *Willmar Republican Gazette*, 26 April 1894; *St. Paul Pioneer Press*, 30 April 1894. Hill wrote directly to at least one sheriff to request him "to disperse and prevent" the striking workers' "assemblages." See Hill to sheriff of Clay county, Minnesota, 28 April 1894, in Great Northern Records.

[74] See a dispatch from St. Paul, dated April 27, printed in the *Willmar Republican Gazette*, 3 May 1894. For the injunction, and argument over what constituted a mail train, see *St. Paul Pioneer Press*, 19, 22, 23 April 1894; and *St. Cloud Daily Times*, 23 April 1894.

[75] Helmes, *John A. Johnson*, 218-225. For later labor conflicts, see Peter Rachleff, "Turning Points in the Labor Movement: Three Key Conflicts," in Clifford E. Clark, Jr., ed., *Minnesota in a Century of Change: The State and Its People Since 1900* (St. Paul, 1989), 195-222.

[76] For praise of Nelson's handling of the strike, see, for example, *Alexandria Post News*, 26 April 1894; and *St. Paul Pioneer Press*, 24 April 1894.

[77] Governor Knute Nelson to J. Billings, telegram, 5 May 1894, in Governor's Records—Knute Nelson. For a description of "Coxey's army" in Fergus Falls, see *Fergus Falls Weekly Journal*, 10 May 1894.

[78] *St. Paul Pioneer Press*, 2, 3, 11, 28 May, 1894; 29 June 1894; 6, 7 July 1894.

[79] *St. Paul Pioneer Press*, 11 July 1894.

[80] *St. Paul Pioneer Press*, 12 July 1894.

[81] *St. Paul Pioneer Press*, 12 July 1894.

[82] Carl H. Chrislock, "Sidney M. Owen, An Editor in Politics," in *Minnesota*

History, 36 (December 1958), 109-126; Chrislock, "Politics of Protest," 232-235, 249-251.

[83] Chrislock, "Politics of Protest," 245-246.

[84] *Marshall County Banner* (Argyle), 2 August 1894.

[85] *Marshall County Banner*, 2 August 1894. Nelson's entire speech was printed in the *St. Paul Pioneer Press*, 30 July 1894; and the *Warren Sheaf*, 9, 16, 23, 30 August 1894.

[86] For the contrast between the cash economy in dairying areas and the credit economy in wheat-growing areas, see *Freeborn County Standard*, 30 June 1897; and Keillor, "Minnesota's Rural Cooperatives, 1865-1917," 420-421, 448-450.

[87] *Marshall County Banner*, 2 August 1894.

[88] Alan I. Marcus, *Agricultural Science and the Quest for Legitimacy: Farmers, Agricultural Colleges, and Experiment Stations, 1870-1890* (Ames, Iowa, 1985), 13-27; Keillor, "Minnesota's Rural Cooperatives, 1865-1917," 691.

[89] Keillor, "Minnesota's Rural Cooperatives, 1865-1917," 684-741.

[90] Keillor, "Minnesota's Rural Cooperatives, 1865-1917," 357, 371, 440-442,

[91] Chrislock, "Politics of Protest," 253.

[92] *Marshall County Banner*, 2 August 1894; *St. Paul Representative*, 15 August 1894. For Nelson's entire speech and Donnelly's entire rebuttal, see *St. Paul Representative*, 8, 15, 22 August, 1894.

[93] *Rodhuggeren* (Fergus Falls), 7 August 1894. For *Rodhuggeren's* Populist politics, see Soike, *Politics of Dissent*, 105-110.

[94] *New York Evening Post*, 6(?) August 1894, clipping in Nelson Papers.

[95] *Alexandria Post News*, 9 August 1894.

[96] *Duluth News Tribune*, 4 September 1894; Grace Stageberg Swenson, *From the Ashes: The Story of the Hinckley Fire of 1894* (Stillwater, Minnesota, 1979), 114, 120; Folwell, *History of Minnesota*, 4:388. Commission members lent $15,000 of their own money to fund relief efforts, but were later reimbursed by the state.

[97] *Duluth Herald*, 7, 8 September 1894; *Duluth News Tribune*, 8 September 1894; Swenson, *From the Ashes*, 108, 142.

[98] Swenson, *From the Ashes*, 116-119, 132; *Duluth Herald*, 7, 8 September 1894; *Duluth News Tribune*, 8 September 1984; *Hinckley Enterprise*, 19 December 1894.

[99] Swenson, *From the Ashes*, 157-159, 215-217. Christopher C. Andrews, who became Minnesota's first forestry commissioner, was the main reformer. Folwell, *History of Minnesota*, 4:386-402.

[100] Swenson, *From the Ashes*, 147, 149.

[101] *St. Paul Pioneer Press*, 4 November 1894; *St. Paul Pioneer Press*, 12 July 1882.

[102] Bruce M. White *et al.*, compilers, *Minnesota Votes: Election Returns by County for Presidents, Senators, Congressmen, and Governors, 1857-1977* (St. Paul, 1977), 82-84, 168-169; Chrislock, "Politics of Protest," 254-255.

Chapter Ten

[1] *St. Paul Representative*, 8 August 1894.

[2] Samuel Hill to J.J. Hill, 21 March 1894, in General Correspondence, Hill Papers, James J. Hill Reference Library. In his biography of James J. Hill, Albro

Martin has seriously misinterpreted this letter to suggest "chicanery" on Nelson's part, namely, an offer "to go easy on the railroads in pending rate cases" in exchange for Hill's support for the Senate. Nelson merely indicated a hands-off position regarding an upcoming decision of the Minnesota Railroad and Warehouse Commission. The conversation was not at all a bid for Hill's support. See Martin, *James J. Hill*, 409.

[3] W.D. Washburn to Frank A. Day, 28 March 1894, in Frank A. Day Papers, MHS.

[4] *New York Evening Post*, 6[?] August 1894, clipping in Nelson Papers.

[5] Larry Millett, *Lost Twin Cities*, 168; Folwell, *History of Minnesota*, 3:328-329.

[6] St. Paul Globe, 5 September 1895; Millett, *Lost Twin Cities*, 168-169. Folwell, *History of Minnesota*, 3:494-495. The quotation from the *Globe* is taken from Millett's description of Washburn's estate.

[7] Folwell, *History of Minnesota*, 3:84; Larson, *White Pine Industry in Minnesota;* Blegen, *Minnesota: A History*, 354-356.

[8] For the explicit contrast, see *St. Paul Pioneer Press*, 9 January 1895.

[9] Folwell, *History of Minnesota*, 3:495.

[10] Millett, *Lost Twin Cities*, 168, Folwell, *History of Minnesota*, 3:494-495; *Heron Lake News*, 25 November 1893. In 1892, for example, Washburn complained bitterly after giving a two-and-one-half hour speech, that "not a newspaper in Minneapolis has even alluded to the fact that I had made a speech at all, much less say a kind word for me." Washburn to Hale, 17 July 1892, in Hale Papers.

[11] Washburn to Hale, July 1894, in Hale Papers. For a brief account of Davis's career, see Barbara Stuhler, *Ten Men of Minnesota and American Foreign Policy, 1898-1968* (St. Paul, 1973), 15-31.

[12] Quoted in Ridge, *Ignatius Donnelly*, 261.

[13] Washburn to "Dear Major Hale," 26 June, 1, 16 July, 1 August, 1894, all in Hale Papers. The Hale Papers are the best single source for the Washburn re-election campaign in 1894-1895. Washburn, or his family after his death in 1912, destroyed his personal papers. As with the 1882 and 1892 papers, so too, Nelson's protectors destroyed nearly all his 1894-1895 political correspondence. Unfortunately for the historian, the papers of Nelson's chief aides, such as Tams Bixby, have not been preserved.

[14] Washburn to Hale, 1 August 1894, in Hale Papers.

[15] Washburn to Elmer Adams, 28 June 1894, in Elmer E. Adams Papers, MHS.

[16] *Red Wing Daily Republican*, 21 June 1894; Washburn to Hale, 27, 29 June, 1894, in Hale Papers. The successful candidate, O.J. Wing of Wanamingo, later voted for Nelson for the Senate. Washburn subscribed to a statewide newspaper clipping service for 1893-1894, and many stories in his file talked of a possible Nelson candidacy for the Senate. See the Stanley Washburn Papers, MHS, for the scrapbook.

[17] Washburn to Hale, 1 July 1894, in Hale Papers. Years later, Foote confirmed that he had been working to defeat Washburn. He recalled that, at Washburn's request, Nelson "called me in and told me he had promised the Senator that he would not do anything to prevent his election." Foote maintained that Nelson did not act as a Senate candidate until January 3, 1895, but elsewhere in the let-

ter he attempted to guard the reputations of anti-Washburn men, and he may be doing the same for Nelson. See Foote to W.W. Folwell, 19 June 1924, in Box 51, William Watts Folwell Papers, MHS.

[18] *Mankato Review*, 9 April 1895; 1909 House Committee on Public Accounts and Expenditures, Testimony, pp. 16-17, Legislative Records, State Archives, MHS.

[19] One such deputy was George W. Neff, publisher of the *Lake Crystal Union*. In January 1895, he asked Nelson to reappoint him deputy oil inspector for Blue Earth and Watonwan counties. Though his first year fees were only $400, they were "the power that kept the wheels of the *Union* running turning out good Republican principles." See Neff to Nelson, 1 January 1895, in Governor's Records—Knute Nelson. For Neff's editorial support for Nelson in the Senate battle, see *Lake Crystal Union*, 9 January 1895.

[20] Washburn to Hale, 1 July 1894, in Hale Papers; Hiram W. Foote to W.W. Folwell, 19 June 1924, in Box 51, Folwell Papers.

[21] Washburn to Elmer Adams, 28 June 1894, in Adams Papers.

[22] Washburn to "Dear Major Hale," 26 June 1894, in Hale Papers.

[23] A.C. Wedge to Hale, 6 August 1894, in Hale Papers.

[24] *Red Wing Daily Republican*, 21 June 1894; *Nordstjernen* (Red Wing), 18 January 1895.

[25] Hugh Thompson to "Friend Comstock," 26, 29 July, 8 August, 1894, all in Comstock Papers, NWMHC, Moorhead.

[26] Washburn to Adams, 27 September 1894, in Adams Papers.

[27] Louis O. Foss to Washburn, 15 October 1894; George F. Potter to C.C. Gram or Major Hale, 16 October 1894; E.A. Zuver to Washburn, 20 October 1894; Otis Staples to Hale, 27 October 1894; and E.A. Zuver to Hale, 29 October 1894, all in Hale Papers.

[28] Wedge to Hale, 6 August 1894, in Hale Papers.

[29] *Freeborn County Standard*, 26 September 1894; *Albert Lea Enterprise*, 27 September 1894.

[30] *Minneapolis Journal*, 24 September 1894. Neither the *Pioneer Press* nor the *Minneapolis Tribune* featured this story. John S. McLain edited the *Journal* from 1885 to 1908. He later called Washburn's defeat "a dishonorable piece of business. . . . It was a long time before I could forget that deal." John Scudden McLain to Adams, 15 May 1923, in Adams Papers.

[31] *Minneapolis Journal*, 24 September 1894.

[32] Quoted in H.P. Hall, *H.P. Hall's Observations*, 214-242. Hall noted that "a committee of Washburn's friends signed a statement" that these were Nelson's exact words. They, especially the key phrase "some other good Republican," were later confirmed by both Nelson and Washburn supporters. See *St. Paul Pioneer Press*, 4, 6, 12 January, 1895. For an editorial stressing that phrase, see *Red Wing Daily Republican*, 10 January 1895.

[33] *Freeborn County Standard*, 26 September 1894. The *Standard's* interpretation is persuasive. It came long before the January controversy, and from a paper friendly to neither candidate. For other country editors' interpretations, see Folwell, *History of Minnesota*, 3:490.

³⁴ See, for example, Washburn to "My dear Major Hale," 11 December 1894, in Hale Papers. Immediately after Nelson's "withdrawal" at Albert Lea, Washburn sounded confident, but that feeling was gone by December. See Washburn to Cushman K. Davis, 28 September 1894, in Cushman K. Davis Papers, MHS.

³⁵ Unidentified correspondent to Major Hale, 1 December 1894; H.G. Stordock to Washburn, 12 December 1894, both in Hale Papers.

³⁶ Washburn to Hale, 11, 15 December 1894, both in Hale Papers.

³⁷ Stephenson, *John Lind of Minnesota*, 98-99.

³⁸ Stordock to Washburn, 12 December 1894, in Hale Papers; Ira B. Mills to S.G. Comstock, 12, 23 November 1894; D.C. Lightbourn to Comstock, 27 November 1894, both in Comstock Papers. Railroad and Warehouse Commissioner Mills, a Nelson appointee, may have been innocent of any deceit here, for he seemed sincerely concerned that Comstock and Nelson come to "an understanding" about the Senate seat. See Mills to Comstock, 17 December 1894, in Comstock Papers.

³⁹ Washburn to Davis, 1 December 1894, in Davis Papers; James A. Tawney to Frank A. Day, 1 December 1894, in Frank A. Day Papers, MHS.

⁴⁰ *St. Paul Pioneer Press*, 21 December 1894.

⁴¹ Washburn to "My dear Major Hale," 10 December 1894,in Hale Papers.

⁴² Washburn to Hale, 10, 12 December 1894, both in Hale Papers.

⁴³ *Alexandria Post News*, 27 December 1894.

⁴⁴ Folwell, *History of Minnesota*, 3:492; *Minneapolis Tribune*, 2 January 1895.

⁴⁵ *Minneapolis Tribune*, 2 January 1895.

⁴⁶ Folwell, *History of Minnesota*, 3:492.

⁴⁷ *Minneapolis Tribune*, 4 January 1895; *Fergus Falls Weekly Journal*, 10 January 1895; *St. Paul Pioneer Press*, 4 January 1895. Apparently, Washburn was the newspapers' only source for the conversation. He may have slanted his story for his own purposes. The Minneapolis newspapers' (*Tribune, Journal,* and *Times*) accounts of the confrontation were detailed—as if reporters were present and taking shorthand, which they were not. For Washburn's attempts to manipulate news coverage and editorials of the Minneapolis newspapers, see Washburn to "Dear Major Hale," 1, 20 July, 10 December, 1894; and George Thompson to Washburn, 31 July 1894, all in Hale Papers.

⁴⁸ *St. Paul Pioneer Press*, 4 January 1895.

⁴⁹ *St. Paul Pioneer Press*, 9 January 1895. For a description of St. Paul's Merchants and Ryan hotels, see Millett, *Lost Twin Cities*, 62-63, 170-171.

⁵⁰ *St. Paul Morning Call*, 6 January 1895.

⁵¹ *St. Paul Pioneer Press*, 5, 6, 13 January, 1895; William D. Hale Diary, 1895, in Vol. 125, Hale Papers; Stephenson, *John Lind of Minnesota*, 99.

⁵² *St. Paul Morning Call*, 4 January 1895; *St. Paul Pioneer Press*, 6, 9 January 1895; *St. Paul Pioneer Press*, 4 January 1895; "Report continued from Monday Jan 21— 8 P.M.," handwritten manuscript on Windsor Hotel stationery, in Hale Papers. This last-named source is the spy's report on the Nelson camp. For a charge that Nelson men hired "detectives and spies" to shadow John Lind, see *New Ulm Review*, 23 January 1895.

⁵³ *St. Paul Morning Call*, 6 January 1895; *Alexandria Post-News*, 21 February 1895.

[54] *St. Paul Pioneer Press*, 9 January 1895.

[55] *Minneapolis Tribune*, 25 January 1895; *Mankato Review*, 29 January 1895.

[56] *Little Falls Transcript*, 1 February 1895. S.S. Brown, Henry's brother, was reappointed surveyor general in the Second District; John W. Mason, an insane asylum trustee; and G.W. Ward of Alexandria, who had worked for Nelson in St. Paul, director of the state normal schools.

[57] *St. Paul Morning Call*, 8 January 1895; James Compton to "Dear Maj[or Hale]," 24 November 1894, in Hale Papers. For Senator Iltis' vote, see *Minneapolis Tribune*, 19 January 1895; and *Minneapolis Journal*, 22 January 1895.

[58] *Minneapolis Tribune*, 25 January 1895, quoted in *Mankato Review*, 29 January 1895.

[59] *Minneapolis Journal*, 17, 21 January 1895; *Minneapolis Tribune*, 22 January 1895; "Report continued from Monday Jan 21—8 P.M.," in Hale Papers. Dahl voted for Washburn. In 1925, he wrote to Folwell, "Evidence of strong circumstantial character ... convinced me that money was freely used to elect Knute Nelson to the senate in 1895." The spy's report (he had no interest in exonerating the Nelson workers) seems more trustworthy than Dahl's recollections thirty years later. However, if Dahl later accepted money from Nelson's operatives, that would be very strong circumstantial evidence! See Dahl's note on Folwell to John F. Dahl, 4 February 1925, in Box 51, Folwell Papers.

[60] Washburn to "Dear Major Hale," 15 December 1894, in Hale Papers.

[61] Washburn to "Dear Major Hale," 19 February 1895, in Hale Papers. Earnest Arnold was co-owner of a lumber company with an office in Minneapolis. See *Davison's Minneapolis Directory 1893-94*, 166, 1279; and *St. Paul Pioneer Press*, 7 November 1942.

[62] There was widespread suspicion that Washburn had freely used money to defeat Sabin in 1889, so the same actions were suspected in 1895. *St. Paul Pioneer Press*, 24 January 1895. Charges of boodle were seldom investigated, for such rhetoric was normal and expected. Undoubtedly, in both 1889 and 1895, boodle did flow, in the form of after-election business contracts, franchises, and cash transfers. The latter were probably fewer than popularly imagined.

[63] Samuel Hill to Adams, 14 September 1924, in Adams Papers; *St. Paul Morning Call*, 22 January 1895. To date, no evidence has surfaced to prove that Hill's money was used in the battle. Samuel Hill met with D.M. Sabin on November 11, 1894, and with David Clough after the contest, on January 28, 1895. What was discussed is unknown. See Samuel Hill to Sabin, 10 November 1894, and Hill to Clough, 28 January 1895, both in Samuel Hill Letterpress Book—Personal, Eastern Railway Company of Minnesota Papers, Great Northern Records.

[64] One political scientist has implied that such elections meant the Senate lacked the "democratic legitimacy" of the House. Walter Dean Burnham, "The System of 1896: An Analysis," in Kleppner *et al.*, *The Evolution of American Electoral Systems*, 149-150, 167.

[65] Bryce, *American Commonwealth*, 96.

[66] [St. Paul] *Midway News*, 9 December 1894. The *Midway News* scoffed at the *Northfield News'* view that "public sentiment" ruled in county and state conven-

tions. "The weight of state patronage and the prestige of a barrel" ruled. "The people are not in it."

[67] *Fergus Falls Weekly Journal,* 24 January 1895; *Spring Grove Herald,* 24 January 1895; *Mankato Review,* 22 January 1895; *St. Paul Pioneer Press,* 12, 13 January 1895; *St. Paul Morning Call,* 18 January 1895; *New Ulm Review,* 23 January 1895.

[68] *New Ulm Review,* 23 January 1895; *St. Paul Pioneer Press,* 9 January 1895; *Little Falls Transcript,* 11 January 1895. The pro-Nelson *St. Paul Pioneer Press* ran the Little Falls story on its front page. For a similar meeting at Frazee City, see *St. Paul Pioneer Press,* 12 January 1895.

[69] *Minneapolis Journal,* 16 January 1895; *Red Wing Daily Republican,* 17 January 1895; *South Minneapolis Telegram,* 19 January 1893.

[70] *St. Paul Morning Call,* 12 January 1895.

[71] *Minneapolis Journal,* 17 January 1895.

[72] *Granite Falls Tribune,* 22 January 1895; *St. Paul Pioneer Press,* 13 January 1895; *Little Falls Transcript,* 11 January 1895; *New Ulm Review,* 23 January 1895. In late December 1894, Washburn urged Fergus Falls editor Elmer Adams to come to St. Paul for some "missionary work," and to bring as many Otter Tail county friends as possible. See Washburn to Adams, 28 December 1894, in Adams Papers, MHS.

[73] *Le Sueur News,* 17 January 1895.

[74] See, for example, *St. Paul Pioneer Press,* 13 January 1895; and *Minneapolis Journal,* 15 January 1895.

[75] David M. Brown to E.A. Bickford, 27 December 1894, in Vol. 2, Box 3, David M. Brown Papers, MHS. Nominated, supported, and probably funded by Washburn men, but elected by a pro-Nelson county, Bickford faced strong pressure, which he side-stepped by voting for Comstock. See Adams to "My dear Major [Hale]," 25 November 1894, in Hale Papers; Bickford to Adams, 25 and 28 December 1894, both in Adams Papers; *Minneapolis Times,* 16 January 1895; and *Minneapolis Journal,* 22 January 1895.

[76] See, for example, *St. Paul Pioneer Press,* 4, 7, 12 January, 1895.

[77] *St. Paul Morning Call,* 15 January 1895; *Red Wing Daily Republican,* 17 January 1895; *Minneapolis Journal,* 15 January 1895.

[78] *St. Paul Pioneer Press,* 5, 15 January 1895; *Nordstjernen* (Red Wing), 18 January 1895.

[79] *St. Paul Pioneer Press,* 12 January 1895. See also *Morris Sun,* 17 January 1895.

[80] *Red Wing Daily Republican,* 12 January 1895.

[81] *St. Paul Pioneer Press,* 12 January 1895.

[82] *Sherburne County Star News* (Elk River), 10, 31 January 1895; *New Ulm Review,* 9 January 1895. See also *Fergus Falls Weekly Journal,* 10 January 1895; *Rock County Herald* (Luverne), 11 January, 1 February 1895; and *Granite Falls Tribune,* 8 January 1895.

[83] See, for example, *St. Paul Pioneer Press,* 4 January 1895; and *Freeborn County Standard,* 23 January 1895.

[84] *St. Paul Pioneer Press,* 4, 7, 9, 10 January, 1895; *Lake Crystal Union,* 9 January 1895.

[85] *Fergus Falls Ugeblad,* 9, 16 January 1895.

[86] "Speech by Ole T. Torkelson. Nominating Knute Nelson for President in 1896. [From the Mayville (North Dakota) Tribune]," in *Mankato Review*, 22 January 1895. The *Review* was a Democratic paper, so it could safely use an out-of-state attack on a Republican candidate.

[87] Reprinted in *Mankato Review*, 15 January 1895. These two articles are examples of what one Norwegian-American pastor characterized as "Americans' inborn national pride," which meant they "will never except of necessity share the spoils [of office] with 'foreigners.'" See J.A. Ottesen to Nelson, 30 January 1895, in Nelson Papers.

[88] Fergus Falls *Ugeblad*, 9 January 1895.

[89] *St. Paul Pioneer Press*, 13 January 1895; *St. Paul Morning Call*, 23 January 1895.

[90] J.A. Ottesen to Nelson, 30 January 1895, in Nelson Papers. Jacob Aall Ottesen was one of those Norwegian Synod pastors whose Civil War stance on slavery Nelson had so strongly condemned. See Lovoll, *Promise of America*, 99; and Blegen, *American Transition*, 423-440.

[91] E.W. Anderson to Nelson, 20 January 1895, in Governors' Records — Knute Nelson, State Archives. Anderson claimed that local Swedish Americans were opposed to Nelson, but favored John Lind.

[92] *Nordstjernen* (Red Wing), 25 January 1895.

[93] *Minneapolis Journal*, 15 January 1895; *Granite Falls Tribune*, 22 January 1895; *St. Paul Pioneer Press*, 14 January 1895. So sensitive was the local ethnic division that the *Tribune* did not mention that the "bitterness" was ethnic in origin.

[94] *Spring Grove Herald*, 10 January 1895; *St. Paul Pioneer Press*, 11 January 1895; *Winthrop News*, 17 January 1895. For Roverud's early support of Washburn, see *St. Paul Pioneer Press*, 6 January 1895; and *St. Paul Morning Call*, 5, 15 January 1895. In early December, Roverud wrote to Nelson asking to be named chairman of the Senate Committee on Taxes and Tax Laws. See Roverud to Nelson, 3 December 1894, in Governors' Records — Knute Nelson, State Archives.

[95] For the caucus balloting, see *Minneapolis Tribune*, 19 January 1895. For the formal legislative votes, see *Minneapolis Journal*, 22 and 23 January 1895.

[96] *Minneapolis Journal*, 17, 18 January 1895; Hale Diary — 1895 (Vol. 125), entry for January 18, in Hale Papers.

[97] *Minneapolis Tribune*, 19 January 1895; *Minneapolis Journal*, 19 January 1895; *Minneapolis Tidende*, 25 January 1895; Hale Diary — 1895 (Vol. 125), entry for January 19, in Hale Papers.

[98] Hale Diary — 1895 (Vol. 125), entry for January 20, in Hale Papers.

[99] *Minneapolis Tribune*, 23 January 1895; Hale Diary — 1895 (Vol. 125), entry for January 22, in Hale Papers.

[100] *Nordstjernen* (Red Wing), 25 January 1895; *Minneapolis Journal*, 23 January 1895.

[101] *St. Paul Pioneer Press*, 24 January 1895; *Minneapolis Journal*, 23 January 1895.

[102] *Minneapolis Tidende*, 1 February 1895 (quoting the *Minneapolis Times*); *Mankato Review*, 29 January 1895 (reprint of *Minneapolis Tribune* editorial).

[103] Hale Diary — 1895 (Vol. 125), entry for January 25, in Hale Papers; *Minneapolis Tribune*, 25 January 1895.

¹⁰⁴ See, for example, *New Ulm Review*, 30 January 1895; and *Alexandria Post News*, 30 January 1895.

¹⁰⁵ *Minneapolis Tidende*, 1 February 1895. *Tidende* called for Scandinavian legislators to support Nelson, despite "American newspapers'" anger "that Scandinavians rally around Nelson, because they take a little bit of notice to nationality and think that it would be an honor to have such a countryman as a member of the United States Senate." *Minneapolis Tidende*, 25 January 1895. This call, however, came after the legislature voted.

¹⁰⁶ *Nordstjernen* (Red Wing), 25 January 1895; *Fergus Falls Ugeblad*, 30 January 1895.

¹⁰⁷ Ottesen to Nelson, 30 January 1895, in Nelson Papers.

¹⁰⁸ Nelson to Rasmus B. Anderson, 25 January 1895, in Anderson Papers, State Historical Society of Wisconsin, Madison.

¹⁰⁹ *Alexandria Post-News*, 21 February 1895.

Chapter Eleven

¹ *Minneapolis Tidende*, 26 April 1895 (quoting the *Milwaukee Sentinel*); Charles M. Reese to Nelson, 19 June 1895, in Nelson Papers. Reese translated the Evanger address, which was signed by A. Kvilekval, Brynjulf Mugaas, M. Mugaas, and G. Brokhus.

² The *Globe* story is reprinted in the *Alexandria Post-News*, 5 September 1895.

³ *Alexandria Post-News*, 17 October 1895, quoting the *Warren Register*.

⁴ *New Haven Register*, 9 December 1895, clipping in Nelson Papers; *Alexandria Post-News*, 29 July 1897, quoting the *Philadelphia Times* of 18 July 1897; *St. Peter Herald*, 20 January 1899. The *New Haven Register* claimed that Nelson had "such great difficulty in talking Norwegian" that he could hardly solicit Scandinavian-American votes. That was a gross exaggeration of his Americanization.

⁵ *St. Paul Pioneer Press*, 11 November 1895; *Skandinaven*, 13 November 1895; Nelson to "Kjære Moder," 18 February 1863, in Nelson Papers; Per Fuglum, *Norge i støpeskjeen, 1884-1920*—vol. 12 of *Norges Historie*, ed. Knut Mykland (Oslo, 1978), 86-93.

⁶ *Congressional Record*, 54:1:442-443 (31 December 1895); *Minneapolis Tidende*, 3 January 1896. For an earlier and fuller expression of his views, see *Alexandria Post-News*, 13 June 1895. He delivered another currency speech on January 27, 1896. See *Minneapolis Tidende*, 31 January 1896; and *Chicago Tribune*, 29 January 1896.

⁷ For the Committee's petition and an editorial favoring their cause, see *Minneapolis Journal*, 30 January 1896.

⁸ *Rodhuggeren* (Fergus Falls), is an excellent source for left-wing, Populist attacks on Nelson. It ceased publication in May 1898.

⁹ *Evansville Enterprise*, 10 April 1896.

¹⁰ *Skandinaven*, 10 June 1896; *Congressional Record*, 54:1:5715-5716 (26 May 1896), 54:1:6100-6101 (3 June 1896), and 54:1:2379-2380 (3 March 1896).

¹¹ *Congressional Record*, 54:1:5221-5226 (14 May 1896); *Skandinaven*, 20, 27 May, 1896. Nelson was a member of the Senate Committee on Immigration. He used

standard pro-immigration arguments, for example, that immigrants did not lower American wages but took jobs the native-born did not want.

¹² *Alexandria Post-News*, 6 August 1896; *St. Paul Pioneer Press*, 3 August 1896. The *Pioneer Press* printed the complete text of Nelson's speech.

¹³ *St. Paul Pioneer Press*, 3 November 1896; White *et al.*, *Minnesota Votes*, 169-170; "Hon. Knute Nelson," typewritten speaking schedule, filed in Nelson Papers under 2 November 1896.

¹⁴ For Nelson's successful efforts to pass his bankruptcy proposal, here and below, see *Congressional Record*, 54:2:1428-1429 (2 February 1897), 55:1:663-672 (8 April 1897), 55:1:764-772, 799-801 (20 and 22 April 1897), and 55:2:6296-6298 (24 June 1898); and *St. Paul Pioneer Press*, 29 January 1897, 25 June 1898. Sources for specific quotations are noted below.

¹⁵ *Congressional Record*, 54:2:1429 (2 February 1897).

¹⁶ *Congressional Record*, 55:1:664 (8 April 1897).

¹⁷ *St. Paul Pioneer Press*, 25 June 1898. This long article gives an excellent history of this legislation.

¹⁸ *St. Paul Pioneer Press*, 25 June 1898.

¹⁹Jas. J. Hill to C.K. Davis, Knute Nelson *et al.*, 30 March 1898, and Nelson to Hill, 31 March 1898, both in James J. Hill Papers. Nelson's response is quoted in John L. Offner, *An Unwanted War: The Diplomacy of the United States and Spain Over Cuba, 1895-1898* (Chapel Hill, North Carolina, 1992), 153.

²⁰ *Congressional Record*, 55:2:3984 (16 April 1898).

²¹ Nelson to Søren Listoe, 1 June 1898, in Nelson Papers.

²² Lind claimed not to have wanted the Democratic-Populist nomination, but he subscribed to a statewide clipping service that saved all Lind stories. Despite his reforming stand, he believed in capitalism, speculated in a Utah coal mine and Minnesota lands, and owned shares in the Brown County State Bank. See Lind to "My dear son [Norman]," 12 June 1898; Lind to "dear children," 12 July 1898; and Lind to Musser, 28 June 1887, all in John Lind Papers. For the campaign, see Stephenson, *John Lind*.

²³ Quoted in Bailyn *et al.*, *Great Republic*, II:267.

²⁴ Nelson's speech and his debate with his questioners are found in the *Congressional Record*, 55:3:831-838 (20 January 1899). For a brief description of the debate, see *Washington Post*, 21 January 1899.

²⁵ *Congressional Record*, 55:3:831-833 (20 January 1899).

²⁶ Tillman's words are quoted in Stanley Arnow, *In Our Image: America's Empire in the Philippines* (New York, 1989), 137, as an example of the racist rhetoric surrounding the American annexation of the Philippines.

²⁷ The entire debate is found in *Congressional Record*, 55:3:831-838 (20 January 1899).

²⁸ *St. Paul Pioneer Press*, 7 February 1899; Stuhler, *Ten Men of Minnesota*, 24-31; Karnow, *In Our Image*, 136-142.

²⁹ *Minneapolis Tidende*, 7 April 1899. Section 9 of Article I would seem to allow the acceptance of such honors with "the consent of Congress."

³⁰ S.C. Hammer, *Georg Stang. Et blad af Norges nyeste historie* (Christiania, 1912), 52-56, 65-73. The quotation is on p. 66. For Georg Stang's advocacy of strength-

ened defenses against Swedish attack, see also Fuglum, *Norge i støpeskjeen*, 107-108. Stang's goals for his trip to Washington are inferred from his actions as defense minister.

[31] *St. Paul Pioneer Press*, 23 July 1899; *Minneapolis Tidende*, 28 July 1899. Nelson apparently left New York on July 29 on the Holland-America Line ship *Statendam*. See E.F. Droop & Sons to Nelson, 20 July 1899, in Nelson Papers.

[32] *Minneapolis Tidende*, 28 July 1899.

[33] *Amerika*, 13 September 1899, quoting *Bergens Aftenblad*. It starts out, "Millom Bakkar og Berg ut med Havet," and those are the words Nelson cites when he describes his first impression. For Aasen's poem, see Ivar Aasen, *Dikting* (Oslo, 1946), 27-28. For its popularity as a song, see Edvard Beyer, Ingard Hauge, and Olav Bø, *Fra Wergeland til Vinje*, Vol. 2 of *Norges litteraturhistorie*, ed. Edvard Beyer (Oslo, 1974), 389-390.

[34] For Nelson's use of this term, see *Minneapolis Tidende*, 13 October 1899, quoting from *Verdens Gang* (27 September).

[35] Fuglum, *Norge i støpeskjeen*, 52-53, 57-68, 143-145.

[36] For the language controversy, see Fuglum, *Norge i støpeskjeen*, 412-416; and Harry Eckstein, *Division and Cohesion in Democracy: A Study of Norway* (Princeton, 1966), 43-46.

[37] T.K. Derry, *A History of Modern Norway, 1814-1972* (Oxford, 1973), 141-142, 148-149, 154; Fuglum, *Norge i støpeskjeen*, 83-93, 106-107. For a cartoon of the Swedish flag (with Union emblem) atop a grenade or bomb, see *Svenska Amerikanska Posten*, 10 October 1899.

[38] *Amerika*, 13 September 1899, quoting *Hordal*.

[39] *Minneapolis Tidende*, 22 September 1899, quoting from *Bergens Aftenblad*; Fuglum, *Norge i støpeskjeen*, 150-151. The following paragraphs are also based on *Amerika*, 13 September 1899, also quoting from *Bergens Aftenblad*; and (Christiania) *Morgenbladet*, 26 August 1899.

[40] *Minneapolis Tidende*, 13 October 1899, quoting *Verdens Gang* for 27 September 1899. A search of *Svenska Amerikanska Posten* for mid-September through early November, 1899, failed to turn up any news of his Stockholm trip.

[41] *Morgenbladet*, 26 August 1899; *Minneapolis Tidende*, 22 September 1899, quoting at length from *Bergens Aftenblad*. *Aftenblad*'s correspondent gave a verbatim report; *Morgenbladet*'s paraphrased and partly respected Nelson's request of confidentiality.

[42] *Amerika*, 27 September 1899, quoting *Vestlandsposten*; *Amerika*, 13 September 1899, editorializing and quoting from an interview in *Bergens Aftenblad* for 22 August; and *Amerika*, 4 October 1899, quoting *Superior Tidende*. Anderson called *Vestlandsposten* a *Høyre* newspaper, but Fuglum (p. 54) describes it as *Moderate Venstre*'s "chief organ." For Norwegian Americans' sympathies in Norwegian politics, see Lovoll, *Promise of America*, 133.

[43] *Minneapolis Tidende*, 13 October 1899, quoting *Verdens Gang* for 27 September; (Christiania) *Dagbladet*, 22 September 1899; *Morgenbladet*, 22 September 1899; *Amerika*, 13 October 1899, also quoting *Verdens Gang* for 27 September. There is some confusion about the date of this *Verdens Gang* article. *Tidende* gives it as 21 September, while *Amerika* renders it 27 September. It is unclear which is correct.

⁴⁴ *Minneapolis Tidende*, 13 October 1899, quoting *Verdens Gang* for 27 September.

⁴⁵ *Minneapolis Tidende*, 13 October 1899, quoting *Verdens Gang* for 21 September 1899; *Minneapolis Tidende*, 27 October 1899, quoting (Copenhagen) *Dannebrog* for 6 October 1899; Fuglum, *Norge i støpeskjeen*, 66; Carl Berner to Nelson, 24 September 1899, in Nelson Papers. Thommessen describes Nelson's 1899 visit in his 1927 lecture on Nelson ("Vår Største Emigrant") in O. Thommessen, *Tidens guder* (Oslo, 1928), 41-65, especially pp. 57-60.

⁴⁶ Charles E. Flandreau to Nelson, 29 October 1900; Swenson to Nelson, 24 August 1898 and 24 February 1899, all in Nelson Papers; and *Minneapolis Tidende*, 27 October 1899, quoting *Dannebrog* for 6 October 1899. This account of his visit to Denmark is based on the *Dannebrog* article. These Minnesotans did not necessarily owe their posts just to Nelson's influence. Senator Davis played a part too. It is not clear exactly when Nelson and Søren Listoe were reconciled after the 1882-1883 unpleasantness.

⁴⁷ *Minneapolis Tidende*, 22 September 1899, quoting *Bergens Aftenblad*.

⁴⁸ *St. Paul Pioneer Press*, 18 October 1899.

⁴⁹ *Times* (London), 18 October 1899.

⁵⁰ *St. Paul Pioneer Press*, 18, 20 October 1899. Nelson may not have attended the second day's session, at which the humorous exchange occurred.

⁵¹ For a complete account of this affair, see Kenneth O. Bjork, "Reindeer, Gold, and Scandal," in *Norwegian-American Studies*, 30 (1985), 150-185. For the North Dakotans' side of the story, see *Minneapolis Journal*, 27 April 1900.

⁵² Nelson to Simon Michelet, 21 May 1900; James A. Peterson to Nelson, 22 June, 1 September 1900; Charles L. Smith to Nelson, 24 June 1900; Søren Listoe to Nelson, 25 July 1900; Nelson to Michelet, 28 October 1900; A.C. Aaby to L.S. Swenson, 2 July 1900; Swenson to Nelson, 12 July 1900, all in Nelson Papers.

⁵³ *St. Paul Pioneer Press*, 2 September 1900; *Alexandria Post-News*, 6 September 1900; *Alexandria Citizen*, 6 September 1900. The *Pioneer Press* printed the speech in full. Senator Davis gave it high praise also. See Davis to Nelson, 8 September 1900, in Nelson Papers.

⁵⁴ For the 17 July speech to the convention, which Roosevelt also addressed, see *St. Paul Pioneer Press*, 18 July 1900.

⁵⁵ Bailyn et al., *Great Republic*, II:207.

⁵⁶ The word "Roosevelted" is taken from an editorial in the *Minneapolis Journal*, 11 September 1900 — though the editorial uses it in a different sense than is intended here.

⁵⁷ *Minneapolis Journal*, 10 September 1900; *St. Paul Pioneer Press*, 11 September 1900; *Winona Republican*, 10 September 1900.

⁵⁸ For this and the following paragraphs on the South Dakota trip, see reporters' accounts in *St. Paul Pioneer Press*, 12-15 September 1900; *St. Paul Globe*, 12 September 1900; *Minneapolis Journal*, 11-15 September 1900; and the trip schedule, typewritten ms., with handwritten heading "Hon. Henry C. Payne from South Dakota" [n.d., but September 1900], in Nelson Papers.

⁵⁹ *St. Paul Pioneer Press*, 20 October 1900; (East Grand Forks) *Saturday Valley View*, 20 October 1900; John Elleson to Nelson, 22 October 1900, and attached

clipping, in Nelson Papers; *Minneapolis Tidende,* 2 November 1900. In describing Roosevelt's trip to North Dakota, the *Minneapolis Journal* 14, 15 September 1900, does not mention Nelson's name.

[60] Stuhler, *Ten Men of Minnesota,* 30; *Alexandria Post-News,* 24 September 1900. Ida Nelson said the one-and-one-half hour speech was excellent but too short!

[61] Nelson to Simon Michelet, 28 October 1900, in Nelson Papers.

[62] *St. Paul Pioneer Press,* 6 November 1900. To this meeting, Davis sent what may have been his last political message, praising Nelson as "the most distinguished Scandinavian that these liberty-loving countries of Northern Europe" had sent to America.

[63] Henry's was hardly a successful political career. Years later, the father expressed disappointment over the "fast crowd" into which Henry K. Nelson drifted while in St. Paul. See Nelson to Emilie Smith, 1 January 1915, University of Oslo Library.

[64] Nelson to Simon Michelet, 7 December 1900, in Nelson Papers.

[65] Nelson to Simon Michelet, 24 January 1901, in Nelson Papers.

[66] John Goodnow to Nelson, 18 September 1901; "A bereaved wife & a bereaved nation . . . ," handwritten ms. (Nelson to the *New York Tribune*), [n.d., 14 September 1901]; Nelson to Listoe, 28 October 1901, all in Nelson Papers.

Chapter Twelve

[1] For Nelson's use of the phrase "on the jump," see, for example, Nelson to Søren Listoe, 30 June 1905, in Nelson Papers.

[2] *Duluth News-Tribune,* 14, 15 October, 1902; *Iron News* (Two Harbors), 17 October 1902; *St. Paul Pioneer Press,* 15 October 1902.

[3] McCormick, *Party Period and Public Policy,* 270-272, 317-318. For Progressivism as, in part, a popularization of the old Mugwump reform, see Richard Hofstadter, *The Age of Reform: From Bryan to F.D.R.* (New York, 1955), 142-145.

[4] McCormick, *Party Period and Public Policy,* 272, 275, 327, 341-342.

[5] For an analysis of Progressivism in Minnesota, see Chrislock, *The Progressive Era in Minnesota, 1899-1918* (St. Paul, 1971), 22-32. These four categories are not derived from Chrislock, however. For an argument that the term "Progressive" is still usable, despite the very disparate groups it embraces, see McCormick, *Party Period and Public Policy,* 263-269.

[6] Beveridge to Nelson, 9 August 1902, in Nelson Papers. The standard biography of Beveridge is Claude G. Bowers, *Beveridge and the Progressive Era* (New York, 1932).

[7] Robert W. Larson, *New Mexico's Quest for Statehood, 1846-1912* (Albuquerque, 1968), 55-57, 221; Howard Roberts Lamar, *The Far Southwest, 1846-1912: A Territorial History* (New Haven, 1966), 486-487, 490-491.

[8] Beveridge to Nelson, 9 August 1902, in Nelson Papers. For Nelson's view that Arizona and New Mexico were "not fit for statehood," and for his account of his work on "a substitute bill" per Beveridge's request, see Nelson to Søren Listoe, 20 December 1902, in Nelson Papers.

[9] Lamar, *Dakota Territory, 1861-1889: A Study of Frontier Politics* (New Haven,

1956), 5. Jack Eblen disputes this contention in his *The First and Second United States Empires: Governors and Territorial Government, 1784-1912* (Pittsburgh, 1968), 13.

[10] Lamar, *Far Southwest*, 504.

[11] James L. Penick, Jr., *Progressive Politics and Conservation: The Ballinger-Pinchot Affair* (Chicago, 1968), 1-2, 5-11; Gifford Pinchot, *Breaking New Ground* (New York, 1947), 10-22, 109-110.

[12] Lamar, *Far Southwest*, 487-488.

[13] Lamar, *Far Southwest*, 487-489; Jay J. Wagoner, *Arizona Territory, 1863-1912: A Political History* (Tucson, 1970), 408, 410-412; Larson, *New Mexico's Quest*, 267.

[14] Beveridge to Nelson, telegrams dated 2 and 13 November 1902, and Nelson to Beveridge, 5 November 1902, all in Nelson Papers; Wagoner, *Arizona Territory*, 408; Lamar, *Far Southwest*, 491-492; Larson, *New Mexico's Quest*, 209-213. For the story that Beveridge's subcommittee discovered one county school superintendent who did not know Christopher Columbus had died, see H.B. Hening, ed., *George Curry, 1861-1947: An Autobiography* (Albuquerque, New Mexico, 1958), 191-192.

[15] *Congressional Record*, 57:2:492-499 (5 January 1903), 525-527 (6 January 1903), 568-574 (7 January 1903), and 674-679 (12 January 1903).

[16] Quoted in Wagoner, *Arizona Territory*, 410-411.

[17] *Washington Post*, 8 January 1903; Larson, *New Mexico's Quest*, 218-219.

[18] *Congressional Record*, 57:2:1938-1941 (9 February 1903). For Foraker's support of statehood, see Larson, *New Mexico's Quest*, 219.

[19] Wagoner, *Arizona Territory*, 412; Bowers, *Beveridge*, 200-201; Larson, *New Mexico's Quest*, 223.

[20] Richard White, *"It's Your Misfortune and None of My Own": A History of the American West* (Norman, Oklahoma, 1991), 172-173, 176-177; Lamar, *Far Southwest*, 498-499. For the Santa Fe Ring, see Larson, *New Mexico's Quest*, 141-146.

[21] For the story of the merger-in-progress, see *St. Paul Pioneer Press*, 13, 14 November, 1901; and *Minneapolis Journal*, 29 October 1901. For Van Sant's and Roosevelt's actions, see *St. Paul Pioneer Press*, 1, 8 January, 21, 24 February, and 1 March, 1902. For the Northern Securities case and Roosevelt's administration, see John Milton Cooper, Jr., *Pivotal Decades: The United States, 1900-1920* (New York, 1990), 43-44.

[22] For the Nelson-Douglas correspondence, see "Railroad Merger Case," Senate Document No. 255, 57th Congress, 1st Session; Douglas to Nelson, 14 March 1902; and Nelson to Douglas, 20 March 1902, all in Nelson Papers.

[23] *St. Paul Pioneer Press*, 15 March 1904; Chrislock, *Progressive Era*, 15-17; Cooper, *Pivotal Decades*, 44.

[24] *St. Paul Pioneer Press*, 2 July 1902; *Duluth News Tribune*, 14, 16 October, 1902.

[25] *St. Paul Pioneer Press*, 15 February 1903; Cooper, *Pivotal Decades*, 46. For an argument that this bill "passed with conservative support and was motivated by conservative intentions," see Gabriel Kolko, *The Triumph of Conservatism: A Reinterpretation of American History, 1900-1916* (New York, 1963), 69-72.

[26] Beveridge to Nelson, 8, 20 April, 1903, in Nelson Papers. The Senate

sergeant-at-arms, David M. Ransdell, two Senate secretaries, and a senator's brother also accompanied the subcommittee — along with John S. McLain.

[27] W.P. Dillingham to Nelson, 6 May 1903, in Nelson Papers; Ernest Gruening, *The State of Alaska* (New York, 1954), 118.

[28] John S. McLain to Nelson, 13 May 1903; (copy) W.P. Dillingham to Senator T.M. Patterson, 27 May 1903, in Nelson Papers; John Scudder McLain, *Alaska and the Klondike* (New York, 1905). McLain's articles appeared in the *Minneapolis Journal* on successive Saturdays from 12 September to 24 October 1903. For a good scholarly account of turn-of-the-century Alaska, including descriptions of many places visited by the subcommittee (Holy Cross, Dawson, Anvik, etc.) see Melody Webb, *The Last Frontier* (Albuquerque, New Mexico, 1985).

[29] Dillingham to Patterson (copy), 27 May 1903, in Nelson Papers; *Minneapolis Journal*, 12 September 1903.

[30] *Congressional Record*, 58:2:3091 (10 March 1904).

[31] Jeannette Paddock Nichols, *Alaska: A history of its administration, exploitation, and industrial development during its first half century under the rule of the United States* (Cleveland, 1924), 71-72, 167, 180.

[32] *Minneapolis Journal*, 12, 19 September, 1903; Nichols, *Alaska*, 214-215; Gruening, *State of Alaska*, 121. The complete subcommittee report and transcript of testimony is given in "Conditions in Alaska," *Senate Report* No. 282, 58th Congress, 2nd Session (4570).

[33] Nichols, *Alaska*, 63-64, 140, 151-154, 172-174, 215; "Conditions in Alaska," 22, 28.

[34] *Minneapolis Journal*, 19 September and 24 October, 1903. A boundary dispute still raged between Canada and the United States over the exact boundary line north and east of Skagway.

[35] "Conditions in Alaska," 10-11; Nichols, *Alaska*, 190-192; *Minneapolis Journal*, 3 October 1903.

[36] *Minneapolis Journal*, 19 September, 3 October, 1903. See also Nelson's small pocket diary of the trip, which is Volume 13, in Box 79 of the Nelson Papers. See the entries for July 8 through July 17, 1903.

[37] *Minneapolis Journal*, 10 October 1903; Nelson diary, entries for July 20-23, 1903, in Nelson Papers.

[38] Nichols, *Alaska*, 222-223. Nichols pointed out that "Alaska's immensity" made "the hearing method" a questionable and inadequate means of obtaining "a complete understanding" of conditions in Alaska.

[39] "Conditions in Alaska," 124, 201-202, 230; *Congressional Record*, 58:2:3091 (10 March 1904); Nelson diary, entry for 25 July 1903.

[40] *Minneapolis Journal*, 17, 24 October 1903; Nelson diary, entry for 29 July 1903, in Nelson Papers; "Conditions in Alaska," 24-25; Nichols, *Alaska*, 192-193, 199n.

[41] McLain, *Alaska and the Klondike*, 176-184.

[42] McLain, *Alaska and the Klondike*, 199-212.

[43] McLain, *Alaska and the Klondike*, 217-218, 228-230, 245-246; "Conditions in Alaska," 11-12. McLain emphasized the possibilities of a railroad from Valdez to Eagle, but the subcommittee only proposed that the government build the road, and let entrepreneurs build the railroad.

44 *Alexandria Post News*, 3 September 1903.

45 Quoted in Gruening, *State of Alaska*, 327.

46 Nichols, *Alaska*, 216, 223, 224-227, 230, 231-233, 318; *Congressional Record*, 58:2:3087-3092 (10 March 1904). In 1906, Nelson succeeded with his bill for an elected delegate. Also, he compromised with the anti-corporate Wickersham despite some personal differences with the Alaska delegate. See Nichols, 261-262, 315, 318. For an expression of appreciation, see Valdez Chamber of Commerce to Nelson, 22 April 1905, in Nelson Papers.

47 Paul E. Storing, "United States' Recognition of Norway in 1905," in Sigmund Skard, ed., *Americana Norvegica: Norwegian Contributions to American Studies* (Philadelphia, 1968), 161; Fuglum, *Norge i støpeskjeen*, 110-116.

48 *Nordvesten*, 8 June 1905; *Minneapolis Tidende* (Weekly), 2 June 1905.

49 *Nordvesten*, 8 June 1905; *Minneapolis Tidende* (Weekly), 2 June 1905; Storing, "United States' Recognition," 172-173; Henry Bordewich to Nelson, 15 July 1905, in Nelson Papers.

50 *Nordvesten*, 8 June 1905; Bordewich to Nelson, 15 July 1905; Magnus Andersen to Nelson, 19 June 1905; Nelson to Søren Listoe, 30 June 1905; Listoe to Nelson, 19 July 1905, all in Nelson Papers. *Minneapolis Tidende* protested against *Nordvesten*'s far-fetched excuses. See *Minneapolis Tidende* (Weekly), 16 June 1905. Nelson tried unsuccessfully to place Swenson as Minister to Sweden-Norway, but the Swedish government refused to have an American minister of Scandinavian descent. Nelson succeeded in placing his crony from 1882, Charles H. Graves, in the Stockholm post. See Nelson to Listoe, 30 June 1905.

51 Storing, "United States' Recognition," 161-171, 173; Fuglum, *Norge i støpeskjeen*, 116-117; Lars Haukaness to Nelson, 9 June 1905; Dr. Henrik Nissen to Nelson, 10, 14 June 1905; Andrew Bromstad to Nelson, 10 June 1905, all in Nelson Papers. The fact that Nelson prepared a form letter ("Dear sir") to respond to these requests suggests that there were many of them. See Nelson to "Dear sir," 12 June 1905. The quoted passages are from Nissen's June 10th letter.

52 Nelson to "Dear sir," 12 June 1905, in Nelson Papers; Storing, "United States' Recognition," 173. It is, of course, possible that Nelson *did* appeal to Roosevelt to recognize Norway's independence and that no written record of the private conference has survived. Yet it seems odd that he would not mention that to old confidants like Listoe. He did forward a petition to Roosevelt "praying" the United States government to recognize Norway. See Alvey A. Adee to Nelson, 7 August 1905, in Nelson papers.

53 Nelson to Listoe, 30 June 1905, in Nelson Papers.

54 Magnus Andersen to Nelson, 19 June 1905, in Nelson Papers.

55 David P. Thelen, *Robert M. La Follette and the Insurgent Spirit* (Boston, 1976), 1-7, 8-9, 16-20; Soike, *Politics of Dissent*, 122-123. Unfortunately, there appears to be no written account of Nelson's personal feelings toward La Follette. This analysis is based on their known characteristics and Nelson's likely response.

56 I have taken the idea of a first (1840s-1850s emigration), second (1865-1880), and third (1880-late 1890s) generation from Soike, *Politics of Dissent*, 44-47.

57 Thelen, *Robert M. La Follette*, 52-54.

58 A. Maurice Low, "The Oligarchy of the Senate," in *The North American*

NOTES

Review, February 1902, 231-244; S.W. McCall, "The Power of the Senate," in *Atlantic Monthly,* October 1903, 433-442; David Graham Phillips, *The Treason of the Senate* (Chicago, 1964), edited and with an introduction by George E. Mowry and Judson A. Grenier, 22-25.

⁵⁹ George H. Haynes, *The Election of Senators* (New York, 1906), 92-97. Expert Haynes derived his ranking from a survey of five Washington observers. He felt constrained to defend "the scientific character of such an inquiry" against objections that it represented opinions not facts. (See pp. 90-91.)

⁶⁰ *Marshall News-Messenger,* 29 September 1905. Before 1895 he had added on a downstairs parlor and bedroom, and an upstairs bedroom and bathroom. Author's tour of Knute Nelson house and conversation with Barbara Grover, 29 September 1993.

⁶¹ For Heatwole's career, see Charles B. Cheney, *The Story of Minnesota Politics: High Lights of Half a Century of Political Reporting* (Minneapolis, 1947), 22-24; and *Northfield News,* 9 April 1910.

⁶² Joel P. Heatwole to Nelson, 17 September 1904, in Nelson Papers. Nelson's move against Verity came a little more than a week after this letter. See *Minneapolis Times,* 29 September 1904; *St. Paul Pioneer Press,* 29 September 1904; *Northfield News,* 1 October 1904; and Cheney, *Minnesota Politics,* 23-24.

⁶³ *Northfield News,* 30 June, 4, 11 August, 27 October, 1906. On some of these pages, Heatwole reprints anti-Nelson articles from other Minnesota newspapers.

⁶⁴ Nelson to Theodore Roosevelt, 18 July 1906, in Nelson Papers. For an emphasis on the publicity uses of the amendment, see Kolko, *Triumph of Conservatism,* 70-71. The term "wily Alexandrian" is Heatwole's. See *Northfield News,* 27 October 1906.

⁶⁵ Roosevelt to Nelson, 21 July 1906, in Nelson Papers. The *Journal* editorial is reprinted and unconvincingly rebutted in *Northfield News,* 4 August 1906. See also, *Minneapolis Journal,* 28 July 1906.

⁶⁶ *Northfield News,* 3 November 1906. Heatwole again disputed Roosevelt's defense of Nelson in that issue. For educational developments, see Cooper, *Pivotal Decades,* 136-137; and Clarke A. Chambers, "Educating for the Future," in Clifford E. Clark, Jr., ed., *Minnesota in a Century of Change: The State and Its People Since 1900* (St. Paul, 1989), especially 477-478 and 488-491.

⁶⁷ *Northfield News,* 3 November 1906.

⁶⁸ Phillips, *Treason,* 28-30, 194-196, 206; McCormick, *Party Period and Public Policy,* 311, 332-339. McCormick's essay is entitled "The Discovery That Business Corrupts Politics: A Reappraisal of the Origins of Progressivism."

⁶⁹ Thelen, *Robert M. La Follette,* 57-58; *St. Paul Daily News,* 1, 2 October, 1906; *Hutchinson Leader,* 5 October 1906; *Hutchinson Independent,* 3 October 1906.

⁷⁰ *Fergus Falls Ugeblad,* 18 October 1906. It was a man who heard Nelson speak, not the editor, who said he was "twenty years behind the times." The professor was "a graduate of Albion college." See *Fergus Falls Daily Journal,* 11 October 1906.

⁷¹ Soike, *Politics of Dissent,* 134-141.

⁷² *St. Paul Pioneer Press,* 30 September 1906.

[73] *St. Paul Pioneer Press*, 6 November 1906. Old W.D. Washburn complimented Nelson on his "moral courage" in refusing to be hauled around the Mill City in an automobile. See Washburn to Nelson, 10 November 1906, in Nelson Papers.

[74] *St. Paul Pioneer Press*, 23 January 1907.

[75] Nelson to Emilie Smith, 1 January 1915, University of Oslo Library; Eugene Roth to June D. Holmquist, 9 December 1969, in Nelson Biographical Papers (P939), MHS; Henry Nelson to S.C. Rugland, 21 March 1906; Henry K. Nelson to First State Bank of Ashby, 4 June 1906, both in Nelson Papers. The *Ashby Post* frequently referred to Henry in 1903-1904, sometimes listing his business activities as in Elbow Lake, sometimes in Ashby. See *Ashby Post*, 14 November and 11 December, 1903; and *Ashby Post*, 6 May, 1 July, 26 August, 4, 11 November, and 2 December, 1904. The December reference is the last.

[76] Nelson to Søren Listoe, 21 August 1907; Amos R. Solenberger, M.D., to Nelson, 30 August and 20 October 1907, all in Nelson Papers.

[77] Nelson to Listoe, 17 February 1908, in Nelson Papers; *Alexandria Post-News*, 26 March 1908.

[78] *Alexandria Post-News*, 1 October 1908; *Fergus Falls Daily Journal*, 28 September 1908; *Norman County Index* (Ada), 1 October 1908; *Crookston Times*, 28 September 1908.

[79] Cooper, *Pivotal Decades*, 47-49; Penick, *Progressive Politics and Conservation*, 1-18; White, *"It's Your Misfortune and None of My Own"*, 407-409; Theodore Roosevelt to "My Dear Senator" [Knute Nelson], 8 June 1908; Pinchot to Nelson, 8 June, 10, 19 November, 1908, all in Nelson Papers.

[80] Penick, *Progressive Politics and Conservation*, 4-6; White, *"It's Your Misfortune and None of My Own"*, 407-408; Pinchot, *Breaking New Ground*, 211-212. Nelson had joined with G.G. Hartley (of the 1882 campaign) in opposing Forest Service policies in the new Minnesota National Forest Reserve in northern Minnesota. See Pinchot, 203-212.

[81] Penick, *Progressive Politics and Conservation*, 19-34.

[82] This and the following paragraph are based on Penick, *Progressive Politics and Conservation*, 41-146, the best single account of the controversy. The quoted passage is from p. 114. Other accounts, such as in Alpheus T. Mason's *Bureaucracy Convicts Itself* and Pinchot's *Breaking New Ground*, suffer from a decided pro-Pinchot bias or a tendency to read Brandeis' later greatness back into this case.

[83] *Washington Post*, 7 February 1910. There is no indication she ever delivered her "great surprise."

[84] *New York Times*, 6 January 1910; *Washington Post*, 23 January 1910.

[85] Here and below, see *St. Paul Pioneer Press*, 27 January 1910; *Washington Post*, 5 February 1910; *The Outlook*, 28 May 1910; and Mrs. Omar Harrison to Nelson, 21 January 1910, in Ballinger-Pinchot File, Box 78, Nelson Papers. It is assumed that the "3,000 misguided Michigan women" (*Post*) are the same as the 3,000 Federation club members (Harrison).

[86] *The Outlook*, 28 May 1910, 140-141; Pinchot, *Breaking New Ground*, 465; William Manners, *TR and Will: A Friendship That Split the Republican Party* (New York, 1969), 125-127; Penick, *Progressive Politics and Conservation*, 140, 145, 146; Nelson to Louis W. Hill, 19 July 1910, in Nelson Papers.

[87] George W. Pepper, *Philadelphia Lawyer: An Autobiography* (Philadelphia, 1944), 84, 85; Manners, *TR and Will*, 123-125; Louis J. Paper, *Brandeis* (Englewood Cliffs, New Jersey, 1983), 115, 126; Penick, *Progressive Politics and Conservation*, 143-146; *Washington Post*, 26 January 1910; *New York Times*, 11 May 1910; Paolo E. Coletta, *The Presidency of William Howard Taft* (Lawrence, Kansas, 1973), 95-96.

[88] Cooper, *Pivotal Decades*, 178; Melvin I. Urofsky and David W. Levy, eds, *Letters of Louis D. Brandeis, Vol. II (1907-1912): People's Attorney* (Albany, New York, 1972), 317-318.

[89] *New York Times*, 2 April 1910; *Washington Post*, 2 April 1910; *Hearings Before Committee. Investigation of Interior Department and Bureau of Forestry*, Senate Document 719, 61st Congress, 3rd Session, Vol. 6 (1910), 2425-2430.

[90] *New York Times*, 1 May 1910; *Letters of Louis Brandeis* 2:333; Paper, *Brandeis*, 127-128; *Hearings*, 7:3624-3632.

[91] *Hearings*, 7:4070-4071; *New York Times*, 11 May 1910; *Washington Post*, 11 May 1910; Paper, *Brandeis*, 126-127.

[92] *New York Times*, 15 May 1910; Penick, *Progressive Politics and Conservation*, 158-162; Manners, *TR and Will*, 129-135; Coletta, *William Howard Taft*, 96-97; Paper, *Brandeis*, 128-131; Archie Butt, *Taft and Roosevelt: The Intimate Letters of Archie Butt, Military Aide* (Garden City, New York, 1930), 1:348-349; *Hearings*, 7:4136-4137, and 8:4395-4396.

[93] Here and below, see *Hearings*, 8:4395-4400, 4406-4407; *New York Times*, 16, 17, 18 May, 1910; Cooper, *Pivotal Decades*, 157, 158-159.

[94] Here and below, see Penick, *Progressive Politics and Conservation*, 172, 173; Cheney, *Minnesota Politics*, 4; *Minneapolis Journal* 6, 7, 9 September, 1910; and Manners, *TR and Will*, 127.

[95] Butt, *Taft and Roosevelt*, 2:692.

Chapter Thirteen

[1] P.V. Collins to Nelson, 19 September 1912, in Nelson Papers; Hanford L. Gordon to General A.B. Baker, 10 February 1912, in Gordon Papers.

[2] *Congressional Record*, 61:3:2939-2950 (20 February 1911), especially pp. 2942, 2945-2947.

[3] Nelson to Ole Canestorp, 9 March 1911; P.V. Collins to Nelson, 5 June 1911; Farmers' Society of Equity, open letter, 29 June 1911, all in Nelson Papers.

[4] Grevstad to Nelson, undated; William H. Taft to Nelson, 6 and 7 July, both 1911, all in Nelson Papers; R. Newell Searle, *Saving Quetico-Superior: A Land Set Apart* (St. Paul, 1977), 41-44.

[5] Ray Stannard Baker, "Is the Republican Party Breaking Up?: The Story of the Insurgent West," in *The American Magazine*, 69:4 (February, 1910), 431, 440-443.

[6] *Minneapolis Tribune*, 3, 5 January, 1912, and 12 April 1918; *Minneapolis Journal*, 5 January 1912. For a summary of Peterson's career, see Carl G. O. Hansen, *My Minneapolis* (Minneapolis, 1956), 267-269.

[7] Cooper, *Pivotal Decades*, 169-175; Nelson to Michelet, 27 June 1912; William H. Grimshaw to Nelson, 7 August 1912, both in Nelson Papers; Millard L. Gieske, "The Politics of Knute Nelson, 1912-1920" (Ph.D. dissertation, University of Minnesota, 1965), 51. Michelet was a hard friend to stand by. He

traveled to Mexico and speculated in Mexican lands in hopes that American intervention there would raise land values. Reporting on Michelet's ten-day trip to Mexico, Grimshaw observed, "any man who wanted to raise the price of real estate by instigating a war with another country had a very limited idea of what was right."

[8] Grimshaw to Nelson, 7 August 1912; Nelson to W.H. Eustis, 16 July 1912; Nelson to Michelet, 31 July 1912; John S. McLain to Nelson, 31 July 1912; H.V. Jones to Nelson, 31 July 1912; A.A.D. Rahn to Nelson, 22 August 1912; A.E. Rice to Nelson, 29 August 1912; Henry Rines to Nelson, 27 August 1912, all in Nelson Papers; Gieske, "Politics of Knute Nelson," 68-76.

[9] *La Follette's Weekly*, 4:35 (31 August 1912), 5-6, 12-13; *Dawson Sentinel*, 23 August 1912; *St. Paul Daily News*, 4, 6 September, 1912; Gieske, "Politics of Knute Nelson," 81. For future governor Theodore Christianson's editorial attack on Nelson, see his *Dawson Sentinel*, 23 August and 6 September, 1912.

[10] Grimshaw to Nelson, 7, 23 August, 1912; Frank Clague to Nelson, 24 August 1912; I.A. Caswell to Nelson, 27 August 1912; O.P.B. Jacobson to Nelson, 26 August 1912, all in Nelson Papers; Gieske, "Politics of Knute Nelson," 82-89.

[11] Gieske, "Politics of Knute Nelson," 87-88. The newspaper quoted was the *St. Paul Pioneer Press*.

[12] *Minnesota Legislative Manual—1913*, 342-343; Grimshaw to Nelson, 7, 23 August, 1912, both in Nelson Papers. The six counties were Chisago, Kanabec, Kandiyohi, Mahnomen, Meeker, and Wright. Mahnomen was the site of the White Earth Indian Reservation, where Michelet had served as Indian Agent.

[13] J.A.O. Preus to Nelson (telegram), 17 October 1912; Michelet to Nelson, 18 October 1912; Nelson to Michelet, 21 October 1912; John Ireland to Nelson, 25 October 1912; Preus to Nelson, 26 October 1912; Charles D. Hilles to Nelson (telegram), 25 October 1912, all in Nelson Papers; Gieske, "Politics of Knute Nelson," 96-104; *Osakis Review*, 31 October 1912; *Alexandria Post News*, 31 October 1912; *Fergus Falls Journal*, 28 October 1912; *Minneapolis Journal*, 28 October 1912.

[14] White *et al.*, *Minnesota Votes*, 18, 33-34; Chrislock, *Progressive Era*, 55-56; Gieske, "Politics of Knute Nelson," 109.

[15] *Minneapolis Journal*, 21, 22 January, 1913; *Minneapolis Tribune*, 22 January 1913.

[16] *Minneapolis Tribune*, 2 February 1913. Of course, it was actually his 71st birthday, not his 70th, for he was born in February, 1842. No one seems to have realized this at the time, however.

[17] *Minneapolis Tribune*, 17 January, 4 February, 1913; *St. Paul Pioneer Press*, 4 February 1913. The federal government began investigating White Earth in 1911, apparently to learn if Michelet and Victor Johnson had acquired an interest in Indian allotments there. "I trust that you have done nothing that will prove embarrassing to you," Nelson wrote, but his trust was misplaced. See Nelson to Michelet, 27 September 1911, in Michelet Papers.

[18] Cooper, *Pivotal Decades*, 190-196; Nelson to Edward W. Decker, 16 August 1913, in Nelson Papers.

[19] George Green, "Financial Intermediaries," in Glenn Porter, ed., *Encyclopedia*

of American Economic History, 717-720; Eugene Nelson White, *The Regulation and Reform of the American Banking System, 1900-1929* (Princeton, New Jersey, 1983), 90-97; Cooper, *Pivotal Decades*, 197.

[20] Joseph Chapman, Jr. to Nelson, 16 April 1913; Nelson to Chapman, 19 April 1913; Nelson to John McHugh, 7 June 1913, all in Nelson Papers; *Minneapolis Tribune*, 27 May, 21 June, 24 August, 2 September, 11, 16 November, 1913; Gieske, "Politics of Knute Nelson," 135-141.

[21] Gieske, "Politics of Knute Nelson," 152-156; *Minneapolis Tribune*, 9 December 1913; Kolko, *Triumph of Conservatism*, 234-242; Robert H. Wiebe, "Business Disunity and the Progressive Movement, 1901-1914," in *Mississippi Valley Historical Review*, 44:4 (March 1958), 666-673. For an overly optimistic letter claiming Nelson thought the Senate Committee would pass the Federal Reserve bill unanimously, see Senator Henry F. Hollis to Woodrow Wilson, 17 October 1913, in Arthur S. Link, ed., *The Papers of Woodrow Wilson*, 28 (Princeton, New Jersey, 1978), 414.

[22] George Green, "Financial Intermediaries," in Porter, ed., *Encyclopedia of American Economic History*, 719-720; Trescott, *Financing American Enterprise*, 158-160; Bailyn *et al.*, *Great Republic*, 250; James Livingston, *Origins of the Federal Reserve System: Money, Class, and Corporate Capitalism, 1890-1913* (Ithaca, New York, 1986), 26, 228.

[23] Kolko, *Triumph of Conservatism*, 261-268; Cooper, *Pivotal Decades*, 199-201.

[24] *Congressional Record*, 63:2:11,298 (29 June 1914), 63:2:12,031 (14 July 1914), 63:2:12,724 (25 July 1914), and 63:2:15,934-15,946 (30 September 1914); Jon Wefald, *A Voice of Protest: Norwegians in American Politics, 1890-1917* (Northfield, Minnesota, 1971), 83. Nelson's bills were S.4381 and S.4647. See *Congressional Record*, 63:2:3023 (6 February 1914) and 63:2:4004 (27 February 1914); *New York Times*, 7 February 1914; and *Minneapolis Tribune*, 8, 28 February, 1914.

[25] Lovoll, *Promise of America*, 163-164; Belle La Follette, *Robert M. La Follette*, 521-536; Cooper, *Pivotal Decades*, 201-202.

[26] Cooper, *Pivotal Decades*, 216-217; Gieske, "Politics of Knute Nelson," 245-247; Grevstad to Nelson, 29 January 1916; John J. Vertrees to Nelson, 29 January 1916, both in Nelson Papers; Alpheus T. Mason, *Brandeis: A Free Man's Life* (New York, 1946), 465-505; *American Jewish World*, 3:14 (9 June 1916), 696. See also, *American Jewish World*, 4 February (407-408), 25 February (451, 462-463), 24 March 1916 (519) and 12 May 1916 (631-632).

[27] *New York Times*, 14 June 1914.

[28] Tour of Nelson house by Barbara Grover, 28 September 1993.

[29] *Minneapolis Journal*, 7 May 1915; *St. Paul Pioneer Press*, 7 May 1915. Governor Winfield Scott Hammond, a Democrat, was as unlikely to appoint a Republican as the "drayhorse" Nelson was to retire.

[30] Cooper, *Pivotal Decades*, 233-234; Gieske, "Politics of Knute Nelson," 334, especially note 16; Chrislock, *Progressive Era*, 66-76; *Rock County Herald* (Luverne), 2 July 1915.

[31] *Minneapolis Tribune*, 5 July 1915.

[32] "Shy Senator Shuns Sly Camera," *Minneapolis Journal*, 5 July 1915.

[33] *Minneapolis Tribune*, 6, 8 December, 1915. Nelson thought Wilson's message

was "made up largely of glittering generalities." Earlier, "Minnesota business leaders" had formed "a local branch of the National Security League . . . the nation's leading interventionist pressure group." See Chrislock, *Progressive Era*, 94.

[34] *Minneapolis Tribune*, 6, 8 January, 1916; *Fergus Falls Ugeblad*, 2 February 1916; Nelson to "Dear Sir," 11 January 1916; Nelson to Dr. A.W. Hanson, 12 January 1916; Julius Moersch to Nelson, 13 January 1916; Nelson to Moersch, 17 January 1916; Nelson to Peter Shippman, 10 March 1916, all in Nelson Papers. Moersch headed the German-American Alliance of Minnesota. The quotation is from Nelson to Shippman.

[35] Cooper, *Pivotal Decades*, 242-243; Chrislock, *Progressive Era*, 104; Gieske, "Politics of Knute Nelson," 228-230.

[36] *Bemidji Herald*, 16 March 1916. Surprisingly, Art Lee fails to mention Paul F. Dehnel's antiwar *Herald* in his treatment of Bemidji in World War I. See Art Lee, "Hometown Hysteria: Bemidji at the Start of World War I," in *Minnesota History*, 49 (Summer, 1984), 65-75.

[37] Evjen to Nelson, 5 March 1916, in Nelson Papers; *Minneapolis Tidende*, 13, 20, and 27 January, 3 February, and 23 March, 1916; *Fergus Falls Ugeblad*, 2 February 1916; Gieske, "Politics of Knute Nelson," 340-350.

[38] Chrislock, *Progressive Era*, 104-105; Nelson to Judge John F. McGee, 4 February 1916, in Nelson Papers.

[39] Stuhler, *Ten Men of Minnesota*, 99-102; Chrislock, *Progressive Era*, 125-127; Gieske, "Politics of Knute Nelson," 267-317. For an inconclusive debate over whether the Kellogg forces secretly induced Lindbergh to enter the race in order to divide Insurgent support, see Gieske, 291-292, and Bruce L. Larson, *Lindbergh of Minnesota: A Political Biography* (New York, 1973), 191-192, 326-327.

[40] Here and below, see *Willmar Tribune*, 4, 11 October, 1916; *St. Paul Pioneer Press*, 1 October 1916; Interview with Dr. Fleming, Oral Interview Tape, Douglas County Historical Society, Alexandria; and Keillor, "Democratic Coordination in the Marketplace," 529.

[41] *Fargo Forum*, 23, 25 October, 1916; Robert L. Morlan, *Political Prairie Fire: The Non-Partisan League 1915-1922*, (Borealis Reprint Edition, St. Paul, 1985), 86, 88.

[42] Morlan, *Political Prairie Fire*, 22-25, 27-31, 34. "League organizers convinced the farmers that there were too many of them to act efficiently as a group on important matters . . . . leaders must therefore be trusted to do the job, and be given full authority and adequate funds." (p. 34)

[43] Morlan, *Political Prairie Fire*, 26, 32-34, 92-93, 96-99.

[44] Morlan, *Political Prairie Fire*, 93, 126; Millard L. Gieske, *Minnesota Farmer-Laborism: The Third-Party Alternative* (Minneapolis, 1979), 13, 15-16.

[45] Gieske, *Minnesota Farmer-Laborism*, 5-10; Chrislock, *Progressive Era*, 115, 116-118, 106-109; Clark, ed., *Minnesota in a Century of Change*, 197-204.

[46] Quoted in Chrislock, *Ethnicity Challenged: The Upper Midwest Norwegian-American Experience in World War I* (Northfield, 1981), 38. See also, John Higham, *Strangers in the Land: Patterns of American Nativism, 1860-1925* (New Brunswick, New Jersey, 1955), 195-201.

[47] For an excellent discussion of this, see Chrislock, *Ethnicity Challenged*, 37-47, 50. Chrislock observes that cultural preservationist Waldemar Ager published

Oberst Heg og hans gutter at this time "to underscore the patriotism of Norwegian immigrants in the Civil War era."

[48] Cooper, *Pivotal Decades*, 260-266; Chrislock, *Watchdog of Loyalty: The Minnesota Commission of Public Safety During World War I* (St. Paul, 1991), 40-44; *Minneapolis Tribune*, 6 March 1917. Chrislock (pp. 13-24, 28-39) has an excellent discussion of the background to the wartime antagonisms.

[49] A.G. Johnson to Frank B. Kellogg, 2 April 1917; Nelson to Johnson, 7 April 1917; Johnson to Nelson, 12 April 1917, all in Nelson Papers.

[50] *Washington Post*, 4, 5 September, 1917; *St. Paul Pioneer Press*, 5 September 1917. This was not a Union army uniform, but merely a blue civilian suit. Nelson was not one to "dress up" in a costume.

[51] *Congressional Record*, 65:1:838-840 (19 April 1917), 64:2:3488 (17 February 1917); Bailyn, *Great Republic*, 1:644-645. He also used the Civil War song in addressing a loyalty rally in St. Paul. See *Minneapolis Weekly Tidende*, 20 December 1917.

[52] Nelson to Rev. J.A.O. Stub, 17 December 1917, in Nelson Papers; Chrislock, *Ethnicity Challenged*, 84-85.

[53] Chrislock, *Watchdog of Loyalty*, 160-161; Chrislock, *Ethnicity Challenged*, 68-71. For an excellent analysis of the predominantly pro-Allied views of Norwegian-American newspapers, see *Ethnicity Challenged*, 30-32.

[54] See Chrislock, *Watchdog of Loyalty*, especially 51-57, 60-64, 68, 78-79.

[55] Chrislock, *Watchdog of Loyalty*, 159, 180-182.

[56] *Alexandria Citizen*, 20, 27 December, 1917. Earlier in 1917, it apparently was called the Loyal Americans League of Douglas County. See *Alexandria Citizen*, 20 September 1917.

[57] *Park Region Echo*, 28 August 1917; Constant Larson to Nelson, 10 August 1917; Nelson to A.S. Burleson, 11 August 1917, both in Nelson Papers; Chrislock, *Watchdog of Loyalty*, 131; *Park Region Echo*, 25 September 1917; Gieske, "Politics of Knute Nelson," 416-418. Nelson blamed George Creel, head of the Committee on Public Information, for the Post Office's failure to act. See Nelson to Elmer E. Adams, 28 June 1918, in Nelson Papers.

[58] *Park Region Echo*, 4, 11 September, 1917; *Alexandria Citizen*, 6 September 1917. According to the *Citizen*, only 226 autos were in the parade.

[59] *Park Region Echo*, 18, 25 September, 1917; Larson to Nelson, 10 August 1917, in Nelson Papers.

[60] *Alexandria Citizen*, 20 September 1917. Nelson probably was referring to the Espionage Act and similar moves against sabotage and leaked military information. But his remarks may have encouraged local vigilantes to move again against Wold's *Echo*.

[61] *Park Region Echo*, 25 September and 2 October, 1917.

[62] *Alexandria Citizen*, 27 December 1917; *Park Region Echo*, 1, 8 January, 16 July, and 6 November, 1918; *Alexandria Citizen*, 3 January 1918; Chrislock, *Watchdog of Loyalty*, 131; Chrislock, *Ethnicity Challenged*, 104, 161, n. 65; Chrislock, *Progressive Era*, 161-162.

[63] Quoted in Chrislock, *Progressive Era*, 161-162.

[64] *Alexandria Citizen*, 20 December 1917.

⁶⁵ Nelson to J.A.O. Preus, 10 August 1917; Thomas W. Gregory to Nelson, 11 August 1917, both in Nelson Papers; *Minneapolis Tribune*, 16, 18 September, 1917; Chrislock, *Watchdog of Loyalty*, 160; Gieske, "Politics of Knute Nelson," 418.

⁶⁶ Chrislock, *Watchdog of Loyalty*, 131; Gieske, "Politics of Knute Nelson," 419-420; A. Fick to Nelson, 30 August 1917; Preus to Nelson, 8 September 1917, both in Nelson Papers.

⁶⁷ Edward E. Smith to Nelson, 4 February 1917; John E. Diamond to Nelson, 14 August 1917; Knute Nelson, "To the People of Minnesota," 15 April 1918, in Nelson to Olcott, same date, all in Nelson Papers; Chrislock, *Ethnicity Challenged*, 100.

⁶⁸ John F. McGee to Nelson, 6 July 1917, in Nelson Papers; *St. Cloud Times*, 1 May 1917; O.J. Quane to Nelson, 6 July 1917, in Nelson Papers. Quane edited the Democratic *St. Peter Herald*.

⁶⁹ *Minneapolis Journal*, 12 December 1917; Chrislock, *Ethnicity Challenged*, 100; Link, ed., *Papers of Woodrow Wilson*, 47:53-55, 48:347, and 51:300-301; Chrislock *Progressive Era*, 176; Stephenson, *John Lind*, 339-340; Chrislock *Watchdog of Loyalty*, 202, 204. William B. Colver of the Federal Trade Commission pressed Wilson for a denial, but he clearly had talked to Lind, for he indicated direct knowledge about Lind's potential availability and electability as a Democratic candidate for the Senate. Though conjectural, this assumption of Lind's involvement is consistent with available evidence and Lind's later actions opposing a Democratic endorsement of Nelson.

⁷⁰ Sanford to Nelson, 20 December 1917; Sageng to Nelson, 20 December 1917, both in Nelson Papers. See also Richard O'Connor to Nelson, 19 December 1917; H.V. Jones to Nelson, 24 December 1917; Charles Mitchell to Nelson, 25 December 1917, all in Nelson Papers.

⁷¹ H.V. Jones to Nelson, 24 December 1917, in Nelson Papers.

⁷² Nelson to Gravstad, 31 December 1917, quoted in Chrislock, *Ethnicity Challenged*, 100; *Minneapolis Journal*, 31 December 1917; Nelson, "To the People of Minnesota."

⁷³ *Minneapolis Tribune*, 5, 12, 13, 14, and 20 April 1918; Chrislock, *Ethnicity Challenged*, 101-103, 160, n.55; Chrislock, *Watchdog of Loyalty*, 131; Gieske, "Politics of Knute Nelson," 497, 499-501.

⁷⁴ Chrislock, *Ethnicity Challenged*, 103-104; Chrislock, *Watchdog of Loyalty*, 304-307. For MCPS activities among the citizenry, wee *Watchdog of Loyalty*, especially chapters 10 and 11.

⁷⁵ Gieske, *Minnesota Farmer-Laborism*, 43; Chrislock, *Progressive Era*, 175; Chrislock, *Ethnicity Challenged*, 103-104; *Legislative Manual - 1919*, 250, 252. The other counties were Aitkin and German-American Brown county.

⁷⁶ W.J. Sheldon to Nelson, 19 June 1918; Constant Larson to Nelson, 19 June 1918; Bob to Nelson, 19 June 1918; Nelson to Elmer E. Adams, 28 June 1918, all in Nelson Papers.

⁷⁷ Chrislock, *Progressive Era*, 176; Gieske, "Politics of Knute Nelson," 548-552.

⁷⁸ White *et al.*, *Minnesota Votes*, 35; Gieske, *Minnesota Farmer-Laborism*, 47; Chrislock, *Progressive Era*, 177; Nelson to Mrs. Ingrid B. Emery, 24 December 1918, in Nelson Papers.

[79] Quoted in Chrislock, *Progressive Era*, 177.

[80] Here and above, see *Brewing and Liquor Interests and German and Bolshevik Propaganda: Report and Hearings of the Subcommittee on the Judiciary United States Senate*, 66th Congress, 1st Session, Senate Document No. 62, 1 (7597), iii-v, 3-6; and 2 (7598), 1617-1619, 1622-1624.

[81] Robert K. Murray, *Red Scare: A Study in National Hysteria, 1919-1920* (Minneapolis, 1955), 36-39, 58-64; Terje I. Leiren, "Ole and the Reds: The 'Americanism' of Seattle Mayor Ole Hanson," in *Norwegian-American Studies*, 30 (1985), 75-95 (especially 85-87).

[82] Quoted in Murray, *Red Scare*, 62.

[83] *Congressional Record*, 65:3:2942-2949 (8 February 1919). Nelson's copy of the pamphlet is in Box 75 of the Nelson Papers.

[84] Murray, *Red Scare*, 94.

[85] *Report and Hearings*, Senate Doc. No. 62, 3 (7599), 465-467; Eric Homberger, *John Reed* (Manchester, England, 1990), 130-163, 176-177.

[86] *Report and Hearings*, 465-467; *Washington Post*, 21 February 1919; *New York Times*, 21 February 1919.

[87] *Congressional Record*, 65:3:1168-1171 (9 January 1919). For information on Bryant and Reed, see Homberger, *John Reed*.

[88] Here and below, see *Report and Hearings*, 3:506-517; *New York Times*, 22 February 1919. For Yakov Peters, see Aleksander I. Solzhenitsyn, *The Gulag Archipelago 1918-1956: An Experiment in Literary Investigation* (New York, 1973), 314-322, 630. For confiscations of land and "surplus" crops, see Robert Conquest, *The Harvest of Sorrow: Soviet Collectivization and the Terror-Famine* (New York, 1986), 43-57.

[89] Arne Halonen, "The Role of Finnish-Americans in the Political Labor Movement," (M.A. Thesis, University of Minnesota, 1945), 126.

Chapter Fourteen

[1] Herbert F. Margulies, *The Mild Reservationists and the League of Nations Controversy in the Senate* (Columbia, Missouri, 1989), 1-5.

[2] Margulies, *Mild Reservationists*, 5; Cooper, *Pivotal Decades*, 319; *Minneapolis Tribune*, 11 July 1919.

[3] Margulies, *Mild Reservationists*, 6, 76-77; *Congressional Record*, 66:1:8135 (8 November 1919).

[4] For early Republican opposition to unreserved ratification, see *Minneapolis Tribune*, 4 March 1919.

[5] Gieske, "Politics of Knute Nelson," 614-615; Margulies, *Mild Reservationists*, 17-19; *Minneapolis Tribune*, 4 March 1919.

[6] Gieske, "Politics of Knute Nelson," 616; *Minneapolis Tribune*, 8 May 1919. In early March, Nelson did give his "concurrence" to a proposed speech by Kellogg on the League; however, it seems doubtful that he would have allowed this ambiguous act to commit him. See Margulies, *Mild Reservationists*, 19-21.

[7] Link, ed., *Papers of Woodrow Wilson*, 60 (1989), 42-43; Margulies, *Mild Reservationists*, xi-xii, 19, 35, 46, 52-53, 134. Margulies' detailed account is superb on the delicate and intricate maneuvers attempted by the mild reservationists to

achieve their goals. For a brief account of Kellogg's views on the League, see Stuhler, *Ten Men of Minnesota*, 103-106.

[8] Ralph Stone, T*he Irreconcilables: The Fight Against the League of Nations* (Lexington, Kentucky, 1970), 1; Margulies, *Mild Reservationists*, xii, 98; Cooper, *Pivotal Decades*, 344-346. Margulies calls eight members of Lodge's group "moderates" for they stood somewhere between strong and mild reservationists. See Margulies, xiv.

[9] *Congressional Record*, 66:1:3320-3323 (29 July 1919); *Minneapolis Tribune*, 30 July 1919; *Washington Post*, 30 July 1919.

[10] Margulies, *Mild Reservationists*, 52-53, 177-178; Nelson to S. Listoe, 3 September 1919, in Nelson Papers; *Congressional Record*, 66:1:3322 (29 July 1919). He also may not have been able to tolerate the irreconcilables' appeal to anti-black, anti-Catholic, anti-Japanese prejudice. See Stone, *Irreconcilables,* 100-109. For Nelson's speech, see *Minneapolis Tribune*, 30, 31 July 1919; and *Minneapolis Tidende*, 7 August 1919.

[11] Nelson to S. Listoe, 3 September 1919, in Nelson Papers; Margulies, *Mild Reservationists*, 69-72; Stone, *Irreconcilables*, 123.

[12] Here and below, see Margulies, *Mild Reservationists*, 81; *Congressional Record*, 66:1:4408-4409 (27 August 1919).

[13] Margulies, *Mild Reservationists*, 8, 81; Nelson to Everett P. Wheeler, 27 August 1919; Nelson to William B. Mitchell, 2 September 1919, both in Nelson Papers.

[14] Here and above, see Nelson to Mitchell, 2 September 1919; Nelson to Listoe, 3 September 1919, both in Nelson Papers; Gieske, "Politics of Knute Nelson," 623-627 (misinterpreting Nelson's "he" to mean Wilson, when it meant Lodge); *Minneapolis Tidende*, 25 September 1919. The unnamed senator is quoted in Cooper, *Pivotal Decades*, 349.

[15] Margulies, *Mild Reservationists*, 88, 94-96, 103-108.

[16] *Congressional Record*, 66:1:6616-6618 (9 October 1919); *St. Paul Pioneer Press*, 10 October 1919; *Minneapolis Journal*, 10 October 1919; *Minneapolis Tidende*, 16 October 1919. Though it clearly approved of his remarks, *Tidende* merely reprinted much of them without comment, as if Nelson's words by themselves should convince Norwegian Americans.

[17] Margulies, *Mild Reservationists*, 137-151.

[18] *Congressional Record*, 66:1:8135-8136; *Washington Post*, 9 November 1919; *Minneapolis Journal*, 9 November 1919; *St. Paul Pioneer Press*, 9 November 1919; *Minneapolis Tribune*, 9 November 1919; Margulies, *Mild Reservationists*, 151.

[19] *Washington Post*, 20 November 1919; *St. Paul Pioneer Press*, 20 November 1919; Margulies, *Mild Reservationists*, 163-175; Stone, *Irreconcilables*, 143-146.

[20] *Park Region Echo*, 11 March 1921; *Alexandria Post News*, 25 September 1919.

[21] Interview with Dr. Fleming, Tape, Douglas County Historical Society, Alexandria; Eugene Roth to June D. Holmquist, 9 December 1969, in Nelson Biographical File (P939), MHS.

[22] *Park Region Echo*, 11, 16 March and 8 June, 1921. Mrs. Jacobson testified that Gustaf "said that he would show the Jacobsons that they had to do what he ordered them to do." See *Park Region Echo*, 6 October 1920.

[23] *Alexandria Citizen*, 25 March 1920; *Park Region Echo*, 17 March 1920. The buyer, A.A. Secord, was temporary chairman of the Republican county convention that spring. See *Alexandria Post News*, 18 March 1920.

[24] *Alexandria Citizen*, 11 March 1920; *Alexandria Post News*, 11, 18 March, 1920; *Park Region Echo*, 17 March 1920.

[25] *Park Region Echo*, 17 March 1920; *Alexandria Post News*, 18 March 1920. For Jacke's candidacy in 1918, see *Park Region Echo*, 30 October 1918. Advice on the trials and appeal was given by Stan Keillor, Minnesota Court of Appeals staff attorney specializing in criminal law. The Supreme Court's decision in State vs. Anders Gustaf Nelson (148 *Minnesota Reports*, 285-301) has been frequently cited. It set important precedents on proof of premeditation and admission of a defendant's prior "bad acts" as evidence. Notes of talk with Stan Keillor, 9 June 1994, in author's possession.

[26] *Park Region Echo*, 17 March 1920; *Alexandria Post News*, 18 March 1920; *Alexandria Citizen*, 18 March 1920.

[27] *Park Region Echo*, 17 March 1920.

[28] *Alexandria Citizen News*, 30 September 1920; *Park Region Echo*, 29 September 1920; *Alexandria Citizen News*, 10 March 1921. The *Citizen News* (10 March 1921) charged that Sullivan "regarded this trial as a means by which he would become a popular hero in the eyes of many of the people of this county who had no love for Gustaf Nelson."

[29] Morlan, *Political Prairie Fire*, 255-261, 283-284; *Park Region Echo*, 29 September 1920; Chrislock, *Watchdog of Loyalty*, 317. Constant Larson aided John Sullivan for the defense. John Sullivan was the Democratic candidate for governor in 1942. See White *et al.*, *Minnesota Votes*, 198-200.

[30] Gieske, "Politics of Knute Nelson," 661, 663, 665.

[31] Gieske, *Minnesota Farmer-Laborism*, 55-58; Gieske, "Politics of Knute Nelson," 657-660. Preus had been Nelson's clerk in Washington.

[32] Here and above, see *Park Region Echo*, 29 September and 6 October, 1920; *Alexandria Citizen News*, 30 September 1920; Supreme Court opinion in State of Minnesota vs. Anders Gustaf Nelson, reprinted in *Park Region Echo*, 9, 11, 16, and 18 March, 1921; 148 *Minnesota Reports*, 295,300-301; *Park Region Echo*, 8 June 1921. For farm tenancy, see Keillor, "Democratic Coordination in the Marketplace," 710; and *The Farmer*, 30:41 (12 October 1912), 1211.

[33] *Minneapolis Daily Star*, 21, 25, 29 September and 1 October, 1920; Gieske, *Minnesota Farmer-Laborism*, 59-65; Gieske, "Politics of Knute Nelson," 672.

[34] *Park Region Echo*, 9 March and 8 June 1921; 148 *Minnesota Reports*, 287-301. Knute Nelson was not called to testify at this second trial in June, 1921. The Supreme Court decision noted prosecutorial excesses at the first trial. In the end, manslaughter may have been a more appropriate charge. Notes on 9 June 1994 conversation wtih Stan Keillor in author's possession.

[35] Eugene P. Trani and David L. Wilson, *The Presidency of Warren G. Harding* (Lawrence, Kansas, 1977), 48-49; Gieske, "Politics of Knute Nelson," 678-679; Chrislock, *Watchdog of Loyalty*, 327-333. McGee committed suicide after less than two years on the bench.

[36] Trani and Wilson, *Warren G. Harding*, 178-187.

413

[37] *Minneapolis Tidende*, 10 April 1922; *Alexandria Citizen News*, 17 April 1922.

[38] *Minneapolis Tribune*, 29 April 1923; Gieske, "Politics of Knute Nelson," 677.

[39] Gieske, *Minnesota Farmer-Laborism*, 71-76; *Alexandria Citizen News*, 19 October 1922. Nelson later joined Lenroot for a speech in Minneapolis.

[40] *Detroit Record*, 27 October 1922.

[41] White *et al., Minnesota Votes*, 36, 105, 186; Gieske, *Minnesota Farmer-Laborism*, 76.

[42] Quoted in Gieske, "Politics of Knute Nelson," 676-677. See also, Trani and Wilson, *Warren G. Harding*, 143, 145.

[43] *Minneapolis Tidende*, 4 and 5 February, 1923.

[44] Gieske, "Politics of Knute Nelson," 680-681; *Minneapolis Tribune*, 29 April 1923.

[45] *Baltimore Sun*, 29 April 1923; *Philadelphia Inquirer*, 29 April 1923; *Minneapolis Tribune*, 29 April 1923; Nelson to "Gode foreldre," 28 July 1861; Nelson to "Langt fraverende og bekömrede foreldre," 22 August 1861, both in Nelson Papers.

[46] *Dagbladet*, 30 April 1923; *Minneapolis Tribune*, 29 April 1923.

[47] *Minneapolis Tribune*, 29 April 1923.

[48] Gieske, "Politics of Knute Nelson," 681-682; *Alexandria Citizen News*, 3 May 1923.

[49] *Alexandria Citizen News*, 3 May 1923; Lovoll, *Promise of America*, 59-60, 114.

[50] *Baltimore Sun*, 30 April 1923.

[51] Gieske, *Farmer-Laborism*, 78-80.

Index

415